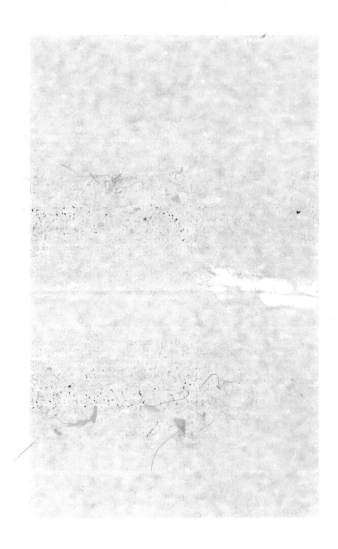

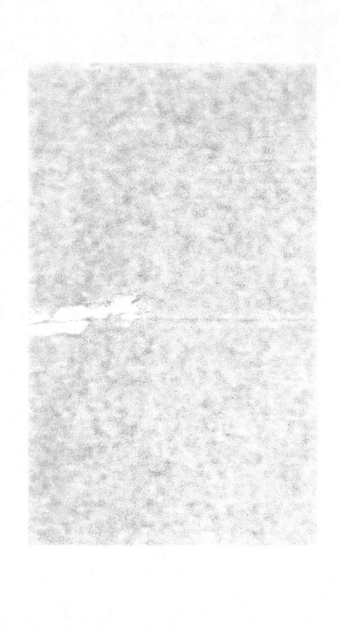

GLOBAL ORDER

FOURTH EDITION

GLOBAL ORDER

Values and Power in International Politics

LYNN H. MILLER

Temple University

Westview Press
A Member of Perseus Books, L.L.C.

Copyright © 1998 by Westview Press, A Member of Perseus Books, L.L.C.

Published in 1998 in the United States of America by Westview Press, 5500 Central Avenue, Boulder, Colorado 80301-2877, and in the United Kingdom by Westview Press, 12 Hid's Copse Road, Cumnor Hill, Oxford OX2 9JJ

Library of Congress Cataloging-in-Publication Data
Miller, Lynn H.
   Global order : values and power in international politics / Lynn
H. Miller. — 4th ed.
      p.   cm.
   Includes bibliographical references and index.
   ISBN 0-8133-6880-4
   1. World politics—1975–1985.   2. World politics—1985–1995.
3. World politics—1989–   .   4. International relations.   I. Title.
D849.M542   1998
909.82'9—dc21   98-5797
                                                                                 CIP

The paper used in this publication meets the requirements of the American National Standard for Permanence of Paper for Printed Library Materials Z39.48-1984.

10   9   8   7   6   5   4   3   2   1

In memory of Linda

Contents

Preface

This book is the product of a consciously normative and value-oriented perspective on world order problems. Often neglected in the standard texts on international politics, such an approach seems to me essential for a number of reasons. First, the game of international politics is played in the normative framework, which provides the parameters within which international actors compete for power and influence. That framework is not an accident of nature but a human invention, created to rationalize and order the relevant social and technological capabilities of increasingly sovereign actors some three hundred fifty years ago and consciously enlarged and adapted to respond to changes in those capabilities ever since. It therefore should be regarded not merely as a footnote or an afterthought in the analysis of international politics but as the ordering, ideal structure that both shapes international behavior and makes its evaluation possible.

Second, the value-oriented perspective encourages analysis of the strengths and weaknesses of the international normative system itself. Such analysis is particularly important now that the system's ability to maintain needed order seems more strongly threatened than at any time in the past. Politics shapes the normative structure, but the normative structure also shapes politics, with potentially disastrous consequences in a world where sovereigns hold weapons of mass destruction and they, and their societies, can inflict perhaps irreparable damage to the earth's environment. The structural reasons for our current peril need to be addressed in ways that are seldom possible in state-based analysis alone.

Third, this approach provides us as students with a critical orientation toward policy, for we are encouraged to judge international political phenomena on the basis of world order criteria. We are forced to examine our own values in the process and to consider whether and why they are congruent or incongruent with what other individuals or groups in the world desire. We are forced to think about global ethics as a result, and we do so with more objectivity than is usually possible when our analysis is heavily state based or oriented toward the outlook of particular decisionmakers.

The basic purpose of this book is to provide a kind of normative guide to the examination of the most important issues on today's international agenda. That is the major substantive component of the book in Chapters 5 through 8, in which the principal agenda items are considered. Chapters 2 and 3, meanwhile, constitute an excursion into the historical basis of our present condition. There the development and logic of the Westphalian system of sovereign nation-states is examined, from its creation at the end of the Thirty Years' War to the present. This component is intended to demonstrate the interplay between values and power in the creation and growth of the world's political system and to suggest what is mutable and what is immutable in the way in which humanity historically has organized itself on the planet. Chapter 1 and especially Chapter 4 attempt to provide the reader with the basic tools for exploring the chaotic world of competing social and political forces as a world order system. Those chapters discuss the world order process in the contemporary period, the relationship between power and values and between power and authority, the relativity of anarchy and order in the international system, and distinctions and connections between politics and law in society.

Nearly everything stated above was said in the preface to earlier editions. Now, nearly a decade after the end of the cold war, some of the first seismic shifts in world order issues, involving the potential and actual use of intergroup force, are being played out. The nuclear balance of terror has given way to the use or threatened use of "conventional" warfare across parts of the former Soviet sphere and elsewhere, the comparative stability of bipolarity having been followed by interethnic conflict and turbulence. As a result, the peacekeeping and peacemaking capabilities of our international institutions have been stretched and strained, and increasingly found wanting. Other major shifts determining humanity's direction since the cold war include the headlong rush toward globalization, with new economic success stories for some and continuing poverty for many others, along with deepening North-South conflicts; major institutional developments in the world's criminal justice system; and new evidence of the human role in global warming, with its perils for us and our descendants.

Earlier editions of this book profited from the useful suggestions of a number of people, especially Peter Bachrach, Lev Gonick, Harold Guetzkow, Robert W. Hansen, Robert C. Richter, and Burns Weston. My colleague Lloyd Jensen has been conscientious and helpful in his advice. I continue to be grateful for the intelligent support of the staff at Westview Press.

I am happy to reaffirm the intellectual debts I acknowledged in earlier editions. There I identified Richard A. Falk as my principal mentor. His work, as well as that of his associates at the World Policy Institute, has left its imprint on these pages. Finally, had it not been for my students, it is unlikely that this book would have been written. Quite unknowingly, they have helped me to develop the issues and ideas that are new to the fourth edition. None of those mentioned need share any of the blame for what follows.

Lynn H. Miller

GLOBAL ORDER

CHAPTER 1

The Best and Worst of Times

It was the best of times, it was the worst of times, it was the age of wisdom, it was the age of foolishness, it was the epoch of belief, it was the epoch of incredulity, it was the season of Light, it was the season of Darkness, it was the spring of hope, it was the winter of despair, we had everything before us, we had nothing before us.

—Charles Dickens, *A Tale of Two Cities*

These famous lines first appeared in 1859, and they have captured the imagination of readers ever since for the way in which they evoke the almost fantastic range of possibilities available in every human experience. Men and women have an enormous capacity for wisdom and enlightenment, an ability to learn all sorts of complex and useful things about the wondrous universe of which they are a part. From the time members of our species learned to domesticate plants and animals until their descendants first journeyed to the moon, humanity's progress in making the physical universe serve its commands has been remarkable, giving rise to hope, happiness, and the sense that we have everything before us. These are among the emotions and the experiences that provide every generation with its own best of times.

Yet humans are not gods nor are they destined to become them, for they are flawed by ignorance and misunderstanding and behave despicably toward each other in their quest for mastery over a confusing and chaotic world. They often inflict misery and death on many while building marvelously complex societies. Yet the oppressors, like their victims, are ultimately vanquished by their own mortality, which guarantees to weak and strong alike their own worst of times.

These are brief descriptions of what appear to be the two extremes of the human condition. Not every human being who has ever lived would

1

describe those extremes in exactly the same way. Some generations have lived at times when the darker prospects for the species seemed to dominate the possibilities for happiness or human progress. Others have been born into a world in which the opposite perception had fertile ground in which to take root and spread. Yet the appeal of Dickens's opening words to *A Tale of Two Cities*—words written in a time and a society that we today tend to see as particularly optimistic—is that they describe what every man and every woman has at some time known to be true.

Pessimistic Versus Optimistic Visions of Human Capability Today

What sorts of things constitute the best and worst of times at the end of the twentieth century? Never before in human history have the best and worst seemed as extreme as they do today and for the near future. We may even wonder if the extremes are not now so great that we must redefine in fundamental ways what traditionally have been thought of as the nature and place of humanity on earth.

   The best visions of what is possible for human life today actually seem to challenge the notion that our mortality is a boundary that we cannot cross. It is now possible to save and prolong life through the use of wonder drugs and other medical and surgical techniques that were unknown a generation or two ago. Hearts and lungs and other vital organs, some artificially created, are routinely transplanted into the bodies of patients to make continued life possible where not long ago it would have been unimaginable. Not yet routine, but even more dramatic in their challenge to death itself, are various developments in genetic engineering that make it possible to clone individuals of a species so as to produce offspring that are exact genetic copies of their parents. The successful cloning of a sheep in 1997 brought cloning of humans a fateful step nearer. It also challenged the public's awareness of the unprecedented moral issues involved. In view of this situation, how can an organism be said to "die" when its carbon copy lives and can itself be cloned and so on, presumably forever? Or consider the geneticist's ability to transfer genes from an organism of one species to another. That power can only be considered godlike, for it suggests incredible possibilities for modifying species in ways that could turn humankind's natural enemies into benign creatures, thereby eliminating much disease, increasing our food supply severalfold, and, no doubt, accomplishing many other miracles as well. The imagination staggers.

   These and other developments in the science of genetics challenge the very mortality of living things, but in other areas too we are frequently assured that any problem can be overcome through a new (or potential) scientific advance. Although the day is fast approaching when no significant reserves of oil will be left underground to keep the world's industrial machine in operation, we can count on the development of truly renewable alternative energy resources. Thus we will never again have to face the problems of either resource scarcity, as in the oil crises of the 1970s, or pollution from the use of such fossil fuels. The sun's energy can be harnessed for our benefit, as can the wind, the waves of the earth's oceans, and even decaying organic matter, which is the waste of the entire life process. The sensible harnessing of such resources seems certain to provide future generations with virtually unlimited amounts of clean power to ensure the indefinite advance of material progress for the species. If these and a myriad of other technological advances do not grant immortality to each of us, they at least seem to promise that our descendants will live and flourish in ways we cannot yet imagine.

The worst of times? It is a jolt to realize that today the worst imaginable future for humanity is not having a future at all—or at least nothing that we would recognize as truly human. As long as nuclear weapons remain scattered about the earth and its oceans, our lives may end any day with the "bang" of thermonuclear explosions that would annihilate millions outright and kill many more through radiation, the poisoning of the earth's food and water supply, and the devastating disruption of social organization across the planet. Although the nuclear arms race of the cold war is now history, a handful of governments still possess enough explosive power to bring death to every man, woman, and child on earth. And even if the threat of nuclear war has receded, the possibility of ending with the "whimper" of a more gradual ecological collapse looms larger. That end might be triggered by further accidents like those at Three Mile Island and Chernobyl, the release of chemical or bacteriological weapons in some future military conflict, the irreparable destruction of the ozone layer, or the continued warming of the planet to the point that it can no longer sustain us. Perhaps the whimpering end may result from other factors already at work—booming growth in populations, the destruction of our tropical forests, the silent extinction of a growing number of animal species—all of which, or a host of other possibilities, already may be leading us toward our doom.

Those of us alive today must live with the fact that in our lifetimes, as never before in the history of the planet, one species has the capacity to make the globe we share with thousands of other living species uninhabitable for us all, with the possible exception of the most primitive forms of plant and animal life. The capacity for unprecedented destruction is also a godlike power, although traditionally we would attribute it to a satanic god.

So there is something unique about our sense of the best and worst possibilities for humanity today. Never before have those opposites extended so far toward the unlimited. Never have they been so unbounded by our physical weakness, which for earlier generations limited what was possible. Never before have human beings had the power at their disposal to act in ways that our ancestors would have regarded not as human but as godlike, with all the terrible responsibilities such power inevitably brings.

The Ethical and Political Challenge of Our Power

This uniqueness in our condition today reminds us of another distinctive quality of the extreme prospects in our time. As we think about our best and our worst capabilities, we are likely to find that our discomfort—horror even—at the satanic power we now hold looms larger than whatever comfort we find in our capacity for good. What is the point of being awed at medical advances if tomorrow vastly more of us may be wiped out in the burst of a few terrible explosives than have been killed in all the plagues of history? Why should we exult in our ability to voyage through interplanetary space when we constantly risk making our home planet largely uninhabitable? Why should we take comfort in the prospect that limitless supplies of energy may soon be available when we consider the destructive applications humans often find for the energy they command?

The more we consider, the more likely we are to see that the worst possibilities we face are more hypnotizing and commanding than the best. If headlong disaster engulfs us, we shall no longer have the leisure to accomplish those marvelous advances in civilized life that otherwise seem to be within our grasp. We shall then have to cope, if we are able, with a human society that has retrogressed so drastically that basic survival values must take precedence over more "civilized" concerns.

But that is not the most troubling consideration we face. We increasingly suspect that the worse possibilities for humanity's continuation on the planet are themselves the direct result of the same forces that have produced what we think of as the best prospects. If the Western world had not undergone its industrial revolution during the past two centuries—a phenomenon that dramatically improved the general standard of living in mature industrial societies before it began to spread to other regions—it would not today have the technology to build atomic bombs as well as automobiles, to poison rivers and streams with pollutants while enabling a single farmer to produce vastly more food than his or her peasant ancestors, or to create the conditions for totalitarian political systems while producing computers and television sets.

We begin to notice that *all* the developments we list as characteristic of the "best of times" and the "worst of times" are somehow related to accomplishments in science and technology. None can be traced to advances in ethics, humanistic studies, or the arts, or what philosophers call metaphysics. No one would dream of suggesting that these final years of the century are the best of times because of breakthroughs we have made in getting human beings to live together peaceably, or in producing the greatest art the world has ever known, or in discovering how to rear children so that they are all smarter, happier, and better citizens than their parents, or because we have exhibited greater love for our neighbors than humans did in the past.

Conversely, when we think about the worst of human behavior, we may note that our century has brought forth some of history's greatest tyrants. But we would not say, when we considered it, that a Hitler or a Stalin established such grim records because they were inherently more evil than certain people in an earlier period. The scope of their evil deeds was possible because of the availability of technologies that have refined spying to a high degree, have controlled people's movement, and have made possible mass murder on a scale unknown to the ancients.

These examples of the power of modern tyrants should remind us of two fundamental facts about the world we live in. First, all our modern technologies are instruments of power. They serve to supplement the comparatively puny ability of even the strongest or most intelligent human being to have an impact on the material world. Every time we call sounds and pictures from the airwaves by turning on a television set or travel in an airplane or switch on an electric light, or do any of the countless other things that draw upon modern technology, we are asserting our mastery over some aspect of the material universe that far exceeds our natural ability. What separates us more than anything else from our primitive ancestors is the immensely greater power over nature that we have acquired.[1]

Second, the technologies themselves are morally neutral: They can be used either for good or for evil and themselves contain no guidelines, no instructions, to tell us which is which. The technologies that enable us to communicate almost instantly with people all over the world can also be used to invade our privacy and otherwise control us in a myriad of ways; the technologies that let us travel faster than the speed of sound can also carry mass destruction to rain death down from heaven; and the technologies that we use to run the vast industrial machine that gives us wealth and power can also make possible both genocide and ecocide— terms that describe two ultimate, cataclysmic events that, not coincidentally, have entered the language only in our time.

Now we have come full circle: The technological developments that today promise us the best of times are also the ones that can provide the very worst. Not long ago nuclear power promised virtually limitless, cheap, and nonpolluting energy for future generations. In the light of disastrous accidents at Three Mile Island and Chernobyl, that hope now seems dated and naive. If the possibilities inherent in genetic engineering excite our imaginations today, we should remember that they also have a dreadful potential to interfere in the life process with consequences no one can yet anticipate.[2] Little imagination is needed to grasp the possibly dire consequences in the misapplication of virtually any promising technology.[3] Moreover, the uniquely human capacity for both the best and the worst to push human capability toward godlike extremes in our time is the direct result of the very nature of technological development: It is cumulative and irreversible. As long as technology does not lead to the destruction or the radical retrogression of the human race, which we all know is more than a small possibility, it proceeds to build on itself in directions that give its creators ever greater power, for good or evil, over the physical universe.

Most of us have not learned to grapple with this situation. Our response is no response at all. We try not to think about it as we go about the pressing business of daily living, which normally does not include confronting matters of eschatology. Or we leave these matters to the experts. (The fact that most people see themselves as nearly powerless in the face of the godlike possibilities open to the human race is an interesting paradox whose implications we shall explore.) We are the children of a scientific age. When confronted with the dangers of our time, we tend to say, "Well, the scientists will discover something." If we use up fossil fuels, scientists will find replacements. If the metal ore necessary to keep the industrial machine going is depleted, scientists will substitute plastics or other synthetics. If the earth's arable land has reached the limit of what it can support, scientists will develop aquaculture. If the planet gets too crowded, we will colonize space. And if nuclear weapons threaten to annihilate us, then we will simply spend billions of dollars more on other high-technology weapons in the mad hope that they can keep us from being annihilated by the push of yet another button.

The Inadequacy of Scientific "Solutions"

These may not all be impossible scenarios, though many of the best minds among us have their doubts. The problem with relying on such developments as "solutions" is that they are not solutions at all—not, at least, to the problems that really matter for the future of humanity on the planet—because these are above all political and economic problems, problems related to the way human beings live and prosper individually and in relationship to other people throughout the globe. Whatever mastery and control over our nonhuman environment technological solutions may provide us, they also give us additional power to destroy that environment and all the species, including Homo sapiens, that draw life from it. Every technological capability we may develop to do greater good for our own and future generations carries with it a capability for evil. What is worse is that we have arrived at a point in our development when we can realistically expect that the dire (if unforeseen) consequences of these new powers will far outweigh their benefits.

"Good" and "evil": We cannot seem to avoid using these terms whenever we consider the applications of our modern technologies. These terms have no meaning outside the realm of human thought and action, for they relate exclusively to how human beings live or try to live. Moreover, they are not concepts that have a place within the postulates of the scientific method, which proceeds from the assumption that the material world is paramount and must be studied and understood agnostically, that is, without a priori prejudices or values to color what may be learned from the facts under investigation. This is not to say, of course, that scientists are more immoral than the rest of us. The greatest of them have been profoundly concerned with the moral issues of their time and have often shown a real sensitivity to the implications of their discoveries for good and evil in human life.[4] Yet the scientist who addresses issues of human value enters a realm that lies beyond science, one that encompasses politics and includes metaphysics.

That realm commands the attention of us all—scientists and nonscientists alike—if we are to save ourselves from the Faustian capabilities we now have at our command. If, in fact, humankind has a future worth hoping for—one in which we are no longer threatened by nuclear explosions, whether accidental or deliberately planned; one in which the genetic material of the species is not irreparably damaged by radiation or other poisoning; one in which mass murder, economic deprivation, and the most extreme forms of political oppression are at least considerably reduced, if not eliminated—it will be because, and only because, we have turned away from the mindless expectation that science will somehow save us and we have moved seriously to try to save ourselves through the only means we have at our disposal: the careful examination of public policy choices, followed by action calculated to advance our chosen values.

The overriding need today is to learn to make ethically informed decisions about the nature and direction of our lives together on the planet. This task cannot be left to experts, although the views of philosophers, humanists, theologians, and, yes, scientists should help to guide us. In an important sense, we all must develop individual expertise in these matters so that together we can make the better possibilities inherent in our situation prevail over the worst. This task is perhaps not as hopeless as it sounds, for although not all of us are geneticists or physicists, every intelligent human being must make ethical choices every day, choices that affect the individual's relationship to others in society. Yet in another sense, "expertise" is the wrong word to choose here because it implies an end product that a specialist strives for, particularly a specialist whose arcane knowledge comes through the pursuit of science. It suggests directives for action built on a complex body of knowledge, acquisition of which points the expert in specified directions discovered through a rigorous, value-free reading of the facts. Yet such expertise does not lead us to our goal of a safer, more humane world. Rather, its orientation allows us to avoid coming to grips with the questions of human value priorities that we have determined are at the root of our current problems.

The Reconciliation of Conflicting Values

If the scientific approach cannot save us from ourselves, what can? On what basis do we make ethically informed decisions? Our first task is to understand that a fundamental difference exists between "scientific" and "nonscientific" problems and that each requires a distinctive kind of mental effort. The late E. F. Schumacher made the difference and its consequences wonderfully clear. As he pointed out, the problems of science call into play the mode of logical thought, of reasoning from one fact or finding to the next, of "working out a problem" in mathematics or science, whether inductively or deductively. Problems of this type constitute humankind's "most useful invention; they do not as such exist in reality, but are created by a process of abstraction. When they have been solved, the solution can be written down and passed on to others, who can apply it without needing to reproduce the mental effort necessary to find it."[5] These are known as *convergent* problems because addressing them includes taking into consideration a variety of factors, which ultimately converge in a solution. Science has advanced so dramatically in recent centuries because of this human invention of looking for convergent solutions.

The other basic kind of problem is *divergent* in nature, requiring us to reconcile conflicting goals and interests in ways that can be lived with. This is the kind of problem we face every time human values enter the picture. It is not possible to provide a clear-cut description of the basic mode of thinking needed to resolve issues of this type, since these problems cannot, by definition, be solved by logic, although logic is needed to help define them and their consequences. If reconciliation works, it is a more or less temporary solution that is limited to a particular historical or social situation. It is subject to being upset when the particularities of the situation change. Divergent problems require us to balance conflicting wants and needs and, where other human beings are involved, as they typically are, their wants and needs become part of the equation. These divergent problems, which are "the true problems of living," in Schumacher's words, "demand of man not merely the employment of his reasoning powers but the commitment of his whole personality."[6] In other words, ethical as well as rational decisions must be made.

Human beings face many divergent problems in their political lives, whenever and wherever they live. The inherent trade-offs in divergent problems are apparent in questions such as the following: Is the loss of freedom in a highly centralized, authoritarian state worth the greater security to a greater number of individuals that may come with it? Does wide participation in making political decisions in a liberal democracy compensate for a lessened efficiency in government? Does the so-called right of national self-determination have any limits, as, for example, when those who identify themselves as a subject nation are scattered, or constitute a very small group, or are not educated for self government? Can the desire to achieve political independence ever justify the use of force against innocent civilians?

These and similar perennial questions about what is good, bad, acceptable, or unacceptable in political life obviously relate to matters of different human values. Different values lead people to make different choices, choices that will not be the same for everyone but will be influenced by one's perspective, one's place within the relevant social situation under discussion, and one's particular view of what is better and what is worse for society. Each question asks some variation on the two opposing concepts of anarchy and order, which makes them characteristically political questions. These questions have no scientific answers; they cannot be resolved for all people in all times and all places. It is certain only that people will always search for an answer within the range in which opposing tendencies can be balanced in some way. Each abstract right or value cited must be limited in practice to avoid its destroying a different or opposing right.[7] Problems of metaphysics simply cannot be resolved like problems in the convergent world of science, and in that sense no comparable kind of progress for humanity can take place in the realm of public policy.

Obviously human values are involved in all matters of human choice. But it does not follow that we must ignore humanly made techniques of convergent problem solving altogether in the study of human behavior. We can learn many things about the way we act by using the scientific method. If that were not the case, we would not have developed the academic disciplines of sociology, economics, anthropology, psychology, and political science—all of which are founded on the assumption that some kinds of human issues can be treated as convergent problems. Rather, we must understand clearly how far the convergent mode can be used and when it must give way to divergent considerations.

For example, if I have enough relevant data at my command, I may be able to explain and even predict the outcome of a U.S. presidential election some days or weeks before it is held and within a small margin of error. Pollsters have produced remarkably accurate forecasts by adhering rigorously to scientific techniques. But I cannot give a scientific rationale for directing an individual citizen to vote for one candidate rather than another. Voters face divergent issues and must balance a variety of values in determining which candidate's victory will most likely advance those currently most important to them as individuals. I may, of course, become an advocate for a particular candidate or political party, and my advocacy may have some impact on other voters. That influence will depend on such things as the extent to which they accept my reading of the likely outcome and whether they view my value goals as congruent with their own. This requires me to be clear about them myself and to have the ability to communicate them to others. But the moment I become an advocate, I abandon the framework of the scientific method (although science may have informed my advocacy) and concern myself, broadly speaking, with matters of metaphysics.[8]

Much of what follows in this book relates to questions of advocacy or, more specifically, to the effort to clarify certain important policy choices as they relate to particular social, political, and economic goals of men and women in our time. To be meaningful, however, such advocacy must be built on as rigorous an analysis as possible of various social trends and patterns, especially those most relevant to the state of world order today. The convergent mode of analysis will let us focus on, and ideally make intelligent and informed decisions about, some of the great divergent issues that we face.

Human Behavior and Value Priorities

The second matter that arises at this point relates to the complex nature of human values themselves and the ways in which they find social implementation. Clearly, some needs are biologically derived: Every living person needs food and shelter at a minimum and therefore places a basic value on securing them. Beyond the bare survival values come a host of others, which relate to the greater and greater realization of human potential.[9] Clearly some of these values are prerequisites to the realization of others: The higher values—such as creative self-expression through poetry writing—obviously cannot be obtained if the value of literacy through education has not first been reached. The basic task of political organization has always been making the survival values attainable to the individuals within the polity. However, it characteristically must do more than that because its general function is the allocation of a whole range of competing values within the system in ways that provide a measure of order for all. That order can never entirely satisfy all who submit to it, although some societies, those we typically regard as comparatively just, do a better job of that than others, which may maintain order through terror and intimidation rather than consent.

Even though all values are at root the goals of individual human beings, we may define some of them as social or political if their implementation can only be sought through the given social or political system. Dominant political values (which are not the same, except perhaps in democratic societies, as those held by a majority of the population) shape particular political systems, which in turn help mold and modify other values. The process is one of continual interaction between the system and the interests held and expressed by the individuals or groups of individuals that live within it.

For instance, most contemporary Americans may naturally suppose that any political system that permits adult citizens a fair amount of participation in the allocation of important values affecting all their lives is superior to a polity where the huge mass of citizens have almost no say in these matters. Yet the contemporary U.S. view has probably been the minority view through most of history—not because men and women have somehow evolved more democratic natures over the course of centuries (after all, democracy is an ancient political invention) but because the polity in which we live today generally reinforces democratic values in a way that other polities have not. The doctrine of the divine right of kings clearly supported the power and values of monarchs within certain European societies in an earlier time. Its real importance was not simply that kings may have been prone to believe it for self-serving reasons. The mass of common people also must have accepted the doctrine as true, which of course reinforced their disinclination to challenge the rule of kings.

Changing Social Values

We see now that the basic normative choices that govern social groups are sociologically derived, that is, particular dominant values are the product of particular historical configurations. This relationship is evident when we look for examples such as the one above. Yet that is something most of us too seldom do, for widespread confusion and misunderstanding exist about which kinds of political behavior and belief are time bound and which, if any, are inherent in human nature.

For instance, many people appear to believe that Homo sapiens is an inherently aggressive animal and that war is therefore an inevitable feature of relations among human groups. But that assertion does not tell us very much that is useful, even if it can be said to be generally true. Certainly it cannot explain how we have managed to create societies that are successful in preventing whatever aggressive instincts humans have from embroiling their own members in constant civil war. Most members of civil societies are by definition at peace with each other most of the time. But perhaps the assertion is meant to apply only to relationships between and not within social groups. If it does, then simply defining those who do not usually go to war as members of the same group, tribe, or nation does not explain anything at all. It merely gives a label to that which is excluded from the generalization (and excluded differently in different historical periods, since the shapes, the sizes, and of course the names of societies within which humans have been pledged to live in peace have changed repeatedly throughout history). But the fact is that competing groups (tribes, nations, and so on) are not perpetually at war. Even if we regard war as one of the characteristic features of what, for lack of more precise terminology, we call international politics, we must acknowledge that it is not a perpetual feature or even the only feature.[10]

Already we have explored one particular truism far enough to suspect that social organization and the values that are advanced in it (as well as the values that are not advanced) play a crucial role in determining whether an aggressive instinct in humans produces war or nonviolent outlets for humanity's energies. Types of acceptable violence, even within societies, are not constant in all times and places. Blood feuds, personal vendettas, and dueling, were once accepted forms of violence between persons within a larger social group, are now almost universally condemned. Even intersocietal conflict, which is characterized by much higher levels of violence than is typically acceptable domestically, is subject to change. What was thought to be the acceptable treatment of one's enemy has shifted over the centuries. When Rome defeated Carthage in the third Punic War, Roman generals destroyed the city completely, even spreading salt about the ruins so that nothing would grow there again. Prisoners in ancient times were routinely murdered, conquered cities were plundered, and the civilian population was enslaved. Whatever abominable practices modern war includes, they generally differ from ancient practices.

Slavery has been a dominant feature of social life through most of human history. Not until the twentieth century was it largely eliminated everywhere on earth. It would be satisfying to conclude that slavery finally met its demise because of principled opposition to it. Appeals to people's higher motives can be extremely powerful. Yet close examination reveals that appeals to conscience are never enough when social conditions combine to encourage perpetuation of a social evil. In modern times, the abolition of slavery in societies where it still existed followed the industrial revolution and the growth of capitalism. These new forces provided economically dominant classes with more of the world's material goods and services than they ever could have had through the mere physical enslavement of people. Hence, complex changes in social and economic forces combined to shift values away from those that once had dominated. Once slavery was abolished, the abolitionist ethic became a part of the dominant normative order, so that what had been accepted by earlier generations as an economic necessity and was therefore excluded from the moral agenda became unthinkable to their descendants.[11]

The processes at work in fundamental social changes of this kind are enormously complex. Only the tip of the iceberg that finally sank slavery has been exposed above. Clearly, political behavior is shaped by the dominant values of a society, which in turn are the product of complex historical forces. Value priorities shift in relation to perceived needs. A group that is physically isolated from its nearest neighbor will develop a foreign policy that is different from the one developed by a group that is constantly subject to attack and subjugation. A society emerging from feudalism into capitalism will probably free its serfs.

But this general rule has an opposite face as well: The larger social organizations become, in general, the slower they are to change. Even when the factors that caused them to advance certain values over others begin to fade, they may continue to behave in the traditional way, even to the point that unthinking habit hobbles self-interest. A state whose traditional isolationism has served it well may cling to such a doctrine even when a greater exercise of its influence in the world might better serve its needs. The received wisdom thwarts adaptation and change. A society may preserve the feudal class structure even when such stratification runs counter to the logic of the new economic organization. The general human reluctance to change behavior gains support from dominant forces within the social system itself, and structural lethargy is the result. The vested interests of once dominant groups or classes are reflected in the laws the society has produced and in the culture more generally, all of which tend to legitimize old values and to shun new ones. In extreme cases, structural lethargy may lead to a sclerotic condition in which the resistance to change is so great that violent revolution becomes the only alternative possible.

The Slowness of Social Change

Perhaps we may now add a third explanation for our perception that the worst prospects for humanity today seem more imperative than the best. The structural lethargy of large-scale social organizations inhibits them from the kinds of rapid adaptations that would let them respond more effectively to the challenges of our time, and they may be ill equipped to prevent the worst from happening. Traditional assumptions that regard military might as essential to security remain firmly in place even though, paradoxically, at least some of our most modern destructive capabilities make us less secure rather than more secure. The planet's atmosphere continues to be treated as a dumping ground for the effluents of the industrial process in the face of mounting evidence that such practices may be contributing to a greenhouse effect and to the destruction of the earth's ozone layer—trends that could render the earth uninhabitable. Flagrant violations of human rights persist in the face of the worldwide public knowledge of them that the modern network of communication has achieved.

These examples point to a fourth reason for our pessimism about the world's future. When we are confronted with these kinds of contrahuman sociopolitical facts, we are inclined to respond to them much as we do to the technological imperative: They are regrettable, but they are beyond our reach. They represent a natural state of things that is impervious to human judgment and action. Although we do well to make ethically informed choices about social problems, we lack the power to advance our goals.

There is no magic formula for overcoming that frustration. It should help to energize us to consider seriously the remarkable power that individual human agents have exercised in combating the lethargy of social systems. Historical examples abound, from St. Paul to Martin Luther to Pope John XXIII, from Joan of Arc to Mahatma Gandhi to Martin Luther King Jr. In the 1980s, Mikhail Gorbachev almost single-handedly brought about the demise of a repressed and lethargic social system, though its problems were so great that the Soviet Union's ending ended Gorbachev's effectiveness as well. Nelson Mandela continues to exert a transformative impact on South African society. Still, most of us are not destined as individuals to effect such changes in social behavior. The best that we can do is to inform ourselves about the likely consequences for the whole society if our value choices were implemented, recognizing that we will no doubt have more failures than successes in moving society, learning as best we can through trial and error what possibilities for change exist at a given time, remaining open and receptive to the goals of others—in short, behaving with conviction tempered by toleration, knowledge balanced by recognition of our own ignorance, and awareness that the effort is the greatest, most typically human effort of our lives.

A basic thesis of this book is that the fundamental reason for our frequent failure to make the right kinds of policy choices in the world today stems from our continued refusal to see the planetary social system as a whole. We know (or should know) that all human beings are members of a single species, with far more similarities in their needs and wants than differences. Yet we behave in most aspects of our political lives as if our separate nations housed separate species. This age-old habit is increasingly anachronistic and may in fact lead to our undoing within the foreseeable future, for it prevents us from effectively addressing most of the life-threatening issues in our worst-of-times scenario. The preceding discussion of values and their implementation applies equally to any social system, including the single global one. In succeeding chapters we will engage in just such an application, for only when we adopt such a perspective do we begin to see the issues that confront the species for what they are—human problems, not simply those of particular tribes or nations.

The fact that most of us continue to think about these matters in parochial terms has far less to do with any inherent limitations on our perception and far more to do with the ways our views of the world have been structured historically, for all our knowledge is sociologically derived. The structural bias of global political and social organization has long emphasized and reinforced all those things, including values, that divide us rather than those that strengthen our commonality as human beings. In the past, recognizing divisions and boundaries was a far less dangerous way of organizing the world politically than it appears to be today. We need to understand what gave rise to this organizational scheme and sustained it if we are to assess how it does and does not serve us in today's world. Therefore, we shall begin by surveying the evolution of the world's basic principles for political organization during the past several hundred years, that of sovereign nation-states coexisting in a normative framework of mutual equality—the Westphalian international system.

Notes

1. Typically, we rejoice in the powers we have acquired through science and technology and assume they mark our own advance over earlier modes of living. But Sigmund Freud, among many others, reminded us that our modern way of life does not necessarily bring happiness but may instead merely provide greater obstacles to its achievement by creating new problems. In *Civilization and Its Discontents* he asked, "Is there, then, no positive gain in pleasure, no unequivocal increase in my feeling of happiness, if I can, as often as I please, hear the voice of a child of mine who is living hundreds of miles away . . . ?" His answer was to note that "if there had been no railway to conquer distances, my child would never have left his native town and I should need no telephone to hear his voice" (New York: W. W. Norton, 1960, p. 35).

2. The dangers are truly incalculable, perhaps especially when the experimentation is intended to be entirely beneficial. David Ehrenfeldt described a case in which experiments were undertaken with genetic transplants into *E. coli* bacteria, the organisms that normally inhabit the human intestine and are needed for our good health, for making the enzyme cellulase. Since cellulase is absent in humans, researchers thought that an ability to manufacture it within the body would give us the capability to break down cellulose, the basic material of plant fiber, and thereby provide humankind with access to food supplies never before available to the species. Yet the experiments were ended when the scientist conducting them discovered that in making digestion of this new material possible, carbon dioxide gas would be released within the gut, which could cause us to swell like balloons

whenever we ate fibrous products. See *The Arrogance of Humanism* (New York: Oxford University Press, 1978), p. 95.

3. One foreshadowing of the possibilities for drastically disrupting the complex operations of a modern society came on March 6, 1992, when the "Michelangelo" computer virus allegedly was introduced to destroy the data banks of computers around the world. Thanks to widespread advance publicity, antiviral precautions were taken in millions of workplaces. Even so, some 1,500 computers were hit in South Africa, and many hundreds or thousands more at widely dispersed sites throughout the world. The prospects for immobilizing much of the commercial, industrial, and research life of a society in this way are obvious. The nuclear arsenals of the world are also susceptible to disruption through computer malfunctions. See Paul Bracken, *The Command and Control of Nuclear Forces* (New Haven, Conn.: Yale University Press, 1983).

4. To take two well-known examples of scientists who played particularly important roles in the development of atomic weapons, Albert Einstein was a lifelong pacifist who agonized over the issue of whether or not the United States should try to develop such a weapon during World War II, and Robert Oppenheimer, who directed the Los Alamos project that eventually produced such a bomb, later found himself in considerable political trouble in Washington for his opposition to the development of the "H-bomb," as it was known at the time, or fusion weapon. Oppenheimer's view was that such a weapon could serve no useful purpose because of its destructive power and therefore should not be produced.

5. E. F. Schumacher, *Small Is Beautiful* (New York: Harper and Row, 1973), p. 97.

6. Ibid., p. 99.

7. The unending need to balance anarchy and order in social life has its counterpart in Freudian psychology, according to which within every human personality there is a conflict between the individual's claim to unrestrained freedom (in the working of the id) and the demands of society (on the superego) for restraints on that freedom for the general social good. See especially Freud, *Civilization and Its Discontents*.

8. For a much fuller exploration of this and other issues involved in the philosophy of science, see Carl Gustav Hempel, *Aspects of Scientific Explanation and Other Essays in the Philosophy of Science* (New York: Free Press, 1965) and Thomas S. Kuhn, *The Structure of Scientific Revolutions*, 2d ed. enl. (Chicago: University of Chicago Press, 1970).

9. Abraham Maslow has developed this idea in *Toward a Psychology of Being* (Princeton, N.J.: Van Nostrand, 1962; rev. ed., 1968), *Motivation and Personality* (New York: Harper and Bros., 1954; rev. ed., 1970), and *The Farther Reaches of Human Nature* (New York: Viking, 1971). Maslow's theory on the hierarchy of human development suggests that basic needs must generally be satisfied before meta needs can be realized. The former range from the physiological requirements to sustain life through those for love, respect, and self-esteem. Meta needs entail self-actualization through the quest for truth, goodness, beauty, justice, peace, and so on.

10. Moreover, Freud and his followers have argued that the aggressive "instinct" is by no means an unmitigated human and social evil, for they view it as the source of energy and creativity in human life, without which most of what we regard as human accomplishment would not have been possible. If that is so, then

we are clearly confronted with one of life's divergent problems: How do we control the destructive capability of human aggression and at the same time give encouragement to its creative potential?

11. Interestingly, much antinuclear writing in the last years of the cold war period used the slavery example to suggest that nuclear weapons could be abolished once their profound risks to the societies possessing them came to be widely understood. Garry Wills used the analogy to slavery to suggest the moral blindness born of presumed necessity that plagued nuclear weapons states in the 1970s. In 1977 he wrote, "If the earth lasts long enough, future generations will look back on us with the uncomprehending horror we feel for slaveholding cultures. They will ask how a nation ever thought it could justify the buildup of instruments for destroying the globe." *The Philadelphia Inquirer,* February 3, 1977, 9A.

Suggested Readings

Baldwin, David, ed., *Neorealism and Neoliberalism: The Contemporary Debate,* New York: Columbia University Press, 1993.

Brown, Seyom, *International Relations in a Changing Global System,* Boulder, Colo.: Westview, 1992.

Bull, Hedley, *The Anarchical Society: A Study of Order in World Politics,* New York: Columbia University Press, 1977.

Deutsch, Karl W., *The Analysis of International Relations,* 3d ed., Englewood Cliffs, N.J.: Prentice-Hall, 1988.

Falk, Richard, *Explorations at the Edge of Time,* Philadelphia: Temple University Press, 1991.

Freud, Sigmund, *Civilization and Its Discontents,* New York: W. W. Norton, 1960.

Hempel, Carl Gustav, *Aspects of Scientific Explanation and Other Essays in the Philosophy of Science,* New York: Free Press, 1965.

Hoffmann, Stanley, *Janus and Minerva: Essays in the Theory and Practice of International Politics,* Boulder, Colo.: Westview, 1987.

Holsti, K. J., *The Dividing Discipline: Hegemony and Diversity in International Theory,* Boston: Allen and Unwin, 1985.

Keohane, Robert O., and Joseph S. Nye Jr., *Power and Interdependence: World Politics in Transition,* Boston: Little, Brown, 1977.

Maslow, Abraham, *The Farther Reaches of Human Nature,* New York: Viking, 1971.

Oye, Kenneth A., ed., *Cooperation Under Anarchy,* Princeton, N.J.: Princeton University Press, 1986.

Rosenau, James N., *Turbulence in World Politics: A Theory of Change and Continuity,* Princeton, N.J.: Princeton University Press, 1990.

Schumacher, E. F., *Small Is Beautiful,* New York: Harper and Row, 1973.

Shattuck, Roger, *Forbidden Knowledge: From Prometheus to Pornography.* New York: St. Martin's, 1996.

Toffler, Alvin, and Heidi Toffler, *Creating a New Civilization: The Politics of the Third Wave,* Atlanta: Turner Publishing, 1994.

Waltz, Kenneth N., *Man, the State, and War,* New York: Columbia University Press, 1954.

CHAPTER 2

The Growth of the Westphalian System

The natural state of nations . . . is . . . one of equality and independence, which establishes an equality of right among them, and pledges them to have the same regard and respect for one another.

—**Jean Jacques Burlamaqui**, *Principes du droit naturel*

The power of declaring war is . . . especially necessary to a state for the purpose of constraining wrongdoers; wherefore, just as the sovereign prince may punish his own subjects when they offend others, so may he avenge himself on another prince or state.

—**Francisco Suarez**, *De Triplici Virtute Theologica, Fide, Spe, et Charitate*

Analysis of the world order system in which we live confronts us at every turn with divergent problems. The essential purpose of any social order is to provide enough regularity in relationships among the individuals within it that values supporting the common good can be achieved, maintained, and advanced, while those most damaging to the common interest are controlled. The common interest almost always lies in a reasonable assurance that individuals will interact peaceably and predictably in important ways, behavior encouraged by the agreed-on rules that govern human interaction. When a man leaves his house to enter a dangerous world, he needs some assurance that his neighbors are not likely to attack him and that he may cross a busy street safely when the light is green. Yet if that same man is oblivious to all considerations of the common good— if he fails, in the words of one of the world's most fundamental ethical precepts, to do unto others as he would have them do unto himself—he

19

may have the physical strength to rob his neighbor of his wallet and almost certainly will be tempted to cross a street against a red light if he deems it safe to do so.

The need for social order—for law to govern our relationships—lives in constant tension with the individual will to exercise power, which is the same as a desire for freedom. Both needs arise directly from the human condition, and balancing their divergent demands is the central task of organized political life.

We have little difficulty grasping these essential facts of our situation. But in general, when we think about how society regulates us as individuals, we probably think first of our national society or our local community, not any global social arrangement. We may even doubt the existence of a truly global political system, since we see little evidence of social solidarity transcending the boundaries of nations. Nor do we find familiar institutions of government in place for the world as a whole. Nevertheless, a worldwide political system does exist, although it is relatively more anarchic than the typical domestic order. In this worldwide system the values that support the common good are less strongly implemented than the ones that give rein to individual, localized interests. It was designed to function in this way at the beginning of the modern period of world history.

The Peace of Westphalia

An international legal system that originated in Europe has dominated the way in which increasing numbers of human beings have ordered global politics down to the current generation. It dates for the most part from the Peace of Westphalia of 1648, one of the most important points demarking the medieval period from the modern period in Europe's development. It arose in the period when Europe was becoming the most dynamic civilization on the planet. Like all such historical benchmarks, Westphalia is in some respects a convenient reference point more than the source of a new, fully formed, normative system. Some elements that characterize the modern world and distinguish it from the Middle Ages were well established long before 1648. Others did not emerge until many years later. Still, the Peace of Westphalia created at least the foundations of a new European system. But it did not become a true world system until the second half of the twentieth century, when it rose out of the ruins of the political structures and the idealized rationale for them that had existed more or less unchanged in Europe for the preceding thousand years.[1]

It is significant, first, that the Peace of Westphalia was created by the many belligerents in the Thirty Years' War—the last and most devastating of the great wars of religion that had wracked Europe for more than a century. That conflict had been complex (a bewildering number of participants had different interests at stake during the war's long course) and anomalous (late in the war Catholic France aligned itself with German Protestant princes against Catholic Austria). Above all, it had exacted a terrible toll in human life, particularly in Germany and Bohemia, where for three decades rival armies roamed the land, plundering, killing, and devastating those societies on a scale that has perhaps never been equaled since. The civilian populations suffered the most, and from the indirect even more than the direct effects of war, from famine, disease, and destruction of property. At least one-third (and perhaps one-half) of the population of those regions perished. An area that had provided religious and cultural leadership throughout northern Europe in the previous century was largely ground into the dust, setting back its development at least a hundred years.

The war saw the collapse of medieval structures that had promoted the common good and the unrestrained contest of individual actors for power. Out of the chaos came a revolutionary change in the way the states of Europe were to order their mutual relations in the future. Indeed, the state system that was created looks so familiar to us today that Westphalia's revolutionary quality may not be immediately apparent. Put most directly, the Westphalia treaties created the basis for a *decentralized system of sovereign and equal nation-states.* Nothing quite like it had ever existed. Although some of its component features had long been familiar, none of those features had been continuously present from the beginning of recorded history.

At first glance, the one unvarying fact of humanity's political life on a global scale has been its *decentralization,* its fragmentation into separate groups without centralized authority. As far into the past as we can see, the human species has been politically divided. But that separation is more apparent to us from our point of view than it was to people living in other times and places.

An Aquitanian grape grower living in the year A.D. 120 may have known very little about the life of a shepherdess in the hills of Cyprus. Yet both owed their allegiance to the same government in Rome, and, more importantly, each no doubt perceived herself and imagined the other as living within a single world society, the Roman one. At about the same time, a resident of Loyang in central China also must have viewed the world as containing a single, overarching political system, although in his case it would have been Chinese. Looking back, we are able to see the Roman and Han Empires as separate political units coexisting on the globe. From the subjective outlook of the inhabitants of either empire, however, the existence of the other mattered not at all. Each was a self-contained universe, a single, "global" system. Clearly, the whole concept of decentralized or pluralistic decisionmaking is meaningless when applied to groups that do not interact or do not know about each other's existence. The fact that ancient Romans and Chinese coexisted on the same planet is irrelevant in terms of social consequences for either polity; it is a nonfact. Nothing in the behavior of either of those communities can be ascribed to it. Erroneous perceptions, when they form the basis for behavior, are more true in their explanatory value than true facts that have no bearing on the way people act and view the world.

In any case, as populations grew and cultures made slow contact over the centuries, the misperception of political unity where none exists has become less and less likely and those who hold it, less relevant to the real world of politics. For example, what about Europe in the centuries prior to Westphalia? A great many political actors made decisions independently of each other, a process that frequently brought them into such conflict that they warred among themselves. Their political system surely was decentralized if any ever has been. Its chief characteristic seems to have been anarchy, the absence of central rule.

The Medieval Conception of Order

Yet the anarchy of the Middle Ages was not the theoretical equivalent of anarchy in the modern world. Westphalia made the absence of central rule the basic condition around which the new international system would be organized, whereas the medieval normative system tried to overcome it by idealizing central rule. Medieval Europeans conceived of their world as being bounded by a unified Christendom and defined by the supreme authority of emperor and pope, the emperor being the final arbiter in matters secular and the pope being the highest spiritual authority. The medieval person's cosmology consisted of a hierarchical system of order in all aspects of human life, as well as in the universe as a whole, in which every individual had an ordained place that carried with it appropriate rights and obligations. All knew precisely where they were in such a social system in relation to everyone else, to whom allegiance was owed and from whom allegiance was due. One's place in the system was determined almost entirely by one's circumstances of birth. Peasants were born to till the fields, princes to rule. Theoretically, the power that the prince held over the peasant was always circumscribed by the prince's obligation to obey greater authority within the system, ultimately, the emperor or the pope, who spoke for all of Christendom.[2]

Although this principle is familiar to us in such hierarchical systems as the Church of Rome (which remains virtually unchanged in its organization since the Middle Ages) or any modern army, we may still be unconvinced of its importance in medieval political thought, for we rightly regard the time as a violent and anarchic epoch of human history. But the anarchy and the violence help explain the force of the notion of the unity of Christendom as an organizing ideal. It guided Europeans for centuries although it was very imperfectly realized. Europe's political disintegration after the fall of Rome in A.D. 476 must rank as one of the most traumatic social upheavals of all time. The highly centralized "world state," which was the only political condition within historical memory, came crashing down at the hands of those who had been subjugated within it. But they were unable to replace it, since they had no comparable political system of their own. Successive generations of Europeans looked back on the fallen empire as the ideal to be revived, since they held that the empire had been merely suspended with the abdication of the last emperor, not ended. Reality may have been divorced from the political ideal to the extent that the ideal was no more than an illusion. But the illusion was so strong that it shaped reality in important ways. A political universe was created that is knowable only in the light of the historical memory and the ideal unity.

The ancient world empire *was* revived, although for little longer than his lifetime, by Charlemagne in A.D. 800. A century later it was revived again, much more imperfectly in terms of the extent of its authority. This time it lasted well into the modern age as the Holy Roman Empire. Before it finally met its end in modern times, the original underlying dream of its maintaining continuity with an ancient past was forgotten. That the Holy Roman Empire persisted as long as it did into the modern age, however, testified to the power and durability of the dream of a unified Christendom.[3]

In spite of the illusion, the Christianized Holy Roman Empire of the Middle Ages and the peripheral political authorities around it bore almost no resemblance to the older namesake. The basic difference between the political worlds of Rome and the Middle Ages was that in the earlier time, power had been highly centralized, whereas in the latter, comparable centralization was never possible. Even at its height, the Holy Roman Empire never achieved more than a fraction of the territorial scope of its model, although actual political unity in Europe was almost nonexistent by our standards. The interlocking and complex patterns of allegiance known as feudalism often failed to check the freedom of self-help through violence.[4] Yet considered as a normative arrangement, feudalism's complex evolution was an ingenious long-term effort to reconcile the fact of a radical dispersal of political power with the ideal of political unity. The feudal order gave that vision of unity a potency for centuries that appears with hindsight to have been a remarkable collective delusion.

The delusion was finally recognized as such in the Peace of Westphalia. Since then, the reality of decentralized, scattered power has been regarded as the legitimate mode of organization, first for the European and then for the global international system. The thousand-year-old dream of Christian unity expressed through something like a world state (never really more than a European state, of course) was seen to be outmoded, that is, no longer an effective legitimizing ideal for the behavior of princes. The separateness that replaced it could only be made legitimate by insisting that the fragmentation of authority now carried with it a new concept, that of the sovereign equality of territorial states.

The Sovereignty of Nation-States

The term "sovereignty" began to achieve some currency several decades before the outbreak of the Thirty Years' War, most notably in the writings of Jean Bodin.[5] Bodin insisted on the absolute authority, or sovereignty, of the monarch within his realm, limited only by the laws of God and nature. Bodin began an argument that virtually every political philosopher of modern times has been forced to join, although most of the debate since Westphalia has focused on the *internal* dimension of sovereignty, that is, limitations on absolutism, justifications for various forms of republican government, for revolution, and so on. In short, much of the most familiar side of the debate has proceeded from the perspective that equates the individual state with the social system under analysis. What is more relevant to our discussion of the single international social system is sovereignty's *external* dimension, which for Bodin was shaped by his determination to deny the continued authority of an imperial or hierarchical conception of world order and to replace it with a legitimized system of sovereign equals.

Since sovereignty may be defined as supreme authority, unhampered by any other, to act within a particular sphere, it follows logically that when the concept is applied to more than one unit or actor, as was the case from Bodin's day onward, then all those defined as sovereigns must be regarded as having equal rights and duties in their interactions. If they are considered to be unequal, then they coexist in a system of dominance and subordination and the supreme authority of the constituent unit is a fiction. Sovereignty, then, begets equality where more than one actor is defined as a sovereign, just as imperialism cannot exist without political inequality and hierarchical organization of the social units, whether in the form of medieval feudalism or modern colonialism.[6]

Why did Westphalia create a new normative system of sovereign equal actors when the territorial units governed by it are manifestly unequal by any material standards of measurement? The answer lies in the development of technologies that began to allow rulers to assert control over fixed territories more effectively than had been possible for many centuries. The arrival of gunpowder from China and the growing ability of kings to raise conscripted armies (itself a mark of the gradual dominance of monarchs over the private military power of their own feudal barons) made it increasingly possible for them to defend the borders of their developing states and thus provide a greater measure of security directly to their subjects than ever before. This new capability had its obvious limits in the power of other kings to control and defend their territories as well. When that emerging fact of life was widely ignored, the result could be the costly retrogression of the Thirty Years' War. So common sense suggested that when a piece of territory was defended well enough to make it very costly to penetrate from outside, it should be considered the sovereign equal of other similar units, regardless of the relative differences of size among them.[7] The alternative would be more or less perpetual violence instigated by the greatest territorial rulers, forever intent on swallowing up the weaker in a centralized system with themselves at the pinnacle of a hierarchical political structure.[8]

The map of Europe showed about two hundred more or less separate but unequal political units at the time of the Thirty Years' War. At the beginning of our century 250 years later, that number had been consolidated into some twenty-five independent states. In general, that consolidation eliminated the greatest disparities in size and capability present in the earlier period. Out of the old order—tiny duchies, counties, electorates, free states, bishoprics, and principalities—it created states large enough to be economically viable and militarily self-reliant. The sovereign units that replaced the older entities have been characterized by their ability usually to defend the core of the new territorial state and its residents, who in turn give the state their allegiance.

Yet even as large territorial states were being consolidated, sovereign actors nevertheless refused to allow the imperial domination of any one of them to be reimposed over the whole. For very practical reasons the creation of a nonhierarchical normative system made sense to European statesmen by the mid-seventeenth century. Its appeal lay in its feasibility and in the hope that to the extent that sovereign actors lived by its rules, violence among them could be reduced to tolerable levels. In that equation, Westphalia sought to reconcile new material capabilities with an essential social value.

The sovereign equality of decentralized units is an abstract conception that theoretically could be applied to interacting components in any social system (it is expressed, for example, in democratic theories of justice that call for the "sovereign" equality of citizens before the laws of the state). But the final characteristic of the Westphalian construct, that the units in question be *nation*-states, is far more time bound. True, the kinds of powerful attachments to an exclusive social group that we think of as characterizing modern nationalism appear to have existed throughout human history. But that attachment is only one of the characteristics of nationalism, which is distinguished above all by the scale of the communities encompassed by it. These communities are larger and more socially complex than extended families, tribes, cities, castes, or other social classes, all of which served in premodern times as the basic units of allegiance. The most important fact for our consideration is that the nation is now firmly wedded to the state as the sovereign unit of international politics.[9] The nation-state purports to make the community's sense of a common history, culture, and language the legitimizing force of its sovereignty and therefore the source of its equal standing with other such units.

As usual, the real-world situation is more ambiguous than the generalization would imply. At present, a number of the more than 180 state actors do not appear to be single nations in any clear-cut sense. The United States is one such anomaly, for it comprises a variety of nationality groups that entered the country in waves of immigration. For most of this century, the Soviet Union, Czechoslovakia, and Yugoslavia seemed to fit the U.S. pattern: "out of many nations, one." But the end of authoritarian and highly centralized rule in the 1990s allowed simmering nationalism to boil over in these multiethnic states. The states consequently disintegrated, revealing how nationalism continues to be the dynamo that drives and energizes sovereign statehood.[10]

These developments are a sharp reminder that it is not enough to speak of nationalism today as a force for unifying large territorial units. Nationalism is a two-edged sword that cuts states apart more frequently than it splices them together. That is particularly the case in Europe and in the former Soviet Union. Throughout much of the rest of the world, where the nation-state system is a much more recent development, the outcome of the battle to determine whether nationalism will be made to serve consolidation or secession is still not clear, even though consolidation tended to carry the day as sovereign states were carved from European empires after World War II. Particularly in Africa, the would-be nation has generally been built on the imperial power's administrative unit, which has meant that subordinated social groups have used the fostering of nationhood within the colony as their principal weapon for reaching and maintaining the goal of sovereignty.

For example, the black majority of a white-ruled colony, Southern Rhodesia, achieved independence in 1980 by subordinating historical divisions and antipathies between the majority Shona and minority Ndebele peoples in a united struggle for majority rule. If Zimbabwe is to survive as a state in its original form, it must transform that successful coalition into something like a traditional nation. Alternatively and perhaps more in keeping with the logic of its history, the state might split apart to form two new units in which the Shona and the Ndebele would form the respective national units. Although either outcome *could* be rationalized as in keeping with the demands of nationalism, those who control the current state would surely resist the secessionist alternative, as the Spanish government resists Basque separatism, as India's rulers oppose the separatism of the Sikhs, and as the government of China is determined to prevent the secession of Tibet. The legitimacy of nationalist movements tends to look very different to the rulers than to the ruled, and therein lies one of the conflicts that may in fact be inflamed, not resolved, by the tension between state and nation when the effort is to marry the two.

The potency of nationalism remains very great. Where sovereignty is still the goal today, nationhood (or its appearance) is the prerequisite. As recently as sixty years ago, there was arguably no such thing as a Palestinian nation, as judged by objective criteria and definitions. Yet as Palestinians have increased their struggle to achieve statehood, they have turned themselves into a nation that is perceived as such by much of the rest of the world, thereby legitimizing their claim to sovereignty. The *intifada*, which began in 1987 on the West Bank, is but one reminder of what the world has seen many times before: Seemingly powerless people under occupation by foreign troops discover that they are not powerless at all once they begin to resist foreign rule as repugnant to their sense of themselves as a nation. And once they take that step, the occupier may soon be made to confront the sense of illegitimacy—by ruler and ruled alike—that now accompanies its unwelcome occupation of another people. The path to statehood leads today, as it has for centuries, first to the creation of a nation.

The Dynamics of Sovereign Equality

As we have seen, the chief characteristic of power capabilities in the modern world system is their fragmentation—their dispersal among many centers of authority. Westphalia's greatest genius lay in its having made the best of that situation by creating a system of order that derives from fragmented capabilities rather than having tried to overcome them through centralization. Westphalia is a blueprint for order based on a factual situation of considerable anarchy. In theory, it needs no central authority, no governmental institutions, to maintain acceptable social order among the component units. Before we consider the kinds of problems arising from that conception of world order, particularly in the current period, we should be clear about its logical implications for state behavior if it is to be an acceptable arrangement for social order.

Among the most basic implications are the mutually supportive ones of self-help and nonintervention. The first describes the directive to the sovereign whose own values are threatened, and the second is meant to prevent the sovereign from threatening the values of others. Together they serve to sustain the decentralization of power and authority and the essential impermeability of the territorial state. Neither precept would receive nearly as prominent a place in the social code of any domestic order, which is characterized by a much greater degree of centralized authority than exists in the Westphalian world. In domestic systems, individuals are strongly discouraged from relying on self-help to redress their grievances. Instead, they are expected to turn to the authorities for such action. By the same token, though individuals are not expected to intervene willy-nilly in the affairs of their neighbors—a precept that generally goes under the heading of respecting the rights of others—they nonetheless are expected to intervene to help stop a crime and to prevent, or at least report, any other violation of the society's laws. What is unacceptable behavior by one citizen toward another within their own state is truly moral for the state authority acting in relation to other sovereigns.

The logic of Westphalia is that it is a positive good to keep the various subjects apart from each other (insofar as possible) with the general understanding that their apartness itself can be maintained only if they all agree on its mutual value for each. Two interrelated examples among the characteristic normative developments of the Westphalian period are the emergence of a doctrine of neutrality for states in time of war between other sovereigns and the gradual abandonment of earlier, pre-Westphalian doctrines that attempted to ascertain the justness of one's cause in war. If nonintervention in the affairs of others is a fundamental directive of the normative order, then these two developments helped maintain it.

A sovereign declaring its neutrality manifests its unwillingness to intervene in someone else's quarrel. In doing so, the logic of sovereign equality is supported (support of neutrality suggests that no sovereign has the right to judge the motivations of fellow sovereigns, including whatever factors have led them into war), and the logic of the system's ordering rationale is maintained (some violence between sovereigns may be unavoidable, but it can be kept within narrow bounds if disinterested sovereigns avoid entering the conflict). Neutrality supports a kind of quarantining of interstate violence so that it does not infect all parts of the system. Similarly, the decline of just war doctrine in the modern world reflects the view that the attempt to determine justice in a conflict is incompatible with a system of decentralized authority. If various sovereigns perceived the justness of a particular conflict variously, the result would be the inevitable widening of the war if they intervened to support their favored belligerent instead of refusing to judge in the matter and remaining aloof.[11] Contrary as it may seem to our own experience within domestic systems of order, the absence of centralized authority in the international system requires that each local authority largely ignore the rights and wrongs of other sovereigns' grievances. The outcome may not be just in any advanced understanding of that term, but it is meant to secure the more basic value, that of the general security of the whole.

The important thing to note is that these behavioral imperatives do not indicate the absence of all social order; rather, they help clarify a different kind of ordering arrangement than we are accustomed to seeing at work in our daily lives. Already some of the implications of these normative precepts for international political behavior should be apparent. Reliance on self-help explains why nation-states typically arm themselves and seldom hesitate to use military force if that appears to be the only means left for achieving their objectives. The fact that most states have such a military capability may also help reinforce the general disavowal of intervention in each other's affairs. And support of neutrality can lead in extreme cases to a general policy of isolationism in which the state carries the effort to keep itself largely apart from its fellows to its farthest possible conclusion. There are, of course, a great many other implications, but this sketch of some basic doctrines of Westphalian order suggests both that it is a true system of law and order and that it bears little resemblance to the hierarchical ordering with which we are all most familiar domestically.

Still another reason for the success of the Westphalian mode, although a lesser one, has been the very simplicity of its ordering logic and of the conditions required for full participation. Once the prerequisites for sovereignty are met—traditionally a government's effective control over a discrete population and territory—recognition by other sovereigns is virtually assured. With that the new sovereign actor can instantly participate within the normative system on an equal footing with all others. Each is ostensibly bound by the same rights and duties, and each, regardless of its relative power, is likely to have a dominant interest in supporting and maintaining them. For the weak, that interest is particularly apparent because the common legal system affords them whatever protections they have against the strong.[12] But the strong have an interest in maintaining the system as well; first, it is *their* system in the sense that it supports a status quo in which they prosper, giving them certain freedoms within both the power and the normative dimensions of their lives that are not available to the weak—most notably in the realm of conflict regulation and in their greater ability to extend their own values and interests beyond their territorial boundaries. Second, however, by providing regularity and predictability in terms of the rules of participation, it thereby ensures the kind of minimum order necessary for the achievement of many of their own goals.

The triumph of the organizing logic of Westphalia became evident by the mid-twentieth century. Then for the first time, the European normative system became a true world system as non-European actors in great numbers achieved statehood. In fact, this globalization of the European order has certainly created new and unprecedented strains within it, so that it is anything but clear that the Westphalian order in any meaningful, traditional sense has triumphed. But the fact that its ground rules for participation have now been so widely accepted is at least a demonstration of their economy and appeal.

Laissez-Faire in World Politics

The Westphalian system must be counted as one of history's success stories in very important respects. Its endurance over more than three hundred years attests to that. The factors that account for that endurance relate significantly to Westphalia's relevance to the real social and physical world this normative system has sought to order. In general terms, Westphalia's success is a function of its utility (at least its helpfulness to dominant political elites) in ordering the realm of power capabilities. Perhaps it is most helpful to our understanding of Westphalia's success if we consider its guiding principles as supporting an international arrangement of considerable laissez-faire.[13]

In its broadest implication, the concept of laissez-faire (literally, "allow to do") supposes that the common good is best served by giving the largest measure of freedom possible to individual actors within society to serve their own interests. Such an outlook is most frequently applied in matters of economics, particularly in association with the work of Adam Smith and other proponents of economic capitalism. Here, laissez-faire theory assumes that less government regulation of the economic marketplace is better because the market itself will act to encourage the profit motive, from which will come investment, growth, and a competition among producers that will assure the consumer of the availability of goods at the lowest possible cost. Underlying these claims is the view that the market is self-regulating when left alone and that governmental intervention simply interferes with and distorts the natural tendency for a free market to provide the greatest economic good to the greatest number within the society.

One might also advocate a political system of considerable laissez-faire if one believed that individuals might best achieve their most important values when left largely alone by governments. The English philosopher John Locke did almost exactly that by arguing that individuals should be freed from the heavy hand of governmental interference beyond what was minimally necessary to maintain basic social order.[14] Locke assumed that such an arrangement would release the creative energies of liberated individuals to generate wealth, culture, and enlightenment—all products that would contribute to the health of the society at large. The modern liberal democratic state owes much of its rationale to Locke in the same way that modern capitalism counts Smith as its founding father.

The Westphalian international system is also best characterized as a laissez-faire system, inasmuch as it too proceeds on the assumption that unrestrained and coequal actors (here nation-states rather than individual persons) should be allowed to help themselves to a great extent to the values of their choice and thereby assist the achievement of the general welfare of all members of the society. The man known as the father of modern international law, Hugo Grotius, stands in relation to the world order system of Westphalia much as Locke does to limited constitutional government and Smith to free enterprise in economics. Each writer emphasized the good that would come to the whole of the respective domain he studied from an absence of strong centralized control and thus a relatively great amount of freedom for the individual actors within the system. Each was an advocate of laissez-faire.

Where the laissez-faire quality of the Westphalian order is concerned, its strength and persistence can be partially explained in the fact that it has served the interests of those who have created, have maintained, and have been subjected to it—the sovereign states themselves. Again, to analogize to the Lockean civil state, which legitimized the rule and values of an ever more powerful middle class, Westphalia created an environment conducive to the free development and growth of sovereign states. There is even a certain similarity in the nature of the law within the two systems. Both regard a primary function of the law to be restraining other actors—including, most obviously in Locke's civil state, community or central institutions—from dominating or coercing the individual actor. The law provides a set of negative constraints against the would-be dominant forces so that individual actors may develop freely. In this respect, the U.S. Bill of Rights, with its emphasis on what the federal government may *not* do to the individual citizen, is philosophically akin to the Grotian doctrine of freedom of the seas, which prohibits any central power from restraining states in their right of access to the seas. Both of these prescriptions are meant to prevent the growth of central regulatory power into areas where private realization of values is regarded as preferable for the individual and, as a result, indirectly the whole society.

Much has been said to criticize the laissez-faire outlook in economics and in the political systems of nation-states. Much of what follows in this book will amount to a critique of laissez-faire as an organizing principle for the world's normative order. But to start, we should be clear about the basic context needed to make any doctrine of laissez-faire, political or economic, appealing and successful. It can best be described as a context of great and perhaps nearly unlimited potential abundance.[15]

Consider the following allegory: Each of two couples has three children, but the first family is poor and the second is extremely wealthy. The first set of parents want their children to have toys but have money to buy only one plaything, not three. The second set of parents feel virtually no limitations at all on the amount of money they may spend for toys for their children. Now the first set of parents, seeking justice and order among their children in their condition of scarcity, will surely buy a toy that all three children can enjoy. And to ensure that end, they may lay down certain rules as to which child is to play with it at what times. A certain amount of authoritarian rule from on high is essential to produce fundamental fairness in this situation of scarcity. Yet the second set of parents may reasonably send each child into the toy store with the happy instruction to buy whatever he or she desires. Leaving aside all questions about the long-term effects such indulgence may have on the children, we may suppose that they will emerge happy with their purchases and without having undergone any conflict among them, for we must suppose that the store has stocked duplicates of toys to avoid the hair pulling that might result if more than one child wished for the same plaything. Laissez-faire in this case has produced mutually satisfactory rewards. All the parents were required to do was to supply the context of abundance.

Underlying Locke's view of what civil society ought to be like is his not always unspoken assumption that the world is a place of nearly unlimited abundance, able to provide sustenance and even riches for all. And if forced to admit that late seventeenth-century England did not always look like such a place, his usual response was to argue that one should then go to America, which for him was almost a metaphor of the boundlessly rich natural state, needing only entrepreneurship to bring forth its bounty.[16]

Similarly, the Grotian view that the seas of the world should be open to all on the basis of reciprocity supposed that the seas themselves were almost endlessly vast and bountiful. No actor could gain a permanent advantage by trying to close off a portion of the sea to others; the sea was too huge for that and the costs entailed not worth the effort. But all sovereigns could benefit mutually through their commerce on the seas, provided all were allowed equal access. If certain states had a natural advantage in the resulting competition for trade, so did certain members of Lockean society within their universe, for in neither instance was it supposed that equal rights necessarily produced equal results for individual actors.

The technology and population density of the seventeenth century were such that both Locke's and Grotius's expectations of great abundance were quite sensible. Neither could have imagined exploitation of the earth's resources on a scale that would have threatened their very continuation by an exploding population that would fill virtually all the land space of the earth. Potential abundance was the reality of the time that nurtured both notions of laissez-faire. Just as the unrestrained individual might, through his unrestricted labor, prosper within domestic societies, so too could the unhampered sovereign turn most of its energies inward when no longer checked by external authority, thereby concentrating on the state's development economically, politically, and socially. At both domestic and international levels of society, the enshrinement of laissez-faire gave free rein to the potential growth of the individual unit acting more or less in isolation from its fellows.

Shared Values and the Double Standard

The Lockean and the Grotian world views were also alike in their optimism that those given freedom to act without serious restraints would not themselves make life intolerable for others, including those over whom they exercised power. Although Locke was the apologist for the rising middle class, he can be read as having supposed that the creative potential of the untettered individual could eliminate class lines, opening successful entrepreneurship to everyone. That at least is the favorite reading of Locke by Americans who find themselves unable to see class divisions in their own, strongly Lockean society.

For Grotius, the issue is somewhat more complex but nonetheless analogous. Grotians had to approach the issue from a reverse path from that of Lockeans: Whereas Locke sought to justify greater limitations on the central authority, Grotius had to consider what kind of justice was possible within a system that had lost its central authority.[17] He and his followers had essentially two sorts of responses. First, they supported the view that even in the absence of centralized institutions in Europe, a large measure of common values made the new normative system possible after all. Therefore, by encouraging actors to recognize their common obligations and responsibilities to each other, those values presumably could be protected. Limitations on the depredations one sovereign actor might do to others would have to flow from the greater pull of recognized shared values.

Second, Grotians recognized and encouraged the growth of the liberal state in civil society. If tyranny and the arbitrary uses of power domestically could truly be ended thereby, then the protection of individual rights could safely be left to the new limited governments themselves, instead of seeking the ephemeral intervention of some higher but by definition weaker body. In keeping with this view, by the nineteenth century strict positivists had found general acceptance of their theory that international law acted only on sovereigns directly and on individuals just to the extent that the law was incorporated into civil law. That view, in turn, was acceptable only because the underlying community of values on which it was built still stood. The bourgeois state of that period was indeed one of more or less limited government, but the state itself was re-markably free of normative restraints from above it (through the reduced authority of the natural legal tradition most evidently) to regulate its con-duct toward those within its jurisdiction.

Both of these sets of expectations proved realistic enough over the two hundred years and more after Grotius wrote to allow Westphalian laissez-faire to function and even to thrive. There were periodic dislocations, as when Napoleon seized on an imperial, pre-Westphalian vision of European order with himself at the apex of authority, but what is notable is that Napoleon did not succeed. When the Congress of Vienna cleaned up after the Napoleonic wars in 1815, its participants were careful to restore the pre-Napoleonic map of Europe so that the game of nation-state coexistence in accordance with laissez-faire rules could be played again. The French em-pire in Europe was dismantled, but France the nation-state was restored to its place as coequal actor. Later in the nineteenth century, the unification of Germany produced several military conflicts among European powers, the most damaging of which was between the emergent German state and France. Yet whatever the long-term injury to French interests, the result was essentially and most importantly the creation of simply one more major na-tion-state capable of participating in the Westphalian order in a way its predecessor principalities and other small sovereigns could not.

For the Europe-centered Westphalia of the early modern period, the con-text of abundance was the rest of the world, the technique for exploiting its resources, imperialism. No doubt the availability of the larger world did much to reinforce standards of nonintervention and mutual respect within the European framework, for these principal state actors never assumed that such standards should apply in their treatment of peoples and territo-ries outside Europe. Their paramount diplomatic concern in this age of ex-tra-European imperialism was the effects of their colonizing and trading activities abroad on their relations with fellow sovereigns, that is, fellow European actors. Once a European power secured its claim to a colonized territory overseas, that region became, in effect, a part of the sovereign's own state from the standpoint of international law and was subject to the same standards of noninterference and nonintervention that applied to the metropolitan territory and population. Seen in this light, the European im-perial powers did not even need to recognize that they were operating on a double standard, for that would have assumed that colonized peoples had been sovereign, or at least were potentially sovereign, in the absence of Eu-ropean imperialism, whereas it was much neater and less troubling to make no such assumptions about those living beyond the bounds of Eu-rope. The rest of the world lived simply in the state of nature, to use the Lockean conception of human existence prior to the formation of society, from which the European order could continue to form itself.

Needless to say, the economic and political conceptions of laissez-faire often coalesced in the history of European imperialism. That is, the process of acquiring colonies abroad was often much less the result of conscious policy at the seat of the European government than it was the result of the entrepreneurial activity of its private or semiprivate citizens. The role of the British East India Company during the eighteenth century in India is an obvious case in point. It became the duty of the state to extend the protection of the flag where the entrepreneurial activity of its citizens demanded it, so long, of course, as such claims were not attempted within the spheres already demarcated to other European sovereigns.

This conception of the operative international rules of the game was flexible enough to permit the occasional and usually gradual addition of new sovereign actors over time. Late in the eighteenth century, English colonists in North America grew weary of being treated as second-class subjects (they objected to the double-standard mentality as it applied to themselves), and after a fight, emerged as a new sovereign within the Westphalian system. More than a century later, Japan was added as a sovereign actor, but not until its government had demonstrated its willingness and ability to play by the rules of the game imposed by Westphalia, a demonstration no doubt made all the more persuasive by the Japanese penchant for adopting many Western styles of behavior in addition to those characteristic of the conduct of diplomacy. Throughout much of this period, Ottoman Turkey, which was neither Christian nor wholly within Europe, played a somewhat anomalous role on the fringes of the system, but gradually it assumed a recognized place within the international order as an imperial power. Finally, by the end of World War I, the logic of Westphalia had triumphed in that region too, creating several new nation-states out of the ashes of the traditional empire.

The place of much of Latin America in this system after it gained independence from Spanish and Portuguese rule early in the nineteenth century reveals Westphalia's ability to accommodate new actors and its inherent tendency (which would become more apparent in the second half of the twentieth century) to foster the proliferation of sovereign states. The success of the liberationist struggle could be tested with considerable objectivity in European capitals, for it entailed, as elsewhere, evidence of effective control by independence-minded political elites in Latin America over populations and territories. Then, however, European recognition of the new nations helped ensure that formal political change in the New World would not also bring radical shifts in the capabilities and influence of core European actors behaving as imperialists there. If Spanish rule had been replaced by, say, French dominion in South America, the general equilibrium of European great powers might well have been shattered. Instead, recognition of the new states clearly supported the maintenance of the European balance by formalizing the hands-off relationship toward them that is fundamental to Westphalian rules.[18]

Balancing Power in a Decentralized World

This example suggests that the tendency toward balancing power may be characteristic of any highly decentralized social system whose actors have diverse interests. What is entailed in the balancing process is a search for allies, that is, other individuals who are perceived to share at least some of the same interests, with whom one can counteract opposing interests from other members of the group. If some approximation of true balance is the result, no one's unwanted values will crowd out the others, which then can be maintained within the group without being imposed on unwilling members. The solution is not a true resolution of the conflict of the values in question but a perpetuation and a reinforcement of the various actors' freedom to pursue their own interests as long as they do not infringe on the right of others to do the same.[19]

Clearly, for some such outcome to work, there must be prior agreement among the contestants on the underlying rules of the game, on the fundamental importance of maintaining the system so that the game may continue to be played. In short, those game-playing values must be shared so that other, diverse interests may be contested in the game itself. That in turn requires that the players, and especially the most important players, remain convinced that they have more to lose by abandoning the game and engaging in a free-for-all than they do by staying within the established rules. For that to happen, they must be reasonably content with their lot already, more willing to defend it than to risk it all in the chance of winning more.

As the history of the modern state system makes clear, the stability of the system demands that most of the most important actors maintain foreign policies essentially oriented toward maintaining the international status quo. That important generalization can be tested by anyone studying the diplomatic history of the European states in the modern period. It does not mean, of course, that satisfied states will never go to war. Rather, they will only (or at least usually) resort to violence as a means of preventing radical shifts in the capabilities of other actors, and as a result, in their own position in the world. In this sense, Westphalia permits the resort to force by states as the ultimate available police power when nonviolent forms of coercion fail. And since force is the ultimate instrument of coercion, its employment by status quo great powers corresponds to their perception of a threat to the stability of the system itself, an effort to overthrow the rules of the game.

The difficulty with these propositions, which have long been generally understood by the leading diplomats of Europe, is not their lack of clarity or logic in principle, but the possibilities for their subjective and therefore varying application in practice—a matter of some consequence in a world of numerous sovereign authorities, all equally entitled to make their own subjective applications of the principles. To take an important example, we may suppose that from the viewpoint of the Prussian Chancellor Bismarck in the 1860s, his policies directed toward the unification of the north German states under the centralized leadership of Prussia were not challenges to the rules of the game. Rather, they were entirely within the logic of nation-state conception that had long prevailed elsewhere in Europe and were intended merely to bring a unified Germany into line, albeit by enhancing Prussian leadership in that process, with the established arrangement of sovereign actors. However, the government of Napoleon III viewed the prospect of enhanced German capabilities as an unacceptable threat to the French status quo, with the ultimate result that France felt compelled to go to war to prevent such a development. In the end, the victory of a united Germany did not destroy the system, although we can say with the vision of a century's hindsight that the nearly complete collapse of the French military effort no doubt resulted in a settlement that in turn changed France from a status quo to a revisionist power, with long-term destabilizing consequences for France, Germany, and the entire world order system of the first half of the twentieth century.[20]

As suggested above, the balance-of-power game traditionally has been played principally, if not exclusively, by the greatest powers within the Westphalian world. That has been so, first, because their greater capabilities permitted them to pursue foreign policy that was more assertive than that of smaller powers (not coincidentally, traditional neutral states in the modern period, e.g., Sweden and Switzerland, have been small powers) and no doubt led their leaders to define the national interest in active terms instead of passive terms. To say this much is little more than tautological, for great power status has always supposed such a state's willingness to play a leading role (that is, a dynamic, far-ranging, and multifaceted one) in international diplomacy. The second reason for great power interest in balancing power is more precise: *Because* they are great powers, leading states typically have the greatest stake in maintaining the established order from which they have clearly profited. Their capabilities combine with their interests to make them the effective managers of the world's political system.[21]

Great Power Concerts

As a result of that special role, great powers sometimes have been able to take a clearer, more highly rationalized position of leadership than the uncertainties of balancing power alone permit. On such occasions, they have consciously formed themselves into a directorate for conflict control, transforming competing alliances into a joint condominium. The classic example was the nineteenth-century Concert of Europe, a somewhat flexible grouping of the greatest powers on the continent and in the world. The Concert had its origins in the Congress of Vienna, which met in 1815 in the aftermath of Napoleon's defeat to restore the map of Europe to its pre-Napoleonic configuration. The earlier success of Napoleon's imperialism, after all, had marked the failure of traditional balance-of-power diplomacy to check his ambitions; now he had been brought down by the concerted action of those with a vested interest in restoring the pre-Napoleonic status quo. Therefore, the creation of the Concert marked the determination of those conservative states not to allow a new imperialist to arise. Its work during the remainder of the century amounted to periodic meetings of its diplomats to find consensus on how to treat international political developments that threatened, in the absence of great power agreement, to disrupt the system.

A sense of the Concert of Europe's successes, and therefore of its importance as a kind of police force for the European system, is apparent in the following comment by Inis L. Claude Jr.:

> The Concert decided on the admission of new members to "Europe," as when it accepted Greece and Belgium as independent states in 1830, and declared that non-Christian Turkey was entitled to full status in the European system in 1856. It undertook ... "to maintain the equilibrium of Europe," and in pursuance of this aim, intervened in such matters as the Russo-Turkish conflicts of the 1850's with a view to preventing the disruption of the balance of power upon which European order was deemed to depend. It assumed the responsibility of formulating certain standards of European public policy, as when it insisted at the Congress of Berlin in 1878 that Serbia could "enter the European family" only if it recognized the religious liberty of its subjects, described as one of "the principles which are the basis of social organization in all States of Europe."[22]

In a very general sense, the Westphalian order had managed to survive its first two centuries because from the beginning it had embodied a rudimentary community of interest among the states of Europe, which alone had kept conflicts within acceptable bounds and perpetuated the basic arrangements of sovereignty. But the creation of the Concert of Europe in the nineteenth century was a clear advance toward greater order within the system, although at the expense of the opposite of order: freedom for the individual units to go their own way. The Concert was made possible only because the great powers of the period perceived themselves as sharing a considerable pool of common interests in their foreign policies, not the least of which was their mutual desire to maintain their own exalted positions within the international arena.

Yet even when the Concert was at its height, the separate pulls of sovereignty generally guaranteed enough simultaneous distrust among the great powers to prevent them from becoming dictators in all aspects of the lives of lesser or excluded nations. A complex range of interests and capabilities, some competing, some in harmony, converged to create an acceptable middle ground between rigid, centralized control and disintegrative freedom for Europe and the rest of the noncolonized world. The twentieth-century world has seldom succeeded in replicating this situation, certainly not with the success or the longevity of that in the nineteenth century. Whatever the injustices of international politics that accompanied the reign of the Concert—and there were many—it was, when measured in terms of the comparatively low levels of interstate violence in the period, the most successful ordering arrangement yet devised by the Westphalian world.

Notes

1. For a discussion of Westphalia's importance, see Leo Gross, "The Peace of Westphalia, 1648–1948," *American Journal of International Law* 42, 1 (January 1948):20–41. A lucid account of the different normative system of medieval Europe is contained in Ernest Barker, "Introductory: Mediaeval Political Thought," in *The Social and Political Ideas of Some Great Mediaeval Thinkers*, ed. F. J. C. Hearnshaw (New York: Barnes and Noble, 1923), pp. 9–33.

2. Ernest Barker reminded us that "when we speak of Church and State in any consideration of the Middle Ages, we must remember that we are not speaking of two societies, but rather of the two governments of a single society.... It was a single *Respublica Christiana*, in which churchmanship was coextensive with citizenship. You could not be a member of a political society unless you were a baptized Christian; and if you were excommunicated by the Church you lost all legal and political rights" (ibid., p. 14).

3. The Holy Roman Empire is a classic example of a political arrangement that long outlived the values that gave rise to it, so much so that by the eighteenth century its by then anachronistic quality prompted Voltaire's famous quip: The Holy Roman Empire, he said, was neither holy, nor Roman, nor an empire.

4. In Barker's words, "There was no organized State to confront the clergy. It has often been said that in the Middle Ages there was no State; and at any rate we may say that . . . there were only feudal communities, dissipated in fiefs and communes, with no regular officials or organized methods of action" ("Introductory: Mediaeval Political Thought," p. 16). For a more recent analysis of the origin and meaning of feudal anarchy, see Gianfranco Poggi, *The Development of the Modern State* (Stanford, Calif.: Stanford University Press, 1978), p. 31.

5. Bodin's writings, *Six Books of the Republic*, are summarized in George H. Sabine, *A History of Political Theory*, 4th ed., rev. Thomas Landon Thorson (Hinsdale, Ill.: Dryden, 1973), Chapter 21.

6. Modern colonialism, i.e., that which was widely engaged in by the great European powers until very recently, of course coexisted with sovereign equality in

the international legal system for centuries. The jurisprudential argument was that colonial holdings, which by definition were not sovereign, had their interests represented by the imperial (and sovereign) metropoles. It could not very well be argued that colonial peoples were treated by their own sovereigns on an equal basis with citizens of the metropole, but not until late in the colonial period did such an observation develop an irresistible moral force. In purely legalistic terms, there are no difficulties in rationalizing the double standard as stemming from the separate facts of sovereign equality for the international actors on the one hand and inequality within domestic, imperial structures on the other.

7. For an excellent discussion of the way in which the great German philosopher of the early modern period, Baron von Leibniz, defined sovereignty as dependent on the essential impermeability of the territorial state, see John H. Herz, *International Politics in the Atomic Age* (New York: Columbia University Press, 1959; Columbia Paperback Edition, 1962), pp. 49–61, 1962 ed. In this context, impermeability means the ability of the territorial ruler (the sovereign) to constrain his subjects while not being so constrainable by superior power. By the time Leibniz wrote, whatever loyalty the emperor still commanded from his princes had become largely a matter of personal fealty. He generally could no longer constrain them into doing his will.

8. The European wars of religion had been motivated by the mutual desire of Protestants and Catholics to suppress—even eliminate, for the most zealous among them—the other, which would have required dominant or hierarchical control. The great ideological achievement of Westphalia was to secularize Europe's international politics thereafter through adoption of the principle *cuius regio eius religio* (whose the region, his the religion), which paved the way for genuine religious toleration in political affairs. That achievement was in an important sense the result of the perceived destructive cost of religious warfare and was supported by Westphalia's more general principle of nonhierarchical organization.

9. A classic work on this subject remains Carlton H. J. Hayes, *The Historical Evolution of Modern Nationalism* (New York: Macmillan, 1931). The reader should note that nationalism had scarcely begun to break the bounds of the European world when Hayes wrote this work.

10. Imperial states lasted much longer in Eastern than in Western Europe. Indeed, the Soviet Union, which was created in 1917, was the inheritor of the empire of the Russian tsars that it succeeded. Czechoslovakia and Yugoslavia were formed after World War I out of the ruins of the Austrian (Hapsburg) and Turkish (Ottoman) empires. One aspect of those imperial legacies was that ethnic communities tended to be far more intermixed in these regions than they were further to the west, where the nation-state had been invented two to three centuries earlier.

11. For a brief analysis of the emergence of a just war doctrine in the early modern period, its subsequent demise, and its revival in the nuclear age, see Lynn H. Miller, "The Contemporary Significance of the Doctrine of Just War," *World Politics* 16 (January 1964):254–286. For a more detailed analysis of the continuing importance of the doctrine and its new relevance today, see Michael Walzer, *Just and Unjust Wars* (New York: Basic Books, 1977).

12. As much a truism for states as for individual human beings are the words of a member of the French National Assembly in 1848, "Entre le fort et le faible c'est

la liberté qui opprime et la loi qui affranchit" ([in relations] between the strong and the weak, liberty oppresses and law sets free).

13. Richard A. Falk has frequently made use of the term "laissez-faire" to describe the basic organizational principle of Westphalia, and I am indebted to him for its explanatory value in this context. See, for example, Falk's *This Endangered Planet* (New York: Random House, 1971).

14. John Locke, *Of Civil Government: Second Essay* (Chicago: Gateway Editions, 1955), especially Chapters 9–13, 15, 18, and 19.

15. In the words of Richard A. Falk, "Any laissez-faire system of organization presupposes the absence of scarcity as a basic condition. Scarcity calls for allocation; excess capacity in a system of automatic checks is consistent with unrestricted use" ("Toward Equilibrium in the World Order System," *American Journal of International Law* 54, 4 [September 1970]:217–224).

16. Locke, *Of Civil Government*, Chapter 5 ("Of Property"), pp. 25, 29–30. I am indebted to Peter Bachrach for calling my attention to Locke's metaphorical references to America in this regard.

17. This issue is explored in Cornelius J. Murphy, "The Grotian Vision of World Order," *American Journal of International Law* 76, 3 (July 1982):477–498.

18. As always in my effort to elucidate basic rules of the game for sovereign actors, this account deliberately ignores the incentives for actors to disregard them in their maneuvering for increased capabilities. The diplomatic history of this period makes clear that certain European great powers did attempt to extend neoimperial influence into Latin America after its general independence and that for the most part the efforts of the Holy Alliance in these directions were opposed by Great Britain and the United States, a policy the latter country articulated in its Monroe Doctrine. There is no reason to argue that the British and U.S. policy was any more high-minded or motivated by devotion to the rules of the game than that of the continental European powers. Their own interests, they determined, could be best supported by opposing radical shifts in the international power balance of the kind that might have resulted from ignoring Holy Alliance power plays in Latin America. The historical record merely supports the generalization that the Westphalian mode of organizing world politics strongly encourages the balancing of power relationships.

19. Students of U.S. politics will note the similarity between the operations of the balance of power internationally and the theory of pluralism as an explanation of how democracy operates within the United States. The authors of *The Federalist* were the classic pluralists in the American tradition. See also twentieth-century writings that take a similar point of view, for example, Edward C. Banfield, *Political Influence* (New York: Free Press, 1961); Robert A. Dahl, *Pluralist Democracy in the United States* (Chicago: Rand McNally, 1967); and E. E. Schattschneider, *The Semi-Sovereign People* (New York: Holt, Rinehart and Winston, 1960).

20. France's humiliating defeat included the proclamation of the new German empire, not in Berlin, but in Paris and, more substantively, Germany's annexation of the French provinces of Alsace and Lorraine. Thereafter, France and Germany became long-term enemies, a condition that naturally prevented them from becoming even temporary allies as they sometimes should have been in keeping

with balance-of-power requirements over the next seventy years. On this point, see Morton A. Kaplan and Nicholas deB. Katzenbach, *The Political Foundations of International Law* (New York: John Wiley, 1969), pp. 36ff.

21. Harold Nicolson, *The Evolution of Diplomacy* (New York: Collier Books, 1962), pp. 99–105.

22. Inis L. Claude Jr., *Swords into Plowshares*, 4th ed. rev. (New York: Random House, 1971), p. 26.

Suggested Readings

Claude, Inis L., Jr., *Power and International Relations*, New York: Random House, 1962.

Deutsch, Karl W., *Nationalism and Social Communication: An Inquiry into the Foundations of Nationality*, New York: John Wiley, 1953.

Gierke, Otto F. von, *Natural Law and the Theory of Society, 1500–1800*, translated by E. Barker, Cambridge: Cambridge University Press, 1958.

Hobsbawm, Eric J., *Nations and Nationalism Since 1780*, Cambridge: Cambridge University Press, 1990.

Hobson, John A., *Imperialism: A Study*, Ann Arbor: University of Michigan Press, 1965.

James, Alan, *Sovereign Statehood*, London: Allen and Unwin, 1986.

Kennedy, Paul, *The Rise and Fall of the Great Powers*, New York: Random House, 1987.

Kissinger, Henry, *A World Restored: Metternich, Castlereagh and the Problem of Peace, 1812–22*, Boston: Houghton Mifflin, 1957.

McNeill, William F., *The Rise of the West*, Chicago: University of Chicago Press, 1963.

Murphy, Cornelius J., "The Grotian Vision of World Order," *American Journal of International Law* 76, 3 (July 1982):477–498.

Olson, Mancur, Jr., *The Logic of Collective Action: Public Goods and the Theory of Groups*, New York: Schocken Books, 1968.

Poggi, Gianfranco, *The Development of the Modern State*, Stanford, Calif.: Stanford University Press, 1978.

Rosecrance, Richard, *The Rise of the Trading State*, New York: Basic Books, 1985.

Rothstein, Robert L., *The Weak in the World of the Strong*, New York: Columbia University Press, 1977.

Tilly, Charles, ed., *The Formation of National States in Western Europe*, Princeton, N.J.: Princeton University Press, 1975.

Ullmann, Walter, *Principles of Government and Politics in the Middle Ages*, New York: Barnes and Noble, 1966.

Walzer, Michael, *Just and Unjust Wars*, New York: Basic Books, 1977.

CHAPTER 3

The Twentieth-Century Challenge to Westphalian Order

The record of Sumerian, Hellenic, Chinese, and medieval Italian history demonstrates that a set of local sovereign states can be no more than a transitory political configuration.

—Arnold Toynbee, *Mankind and Mother Earth*

We have seen how a group of treaties negotiated three and a half centuries ago in Western Europe became the constitutional basis for the conduct of all states in their relations with each other down to the present day. Although that is a true depiction of the ongoing international order in fundamental respects, now we must explore the extent to which it may no longer be the whole truth. The past eighty or ninety years have seen many striking changes in the way we live, in the issues that find their way to the top of the international agenda, and therefore in the values that have helped to shape the content of international relations. Are these changes evidence that the traditional international order has been undermined? Or should we suppose that the altered agenda of international politics (which still shares something with that of the past) has little bearing on the underlying constitutional system of states, that issues come and go while the basic mode for dealing with them stays essentially the same?

One of the major problems we have in assessing the continuing power of the Westphalian order stems from the limitations of our own perspective as creatures of our time. We are so much a part of the late twentieth century that we cannot be certain whether, for instance, any of the important multilateral treaties of our era, such as the UN Charter, will one day be regarded as the Peace of Westphalia is now regarded—as altering in fundamental ways the rules of the game for international society and even of the nature and relationships of the actors within the world system. Many intelligent observers have insisted that no such fundamental change has taken place.[1] They caution against allowing wishful thinking to mislead us into supposing that basic changes have actually taken place if state behavior has changed little, regardless of some apparent novelties in formal commitments. To pursue the example of the United Nations, they might point out that even though the Charter grants the Security Council the authority to act to maintain international peace on behalf of all UN members—a novelty in Westphalian terms—the record makes clear that the Council seldom has been able to reach agreement on important peace-threatening matters, let alone enforce its decision.

That kind of skepticism regarding the formal commitments of states without attention to their behavior is perfectly justified, and any analysis of the real world of international politics that ignores it is doomed to failure. At the same time, the possibility also exists that our timeboundedness may present us with the perennial problem of not being able to see the forest for the trees. When considering important social change throughout the world, one can be far less sure of the significance of what is happening in one's own lifetime than in the more distant past. The Anglo-American world has long given homage to Magna Charta, for example, as the first great constitutional restraint on arbitrary government in our common history. Yet if we imagine ourselves in the place of, say, a small farm family of England in the year 1220 or 1250 or even later, we may doubt that they had any reason to celebrate the signing of that document in 1215 at Runnymede, assuming they even knew of the event. It would be many centuries before the descendants of those farmers would feel the impact of Magna Charta on their lives.

Even though it may be a very long time before future generations are able to find with assurance comparable benchmarks in our century, we can start to assess their presence by examining the major historical developments in international politics in recent decades as they appear to us today.

World War I and the Collapse of the Balance of Power

Much of the evidence now available suggests that World War I should be regarded as one of the most important conflicts in human history, a rare watershed event that ended an era in international politics and ushered in a new one. It was the first general European war in more than two and a half centuries, more like the Thirty Years' War in that respect than any of the other conflicts separating those two great events. As such, it marked both the triumph and the collapse of the balance-of-power policies that had been developed to a high degree during the nineteenth century. The balance of power triumphed in the fact that the alliance commitments of various European powers were honored: Russia supported Serbia, as it had pledged to do, in the face of an ultimatum against the little Balkan republic by Austria-Hungary; Germany thereby honored its commitment in the Dual Alliance by supporting Austria; France and ultimately Britain joined Russia, their ally in the Triple Entente, in the fight against the central powers, and World War I was under way.[2]

Since that is not at all the way balance-of-power politics were intended to work, the general outbreak of war also signaled the failure of those policies. An ominous prelude had been sounded in 1907 when British officials felt compelled to abandon their traditional aloofness in the political rivalries of the European continent—a posture that had permitted them to play the role of balancer and peacekeeper throughout the nineteenth century—by aligning themselves with France and Russia in opposition to the growing militarism of Kaiser Wilhelm II. Thus the conflict spread quickly once it started. In the absence of an effective balancer, the logic of counterbalancing power with power had become perverse. The coalitions were *too* evenly matched now, and neither could be intimidated into forsaking the battlefield by the threat of overwhelming opposing force. The honoring of commitments ineluctably closed off other avenues of choice, and states played out their roles as if caught up in a Greek tragedy.[3]

As the war ground on, its tragic aspects became apparent to many. Among the most articulate critics of the failure of the balance of power was U.S. president Woodrow Wilson. Once the United States finally entered the war, thus ensuring the defeat of the Central Powers, Wilson repeatedly called attention to the need to prevent such a catastrophe from happening again. He insisted that once peace was restored, what the world needed was "not a balance of power, but a community of power, not organized rivalries, but an organized common peace."[4] The logic of his position was based on a shrewder assessment of the balance-of-power politics long practiced by major European states than his later critics sometimes credited him with. He noted in effect that the balance of power was a double-edged sword and one whose destructive power more than offset whatever ability it once had had to keep the peace. When such policies worked, as undeniably they had in the past, they did so only by threatening war, a paradox that no doubt troubled Wilson at least in part on moral grounds. How humane was it, he might have asked himself, to maintain order through the threat of unacceptable disorder, to try to build peace on policies that emphasized states' differences rather than their common ground?

But certainly Wilson's most telling critique of the balance of power was unarguably realistic. As with any system of order built on deterrence, it lost all credibility once it failed, for in its failure it produced conflicts vastly wider and more devastating than could be expected by unprincipled behavior alone. If one can imagine a pre–World War I Europe in which *no* alliances existed and, further, where no major actor was willing to offer the slightest assistance to any state threatened by a fellow sovereign, then one can also picture a situation in which the assassination of the Archduke Ferdinand at Sarajevo would have produced, perhaps, the crushing of Serbia's independence by an outraged Austria-Hungary—and nothing more! We may regret such a hypothetical outcome for the Serbians, but in a world where one must always attempt to pursue the lesser and avoid the greater evil, it is difficult to argue that such a fate would not have been preferable for the larger human society than the actual outcome.

As we know, Wilson did not argue that such an outcome would have been preferable.[5] He called instead for the nations of the world to make not just a different, but an opposite, commitment from that of turning their backs on their neighbors. They should form themselves into a worldwide community pledged to assist each other mutually in restraining any would-be violator of the peace. They should transform their rival alliances, whose results were so disastrous when they failed to deter, into a single, overarching global alliance whose deterrent capabilities would be unquestioned because of the evident overwhelming force available to it. They should create a collective security system to replace the vagaries, the uncertainties, and the dangers of balance-of-power politics.

The Wilsonian vision was not, in fact, particularly original to Woodrow Wilson. From the earliest days of the Westphalian order, a number of thinkers had advanced similar views of a collective security alternative to what they saw as the dangerous every-state-for-itself permissiveness of the European normative system.[6] None of these earlier proposals had ever received serious attention by sovereign decisionmakers, so it is easy to dismiss them as unrealistic within the context of their times.[7] In the cataclysm of World War I, however, many people, including many leaders of sovereign states, apparently were persuaded that a new commitment to the peace of the whole community was needed as the only discernible way to protect the rights and interests of the individual units. Self-help strategies had brought disaster. Now was the time to create a League of Nations that would embody the historic turn away from self-help toward a worldwide commitment to mobilize whatever power was necessary to keep or restore the peace.

Collective Security: The Hunters and the Stag

A well-known parable seems particularly relevant to the experiences of the League of Nations.[8] A group of hunters, armed with primitive weapons, agree that the only way they can catch a stag is to form a circle around the spot where it is grazing and then slowly close in on it for the kill, after which they will share the spoils. They proceed as planned until one of the hunters sees a hare dart before his path and, calculating quickly that it would provide sufficient food for his immediate wants, breaks from the circle to capture it. When he does so, the stag is able to escape through the breach and the other hunters go hungry. The collective effort has been thwarted by the selfish act of one.

The parable demonstrates a critical truth about the concept of collective security. If it is to succeed, the element of free choice to opt out must be virtually eliminated once the commitment to the common good has been made. How such a state of affairs is dependably produced is an issue that goes to the very heart of community building at any level. Clearly, there is no single, simple technique of the sort a chemist may use to produce compounds of the elements in a laboratory. But just as clearly, the creation of such a social contract is not impossible, for if it were, no human communities would have been formed throughout our history. Within such communities, typically nation-states in the modern period, we take it for granted that the freedom of individuals to opt out at times and places of their own choosing is severely restricted. We can predict that most citizens will pay their taxes or serve in their nation's armed forces when compelled to do so, to take as examples two of what many consider to be the more distasteful restrictions on their absolute freedom.

The Covenant of the League of Nations, at whose heart lay the collective security commitment, was in form and in theory a social contract among the states that ratified it (covenant = contract). We know through hindsight that it was a failed contract, which left those who had committed themselves to it like the hungry hunters of the parable. In the final analysis, the deeply ingrained compulsion for self-help, for going it, if not alone, then with particular friends of one's own choosing, won out over the more abstract commitment to support the established peace and thereby the long-range interests of all the members. Where do we look for the reasons for this failure?

First, we look to what were no doubt serious flaws in the Covenant itself, flaws that reflected the initial reluctance of those states that created it to subordinate very many of their traditional freedoms to the common good. If universal collective security is to work, the threat of stringent sanctions must be credible to a would-be warring nation in much the same way that the government of any viable state can threaten arrest and prison terms to would-be criminals. Yet the Covenant was somewhat vague on the point of whether collective military action might be needed against an aggressor, nowhere specifying what procedures League members should follow in that case, and was specific only in its depiction of nonmilitary sanctions—

diplomatic and economic—that could be invoked against the outlaw state.[9] In the most well-known and fatally unsuccessful collective action undertaken by the League, that of economic sanctions invoked against Mussolini's Italy for its invasion of Ethiopia in 1935, the rueful conclusion of many was that the League lacked "teeth"; the League's action failed because it became troublingly clear that it was not having the desired effect. Mussolini was not coerced into obeying the law and got away with his illegal action. Therefore it seemed clear enough with hindsight that stronger police powers should have been prescribed in the Covenant, although when the Covenant was written, few participants would have found it realistic, that is, acceptable to their own governments, to commit themselves more fully to support a police power for the world.

The League's constitutional document also contained the rather murky provision that "nothing in this Covenant shall be deemed to affect the validity of . . . regional understandings like the Monroe doctrine, for securing the maintenance of peace."[10] These innocent-sounding words reflected a hard-fought battle at the Paris Peace Conference won by those who frankly did not trust the logic of Wilson's universal collective security commitment, preferring instead to maintain the principle that more traditional, partial alliances of states could continue to maintain the peace as they had attempted to do in the past. The result was a bit like trying to square the circle. The Covenant sought to obligate states under the principle that world peace was indivisible, that every violation of the peace anywhere in the world was everybody's business. But at the same time it suggested that some states would naturally maintain their own priorities—no doubt determined largely by geographical considerations—in deciding which peace-threatening issues would demand more determined responses than others.[11] Carried to its logical conclusion, this concession to regional ordering techniques invited the reestablishment of balance-of-power policies within a framework that would have no chance of maintaining peace if such policies were not forbidden.

These comments on some important weaknesses and inconsistencies in the Covenant in fact are comments on the unwillingness of those who created the League to abandon altogether traditional Westphalian modes of behavior even while they supposedly were committing themselves to a radically new concept. Ironically, even this somewhat timid departure from traditional international patterns proved too radical for Woodrow Wilson's own United States. That country's refusal to become a member of the League struck a serious blow, at least symbolically, to the future practicability of collective security itself. When important actors refuse to be bound by the collective will of the larger community, others are likely to find the temptation overwhelming to follow suit. In fact, out of the total membership of sixty-three states in the League, seventeen, or more than one-quarter, withdrew before the organization collapsed. The hunters' circle developed holes in so many places that it was little wonder the League's major effort at universal sanctions in the Italian case was doomed to failure.

The League did, of course, have some record of success, although in general the successes lay outside the realm of collective security action in the strictest sense. On more than one occasion, League involvement in an international dispute as an objective third party, whose role included the investigation of issues, efforts at mediation, and the like, helped produce a peaceful settlement.[12] Obviously, such techniques, including the extension of good offices and similar offers of help by neutral parties to assist in the settlement of disputes, long predated the creation of the League and are probably as old as diplomacy itself. In this respect, the novel place of the League as an instrument of order within a traditional system may have enhanced its role as peacemaker, but it was evidently not a role reflective of a transformed system. A friend may act as go-between when a marriage appears headed for the rocks and assist at a reconciliation, but not because she can coerce the unhappy couple into a rapprochement that neither wants. That is because the relationships among such parties are those of sovereign equals, capable perhaps of persuading but not of commanding each other. Only a judge has the authority in such a situation to command the couple, and the League never effectively and consistently carried out a judge's role.

Are we then simply to conclude that the Covenant of the League amounted to a false social contract, one that misguidedly purported to reflect the creation of a true world community where none in fact existed? This has been the thrust of much of the realist criticism of both Wilson and the League when its failure became evident.[13] As a sweeping generalization, it is no doubt an accurate conclusion although, as with all such generalizations, countertruths may lie hidden beneath it. What is much more difficult to determine because it is far less susceptible to generalization is the extent to which the League experiment may have nibbled away at some of the characteristic self-help expectations of the traditional Westphalian system, even without demolishing them. Such a possibility no doubt would not have teased our minds for long in, say, 1939 or 1940, for at that time we would have been justified in concluding that the noble experiment had failed and that Hitler's *Realpolitik* appeared to be a more vicious variant for the future of the game of politics characteristic of the past. But now we know that after World War II, a new version of the League was created in the United Nations, and although we may suspect that it too has failed to make the collective security commitment a predictably obligatory force in the contemporary world, we can at least not be so certain that it has been discarded as useless.

For the moment, there appear to be two lessons to keep in mind, their contradictory assertions serving as healthy correctives to each other. First, formal social contracts do not in themselves make a community if the underlying behavioral patterns supporting such an arrangement are not in place. Second, such a contract, even when it fails, may constitute a kind of chart for searching out and strengthening those patterns of behavior that support a developing community ideal.

Interwar Challenges to the Established Order

We can also see with hindsight what could not have been clear at the time the League of Nations was created: The twenty-year period between the world wars was one of unusual and nearly unprecedented challenges to Westphalian rules of the game by various state actors and of extensive ferment on the part of peoples that had hitherto been largely ignored by the Westphalian order. In the aftermath of the Treaty of Versailles, economic and social upheaval in Germany transformed that country into a humiliated, dissatisfied power, the long-term result of which brought the rise of one of the most maniacally aggressive governmental leaders the world had ever known. Meanwhile, tsarist Russia had undergone a sweeping social revolution during the course of World War I, which brought to power a Communist party of a type long feared by political elites in the West, so much so that the new Soviet state was widely regarded as a rogue, not to be trusted or included within international political councils.[14] Italy also produced a dictator who espoused an extremely virulent strain of nationalism with increasingly revisionist demands to make on his neighbors, and in the Far East, the rise of Japanese militarism led that country down a similar path.

The elites of all these states now gave evidence of their unwillingness to accept the general status quo, commitment to which by such great powers had always been critical to the stability of the Westphalian order,[15] just as that status quo orientation remained an essential assumption on which collective security in the League was built. Of the traditional great power keepers of the order, only Great Britain and France continued to play these roles. Austria-Hungary and the Ottoman Empire both had been dismembered in the war, whereas a prospective new great power with a considerable stake in the established order, the United States, refused to have that kind of greatness thrust upon it until after the interwar period had ended.

The result could not have been more unfortunate for developing a strong collective security system within the League, for that principle could work only if most of the great powers that had bound themselves to the Covenant were essentially satisfied powers willing to defend with their like-minded fellows against threats to violent disruptions of the territorial status quo as the cost that must be paid for the peace from which they above all profited. Nowhere was the presumed satisfaction with the status quo more clearly expressed than in the Covenant's Article 10, by which members undertook "to respect and preserve as against external aggression the territorial integrity and existing political independence of all Members of the League." Once revisionists came to power in Germany, Italy, and Japan, they found their policies in conflict with that provision of the Covenant whereupon, one by one, they simply renounced their countries' earlier commitment and left the organization. Only Stalin, in his cynicism, apparently thought that the then moribund League would look the other way for his violation of Article 10, but found his government expelled in 1939 for its attack on Finland.

The interwar period also marked the first chapter in an extended process of opening up the system to new sovereign actors. That phenomenon has produced continuing conflict over the proper goals of world order down to the present. In its immediate post–World War I phase, it complicated the task of responding effectively and with justice to the demands of revisionist great powers. Under the name of self-determination, the World War I peace settlements granted independence to a number of national groups long under the imperial domination of the Austrian Hapsburgs or the Ottoman Turks. Furthermore, the League's mandate system embodied the enlightened view for its time that the colonial dependencies of the defeated great powers (those "not yet able to stand by themselves under the strenuous conditions of the modern world") should not simply be annexed by the victors but should be administered by League members in a kind of public trust, with the eventual goal of self-determination.[16]

The diplomats who struggled with the peace treaties at Paris, as well as their successors down to the present day, discovered that self-determination is a formidable weapon for challenging the established order. National groups, especially in Eastern Europe, did not always live within cohesive territorial regions, particularly not after centuries of alien imperial rule. As a result, officials of the 1920s and 1930s had to wrestle with the attempt to reconcile the new sovereignties they had created with the injustices felt by many at the destruction of the traditional map of Europe. Of the revisionist leaders, Hitler was particularly adept at manipulating the self-determination ethic to support the Nazis' aggressive nationalism. He could point to the situation of the Sudeten Germans within the borders of Czechoslovakia to justify the annexation of large chunks of that country's territory, and when the British, French, and Italian leaders all agreed to his claims at Munich in 1938, they not only sealed Czechoslovakia's fate but also emboldened Hitler to make good on his irredentist claims to

Memel and the Polish Corridor. Within a year came the German attack on Poland and the fateful start of the second world war in the twentieth century.

A somewhat different light is cast on this interwar struggle between self-determination and imperialism when we consider the following. At the end of World War I, Great Britain laid claim to the loyalty of some 500 million people, about one-fourth of the earth's population and a quarter of its territory. The French empire covered only about a third as great an area, but nonetheless encompassed more than 100 million people. In contrast, Germany, Italy, and Japan held total populations about one-third larger than the total home populations of Britain and France, although without any of their overseas imperial territories. What were to become the three Axis powers ruled over a combined territory of less than 1.5 million square miles, as opposed to the British-French control over nearly twelve times that amount of territory. Those facts alone give a sense of the strength of the Axis impulse to acquire empires of their own in this period, especially because—and this is no doubt the most forceful engine of that impulse—the Western democracies obviously had not yet faced up to their own hypocritical postures on this subject. They had given their support to self-determination for national groups within the empires of defeated powers; self-determination for their own colonized peoples was quite another matter.[17]

Seen in this light, the interwar period is one of a global struggle between the two opposing forces—empire building and empire maintenance on one side and national self-determination on the other. World War II may have been above all an ultimately successful struggle to prevent the revisionist states from advancing their new imperial claims, claims that, subsequent history shows us, were truly reactionary, for the outcome of World War II was, ironically, to produce the beginning of the end of British and French imperialism as well. Here we have another of the truly momentous global changes of the twentieth century. After two world wars and several decades of contesting change, the double standard of the traditional order, which had justified inequality between European and non-European peoples, finally was overthrown, although not without one of the most prolonged and often violent struggles of the age.

Westphalia as a Global System

It is tempting today to see the almost complete demise of formal imperialism as historically predestined, but whether or not we take such a view—as, for example, a Leninist interpretation of history requires—we should at least remember that imperialism in various forms has been a recurring phenomenon throughout human history; therefore announcements of its death may well be premature. What we can say is that within our life-times imperialism has lost virtually all the sense of legitimacy it once had, even for those nations that were very recently the major imperialist pow-ers. It is not simply coincidental that the system of international order de-vised by a handful of European statesmen more than three hundred years ago has proved to be so congenial to non-Europeans struggling to assert their equal rights as international actors. The concept of sovereign equal-ity has proved to be as powerful an idea for abolishing twentieth-century imperialism as it was for ending the legitimacy of European feudalism in the seventeenth century.

We should draw two conclusions from this experience to guide our thinking about the Westphalian order's likely future. First, any legal or-der that claims rights for some cannot resist indefinitely the logical con-clusion that they must be granted to all like actors if it is to maintain a claim to any semblance of being a system of justice. As the history of Westphalia shows, those served by the system can deny the logic of such an idea for a very long time simply by defining unequal participants as not truly like themselves and therefore not entitled to participate on an equal footing. Nonetheless, the very idea of equality—whether of sover-eigns or of individual citizens within a domestic order—has proved to be an extremely dangerous idea to let loose on a hierarchical society, for as larger numbers of actors meet whatever requirements are demanded to be treated like equals, the tendency is irresistible to qualify still other members of the society as well.

The second conclusion, which reinforces the first where global ordering arrangements are concerned, is that the concept of sovereign equality, with its comparatively simple and concrete tests to qualify as such an ac-tor, remains the only alternative the modern world has been able to de-vise in opposition to hierarchical governmental principles. The result has not been an unmixed blessing from the standpoint of effective control over social disorder, but it undoubtedly has guaranteed greater freedom for more groups of people than any other kind of legal order known in history.

One paradoxical result today is that spreading the legal order to make it truly global may have stretched it beyond its capacity to do its work, that of maintaining acceptable order. The more actors who must agree be-fore any plan or policy can be implemented, the more cumbersome and difficult is the process of achieving consensus. During the nineteenth cen-tury, no more than half a dozen governments in Europe determined the destinies of several hundred million people in Africa and Asia, and to do so their representatives had to meet face-to-face only on a very occasional basis. In contrast, when by the 1970s it became necessary to try to regulate the exploitation of the ocean's resources, the representatives of 157 states

had to meet over the course of some ten years, during which the delegates were actually in session for a total of ninety-three weeks, before a
treaty could be completed.

But it is not just that widespread participation is more cumbersome.
Democratization has brought new issues and priorities to the agenda of
international politics. This fact may not in itself threaten the way in which
the business of international politics is conducted, but it is often impossible until long after the event to separate the actual impact of a policy goal
from the way in which it is perceived by other, especially hostile, actors.
The dominant Western view of the policy goals of the Soviet Union
throughout most of its history, or of the People's Republic of China in the
1950s and 1960s, was of dangerously revisionist elites bent on destabilizing the international order wherever possible to further their ultimate aim
of world revolution and conquest. Yet an objective reading of the foreign
policy record of either of these powers is at best ambiguous proof of such
motivations, nor is it particularly difficult to read much of those records
as evidence of comparatively restrained and even conservative foreign
policies in keeping with traditional Westphalian values.[18] The question of
the revolutionary or status quo orientation of important Communist governments *was* debatable, as the entire history of the cold war era makes
clear, and those who were inclined to accept the first rather than the second characterization made very different assessments about the extent of
their threat to Westphalian standards.

A converse case was that posed by the rise of Hitler and Mussolini.
Had not so many of their irredentist claims appeared to the elites of other
major actors at the time as examples of somewhat extreme but nonetheless traditional and therefore acceptable goals of major actors, they probably would have been more strongly opposed at an earlier stage, with the
result that World War II might have been averted. Clearly, perceptions of
the goals of other sovereigns may matter even more than their actual
goals—if such matters ever exist in an objective vacuum—in determining
the course of international politics.

Now that the Westphalian system has been opened to embrace the
world, one of the inherent difficulties confronting, especially, traditional
Western actors is that not only of judging the revolutionary or nonrevolu-
tionary character of the demands for change made by the newer states
but, even more important, assessing their likely world order impact if
they are implemented. For example, a basic interpretation of the interwar
period is to characterize the revisionist Axis powers as "have-not" states
that sought the kinds of overseas empires that the Western democracies
had long since acquired. We have some sense of the kinds of injustices to
large numbers of peoples that would have resulted had they succeeded.[19]
Today the continuing contest between much of the industrialized North

and the formerly colonized, underdeveloped South is again one between haves and have-nots. Not surprisingly, the economically dominant Northern states are extremely resistant to demands for the kind of structural change in the world's economic system that would undermine their privileged position. But there the parallels between the interwar and the contemporary situations end, for whatever the consequences if today's international economic order were to be radically reordered along the lines proposed by the Group of 77, it is difficult to suppose that the imposition of a rabid imperialism would be among them.[20]

The East-West split and the North-South conflict—together they are labels for the perception of many that the homogeneity of the Westphalian system, visible to and visibly encouraged by Grotius, vanished as that ordering arrangement was stretched to fit the world's politics over much of the second half of the twentieth century. Now that the East-West split itself is history, our own forest-and-trees dilemma lies in trying to assess whether Westphalian traditions are being renewed as a result, or whether they are still subject to revolutionary change in a world that has left Westphalia ever farther behind. A case against the revolutionary view is readily apparent in the formal operation of the system, for there Westphalia remains triumphant through whatever social change the century has brought. The smallest of the new states has all the formal trappings of its older European counterparts; the rules surrounding diplomatic intercourse today look much as they did to eighteenth-century diplomats; the mode of operation of, say, the UN General Assembly is Westphalian in its purest form.

Yet we know that underneath the formal continuity with the traditional mode, social changes may be transforming a system that looks much as it always has while it is gradually evolving to perform increasingly ceremonial functions. In Britain the queen still "commands" her subjects, even though for centuries the British Parliament and, in modern times, the Cabinet have ruled, in any meaningful sense of the term. The continuity of form in British government during nearly a thousand years does not hide the fact that both the government and the values that support it are radically different today than in the times of either William the Conqueror or Henry VIII.[21] Will future historians discern a transformed international system in our time, perhaps in social change that we are blind to as we focus instead on the traditional trappings of international interaction?

The Emergence of Bipolarity

For some purposes, it is useful to view the two world wars of this century as bracketing an intense period of upheaval initiated by the death of the traditional balance-of-power structure and ending in the novelty of a bipolar configuration in the post–World War II period. In these terms, the three decades from 1914 to 1945 were characterized by immense reordering change whose most immediately apparent outcome was the emergence of two new world actors, the United States and the Soviet Union, and the precipitate decline of the traditional great powers: Great Britain, France, Austria-Hungary, Germany, Italy, and the old Russia. A new term, "superpower," had to be coined to label the two new world actors, for their capabilities and influence left them alone at the center of the world stage for some forty-five years, from 1945 to about 1990.[22]

This development was accompanied by the onset of cold war with all that it implied regarding a vast global conflict for world leadership between two opposing forces. In its crudest terms, and especially in its earliest phases, the cold war was marked by the general attitude in each of the power centers that all who were not publicly committed to its own cause were at best suspect and at worst implacably hostile, a situation that made the prospect of balancing power across ideological lines a clear impossibility.[23] We search in vain throughout the Westphalian period for any parallel condition at the international level.

Only when we examine the European wars of religion of the sixteenth and seventeenth centuries do we begin to see some ominous similarities with the period from 1945 to 1990. Then, as during the cold war, the most zealous ideologues, whether Protestant or Catholic, regarded their opposite number as implacably hostile foes, to be eliminated if they could not be converted. Then, as in the decades after World War II, emotive labels for the enemy—papist, heretic, Communist, or capitalist imperialist— were used as reminders of the impassable gulf that separated one's own community from that of the enemy, even of the other side's lack of common humanity. Then, as in the post–World War II era, some regarded any war as just that could be inflicted on the enemy camp, to the point that the perceived righteousness of the conflict itself could overwhelm considerations of restraint and humane treatment of the enemy once war had broken out. We may find it repugnant that in the earlier conflict those identified as not of the true faith were drawn and quartered or burned at the stake. Yet the cold war also was characterized by its devil myth. The almost infinitely cunning enemy, the devil, was capable of brainwashing our innocent victims, and no doubt of worse, and therefore we felt justified, as some of us did during the war in Vietnam, in dropping them from helicopters or murdering their civilians, because presumably none of "them" was innocent.

These similarities of course do not describe the whole picture of bipolarity in the recent period of cold war. A major difference is that we did not actually see the Eastern and Western camps plunge, except somewhat indirectly, into battle like Protestants and Catholics in the Thirty Years'

War. Yet, to carry the parallel one step further, we know that the Thirty Years' War, more than any other upheaval, transformed medieval Europe into Westphalian Europe. Had the United States and the Soviet Union ever engaged in direct conflict, particularly with nuclear explosives, the modern system of world order surely would have been left in rubble. Now that the threat of such a holocaust has receded very substantially, so has that most nihilistic threat to the continuation of Westphalian order, not to mention to civilization as we know it.

That overarching threat is what made the tendency of the cold war to take on the coloration of religious warfare so frightening. Much of the justification for the growth of nonalignment as an appropriate political stance between the interests and demands of the superpower camps stemmed from the perceived dangers of an ideologically polarized world. Refusal to join irrevocably either of those parties who claimed ideological supremacy became a force working against both claims. Thus nonalignment in the cold war period allows another point of comparison to the early Westphalian age. In the early modern period, the role of the neutral became a respectable, conflict-limiting position in conjunction with the decline in ideological politics. Skepticism as to who is right and wrong in political disputes does not support just wars. Neutralism and nonalignment are the marks of actors who refuse to regard others, or the enemies of others, as devilish, even when they may not agree with them.

Perhaps the development of such skepticism and detachment in any social system at least marks a decline in dangerous polarization within the society and, further, the rise of a sense of toleration that can lead ultimately to a new, if heterogeneous or pluralistic, sense of community built on new dominant values that need not so much defeat as supersede the old ones. In this way, neither Protestants nor Catholics have been driven out of modern European society; rather, the two groups have learned to live together in dependable peace as other, shared values have been allowed to develop. As the cold war began to fade at the close of the 1980s, we witnessed a comparable crumbling of a holy war mentality between long-standing antagonists. The brighter prospect was for a post–cold war world of dependably nonideological politics and shared basic values, and from them, a sense of limited and negotiable competing interests.

From the aftermath of the Cuban missile crisis of 1962 until the mid-1980s, the cold war went through periodic thaws and freezes while remaining a constant feature on the world's political landscape. During the Nixon presidency, Secretary of State Henry Kissinger reestablished normal relations between the United States and China for the first time in twenty-five years so as to raise the specter of a Sino-American alliance before the Soviets and thereby frighten them into concessions in strategic arms negotiations.

That episode was characteristic of Kissinger's conception of détente, as essential not in spite but because of the deep conflict of interests between the United States and the Soviet Union, requiring constant efforts at amelioration if it were not to lead to disastrous, all-out war.[24] His policies also encouraged the growth of Western Europe and Japan as traditional, capitalist economic centers with an increased U.S.-style interest in resisting revolutionary change.[25] Kissinger's entire effort was meant to stabilize the superpower relationship by encouraging tendencies that would counterbalance the Soviets on the part of other actors with a presumed stake in the status quo. His carrot-and-stick approach to the Soviets was predicated on the continuation of cold war; underlying détente was a premise of continued distrust and suspicion of Soviet intentions.[26]

Even so, the very term "détente" fell into disfavor as the superpower relationship again grew colder by the late 1970s. Triggered by renewed fears of the security threat posed by the Soviet Union after its invasion of Afghanistan at the end of 1979, U.S. military spending shot up dramatically and arms control negotiations broke off. President Reagan described the Soviet regime as "the embodiment of evil." Again we were reminded that to base our security on a balance of terror demands that each camp perceive the other as unrelentingly hostile to its interests. That in turn is what sustained the impression of a bipolar world of two self-contained and disconnected societies.

While such self-fulfilling prophecies flourished, the superpowers could seldom acknowledge a mutual responsibility for managing conflict. Instead, each superpower unilaterally attempted to coerce recalcitrant actors within its own neighborhood (the Soviet Union in Afghanistan, the United States in Grenada), whereas on the power frontiers between their spheres of interest, almost no community authority was asserted in the attempt to constrain belligerents (as in the Iran-Iraq War). The UN Security Council, which had been created in 1945 as a sort of latter-day concert of great powers, was again paralyzed by the hostile cleavages among those ordained to resolve world conflicts. The territorial divisions of Westphalia seemed still firmly in place, although at this stage they sometimes hinted ominously at creating armed camps of Orwellian scope.

Alternatives for a Post–Cold War World

By the last half of the 1980s, the world began to glimpse fascinating alternatives to cold war, which soon came to a dramatic end. The cold war's last chapter opened when a few individuals in positions of political power began to speak and act on the need to reorder state priorities in seemingly radical directions. The last Soviet leader, Mikhail Gorbachev, emerged after 1985 as the principal agent for such a viewpoint and

quickly epitomized the call for "new thinking" about world political relationships. Within a remarkably brief period, the ideas he unleashed produced a genuine revolution in East-West relations. Improved relations
with Western leaders were swept along with the much greater openness,
political reform, and, eventually, revolutionary change that occurred
within the Soviet Union and Eastern Europe.

Gorbachev's insistence that he would support greater pluralism within
the Soviet sphere was first put to the test in Poland. In 1989, the newly le-
galized Solidarity trade union movement was asked to form the nation's
first non-Communist government since World War II. That democratic
outcome came to fruition when Gorbachev refused to send Soviet troops
into Poland to keep the Communist regime in power. Prodemocratic
forces elsewhere in Eastern Europe were thereby emboldened to step up
their own pressures against the Communist elites that governed them. By
the autumn of that year came the dismantling of the Berlin Wall and the
generally nonviolent transformation of the Communist-led states of Eastern and Central Europe into systems where non-Communist forces could
quickly come to power.

Meanwhile, the reformist efforts Gorbachev had undertaken at home
revealed both the Soviet Union's serious economic problems and the
deepening political unrest of millions of people, especially non-Russians,
under Soviet rule. When the Baltic states asserted their independence of
Moscow, hard-line Communists pressured Gorbachev to crack down. For
months, the Soviet president seemed to walk a tightrope between ever
more polarized political forces throughout his vast realm.

Then in August 1991, an abortive coup led by members of the old Communist guard briefly toppled Gorbachev. Paradoxically, this desperate effort to restore authoritarian Communism instead provided the coup de
grace to Communist rule, and to the life of the Soviet Union itself. The
most visible leader of the opposition to the coup, Boris Yeltsin, became
the commanding figure in the post-Soviet order, as president of the Russian Republic. On the last day of the year, Gorbachev resigned as the Soviet Union was officially dissolved, and most of the former Soviet republics joined in a loose Commonwealth of Independent States. The new
fact of political life was that out of the ashes of the old Soviet empire were
born more than a dozen new nation-states—several of which would
themselves be rent for some time to come by intra-ethnic conflicts between minority and majority populations within their borders. In the
Transcaucasus, newly independent Georgia had to confront separatist
movements in the 1990s in its territories of Abkhazia and South Ossetia
while Armenia and Azerbaijan clashed violently over the fate of
Nagorno-Karabakh, a predominantly Armenian enclave within the territory of Azerbaijan. Meanwhile, within the Russian Federation on the

northern slopes of the Caucasus, a breakaway Chechnya fought a bloody war with Russia, whose government was heavily criticized for the destruction it unleashed on that minority society.

These outbursts of violence and disorder nonetheless involved governments within the former Soviet Union that were no longer perceived as the ideological adversaries of the West. In other words, a confrontational bipolarity was ended by destroying the authoritarian Soviet system that had been able to maintain a military capability perceived to be the match of that wielded by the United States and its allies. Almost overnight, a political actor that had looked extremely powerful, cohesive, and clear about its agenda in the world had disappeared from the global stage. Now the questions for world politics were how the resulting instability and economic upheaval of the region would affect world order, and what impact the world's ordering arrangement might have on this region's problems.

One of the most hopeful prospects to appear from these historic changes was that the nuclear threat might at last be brought under control. Serious nuclear arms control could begin at last in a way that had never been possible as long as the cold war lasted.[27] The threat to engage in all-out nuclear war had depended for its credibility on maintaining the perception of a world split socially into two enemy communities, each willing to risk its own annihilation rather than succumb to any of the devil's demands. As the Soviet Union began to be transformed late in the 1980s, the enemy came to be perceived in the West as human instead of devilish—in effect, as no enemy at all. Doctrines of mutually assured destruction lost their credibility even before the Soviet Union came to an end. Radical cutbacks in the arsenals of the leading nuclear powers became the stuff of realistic policy goals, not pipe dreams. In June 1992, some six months after Russia succeeded the Soviet Union as a nuclear power, Presidents Bush and Yeltsin agreed to the eventual elimination of all their multiple-warhead, land-based missiles, the nuclear warheads of which were to be reduced by two-thirds within the next decade.

But even as the U.S. and Russian governments backed away from the hair-trigger confrontation of the cold war, a new rationale for maintaining a nuclear deterrent was heard. Officials of the United States, in particular, expressed the view that with the disintegration of the Soviet empire, rogue groups might gain control over nuclear weapons and threaten others. Other revisionist governments might become nuclear terrorists (Iraq, Iran, and North Korea were among the favorite candidates) in the absence of a greater deterrent capability on the part of the only superpower left on earth. Whatever the merit of these new concerns, they precluded the likelihood that the world would be nuclear free at any time within the foreseeable future.[28] They also perpetuated the doctrine that the only road to a reliable peace for the world lay in threatening to unleash unprecedented violence on sizable portions of humanity.

In the 1990s, it often appeared that the end of the cold war meant a revival of the venerable ordering arrangement of Westphalia. Resurgent nationalism, greater pluralism, and a revived balance of power would replace the bipolar confrontations of the recent period. Indeed, much of the Balkan region quickly reverted to the kind of intercommunal conflict that seemed to resemble the area's politics at the start of the twentieth century more than it did those prevailing in the Yugoslavia that had held the region together from 1920 to 1991. Now that one superpower's control over conflicts within its region had ended, the remaining superpower no longer had much incentive to intervene to restore the peace.

Moreover, where the United States *did* see its important interests threatened, as in Saddam Hussein's seizure of Kuwait in the summer of 1990, it was able to turn to the Security Council of the United Nations to lead collective action against the Iraqi aggression. That had never been possible during the cold war, since the Security Council had been constructed before the cold war was in place on the assumption that a concert of great powers should be encouraged to keep the peace. As we have seen, such a concert has been possible historically only when a number of great powers share similar core values—not when two giants see themselves as locked in a zero-sum contest in which every gain for one camp is a loss for the other.

While the world was mesmerized by the collapse of the Soviet Union and the end of the cold war, other factors that had long been growing beneath the surface appeared on the landscape as well. Japan and a dozen or so countries in Western Europe had increased the material well-being of their people astonishingly in just a few decades. All of them, with Japan in the lead, had done so not through the failed territorial imperative of their earlier leaders but by reducing their military capability drastically and setting out to secure their well-being through trade.[29] By 1991, Japan became the society with the second-largest gross domestic product in the world. Its example strongly suggested that the next stage of economic development for many (perhaps most) societies will require increasing numbers of transactions across state boundaries, a situation that demands reliably peaceful relationships with trading partners. Indeed, one of the factors that helped to undermine the cold war was the growing economic and social interdependence of the most economically advanced societies from the 1950s through the 1980s, and the way in which the Communist world had been excluded from so much of that.

These changes have been accompanied by the rise of new issues on the world's political agenda, issues that are almost wholly irrelevant to traditional geopolitical rivalries. They include recalcitrant problems of poverty for at least two-thirds of humanity, questions of how to manage our global commons, the globalization of economic life, the impact of our industrial activities on the very life of the planet, and much more. Before examining them more closely, it may be useful to bring these summaries of recent trends in world political developments into sharper focus by generalizing about the two alternatives they suggest.

The policies of most contemporary leaders are strongly rooted in the traditional Westphalian outlook. They seldom question whether nation-states are the immutably important actors of international politics—particularly not when they happen also to serve the governments of great powers. States are perceived to have interests that change little over time and are in conflict with those of other states with which temporary accommodations may nonetheless be possible. Such accommodations are required by respect for the basic rules of the game, but they are never perceived as transforming or eradicating basic interests or traditional state-based values. This vision is no doubt still shared very widely, if unthinkingly, by the world's public, for the simple reason that it is the least imaginative way to address the world. It accords with many of the fundamental realities of the past three centuries and therefore may be supposed by those without a view of history that predates the modern period to apply to the present and the future as well.

The other alternative is only hinted at in some of the most recent developments just discussed. It assumes that at this stage in our history, many of the emerging goals of humanity require new modes of social interaction, with novel social structures likely to be the eventual result. These new goals and the evolving social needs on which they are based must compete with the traditional thinking of Westphalian statecraft. Perhaps the greatest unanswered question at the moment is whether the new thought and action can prevail against the old. That prospect seems particularly difficult, since much of the change apparently must be engineered by those very representatives of states who are *expected* to advance traditional Westphalian interests rather than encourage novel social arrangements.

For example, is it possible to create a reliable world police power capable of ending the kind of internecine violence that since the end of the cold war has produced fighting and death across parts of Europe, Africa, and Asia, and to do so without its becoming the instrument of new oppression in some continuing contest for territory and domination? Can the leaders of all nation-states recognize the common human interest in their acting so as to save the planet from destruction instead of passing each of their own society's harmful practices off on others on grounds that as governmental leaders they are responsible only for one segment of humanity? Above all, can the *public* think and act clearly enough to express the kinds of value preferences that will support those leaders who are committed to improving the world's social and political system? Our future as a species may hinge on the answers.

Global Issues Confront Westphalia

We cannot possibly account for all the factors that may be producing or resisting global change because the normative system we live in is the complex and often unplanned product of human development, evolving continually. What follows is little more than a listing of the most salient social and political concerns on today's international agenda. Each of these issues will be explored for its world order implications in succeeding chapters.

First, the security problem for the globe's citizens today is multifaceted and in very many of its aspects seems to be inadequately treated by the Westphalian system. Westphalia demands that nation states become the locus of sovereignty, but applying that principle to the area that recently was mostly dominated by the Soviet Union has created enormous insecurity for millions. Creating new nation-states in that region has meant the sometimes violent destruction of such multiethnic states as Yugoslavia. Nor can nation building proceed to the satisfaction of all where ethnic communities are intermixed, often forming enclaves within larger groups that themselves may be dispersed among others.[30] If Westphalian imperatives are still very much in place there and elsewhere in the world, they are operating at a terrible cost in human misery.

Clearly, the security that is meant to flow to national communities by attaching them to states requires a government capable of providing it. But a government with the capability to provide security from threats beyond its nation's borders is also one able to engage in repressive action against its own citizens. It is little wonder, therefore, that where the threat of internal repression has been much reduced or removed, a new kind of insecurity—that stemming from civil unrest—frequently has taken its place. From the end of the 1980s, as through much of human history, the gravest instances of violence done to social groups generally have occurred as part of a cycle. First comes a relaxation of rigid governmental control and then civil disturbance, which may be followed in turn by a ruthless reimposition of control from the center. So it has been in China, Burma, Iraq, and elsewhere.

Still, as our recent history shows clearly, the repressive ending is not inevitable. Some societies, including the majority of those within the former Soviet orbit, have achieved greater freedom—even to the point of amicable divorce—without shedding blood. The lesson of those cases apparently is that security for human beings can be maintained on a new and freer basis. Indeed, one of the most powerful ideas of our time is what until now only a minority of societies have known: Democratic government can increase security from violence for its citizens because its fundamental purpose is to allow, as Thomas Jefferson put it, the pursuit of happiness. And the number of countries with democratic systems has grown dramatically since the late 1980s.[31]

In earlier editions of this book I suggested that the nuclear threat constituted perhaps the gravest threat to the security of human beings and even to the very idea of sovereignty itself. The theory of nuclear deterrence that dominated the cold war era threatened sovereignty, and hence the world order system that had evolved over centuries, because sovereigns—including the sovereign government capable of threatening nuclear destruction—could not defend themselves against the power of the atom. Territorial states had become potentially permeable in a way never before encountered in human history.[32]

That assessment remains accurate today, since nuclear arsenals that are capable of ending perhaps all human life on earth still exist. But what has changed dramatically is our diminished perception that a nuclear holocaust will occur. Nuclear powers no longer make that prospect the central consideration of their strategic planning. The salience of the nuclear threat is therefore reduced, although it is unlikely ever to vanish altogether. Even if nuclear weapons cannot be eliminated from the earth, they can and presumably are being relegated to a role in which their only purpose is to stop other actors from using theirs. That still holds dangers for our security, albeit reduced ones. It suggests that a task still awaiting us is to develop a more centrally authorized nuclear control system in the future.

Within this century, the laissez-faire underpinnings of Westphalia have begun to look increasingly inadequate as the basis for addressing other important issues. The developments that help to define these center about the increasing crowding of the planet with the closing of the world frontier and, more or less simultaneously, the growing interdependence of states.[33] The limitless potential abundance presupposed by both Locke and Grotius is now all too evidently limited and finite, a condition exacerbated by enormous pressures on the biosphere created by the frontier beyond which, in the past, there always seemed to be abundant resources for all. The industrial process has entailed such a tremendous increase in the use of fossil fuels that the once seemingly limitless supply of some is now being rapidly exhausted. We are forced to come to terms, for the first time in human history, with the finiteness of the earth's resources.

Moreover, industrialization has ravaged the environment through pollution of the air and water, a phenomenon that has begun to make clear, also for the first time, humanity's awesome ability to make a devastating impact on the life chain. An Olympian view of the earth over the past century reveals that the laissez-faire approach to social organization has allowed enormous energies of individual actors to be unleashed but that their activities have been largely heedless of each other and of the inevitable relationship they have to the nonhuman components of the earth.

An initial response to these kinds of problems generally occurred within advanced industrial states sooner and more easily than across their borders. Early in this century, most such civil societies began enacting legislation designed to curb some of the worst depredations of unrestrained entrepreneurship. Although conflicts over such regulation stir the politics of some of the richest states today, their governments still intervene in the private sector considerably more than they once did to establish standards and enforce them—all as a result of the reaction against an untrammeled laissez-faire. At the international level, such a reaction has not proceeded nearly so far, although it began about a quarter century ago. At present the most serious problems raised by the workings of an international system of laissez-faire arc only beginning to be addressed by effective global arrangements for regulation and control.

We also have begun to see new, international dimensions to the problems of human rights and human welfare. Much of what is new here is the perception that many of these issues now ought to be dealt with by the international normative order, even though traditionally they have been excluded from it. They ought to be included, according to this reasoning, because only by addressing such problems with effective power and authority at a global level will they be alleviated. Sovereigns, after all, have proved to be the principal violators of the rights of individuals. If this practice is to stop, it is sovereigns who must be restrained. And if forces within the state cannot do the job, then it must be done by forces from beyond it.

No doubt many factors have contributed to this perception. Among the most important are the unparalleled (at least in modern times) atrocities governments have engaged in during this century. They have been able to kill and torture on an unprecedented scale, thanks in large part to the more ruthless, totalitarian control of populations that has only become possible in this century and has come to characterize it. Those facts, combined with the speed and global reach of modern communication, have meant that it is becoming possible to mobilize effective action against such behavior from abroad in ways that were not possible much before this century. By the mid-nineteenth century, legal positivism had developed to the point that the dualism of international and national legal systems was generally accepted as adequate to social order. Individuals could be viewed as subject solely to state sovereigns when authoritative structures beyond the state were not developed to a point that international control over sovereign treatment of their subjects could be effective.

However risky, that condition could be tolerated as long as sovereigns generally could be counted on to grant a measure of respect to those they ruled. The normative acceptability, in other words, of much sovereign treatment of the individual may have inhibited the growth of universally enforceable standards to which sovereigns were subject.

But by the 1940s, important actors in the international system asserted for the first time the need to bring egregious sovereign violators of human rights within the purview of community standards. The Nuremberg and Tokyo tribunals were the first, dramatic steps in that process, which continues in the 1990s with tribunals for violations of international humanitarian law in the former Yugoslavia and in Rwanda. This development has necessarily confronted legal positivism with the ancient tradition of natural law, a confrontation that has not in itself confounded the Westphalian approach to order (Grotius and other international lawyers since his time have drawn on the natural law tradition) although it has also raised questions about the Westphalian approach that may yet prove to be fundamental. For example, the 1990s tribunals have been much hampered by their inability to obtain custody over alleged war criminals who are protected by the officials of self-proclaimed states who recognize no obligation to the universal normative standards the tribunals seek to uphold.

Another kind of human rights deprivation has also come to characterize our era. Much that goes under the name of terrorism today is a unique reflection of the unprecedented security dilemmas modern technology has brought us. A tiny amount of a plastic explosive smuggled in a suitcase can blow a jumbo jet out of the sky. No sovereign's military capability can assure a defense against such actions. Just as troubling is the sense that in its frequent randomness contemporary terrorism also reflects a willingness to murder those who traditionally have been considered innocent, ordinary civilians, not state officials who might more reasonably be charged with denying the perpetrators of the violence some passionately held political goal. Both these characteristics further undermine the security pretensions of Westphalian assumptions. Worse, they launch a dreadful cycle, inducing cries for vengeance, repression from governments, and a terrible dehumanization of all involved—terrorists and victims alike.

A number of the developments already considered have helped foster the contemporary global concern with distributive justice. Only in recent decades have many of the poorest segments of the globe's population been enfranchised as their states achieved sovereignty; now their values and demands against an international economic system that appears to them unjust have come to be expressed within the Westphalian framework. The growth of industrialization and economic interdependence has focused attention on the problems of economic inequality, but the Westphalian approach itself has, in general, not proved capable of addressing those problems effectively. Laissez-faire, whether for individuals or sovereigns, must rely on conscience rather than coercion if those who have most of the wealth are to prove willing to share it with those who have little. In this respect, the current debate between the haves and the have-nots over responsibilities and over actions needed to overcome widespread poverty and underdevelopment may be viewed as the opening salvo at the global level to create an international welfare state or society. In the first decade of the post–cold war world, however, the triumph of market forces has nearly drowned out that campaign. At the same time, globalization of the market is overwhelming the abilities of states to control their own economies, and this challenges a fundamental feature of Westphalian order.

Intertwined with several of these growing contradictions of our time is the issue of the shifting locus of political loyalty in the contemporary world. It is surely significant that the consolidation of territorial units that proceeded inexorably from the Peace of Westphalia to about 1900 has been halted and radically reversed.[34] The few dozen sovereign states at the beginning of our century now number nearly 190. That development seems to run sharply counter to the Orwellian prediction that we were headed toward a handful of superstates. It suggests an increase in the opposite risk (particularly now that the bloc politics of the cold war have crumbled), namely, of too much freedom by too many sovereign units for effective order in the world. Moreover, this trend toward the fragmentation of states has increased substantially at the same time that their real self-sufficiency, especially in economic terms, is more than ever a thing of the past. How that can be squared with the Westphalian principle encouraging sovereign independence raises more important questions than ever before.

Some minority dissidence today is almost antinationalistic, at least in the traditional sense, and stems from the kind of cosmopolitanism or class consciousness that has accompanied the enormous acceleration in communication. It is still too amorphous and contradictory a phenomenon to allow precise definition, but it is to be seen in a variety of examples. Black separatism in North America is fueled not merely by black pride (which owes a debt to the independence of Africa in the third quarter of the century) but also by identification with poor, nonwhite populations throughout much of the world. French separatism in Canada arises from the awareness shared by many Quebecois of their inferior cultural status within their own country. Some living in the richest societies feel shortchanged or oppressed by governmental establishments that they despise and are able to connect with like-minded others through the Internet. There has been a reemergence of startling growth in political pluralism within what have recently been some of the most highly centralized and authoritarian societies in the world.

No doubt all of these developments have been encouraged by the perceived emergence in this century of a world-class political elite that is largely Europeanized and basically conservative. It is more fascinated with maintaining and expanding its own powers than with achieving social justice. A common thread through most of these phenomena is that they do not appear to seek anything so simple (in Westphalian terms) as secession and the creation of new sovereign states. Rather, their dissent results from what are seen as certain negative features of the state or of the very state system. Are these developments ephemeral or important? Can they be expected to run their course without serious impact on the Westphalian system? Or will they alter it in fundamental ways?

Perhaps the phenomenon just described can be most sensibly related to an additional development that is characteristic of our time and important in its own right, that of the growth of both private and public international organizations. Whether we refer to the creation and development of international governmental organizations (IGOs), international non-governmental organizations (INGOs), or transnational corporations (TNCs), to use the usual terminology, the increase in the numbers and activities of such organizations in recent decades has been dramatic.[35] That alone does not, of course, tell us much about the real impact of international organization on the world today; nor should it be read as proof of the weakening of the Westphalian system, particularly not when many, although not all, such organizations are clearly the product of the Westphalian mode.

Yet some of the developments in this area look as if they would or could transform the system. That may seem to be most obviously true of those intergovernmental arrangements whose overt purpose is to integrate certain governmental functions at a suprastate level, as, for example, in the European Union. Nonetheless, it is still an open question whether or not such regional integrative movements will only be counted a success if they create a single superstate where several states once existed. If that is the outcome, then Westphalia itself will not have been transformed but merely rearranged with regard to a few of its component actors, the superstates now major powers, perhaps, in a revived version of a balance-of-power system. The activities of multinational enterprises also may seem evidence of the growing inability today of the sovereign state to control and regulate effectively economic activities within the private sector. If that is so, then one of the traditional rationales for modern sovereignty is undermined. Moreover, we may find on closer examination that even those intergovernmental organizations that look to be the servants of the Westphalian system (in the sense of being the clear instruments of sovereign states) may be having a more complex impact on the contemporary normative order.

The novel security challenges, the need to control more effectively the uses of violence, efforts to ameliorate economic disparities at the global level, the promotion of human rights, the threats to the very biosphere in which we live through the practices of modern industrial society—all these are problems that in our time need to be addressed by world order values if we are to survive and flourish.[36] Do we have the social resources at our command, the imagination and the will to make the better possibilities prevail over the worst?

Notes

1. This is typically the position of those described as "realists" or "neorealists" in their analysis of world politics. For a diverse sample of some of the influential literature from this perspective in recent years, along with commentary on it, see Hedley Bull, *The Anarchical Society: A Study of Order in World Politics* (New York: Columbia University Press, 1977); Robert Gilpin, *War and Change in World Politics* (Cambridge: Cambridge University Press, 1981); Robert O. Keohane, ed., *Neorealism and Its Critics* (New York: Columbia University Press, 1986); and Kenneth N. Waltz, *Theory of International Politics* (Reading, Mass.: Addison-Wesley, 1979).

2. See, for example, Luigi Albertini, *The Origins of the War of 1914,* trans. and ed. Isabella M. Massey (London: Oxford University Press, 1952); Sidney Bradshaw Fay, *The Origins of the World War,* 2d ed. rev. (New York: Free Press, 1966); D. F. Fleming, *The Origins and Legacies of World War I* (Garden City, N.Y.: Doubleday, 1968); Richard Langhorne, *The Collapse of the Concert of Europe* (London: Macmillan, 1981).

3. Conservative estimates are that 10 million died and an additional 20 million were wounded in the war, although this figure does not include the large number of civilian deaths in the immediate postwar period from epidemics and starvation.

4. From Wilson's address to the U.S. Senate on January 22, 1917. *The Papers of Woodrow Wilson,* ed. Arthur S. Link (Princeton, N.J.: Princeton University Press, 1982), 40:536.

5. Nor do I want to suggest that an international normative system based rigidly on self-help would have been in any way a realistic alternative by the twentieth century. I wish to demonstrate merely that, in principle, it might have produced less violence than the mixed system, containing some elements of self-help and some of community obligation, that prevailed in 1914. An extreme self-help system assumes the absence of *any* of the features and characteristics of an organized society, and as such, is difficult to imagine in any concatenation of interacting units. No doubt it is the only plausible strategy for the lone individual marooned on a desert island or for larger social groups completely isolated from any other, but for most of recorded history, such situations have been rare. Thus it is little wonder that serious theorists of social order are always inclined to discover both practical and moral limitations on the unrestricted practice of self-help.

6. Included among these were Maximilien de Béthune, Duc de Sully (1559–1641); Emeric Crucé (1590–1648); William Penn (1644–1718); and Charles Irénée

Castel, Abbé de Saint-Pierre (1658–1743). Harold K. Jacobson has described the communal alternatives posited by these and other writers in a way that makes clear their commonality in what today we should describe as the collective security principle: "They all would have forbade organization members to use military force, at least in Europe, except when authorized by the common institution. . . . Military force should be employed to ensure compliance with at least some common decisions, particularly those relating to disputes. . . . Most of the plans relied on military units under the control of organization members, but some . . . provided that the organization would have military units assigned to it" (*Networks of Interdependence* [New York: Alfred A. Knopf, 1979], pp. 28–29). For a fuller discussion of these and other plans for collective maintenance of the peace, see Sylvester John Hemleben, *Plans for World Peace Through Six Centuries* (Chicago: University of Chicago Press, 1943).

7. The adjective "unrealistic" is simply a label for an idea that has not notably influenced relevant behavior; it provides no reasons for that failure. In broadest terms, we can say that the reasons why these peace plans had so little success in earlier centuries lay in the fact that the only actors in international society capable of bringing them into being, the sovereign states, remained unpersuaded that they had a greater interest in subordinating their own freedom of choice, i.e., their sovereignty, to the common good than they did in continuing to go largely their own way, cooperating with fellow sovereigns when that seemed appropriate and fighting with them when that seemed the most likely way to advance their own interests. Underlying that stance was the sovereigns' general conclusion that the costs of going it alone—principally the risks in ending up a loser in a war—were far outweighed by the benefits of freedom from control by some distant authority.

8. Jean-Jacques Rousseau, *The First and Second Discourses* (New York: St. Martin's Press, 1964), pp. 165–167.

9. League of Nations Covenant, Article 16.

10. Ibid., Article 21. For a discussion of the political context at Versailles that underlay the drafting of this and other provisions of the Covenant, see Stephen S. Goodspeed, *The Nature and Function of International Organization*, 2d ed. (New York: Oxford University Press, 1967), pp. 31–33.

11. For a fuller explanation of the pulls of regionalism within the framework of the League's collective security system, see Lynn H. Miller, *Organizing Mankind* (Boston: Holbrook, 1972), Chapter 2.

12. Among the most notable of these were the resolution of a Turkish-Iraqi border dispute in the years 1924–1926, conflicts between Greece and Bulgaria in 1925–1927, and clashes between Poland and Lithuania in 1927. For a full account, see F. P. Walters, *A History of the League of Nations* (Oxford: Oxford University Press, 1964), pp. 305–315, 398–400; and E. H. Carr, *International Relations Since the Peace Treaties* (London: Macmillan, 1937), pp. 103–108.

13. See, for example, Nicholas J. Spykman, *The Geography of the Peace* (New York: Harcourt, Brace, 1944); E. H. Carr, *The Twenty Years' Crisis, 1919–1939* (London: Macmillan, 1946); and Frederick L. Schuman, "International Ideals and the National Interest," *Annals of the American Academy of Political and Social Science* 280 (March 1952):27–36.

14. Ironically, virtually the last act of a disintegrating League of Nations was to expel the Soviet Union, on December 14, 1939, from membership—the only state ever so treated—for its attack on Finland. That action was a symbolic reflection of the wariness with which the Western democracies, in particular, had regarded the USSR since its inception. Britain, France, and the United States all had violated non-intervention standards when they introduced troops into Russian territory in 1918–1920 to try to prevent the success of the Soviet revolution. See George F. Kennan, *Russia and the West Under Lenin and Stalin* (Boston: Little, Brown, 1961). Some have viewed this deep-seated mutual distrust by traditional powers and Russian Communists as, in effect, an international civil war, beginning in the Soviet revolution in 1917 and continuing to the Gorbachev era. See, for example, Arno J. Mayer, *Politics and Diplomacy of Peacemaking* (New York: Alfred A. Knopf, 1967).

15. In the case of the Soviet Union, the elite's revisionist demands on the international order probably were more apparent to traditional governments than real in Soviet eyes, a fact explained by a somewhat irrational fear of the "Red menace" in the West and by extrapolation from the clearly revisionist intentions of the Soviets regarding the construction of Soviet society. Needless to say, the question of the extent of the Soviet Union's revisionist goals for the non-Soviet world was still hotly debated for nearly seventy years after the revolution in Russia, defining, as it did, the dimensions of the cold war and making it probably the greatest controversy in the international political arena of the twentieth century.

16. The quotation is from Article 22, paragraph 1, of the Covenant. The entire article spells out the concept of the mandates system and clearly expresses the Europe-centered attitudes and values regarding colonialism of its time. The reader who reflects on the evident quaintness of its tone today will have noted an example of how dominant world order values do indeed change over time.

17. Parts of the British empire already had become independent sovereign states within the British Commonwealth of Nations, which was created in the Statute of Westminster in 1931. Many other British colonies would take this route in the post–World War II period, which makes clear in retrospect that a model already existed in the interwar period, whether British officials then saw it consistently as such or not, that showed the way to the dismemberment of empire and the creation of new sovereignties without totally severing the links that had developed through the colonial period. This orderly effort at creating sovereign states from British colonies can be traced to the British North America Act of 1867, which became the constitution of the independent "Dominion" of Canada.

18. This was the frequent contention of the revisionist school of cold war historians in the West, who tended to reverse the orthodox U.S. interpretation that viewed this country as peaceful and satisfied, acting only in the international sphere to counter an unacceptable expansionism on the part of the Soviet Union or China. Revisionists generally saw the United States as the initiator of action in the cold war period and their Communist enemies as behaving more defensively. See, for example, Gabriel Kolko, *The Politics of War* (New York: Random House, 1968) and *The Roots of American Foreign Policy* (Boston: Beacon, 1969); William Appleman Williams, *The Tragedy of American Diplomacy* (New York: Delta Books, 1962); and Gar Alperovitz, *Atomic Diplomacy: Hiroshima and Potsdam* (New York: Simon and Schuster, 1965).

19. One need only recall the Nazis' "final solution" to the "Jewish problem" in territories they occupied for the most horrifying suggestion.

20. The Group of 77 is the name still used by the non-European and for the most part formerly colonized nations, whose number today has risen to more than 120, that first caucused as an economic bloc at the first UN Conference on Trade and Development (UNCTAD) in 1964. They have maintained a fair measure of unity and, for more than a decade after 1973, called for the establishment of a New International Economic Order (NIEO).

21. Walter Bagehot noted the continual transformation of the efficient into the ceremonial in the historical evolution of the British governmental system, *The English Constitution* (Ithaca, N.Y.: Cornell University Press, 1966), p. 262. Citing Bagehot, Richard Rosecrance has suggested much of what I argue here: a possible analogy between that trend and the evolution of the Westphalian international system. See *The Rise of the Trading State* (New York: Basic Books, 1985), p. 227.

22. This transformation in the status of important state actors was manifest to most students of the period. It lasted from about 1945 to 1990, although the writings of Morton A. Kaplan pioneered in abstracting and clarifying the basic behavioral and normative requirements of the shift from a balance of power to a loosely bipolar world. For one depiction of those models (as well as other hypothetical model systems), see his "Constitutional Structures and Processes in the International Arena," in *The Future of the International Legal Order*, ed. Richard A. Falk and Cyril E. Black, vol. 1, *Trends and Patterns* (Princeton, N.J.: Princeton University Press, 1969), pp. 155–182.

23. Such views generally were tempered later in the cold war period as nonalignment grew and as the early perception of monolithic loyalties within East-West power blocs was seen to be a myth, particularly after the People's Republic of China parted company from the Soviet Union. Even so, the Reagan reaction in the United States largely embodied a return to cold war primitivism, two decades and more after the early virulence of the cold war had been dissipating fairly steadily. Only after Mikhail Gorbachev came to power in the Soviet Union did the final thaw in the cold war begin.

24. Henry Kissinger, *White House Years* (Boston: Little, Brown, 1979). For an incisive review of this first volume of Kissinger's memoirs and an analysis of his foreign policy, see Stanley Hoffman, "The Case of Dr. Kissinger," *New York Review of Books*, December 6, 1979, pp. 14–29. The second volume of the Kissinger memoirs is entitled *Years of Upheaval* (Boston: Little, Brown, 1982).

25. Kissinger's lack of interest in international economic matters is apparent in the comparatively miniscule attention he devotes to them in the two volumes of his memoirs.

26. It is no coincidence that Kissinger strongly admired the policies of the early nineteenth-century Austrian statesman Metternich, who was the principal architect of the Congress of Vienna in 1815. It ushered in the long period of the great powers' management of a status quo that preserved their dominant positions in Europe and around the world. Kissinger's doctoral dissertation on Metternich was published under the title *A World Restored: Metternich, Castlereagh and the Problem of Peace, 1812–22* (Boston: Houghton Mifflin, 1957).

27. One early, if small-scale, evidence of the ending of the cold war was the U.S.-Soviet Intermediate-range Nuclear Force (INF) agreement of 1987. By 1991,

the former antagonists agreed to significant cuts in a Strategic Arms Reduction Treaty (START I), and that was followed a year later by the Bush-Yeltsin agreement (START II) meant to reduce U.S. and Russian arsenals by some two-thirds from 1992 levels. As of early 1998, however, START II still had not been ratified by the Russian Duma, where Communists and others opposed to Yeltsin's cooperative behavior with the West had considerable strength.

28. Although no clear alternative to a continued reliance on nuclear weapons for their deterrent value had emerged by the late 1990s, they were beginning to be viewed by the principal nuclear weapons states "as more a liability than an asset," in Freeman Dyson's words. See his "The Arms Race Is Over," *The New York Review of Books*, March 6, 1997, p. 4, and the discussion of this issue in Chapter 5 herein.

29. The growing importance of trade as a way of overcoming the violence of the Westphalian territorial system is the provocative thesis of Richard Rosecrance's *The Rise of the Trading State* (New York: Basic Books, 1985).

30. In Bosnia-Herzegovina, for example, Croats, Serbs, and Muslims were intermixed when the republic's independence was declared early in 1992. In the former Soviet Union at about the same time, South Ossetians fought ethnic Georgians in an effort to secede from Georgia and unite with North Ossetia, across the border in Russia. And in 1994, many thousands of people making up the Tutsi majority in Rwanda were massacred by members of the Hutu majority. Hutus and Tutsis were also the major ethnic groups in neighboring Burundi, where their conflict, spilling over from Rwanda, threatened that society's stability, as well.

31. According to Freedom House, the number of democracies grew from 41 percent of the total in 1985–1986 to 61 percent in 1995–1996 (See December 19, 1995, press release of the *Cooperative Survey of Freedom*).

32. See John Herz, *International Politics in the Atomic Age* (New York: Columbia University Press, Columbia Paperback Edition, 1962), especially Chapters 2–3, 7–8.

33. This development reminds us of the much debated significance of the closing of the American frontier at the end of the nineteenth century, a debate stimulated by Frederick Jackson Turner's famous essay, "The Significance of the Frontier in American History." It has been reprinted, with commentary, in *The Turner Thesis*, in the series *Problems in American Civilization* (Boston: D. C. Heath, 1956). Turner ascribed many of the characteristic ideas and values of the American democratic experience over several centuries to the influence of the westward-moving frontier, a historical condition that had just ended when he wrote with, he presumed, far-reaching consequences for future American development. See Chapter 8 of this book.

34. It should be remembered that the long period of consolidation of territorial units, especially outside Europe, corresponded to the era in which Europe increasingly dominated the globe, that is, consolidation went hand in hand with European imperialism. Paul Kennedy has pointed out that "in the year 1800, Europeans occupied or controlled 35 percent of the land surface of the world; by 1878 this figure had risen to 67 percent, and by 1914 to over 84 percent" (*The Rise and Fall of the Great Powers* [New York: Random House, 1987], p. 150). Today, however, Europeans control almost no territory outside Europe, which constitutes less than 10 percent of the world's land surface.

35. On the eve of World War I, there were about 50 intergovernmental organizations; by the outbreak of World War II, about 80; by the 1970s, between 250 and 300.

Nongovernmental organizations began to appear in the nineteenth century. By World War I, there were approximately 330, by World War II more than double that number, and by the 1970s, some 2,500. Not until the 1960s did it become common, because of the great expansion in corporate activity worldwide, to use the newly coined terms "transnational" and "multinational corporations" to refer to the actors involved in that phenomenon. See Jacobson, *Networks of Interdependence*, pp. 10–11.

36. These are essentially the same problem areas that the World Order Models Project of the Institute for World Order placed at the top of its agenda of issues demanding greater worldwide normative attention. See the editor's introduction in Saul H. Mendlovitz, ed., *On the Creation of a Just World Order* (New York: Free Press, 1975).

Suggested Readings

Buchheit, Lee C., *Secession: The Legitimacy of Self-Determination*, New Haven, Conn.: Yale University Press, 1978.

Camilleri, Joseph A., Anthony P. Jarvis, and Albert J. Paolini, eds., *The State in Transition: Reimagining Political Space*, Boulder, Colo.: Lynne Rienner, 1995.

Fleming, D. F., *The Origins and Legacies of World War I*, Garden City, N.Y.: Doubleday, 1968.

Furedi, Frank, *Colonial Wars and the Politics of Third World Nationalism*, New York: St. Martin's Press, 1994.

Gaddis, John L., *The Long Peace: Inquiries into the History of the Cold War*, New York: Oxford University Press, 1987.

Hayes, C. J. H., *The Historical Evolution of Modern Nationalism*, New York: Macmillan, 1945.

Herz, John H., *International Politics in the Atomic Age*, New York: Columbia University Press, Columbia Paperback Edition, 1962.

Jacobson, Harold K., *Networks of Interdependence*, 2d ed., New York: Alfred A. Knopf, 1984.

Kennan, George F., *Russia and the West Under Lenin and Stalin*, Boston: Little, Brown, 1961.

Kohr, Leopold, *The Overdeveloped Nations: The Diseconomies of Scale*, New York: Schocken Books, 1977.

Langhorne, Richard, *The Collapse of the Concert of Europe*, London: Macmillan, 1981.

Mandlebaum, Michael, *The Fate of Nations: The Search for National Security in the 19th and 20th Centuries*, New York: Cambridge University Press, 1988.

Nincic, Miroslav, *Anatomy of Hostility: US-Soviet Rivalry in Perspective*, New York: Harcourt Brace Jovanovich, 1989.

Pachter, Henry M., *The Fall and Rise of Europe: A Political, Social, and Cultural History of the Twentieth Century*, New York: Praeger, 1975.

Pfaff, William, *The Wrath of Nations: Civilizations and the Furies of Nationalism*, New York: Simon and Schuster, 1993.

Walker, Rachel, *Six Years That Shook the World: Perestroika—The Impossible Project*, Manchester: Manchester University Press, 1993.

Wallerstein, Immanuel, *The Modern World-System*, New York: Academic Press, 1974.

Wardlaw, Grant, *Political Terrorism*, New York: Cambridge University Press, 1983.

CHAPTER 4

Power and Values
in World Society

No change of system or machinery can . . . secure that men live up to their principles. What it can do is to establish their social order upon principles to which, if they please, they can live up and not live down. It cannot control their actions. It can offer them an end on which to fix their minds. And, as their minds are, so in the long run and with exceptions, their practical activity will be.
                                        —R. H. Tawney, *The Acquisitive Society*

Our task is to explore some of the possible directions in which the world may be heading in the near future, as well as the ways in which its course may be directed by intelligent human action. We cannot usefully begin, however, without first clarifying two fundamental aspects of the human condition in all times and places, both of which are implied in the previous sentence. These can be given a variety of labels such as those that make distinctions in ethics between the *is* and the *ought;* in philosophy between the *real* world of the physical universe and the *ideal* realm of human thought; in religion between the *material* and the *spiritual* sides of our existence; and so on. In the study of world politics, it is often useful to describe this dialectical distinction in terms of *power* as opposed to *normative* considerations of the issues.

This linking of concepts that describe apparently quite different phenomena is a basic and recurrent theme in the whole history of human thought simply because these distinctions arise from the very stuff of every human life. We are indeed physical, material creatures, part of a substantial universe that we can experience in a limited way through our senses. Our basic needs are physical, and these must be satisfied if we are to live. But we also possess minds that let us know (or try to know) the cosmos through our ideas and imaginations, minds that help us link the disparate, chaotic experiences of our senses into coherent patterns that "explain" them in ways that are more or less satisfactory to us. Without ideas, the physical universe would be largely formless, for ideas, and ideas alone, bring us a sense of order out of chaos. Ideas permit us to master, to the extent we can, the material universe. Thus the link between the ideal and the real is critical to our knowledge.

Politics: Power and Normative Orientations

Nowhere is this more apparent than in the political dimension of our lives. Politics is "about" the exercise of power and control over human societies to further specific social values or ideals. Our lives assume a political dimension only with the wedding of capability (power) and value (normative) factors relevant to human society. The articulation of any social value is the attempt to legitimize the quest for power. Conversely, the will to power must be accompanied by the articulation of a social value, or set of values, if it is to assume a political quality. When we say that certain political ideas are powerful, we mean that they have succeeded in mobilizing substantial numbers of people to seek to advance them by achieving the means to implement them in society.

The burglar who survives by robbing people's homes undoubtedly wields a kind of power over the physical universe (as long as he is not caught), but his power is outside the political process because he has not articulated any social purpose for his actions. Conversely, the ascetic hermit who withdraws to a cave may live in considerable harmony with his own ideals by making the choice not to interact with the material world, including other human beings, around him. Yet his withdrawal also removes him from the political process because he has left the dimension of power over others behind him. However, as soon as either of these individuals incorporates the missing dimension in his life, he begins to move into the political realm. So we may imagine that the burglar justifies his theft on grounds that, say, unjust political institutions force him to steal. To the extent that, like Robin Hood, he can persuade others to follow his own example, he may become part of a political force in which his idea is tested ever more widely within the society. The hermit, on the other hand, may persuade so many others to follow his ideals about how people ought to live, as did Buddha, that eventually the world must take notice of them and respond in some way to the values they articulate.

Although the distinction between the power and the normative dimensions is a clear one, they always coexist within the realm of politics. They may sometimes seem to be dichotomous features of human life, yet they are inextricably linked, molding and directing each other. All political activity must encompass both dimensions, as must all political analysis. The interesting questions in the interpretation of international political phenomena always revolve about what is thought to be the correct mix of power and normative orientations.

A need exists today for analysis with a stronger sensitivity to normative factors than is typical in the study of international politics. This is so in a basic sense because ideas permit us to generalize and theorize about real-world phenomena, and therefore more attention to normative factors should deepen our understanding of the possibilities inherent in world political behavior today. But more particularly, the need exists to correct the dominance of power-oriented analysis in much of the literature of international politics in recent decades, a dominance that may have biased our understanding of the important trends and possibilities that are removed from a grasp of immediate, empirical reality.

Realism Versus Idealism in International Politics

In U.S. academic circles, a great debate began at about the time of World War II among students of international politics between so-called realists and those they labeled as utopians or idealists. By the 1950s, the realist critique had clearly triumphed; its victory proved so large that it dominated most of the analysis of international politics at least until the 1990s.[1]

Realists first got a hearing through their criticism of what was seen to be an overemphasis in much of the interwar period on the kinds of ideas that ought to govern international relationships, most notably the Wilsonian vision of a League of Nations that would keep the peace through collective security. Realist criticism of Wilsonian thinking began by noting its strong emphasis on moral solutions to the world's problems that failed, according to this view, to take sufficient account of some unchanging realities about international politics, particularly the unwillingness of states, regardless of their formal commitments, to abdicate their time-honored ability to act freely and independently of one another as sovereigns. In simplest terms, the realist critique viewed the commitment to the new international normative standard as ephemeral, perhaps even insincere, given the unwillingness of states to forego the exercise of accustomed power. Adherence to the League Covenant amounted to little more than lip service to an ideal that did not move fundamentally important behavior in the same direction as the new standard.[2]

What was especially dangerous about this, according to the realists, was that the acceptance of these normative commitments at face value had amounted to wishful thinking and the triumph of an illusion. It had lulled many into supposing that solutions had been found to world problems through the stroke of a pen, when in fact the problems and the nation-states' responses to them had remained much the same as in the past.

Throughout the League's existence, states had continued to be driven by the quest for power, which ensured continuing competition among them to advance their diverse interests. At some time in the future that competition would result, as it had in the past, in war.

The realists typically urged us to note that all states sought security for themselves, first and foremost, and that their most durable interests (a favorite term of realist analysis) therefore were those most closely tied to the facts of their physical place in the world. To take one characteristic example, a realist analysis of Soviet foreign policy in the aftermath of World War II was likely to argue that Russian geography long had induced its leaders to search for secure warm-water ports, particularly in Eastern Europe and the Middle East, as a way of improving its strategic position in a world in which it had such limited access to the sea.[3] In this respect, the actions of the Soviet government differed little from what the tsars had long attempted; traditional Russian interests were what mattered regardless of who controlled the Russian state. Analysis of those interests had more explanatory power than, as an idealist interpretation might have assumed, such matters as the revisionist ideology of the Soviets, their presumed revolutionary fervor, or their suspicions of the motives of bourgeois states.

Undoubtedly, the realist critique was a healthy corrective to some of the more naive and optimistic expectations held by many people in the Western democracies, and perhaps especially in the United States,[4] in the earlier decades of this century. Realist interpretations triumphed when they did because they fell upon fertile ground. The leaders of the major revisionist powers between the wars appear to have been about as cynical in the pursuit of power and as devoid of socially acceptable values in that search as any in modern times. For them, the mix of power and normative considerations in their own careers contained overwhelmingly more of the former than the latter.

Even in a world whose leaders behaved more morally, we should be well advised to keep in mind the realists' most important lessons, among which are the following: (1) the leaders of any nation-state have a primary responsibility to provide it with security; it follows, therefore, that (2) they will perceive a duty to try to maintain or, if possible, enhance their own state's position vis-à-vis others through competition, diplomacy, and, when all else fails, the use of force; (3) all such sovereign leaders, whether their interests are revisionist or status quo in orientation, are certain to be conservative in the basic sense that they have a mutual interest in maintaining their individual states and collectively the state system; finally, (4) state leaders are bound to advance value systems peculiar to their positions in the world, values that place extraordinary emphasis on self-interest and comparatively little on obligations to those beyond the nation-state, or even to those within the state who do not share their statist outlook. Unquestionably these are important lessons precisely because they embody insights that explain many important facts about the continuing nature of international politics in our time. Any consideration of how to make a better world that ignores those lessons does so at its peril.

Yet it is just as important to recognize that the realist analysis does not provide absolute truths about the nature of international politics. There are no absolutes in this realm because of the fundamentally divergent nature of politics themselves. Sound political analysis must search for the correct mix of realist and idealist considerations, and the rightness of the mix will always be determined within a particular historical context and even then will vary with the analyst's own biases and purposes.

Statism: The Realist Bias

One of the clear biases of the realists is their (usually unstated) assumption that the traditional interests of states are also their unchanging interests and that the determination of what those interests are also changes little if at all over time. If neutrality for, say, France and Great Britain was a sensible policy for them in the Russo-Japanese War of 1904–1905 (even though France was an ally of Russia and Britain of Japan at the time), then neutrality presumably would remain in their interest in a comparable conflict in the future, regardless of any other normative considerations that might have arisen in the meantime.

An example used by one of the most influential writers of the realist school, Hans J. Morgenthau, illustrates the point. He cited the Soviet attack on Finland in 1939 as presenting France and Great Britain with two issues, one he calls legal (and I term normative) and the other political, that is, power (Morgenthau often *equated* the power factor with what he called the political, as he did here, thereby relegating normative considerations to a kind of nonpolitical limbo). In his terms, the legal issue was whether or not the attack violated the Covenant of the League of Nations, which was easily answered in the affirmative, "for obviously the Soviet Union had done what was prohibited by the Covenant." The political issue entailed assessing the attack on the interests of the two Western democracies, including what it would mean for "the future distribution of power" in Europe.

According to Morgenthau, Britain and France muddled legal and political considerations when they not only saw to it that the Soviet Union was expelled from the League (the appropriate legal response, evidently) but also planned to join Finland in the war against the Soviets, an action that was thwarted by Sweden's refusal to allow their troops to pass through Swedish territory on the way to Finland. Morgenthau concluded: "The policy of France and Great Britain was a classic example of legalism in that they allowed the answer to the legal question, legitimate within its sphere, to determine their political action. Instead of asking both questions, that of law and that of power, they asked only the question of law; and the answer they received could have no bearing on the issue that their very existence might have depended upon."[5]

It is assumed in this assessment that had the two countries asked the right political or power question, they would have known it was contrary to their interests to enter a war with the Soviet Union at the same time they were fighting Germany. That assumption seems to mean they would have seen that they could not win both contests and hence should not have entered the second one. But Morgenthau's conclusion tacitly ensures that what he calls the legal issue shall forever remain a trivial consideration in the world of international politics, for he has separated it from political considerations and thereby decreed its impotence. He seems to argue that it was acceptable for Britain and France to work to expel the Soviet Union from the League but that it was unacceptable for them to attempt the kinds of sanctions (i.e., the use of their power) called for by the Covenant to make the collective security system an effective police agent.

By the time of the Soviet attack on Finland, the reversion to traditional power politics through the use of military force may already have proceeded too far for the Western democracies reasonably to expect to succeed in supporting League principles. Yet their willingness even at that late date to try to take collective security action can be read as resulting from their own realistic assessment that their national interests now lay in opposing aggression, collectively, if possible. One of the interests their leaders may have come to see, however belatedly, was the creation of an effective security system; however, such a system could not have been regarded as a traditional interest, for traditionally the logic of Westphalia encouraged noninvolvement in other sovereigns' quarrels. It became a possibility only with the creation of the League. Had these two countries consistently used their capabilities to support collective security during the 1920s and 1930s, the legal issue would have been far less separable from that of power calculations in European capitals by 1939. A new normative factor would have mobilized effective power in a novel, useful way. Had that occurred, no rational Soviet leader would have been nearly so sanguine about the use of force against its small neighbor as was Stalin. The point is that nothing was preordained in nature to prevent that occurrence, although Morgenthau's interpretation comes very close to implying that something was.

Statist Versus World Order Perspectives

Morgenthau's analysis of the Finnish case is typical of the realist point of view. Implicit in his critique of the British-French decision is the assumption that one and only one standard exists for the evaluation of action in the international arena: that of whether or not it serves the interests of the particular nation-states under scrutiny. Leaving aside the question of the ambiguity involved in determining just what such an interest truly is, the realist approach always proceeds from the point of view of state actors, never from the standpoint that would regard states as subordinate units within the single, larger international community.[6] What results is the inevitable bias of a particular level of analysis or point of view.[7]

Analysis that proceeds from a global perspective will produce different biases of its own, as my own critique of Morgenthau should show. The world outlook is essentially that of the space traveler who looks back on the earth from a great distance. From such a viewpoint many detailed features of the globe's topography are invisible or blurred, the boundaries between states are nonexistent, and the main impression is that the various parts of the earth's surface form a harmonious whole. The foreign policy analyst in contrast is fixed firmly within the territory of a particular state, whose importance naturally looms largest for him or her. The more distant points on the globe's surface assume less importance than those close at hand. Unable to see the whole sphere, this person will naturally see his or her own domain as central to the world.

It follows that those who take the world view are more open to the charge of idealism than are those who start from the foreign policy outlook of particular states. This results because the statist view is so much more strongly rooted in the concrete reality of our everyday experience, so much more attuned to physical nuance and detail than is the world view. Throughout human history, experience with one world has been minimal in the social sense; most of us live and die within a particular locality and only have occasion to grasp the larger whole imaginatively, if at all. Conversely, it is no accident that the world's greatest ethical and religious systems are strongly universalistic in their metaphysics, which is exactly what has stimulated the human imagination about what might or ought to be when we find ourselves living in an imperfect material world.

We need only consider for a moment the way in which the student of international affairs typically receives information about these matters to sense the ways in which realist perspectives far overbalance idealist or normative considerations. Virtually all that information comes through the news media. Characteristically, these media report the immediate, the particular, and the concrete events of international politics. They select as newsworthy those daily happenings that bring political groups into conflict rather than harmony (surely nothing is more newsworthy than the outbreak of a war, nothing less so than another day of peace between Manitobans and North Dakotans). Regardless of their efforts at objectivity, their reports reflect the values of the society that produces them, al-

most always reinforcing the parochial at the expense of the global outlook. As a result, it is little wonder that most of us, including those who
are well informed in the usual sense about world events, are inclined to
regard the international arena as nothing but a jungle and therefore are
discouraged from turning our minds toward the effort to improve it.

Power and Law in World Society

In sum, a sensible regard for what is possible and preferable in the way of
international conduct must always seek not the divorce but the marriage
of some form of the ideal with the real or practical. We are quite accustomed to this kind of joining in the politics of vigorous and viable domestic societies; in fact, it is the relative success of that joining of the normative with the power dimension that makes them viable and vigorous.
When the United States, for example, enacted far-reaching civil rights legislation during the 1960s, no intelligent observer supposed either that the
laws were meaningless, in the sense that they would have no effect on
real behavior of Americans, or that they would make all behavior instantly conform to the new standard. What they correctly expected was
that the power of the federal government would now be marshaled at
least to nudge behavior into the directions specified in the legislation,
changing attitudes in the process.

It may be argued that this example, drawn from a domestic rather than
the international social order, is misleading. After all, the existence of a
stronger normative cohesion is what chiefly separates a domestic polity
from world society. True enough, but the difference is one of degree and
not kind. Just as not all political behavior within a domestic society is controlled by the normative order, neither is all international behavior devoid of normative concerns. It is useful to think of all activity within both
spheres, domestic and worldwide, as falling somewhere along a continuum that runs from the most extreme form of the exercise of raw power
we can imagine at one pole to the most rigid kind of normative control at
the other. Even though these are analytic constructs only, since in the
world of human experience some mix of these factors is always present,
certain thinkers have found it useful to imagine each force in isolation for
what it can teach us about the world we actually inhabit. The following
two polar visions happen to have had profound effects on Western
thought, although they are by no means the only such models that might
have been selected from the intellectual storehouse of our inheritance.

The seventeenth-century English writer Thomas Hobbes imagined a
time before humans formed civil societies, in which each individual was
motivated by the mechanistic impulse to gain such power over nature as
was needed to survive. In that "state of nature," each person was neces-

sarily at constant war with all other individuals in the battle for life, a condition so terrible that it made the lives of all "nasty, brutish, and short."[8] No evidence exists to suggest that Hobbes's state of nature is a true picture of any actual historical condition known to members of the species. It is even difficult to imagine it as a literal description of the condition of our prehuman ancestors, who must have cooperated with each other for their own survival, however primitive or instinctual such cooperation might appear to us today. It demonstrates, however, by painting the intolerable quality of such a state of things, why humans do *not* live in the power dimension alone. In their mutual relationships they must advance the kinds of values that permit them to live together in a more or less orderly way if they are to survive not just randomly as individuals but as a species.

The opposite extreme of total social order, entirely freed from considerations of power advantages, is at least vaguely known to Christians in the image of the kingdom of heaven. The first great Christian theologian, St. Augustine, related that vision to the temporal world in his work *The City of God,* in which he took the view that God was preparing through history two mystical cities, one of God and one of the devil. The duty of the Christian was to try to live so that he or she would enter the City of God—the perfect, ideal kingdom. That meant avoiding the corruption, the "unreality" of the imperfect physical world, that of the devil. While on earth, Christians could not expect the perfection of the City of God, but they could, through their devotion, try however imperfectly to emulate it.[9] From this great work, and from the Platonic idealism that had so influenced Augustine, grew the Western tradition of natural law. That tradition assumes the existence of ideal laws in nature that govern, or ought to govern, human relations on earth, it being our duty to discover those laws—principally through the use of our ability to reason—and try to live by them.

Today when we view global society as a whole, we naturally see that in terms of our continuum it seems much closer to the Hobbesian or power pole than it does to the Augustinian or normative pole. It displays more exercise of power politics than evidence of dependable legal order. This perception is no doubt accurate regardless of any criticisms we might have of realist analysis, in which the self-interest of the individual state can be seen as analogous to that of the individual person in Hobbes's state of nature. If we have not attained the City of God in our domestic societies, how much farther are we from that ideal state at the world level! Nonetheless, we are only *relatively* closer to the Hobbesian pole internationally than domestically, for international behavior is guided by normative concerns that remove it from the absolute of nature, as our overview of Westphalian principles demonstrated, even though these are often less commanding and less obvious to the untrained eye than their domestic counterparts.

The International Order, Agency, and Change

The Westphalian order, while weak in terms of Augustine's ideal, embodies the principal normative constraints for state actors, the dos and don'ts of their interactions. Westphalia is a social *structure* whose goal is *order.* The traditional wielders of power in the world are Westphalia's subjects, nation-states, which are also the principal *agents* of political dynamism and *change.* System and subjects are essentially connected, for neither would exist as we know it without the other. Yet tension between the system and its subjects is also inherent in the way that tension is always present between the normative and capability dimensions of political life. Here the normative system works to constrain antisocial behavior, as judged in Westphalian terms, by individual states. Yet states—and increasingly today other "subjects" of the normative order, such as groups and movements, in addition to governmental leaders—are the agents of change, including not merely change that goes against norms but also change that attempts to further social values other than those traditionally upheld by the normative order.

This situation produces a never-ending dilemma, for we need *both* order and change. When too little order is present in the world, there are no dependable, harmonious relationships among individuals, and there is no peace. But when too little change is permitted, there may be much injustice and none of the growth that is essential to the life process. As we explore important issues on the agenda of world politics today, we shall see that all of them confront us with divergent problems of decisionmaking and pose important questions.

First, when should we try to insist on making the capability of some agent or group of agents conform, perhaps more stringently than it usually does, to existing community standards? For example, do the destructive capabilities of governments today require a more effective ban on the initiation of force against other states than has been possible (or seemed necessary) in the past? Do the terroristic practices of some private agents amount to a threat to the integrity of the Westphalian order that can best be met through collective state sanctions?

Second, and conversely, when should we expect to advance important contemporary values by encouraging normative change? Would the cause of individual human rights be better served if various external agents were allowed a greater role in humanitarian intervention into offending societies than has traditionally been the case? Is the Westphalian order too weak to provide the amount and kind of regulation needed to preserve the biosphere from the assaults our laissez-faire practices have allowed and perhaps even encouraged? If so, what agencies should we seek for effective change?

Third, when the agent of change is the government of a very powerful nation-state, with its inherent self-interest either in a perpetuation of the existing order or else in a structural "reform" that furthers its capability, how is it possible to encourage real reform of the sort that empowers groups previously excluded, and most important, those that are not merely other state governments? An example of the problem was seen when the U.S. government under both Carter and Reagan proposed changes in the organization and structure of the United Nations. These proposals were touted as reforms meant to realign effective power with UN goals more fully than had come to be the case. But the only kind of power/value realignments they sought not only reemphasized the cruciality of states as the only life force behind the UN Charter; they also sought to institutionalize the uniquely great economic and financial power of the United States (and of other large, rich nations) within the constitutional structure of the UN system.[10] The proposed changes naturally were objected to—also on statist grounds—by many other members, particularly the huge number of poor, small countries, whose Westphalian power lay not in their ability to contribute more than the United States to UN programs, but in the combination of their votes as many separate sovereigns.

The concluding chapter of this book attempts to explore ways of achieving realistic change of a kind that may help us realize important values of our time. Meanwhile, we must not forget that human agents are not mere cogs in structural machines, programmed to act only as their predecessors have acted for as far back into history as they can peer. Humans can demonstrate imaginative and courageous leadership and moral choice, even if the possibilities open to them in these respects are always somewhat limited by the historical and social context of their time. Whatever the rigidities of today's social and political structures, we live in an era when, thanks to increased education about the nature and condition of the world we inhabit and the explosion in our capability of making our voices and our values heard around the globe, the power of human agency may be potentially greater than ever before.

We should also remember that whatever the limitations on our efforts to reform the world, the prospective dangers of business as usual loom larger before us all—government officials and private citizens—almost every day and are more and more difficult to ignore. In the words of Stanley Hoffmann, "The fear of violent death and the fear of economic collapse are the international relations equivalent of that famous threat of hanging which so powerfully concentrates the mind."[11] Before undertaking a fuller examination of the issues that threaten us, we need to concentrate our minds next on the growth and change in a normative order within the international arena that may, in fact, have been occurring all around us without our much noticing it.

Formal Governmental and International Institutions

What can easily mislead the untrained eye is the apparent absence of governmental structures at the world level, when governments apparently go hand in hand with normative order inside every sovereign state. Governments are the channels through which flow social power and values, there to be stirred into a legitimate mix before flowing back as the dominant current over society. States have created such institutions as congresses, parliaments, revolutionary councils, and the like and have given them clear and accepted responsibilities for declaring what is the law of the particular society. They have created judges and other tribunals to assist in definitive rulings as to what constitutes the law in the face of conflicting claims by its subjects, and they have given executives and other heads of state the responsibility and the right to enforce it. Governments are the product of a legal system as well as its maker. They are what shape and sustain the legal order. They embody the sovereign's ability to command the members of society.[12]

We look about the international arena and see nothing comparable in the way of governmental structures. There are, it is true, in our day a number of international institutions that look a bit like the governmental structures of our domestic societies. For Americans, it is not hard to see a resemblance between the UN Security Council and General Assembly and the two houses of Congress. Perhaps we note too that the UN secretary-general looks like the organization's chief executive, and the International Court of Justice (ICJ) sitting in The Hague a bit like a world supreme court.

But we rightly suspect that these comparisons are misleading. These international institutions do not seem truly governmental in the sense that they can command individuals to obey their orders. They do not simply represent the sovereign states of the world; they evidently embody the conflicting interests of those states, institutionalizing their traditional freedom to disagree with each other. They evidently have little more authority over states than each sovereign seems to submit to voluntarily. The International Court of Justice (more informally known as the World Court), for example, has no power of compulsory jurisdiction and only hears cases that state governments volunteer to bring before it. And once the court decides such cases, it cannot turn to a world executive with a monopoly of police powers to enforce its decision. This, at least, is our conclusion when we, first, equate legal authority with a social process of subordination, in which the authority commands the subject to obey its decree, and, second, identify such an arrangement as possible only where institutional structures exist to mark the hierarchical authority.

Yet this conclusion has taken us too far. We have forgotten that the pole of power and the pole of order are joined in the continuum of politics, internationally as well as domestically. We have fallen into the common error of supposing that the usual features of a domestic legal order are the necessary prerequisites for *any* legal order.[13] Few international institutions today have the power to command that is generally characteristic of domestic governments, but it does not follow that they are without any ability to persuade international actors, that they have no impact on the articulation and advancement of particular social values relevant to ordered international behavior. The extent of their ability to shape the international order varies with the situation. It is tested by the extent to which nation-states and other international actors act on the directives expressed through the international institutions, directives to which the states themselves have contributed, of course.

Examples relating to four different international institutions help illustrate this point. For a number of years, the UN Security Council refused to recognize the unilateral independence of the white minority government of Rhodesia (now Zimbabwe), which prevented universal suffrage in that formerly British colony and with it the inevitable coming to power of a black majority. On May 29, 1968, a unanimous Security Council called for mandatory economic sanctions against the white minority regime. Even though the United States was among those voting in favor of sanctions, the U.S. Congress in 1971 adopted the Byrd Amendment to permit the importation of Rhodesian chromium into the United States in clear violation of the UN sanctions. Other members of the United Nations repeatedly objected to this U.S. breach of sanctions and publicly condemned it, but they had no effective means at their disposal to coerce the United States into obeying the directive. What had looked like an authoritative action by the Security Council evidently was not truly governmental in its effect, for one important subject was able to ignore it with impunity.

That is the clearest point at which to leave the story for one bent on demonstrating that the Security Council does not have, in spite of some UN Charter provisions that suggest otherwise, truly governmental capability. But the picture gets somewhat muddled when we note that the Byrd Amendment was strongly opposed by some U.S. political groups, and a new president, Jimmy Carter, succeeded in getting Congress to repeal it. As a result, by March 1977, the U.S. law was once again in compliance with the Security Council directive. And did the Security Council's action succeed in its real purpose of bringing an end to Rhodesia's white minority rule? Certainly not in and of itself. In fact, a cynically realistic analysis would argue that black rule eventually came to Rhodesia because of the force of arms of the Patriotic Front, thereby proving once again the commanding role of force in such cases. A more normatively ordered interpretation might insist that the use of force in this instance should be seen in its relation to the legal directive of the Security Council. From this viewpoint, the Rhodesian Patriotic Front exercised a quasi-police power on behalf of the international community. The realist view is too simplistic—although easier to grasp because it is—whereas the normative analysis points toward the complex and often ambiguous interrelationship of forces in the world order process. If it cannot show that the Security Council behaved like a government in the usual sense, it at least suggests that it was not devoid of any governmental quality whatever in moving the situation toward its preferred outcome.

In April 1984, the government of Nicaragua asked the International Court of Justice to act on its charge that the U.S. mining of Nicaragua's harbors constituted an unlawful action, as did U.S. support for military groups attempting to overthrow the Nicaraguan government. The Reagan administration, anticipating that Nicaragua was about to file such a complaint, had announced three days before it was brought that the United States would not accept the jurisdiction of the ICJ in any Central American dispute for a period of two years. That action underlined the lack of compulsory jurisdiction in the processes of the ICJ and seemed to assure in advance that the Court would be unable to do what courts presumably are meant to do: hear a matter in litigation between two subjects of the law, make an authoritative decision on the merits, and order an appropriate remedy. In fact, however, the Court did agree to hear the case, denying the validity of the U.S. attempt to excuse itself. The case then went forward without the formal participation of one of the disputants. The Court's decision on the merits, handed down in June 1986, generally upheld the Nicaraguan contention and found illegal many of the U.S. actions that had prompted the application.[14]

A realist interpretation might argue the futility of this episode, first as a demonstration of the impotence of the ICJ in the face of opposition by a government determined not to submit to it, and therefore to the unrealism of the Court's having proceeded nonetheless with the case. Without question, these events seem yet another illustration of the little distance the Westphalian world has moved from the pole of power, for what seems clearest here is the Court's inability to assert its normative control authoritatively in the face of a sovereign's determined refusal to be bound.

Once again, however, a more sophisticated reading of the situation shows us that the real outcome was more nuanced than that. One needs to see what really happened by way of changes in U.S. policy (since it is effective state policy that largely shapes the international normative order for good or ill) that may reasonably be connected to these events involving the World Court. What happened first—indeed, before the case was even brought by Nicaragua—was an end to the mining of Nicaragua's harbors by the United States. When, as an interim measure, the Court ordered the United States not to restrict access to Nicaraguan ports, the State Department announced its acceptance of that ruling. The period of the Court's proceedings also saw the U.S. Congress increasingly pull back from continued military support for the contras. In October 1984, Congress cut off additional funding to the Central Intelligence Agency (CIA) as a result of revelations about the harbor minings. And soon after the ICJ's decision on the merits of the Nicaragua case, Reagan's effort there became mired in allegations of domestic illegalities in the form of the Iran-contra scandal.

Much as in the eventual outcome of the Rhodesian case, one could scarcely argue that this result had been directly produced by the authoritative action of an international institution. At the level of rhetoric and symbol, the Reagan administration had effectively denied its responsibility to be bound by the decision of the Court. Yet, by the end of Reagan's term of office, the power of the United States had been considerably retracted from an earlier use against Nicaragua that so clearly defied community norms and values, as these had been restated by the World Court. The very process of litigation had been a contributing factor to that end. There was, in all this, at least a hint that one subject of the world's normative system was more constrained by it than its representatives would admit.

Some analysts have looked to the roles of what they call functional international organizations in our time for evidence of how quasi-governmental functions can develop at the world level when compliance is not likely to demand the kind of coercive force evident in the Rhodesian case.[15] A good example is one of the oldest of these, the Universal Postal Union, which for more than a hundred years has assured us that when a citizen of Japan sends a letter to a friend in Peru, the Peruvian post office will honor the Japanese stamp and deliver it to the correct address. That may not seem a very dramatic example of a governmental capability at the world level, although its importance becomes apparent when we think about the consequences if such a system were not in place today. Significantly, the Universal Postal Union was created once nineteenth-century communication increased to the point that a widely shared value favoring a dependable global arrangement had developed. Governments keep it operating because of the social need it serves.

The Universal Postal Union is by no means a unique example of a functional intergovernmental organization exercising truly governmental powers over societies, even if those powers are limited to particular areas of human life. By the 1980s, smallpox, that dread disease responsible for many of the plagues of earlier periods, had been eradicated throughout the globe, thanks mainly to the governmental power of the World Health Organization (WHO). That power consisted in an ability to monitor the locale and progress of the disease worldwide, to assist nation-states in providing the necessary health and sanitation measures to control it, and so on—all on a scale beyond the reach of particular state governments. It was clearly in the interest of us all to see smallpox ended, and that interest became the basis for WHO's power to act.[16]

These examples from the UN Security Council, the International Court of Justice, the Universal Postal Union, and the World Health Organization all suggest that governmental capability does not always and everywhere rest only with the formal governments of sovereign states.[17] They should remind us too that the government process is more complex than we generally suppose, difficult to trace and hard to describe when we cannot fall back on the customary references to parliaments or presidents, which are only labels for the formal institutions of government, explaining nothing about its meaning or how it functions. How and where should we expect to find it, particularly in its informal guise? What is its place in the contemporary world order system?

Government and the Support of Social Order

Consider the following: We are all accustomed to the place and function of traffic lights in modern cities. They are meant to serve social order by commanding cars to stop and go in patterns that ensure the safety of all, which is our common interest when we drive. Traffic lights may be seen as symbolic or institutional representations of the city government's formal power to command us in the common good. They stand for government in the sense that they represent a kind of socially legitimate power, one that we accept as useful. But what happens when, because of a malfunction of some kind, the traffic lights at a busy intersection suddenly fail? The symbol of government ceases to operate; yet we would not expect every semblance of social order there to break down as a result. The drivers of the cars approaching that intersection still have a mutual interest in their own safety. As a result, they almost certainly will begin to create an ordering, or quasi-governmental, system of their own, perhaps even without any verbal communication. We should expect such drivers at least to slow down when they see the traffic lights not functioning, and then proceed only when they deem it safe. Logically, each will defer to the driver who arrives at the intersection next before him, for if all drivers do that, none will be more than minimally inconvenienced, and a dependable stop-and-go system, clear to all, will be in place.

We should not regard such a system as ideal, partly because we might fear that some drivers will fail to abide by the etiquette or norm tacitly agreed to by most, and will, as if they have reverted to a state of nature, take advantage of some car's slowing to speed on through the intersection at risk to themselves and others. Yet common sense (i.e., perception of the mutual self-interest) will make the system work well enough at least as a temporary measure for everyone's safety.

The situation at a busy intersection is a clear example in which the self-interest of the individual (or person, tribe, nation-state, or other unit) coincides with the interests of the community as a whole. It is like the individual and common human interest in seeing smallpox eradicated. When this kind of clear and evident harmony exists between the self and the social interest, a functional governmental system is likely to develop. It need not be a formal system, though formalization no doubt helps to clarify it, and it need not rest on an evident police power at the top. Each subject's commonsense recognition of its own self-interest induces its compliance.

Yet we have guessed that in the absence of an effective police power, symbolized by functioning traffic lights, some brash driver may charge through the intersection in disregard of the rights of others. It may not be very far-fetched to see such a person as resembling the government of the United States when it violated the Rhodesian sanctions with regard to chromium. If we picture the type of driver most likely to behave antisocially at the intersection, we probably would not expect our culprit to be an elderly grandmother but a virile young male, one that a psychologist might describe as unusually aggressive. To pursue the analogy (perhaps too far), we probably would not expect a small country whose traditional policy has been based on the effort to get along well with its larger neighbors—say Finland or Thailand—to violate a Security Council resolution of this kind. That role would far more likely fall to a great power with a habit of supposing it could generally call the shots in the world arena, particularly when it also doubted if the so-called community interest necessarily coincided with what some formal organization of the community claimed it to be. For such an individual or state the appearance of the police officer with a nightstick may be needed to compel obedience. Short of that, should the individual decide to defer to the community standard, that person will no doubt be convinced that his or her compliance was voluntary, not forced by someone else. Such are the ambiguities surrounding free choice and deference to the standards of the group in all aspects of our lives.

These analogies should remind us that we generally find it easier to obey the police officer's signal than to figure out our own interest in conforming to a tacit ordering arrangement when the formal symbol of government is absent. The police officer's presence eliminates the need for us to engage in analysis of our own interest compared to that of others. That analysis has, in effect, already been done, and we know the answer, as well as the consequences to ourselves if we fail to accept it. That is one reason why formalized, tangible governments are useful things. In the world order system, that kind of evidence of government almost never is present, and when it is, sovereign actors find that its bark is worse than its bite, for it can often be thwarted. The police officer (e.g., the Security Council of the United Nations) has no nightstick and no gun to enforce compliance. That official must persuade us that we should adhere to the general social consensus of interest, and only to the extent that we are successfully persuaded to comply with recognizable patterns of social order will that agent assume a greater sense of legitimacy as an authoritative figure within the legal order. Until that happens, however, we will probably regard this authority as ineffectual and assume our compliance is freely given.

Wherever social values command behavior over time, government emerges, perhaps gradually and with enough behavioral variations to be invisible for a long initial period. Eventually, however, if the patterns persist, the likely end product will be defined and visible institutions: *governments* in the everyday sense of the word. A government is formed when the power available to those whose political values dominate a society is joined to authority, which is the formal grant of competence to wield that power in specified ways and for certain ends. This is nothing more than a particularized version of that continual duality within the social world of the power oriented and the normative, and of the necessity of joining them to form the political—here the governmental—process.

The Congruence of Power and Authority

The greater the measure of congruence between political power and authority, the more we are inclined to regard the resulting government as legitimate. To the extent that one dimension dominates the other, governmental capability is weakened to the point that, as we approach either extreme, we eventually must regard the case as not governmental at all. Some familiar examples will illustrate these imbalances.

The Kellogg-Briand Pact of 1928, formally known as the Pact of Paris, condemned "recourse to war for the solution of international controversies." Although it was ratified by sixty-two nations (nearly all the sovereign states of the day), it stands as a classic example in international law of the creation of a specific authority (declaring the resort to war to be illegal) left essentially unattached to relevant power, for it provided no enforcement measures. As a result, its authority grew hollow and failed to shape behavior. Little more than ten years after its signing, most of the signatories were themselves embroiled in World War II. It assuredly did not govern the international relations of the period in any effective way. At the power end of the spectrum, when the United States intervened in the war in Vietnam in the 1960s, it did so without authorization by any formal institution of the international community and, as a result, could scarcely be regarded, from this perspective, as acting governmentally. Yet the United States clearly had the power to have a considerable impact on the political situation in Southeast Asia. In the one instance, authority without effective power and, in the other, effective power without authority both produced nongovernmental behavior within the world's legal system.

But preoccupation with extreme cases can make us forever blind to the quasi-governmental implications of much international activity that lies between them. In fact, even the above examples can be read as having implications that place them in the ambiguous middle ground between the extremes of power unrelated to authority and the reverse. When the Nazi war criminals were tried at Nuremberg at the end of World War II, one of the charges against them was that they had planned and initiated a war in violation of the international norm set forth in Kellogg-Briand.[18] The Nuremberg tribunal was patently in a position to enforce this interpretation of Nazi criminality, which is to say it began to align relevant power with the authority expressed in the 1928 treaty. Our sense of justice tells us that the creation of governmental capability should at least be evident to all who must submit to it. Therefore, we may argue that the relevant power should have been clearly in place when the authoritative standard was first expressed. We think that we are unfairly treated when a police officer appears at our neighborhood recreation center to arrest us for playing poker on Sunday, since we thought the old blue law that permitted such an arrest had not been operative for years. Yet, like it or not, the slow and painful development of government in any emerging social system seems always to be asymmetrical and uneven and to deprive some people of the sense of fairness advanced legal systems attempt to honor.

In the Vietnam case, the official position of the United States justifying its intervention was that some actor with the capability had the right and responsibility to assist South Vietnam in its effort to repel aggression from beyond its borders. This view saw the Vietcong as having committed the illegal act that demanded the sanction of forcible resistance from some other sovereign if the collectivity of sovereigns embodied in the United Nations could not agree to do so. No doubt there were serious flaws in this argument—South Vietnam was not a sovereign and could be viewed as engaged in a civil war with its northern half, a condition that demanded nonintervention by outside powers according to agreed-on normative standards—but U.S. spokespersons were at pains to articulate the normative implications of their behavior for world order.[19]

As both these cases illustrate, one of the frustrations in trying to understand the contemporary international legal order stems from the absence of those formal governmental authorities at the world level capable of telling us definitively whose interpretation of normative standards and behavior is right and whose is wrong. We must usually make that determination for ourselves, just as the spokespersons for sovereign states do. The situation in Vietnam in the 1960s was like that of two parties to a suit before a local court. We hear the attorneys' arguments for the plaintiff and the defendant, arguments that make very different yet plausible cases from the same set of facts. Then we find that after arguments are heard, no judge is present to make an authoritative decision. We spectators in the courtroom must decide the case, although we are hardly in a position to make our decision stick. Perhaps the moral authority of our collective voice will influence compliance, if we can find a collective voice, but there is also a strong possibility, in the absence of the judge and the coercive power of the state, that the guilty party will refuse to abide by our decision. In that case, a new mix of power and normative factors will flow out into the larger world to be assessed by any actors finding themselves in comparable situations in the future.

Dependable Expectations of Peaceful Change

Individuals and groups are by no means perpetually in conflict with each other within the larger social order, for in many situations the perceived self-interest of the one coincides with that of others to the point that a common interest in identical or comparable behavior is clear to all. In such cases, it is possible to eliminate the threat of smallpox or to deliver the mail without notable coercion from a formal governmental authority. Such activities are in fact so noncontroversial, so evidently right and proper in all our minds, that we rightly regard them as nonpolitical matters even though some intergovernmental direction, through a World Health Organization or a Universal Postal Union, may be necessary to implement our common value.

We have little difficulty, on the other hand, in listing the kinds of issues that are likely to be highly charged politically as least susceptible to this kind of functional international management. Our list would no doubt be headed by the military provocations across international boundaries that lead to war, since issues of war and peace are at the very heart of international politics. The problems of governing such war-threatening issues before they lead to dreadful costs in human lives are clearly much greater. Our experience in the twentieth century suggests that to be successful the effort to control large-scale outbreaks of violence internationally requires at least the following: first, agreement by virtually all actors in the international system on standards of conduct required by all; second, clear articulation of those standards, so that would-be violators and those who judge them will at least be clear about the normative implications of their actions; third, agreement on the kind and scale of sanctions appropriate to impose for various unlawful actions; and fourth, a demonstrable willingness to enforce adherence to the standards through the exercise of a police power.

The importance of these measures in the abstract is not particularly difficult to understand, since in effect they summarize the requirements underlying effective police power at any level of society. Yet our experience with the League of Nations and the United Nations seems conclusive proof that as a world society we have only begun to grapple with the implications of an effective monopoly of authoritative force at some central level. We dimly perceive the logic of the police power imperative but are not yet prepared—thanks to the habitual thinking and values of centuries—to act effectively on it. We have read Hobbes's description of the state of nature but either think that it is too grim a depiction of our place in the world or, more likely, are at a loss to know how to create a world order that will not do unacceptable violence to our treasured, pluralistic freedom of choice.

These problems are critically important for our future as a species. But even as we continue the effort to construct dependable police power to serve the international community, we need to recognize and look for support outside the realm of such formal activity as writing treaties, amending charters, or defining aggression. We need to try to understand how social groups come to develop peaceful interrelationships even where no formal agreements or institutions bind them.

For example, many, even neighboring, states have coexisted over long periods of time in relationships so peaceful that we have not the slightest realistic expectation that they might fall into war.[20] The situation of the United States and Canada is a good example, separated as they are by the world's longest undefended border. The relationship between the two was not always peaceful, and a fundamental difference in political allegiance has divided them from the beginning of their separate histories. Nor are their political and economic relations without conflict today, but no one seriously expects them to settle differences by the force of arms. A pioneering study of the process of social integration across national lines called this a model of a "pluralistic security-community," integrated to the point that there existed between the units "dependable expectations of peaceful change."[21]

By distinguishing such pluralistic communities from "amalgamated" ones, such as the fifty states of the United States, the authors helped us see that this fundamentally important characteristic of an integrated society—that its members coexist in peace—is not necessarily dependent on union under a single, formal government. What is most important about the pluralistic community is that it has somehow produced effective informal government to ensure peaceful change without subordinating all the differences in values, culture, and the like that make the separate units distinctively free and independent. The most fundamental problem of international politics has been resolved without the hierarchical domination and control of the powerful over the weak.

The world unquestionably would be a better place in which to live if all the states that now exist could become a single, pluralistic security-community. That would, by definition, eliminate the large-scale violence we know as war. Utopian? No doubt, for what we know of this process of community formation tells us that it is enormously complex and deeply rooted in a sense of shared historical experience, with all the possibilities for the development of similar values that implies. It cannot be duplicated in the laboratory or manipulated in the short run by a handful of people of goodwill. Still, many lessons are to be learned from the formation of particular security-communities that have application to the larger world.

Pluralistic Integration in Europe

One other such case is worth our attention, if only because of its dramatic move toward peaceful change and away from frequent armed conflict in a comparatively short time. Western Europe has been the site of numerous wars over the course of centuries, none more devastating or with greater reverberations globally than the two world wars of this century. At the root of each of these great conflicts lay Franco-German enmity, which itself had been fed by their war in 1870–1871 that led to the triumph of the German empire and France's humiliating defeat. After World War I, a number of leaders began talking of the need for European unity, but the traditional suspicions and fears dividing France and Germany continued to grow and deepen. Unity seemed an impossible dream. The best efforts of the visionaries were sadly inadequate to stave off another general European war.

Amazingly, however, within a scant twenty or twenty-five years after the end of World War II, France and Germany had become the core of a recognizable security-community, so firmly in place that today no one seriously supposes that they or their neighbors within the European Union will again resort to arms to settle their differences. How did such a fundamental transformation take place within so short a time? The general answer is simply that "the time was ripe" for it, in the sense that huge numbers of Western Europeans, weary of the killing and the destruction,

passionately desired an alternative to the war system and so were susceptible to novel ideas and policies designed to lead toward a preferable alternative. The widespread social upheaval produced by general war can
have revolutionary effects by calling into question the traditional prejudices and values that have led to the general misery.

That still does not say much about the ways in which European integration came about and even less about its implications for the rest of the
world. Among the factors that help explain this development, the following seem particularly important. First, the process of building today's European Union began with a very specific, functional agreement to create
an integrated coal and steel industry for the core countries. Among the
war-threatening issues dividing France and Germany, and threatening
the Low Countries as well, were their competing interests for control of
the important coal-producing regions of the Saar (now in Germany) and
the iron ore of French Lorraine. It was not hard to see that if mining and
processing operations could take place without regard for political
boundaries, a more economical steel industry should result. Therefore, a
West European coal and steel authority was created in a 1951 treaty for
just that purpose.[22] The result was the almost immediate economic gain
of all concerned within the industry, benefits that flowed throughout the
industrial economies of the region, simultaneous with the effective elimination of a traditional source of political conflict among the powers in the
region. That "pocketbook" success no doubt encouraged a habit of cooperation that seemed increasingly sensible from a strict self-interest point
of view to growing numbers of French, Germans, Belgians, and their partners. As a result, within a decade a far more ambitious plan for the general integration of the economies of the participating states was created,
the so-called Common Market.[23]

Second, the creation of the European Coal and Steel Community was itself made possible because the social disruption of the war brought to
power in Germany and Italy elites that clearly rejected the imperialist,
militarist values of those recently defeated. For the first time in living
memory, all the states of the region were governed by parties that were
committed to parliamentary democracy, to the goals of building societies
at least moderately committed to social welfare, to reinvigorating their
economies through considerable encouragement of private enterprise,
and so on. They could "talk the same language" and seek out their common interests in ways their predecessors could not. Even so, they had to
learn by trial and error that the functional route to integration was the
least threatening to traditional attitudes, and therefore the pathway to
success. In 1954, after a very emotional debate, the French National Assembly rejected a proposed treaty whose purpose was to create an integrated European Defense Community (EDC): So radical a change in tra-

ditional security arrangements raised fears in French minds of their army's domination by the Germans. This issue of high politics was too highly charged to find acceptance at the time.[24] In contrast, the integration of a basic industry could proceed without confronting traditional dogmas of national military power.

Third, the new elites had come to power because of the final defeat of the imperialist ethos in World War II. The virulent imperialism of the defeated powers had been eliminated, but just as important, it soon became increasingly clear to the victorious powers—among whom France, Britain, and the Netherlands still held sizable empires—that these traditional sources of their wealth and power could not be sustained indefinitely. They had to find alternatives for their continued economic growth, and the most plausible one was the creation of a common market that would thrive by eliminating all the barriers to trade and economic exchange that had separated their economies in the past.[25] Sweeping new economic and political imperatives served to encourage this break and, once the European Economic Community (EEC) was created, it helped advance the new economic forces that otherwise would have remained nothing more than visions.

Fourth, at every major step the integration of Western Europe has proceeded at a formal level through treaty making that serves to clarify and advance agreement on the governmental capabilities acceptable to all. That is, integration has been a gradualist process, proceeding from the particular and the simplest to the most complex. It has also been a rational process in the sense that participants have known basically what they were doing, submitting voluntarily to the new authority that they themselves progressively created. It has also been a process based on the faith that not all problems had to be solved at once. Problems that looked intractable yesterday may be far less serious by tomorrow, if only because between yesterday and tomorrow a social process of cooperation has continued that may well change the context in which tomorrow's problems must be tackled. Thus the goal of achieving a fully integrated internal market by January 1, 1993, became possible simply because the European Community (as it still was called) had been moving consciously in that direction for many years. The process clearly demonstrated the importance of attending to the normative dimension as a counter to the raw coercive power of integration through conquest. In the beginning, the widespread consent to creation of the European Community reflected the articulation of its goals within a pluralistic setting, with all that suggests regarding the diverse social values that had to be accommodated.

Fifth, the pluralism of this enterprise is such that important political differences remain and no doubt will continue within member societies and among their governments. For instance, the political left has often opposed the way the market purportedly discourages greater economic equality at home while tending to create neoimperial economic relationships with less developed countries abroad. The right has voiced its opposition to the centralization of ever more governmental decisions in the European capital of Brussels and to the corresponding loss of national sovereignty that comes with fuller integration. With the end of the cold war, the EU was presented with unprecedented challenges and opportunities that cut across the political spectrum. These were essentially of three kinds.

One surrounded the dilemma over whether to expand the Union to include virtually all the states of Europe now that no Iron Curtain restricted its potential scope to the western end of the European peninsula. Central and East European states that for more than forty years had been under the influence of Moscow were generally eager to tie their fortunes to the West. But if they joined the EU, as many of them were expected to do by early in the twenty-first century,[26] the Union would have to forgo or at least postpone some of its more ambitious goals for deeper political integration.

A second set of challenges had to contend with the first and stemmed from the conscious effort in the 1990s to move the EU more fully into areas of "high politics." The engine for the boldest of these initiatives, the Maastricht treaty of 1992, was intended to create a common currency (the euro) by 1999 and eventually a common foreign and security policy. Yet its initial impact was to trigger a sustained reaction against such moves in the publics of a number of member countries. One response was acceptance of the view that members could have different timetables for becoming fully integrated into the new financial institutions. A further reaction is that for the first time in its history the EU is abandoning the unified approach to integration and assuming instead the prospect of a "multi-speed Europe" in which integration proceeds for some in a particular area with the expectation that others will join them at a later date.[27] One consequence is that by 1997, progress toward a common foreign policy had scarcely proceeded beyond generalities.[28]

These two developments are deeply entwined with a third, which is the problem of the so-called democratic deficit in the European Union of today. Some of the reaction to Maastricht showed plainly that large segments of the European public felt disenfranchised from important EU decisions and initiatives over which they had little control. For example, even though the European Parliament has long been directly elected by the citizens of member countries, its powers are less legislative than recommendatory. Effective legislation is initiated by the Council of Ministers, where most action must be taken unanimously. That unanimity becomes a more difficult operational requirement with every addition to the Union's membership and, therefore, to its Council. By the same token the Commission, which acts as the executive arm of the European Union, was widely regarded as unwieldy even before many new members were added from Central and Eastern Europe. As a result of popular criticism, initiatives currently are under way to extend majority voting and to decrease the size of the Commission, as are proposals to increase the competence of the Parliament and to create a common social policy. In spring 1997, changes of government occurred after elections in Britain and France that were at least partly referenda on the austerity policies the EU leadership had endorsed to pave the way for monetary union. As a result, soon thereafter EU governmental leaders committed themselves to combat the high levels of unemployment that evidently underlay much of the discontent with the current path of integration in Europe.

An assessment of the EU's prospects today must deal with apparent contradictions. The fundamental accomplishments are clear. The Union has succeeded dramatically in creating a fully integrated common market and a security-community for its fifteen current members. In the words of the president of the EU Commission, "It is something of a miracle that war between our peoples should have become unthinkable. To squander this legacy would be a crime against ourselves."[29] This legacy was achieved by *not* posing serious challenges to the formal political structures of the EU member states and, hence, to the loyalties of citizens. Now, after nearly half a century of evolution, the EU is at a point where certain sovereign prerogatives are being challenged more clearly than ever before. For the moment, that has led to greater dispute than consensus on higher political goals. There is little evidence anywhere in Europe that a transference of loyalties from the national to the European level has been achieved. Does that mean that the further integration of Europe is now in jeopardy? The answer probably depends both on the time frame and on the vision one has of the end state of integration. European integration is currently in a difficult period because of its enormous past success. That so many states now are knocking at Europe's door—and posing questions about how heterogeneous or democratically organized the Union may be in the future—is a mark of the EU's attraction because of what it has accomplished. Similarly, the constraints on national economic decisions imposed by the goal of monetary union are themselves the product of having achieved a fully integrated common market within the EU. European integration, seen in this light, is not so much faltering today as it is finding its way through uncharted waters. Few now imagine—as some once did—a "United States of Europe" that is simply a confederated superstate. Fewer still can posit some alternative end product of the integrative process to which diverse publics would be loyal while retaining loyalty to their national cultures and institutions. It is, therefore, important to recall what European integration already means to Europe and the world by way of placing the current debate in perspective.

As the European security-community has grown, it has worked to strengthen dependable expectations of peaceful change across a region where minority groups have frequently resorted to violence in their quest for greater territorial independence from the larger nation. As economic integration has enriched the lives of Europeans,[30] many have become convinced that such controversies as Italy's control over the German-speaking province of South Tyrol, Spain's sovereignty over Basque country, and the divisions in Ireland all will be eased. In a more integrated region, national minorities will be far more able to interact freely across boundaries that will less and less restrict their domains. Once ethnic violence became a reality to the East in the 1990s, this dynamic no doubt became part of the EU's magnetic pull on countries in Central and Eastern Europe.

Much of what currently challenges the EU reminds us of what has always been most positive in the way the EU has developed. At every step, European integration has proceeded by protecting first the democratic pluralism of the region. The manifestations of that pluralism visible today reveal perhaps the most effective barrier one can imagine to the growth of a highly centralized and authoritarian superstate. Moreover, European integration is taking place with considerable openness, not in isolation from the rest of the world. As North Americans in particular must be aware, their ties to Western Europe are no doubt greater and more complex at many levels today than in any time in the past, so much so that the peoples of both continents are now plausibly integrated in a pluralistic security-community, even though North America is not included in the Treaty of Rome.

Europe's integration to date appears to be producing a set of political and social relationships that are largely unexplainable in Westphalian terms, something truly new under the sun. It would be naive to expect the West European model to apply fully to countries elsewhere in the world. For instance, its success may largely reflect the imperatives of advanced industrial capitalism; certainly, it is built on two thousand years of a common European culture. But whatever the criticisms of the Community's thrust or the problems that it still must face, it shows us that one of the most conflict-ridden regions of the world, long a source of infection in global international politics, can with vision, careful planning, and great sensitivity to the values of different groups be transformed into an area of peace. Not coincidentally, it has shown us in the process that our Westphalian views of sovereignty and separateness are becoming badly out-of-date.

Notes

1. With the ending of the cold war, realism began to receive more widespread criticism than it had for decades. That was largely initiated by its failure, in the eyes of many, either to predict the cold war's end or to provide adequate tools for

analysis of the dynamics of the post–cold war world. See, for example, David Baldwin, ed., *Neorealism and Neoliberalism: The Contemporary Debate* (New York: Columbia University Press, 1993); Charles W. Kegley Jr., *Controversies in International Relations Theory: Realism and the Neoliberal Challenge* (New York: St. Martin's Press, 1995); Luis E. Lugo, *Sovereignty at the Crossroad? Morality and International Politics in the Post–Cold War Era* (Lanham, Md.: Rowman and Littlefield, 1996); and James N. Rosenau, *Turbulence in World Politics: A Theory of Change and Continuity* (Princeton, N.J.: Princeton University Press, 1990).

2. Much of the tone for the realist-idealist debate was set in an important book by E. H. Carr, *The Twenty Years' Crisis, 1919–1939* (London: Macmillan, 1946), which lucidly explored the implications of the idealist versus the materialist bent in a variety of human types and social settings relevant to international politics. A more recent study of realism is Michael Smith, *Realist Thought from Weber to Kissinger* (Baton Rouge: Louisiana State University Press, 1987).

3. See Carr, *The Twenty Years' Crisis,* Chapter 5, for a general realist critique. See also George F. Kennan, *Russia and the West Under Lenin and Stalin* (Boston: Little, Brown, 1960).

4. George F. Kennan criticized what he termed the "legalism-moralism" of U.S. foreign policy in an influential set of lectures published as *American Diplomacy, 1900–1950* (Chicago: University of Chicago Press, 1951). The theme of an ongoing naive idealism in U.S. diplomacy is also the object of criticism in the writings of Stanley Hoffmann. See, for example, his *Gulliver's Troubles* (New York: McGraw-Hill, 1968) and *Primacy or World Order* (New York: McGraw-Hill, 1978).

5. Hans J. Morgenthau, *Politics Among Nations,* 4th ed. rev. (New York: Alfred A. Knopf, 1967), p. 12.

6. Though many younger, neorealist scholars have modified the realist approach by granting more importance than their predecessors did to the structure of the international system and how that influences state behavior. See, e.g., Hedley Bull, *The Anarchical Society* (New York: Columbia University Press, 1977), and Kenneth N. Waltz, *Theory of International Politics* (Reading, Mass.: Addison-Wesley, 1979).

7. The importance of and intellectual considerations inherent in the level of analysis undertaken in international politics are explored in J. David Singer, "The Level-of-Analysis Problem in International Relations," in *The International System: Theoretical Essays,* ed. Klaus Knorr and Sidney Verba (Princeton, N.J.: Princeton University Press, 1969), pp. 77–92.

8. Thomas Hobbes, *Leviathan,* edited with an introduction by C. B. Macpherson (Harmondsworth, U.K.: Penguin, 1968).

9. St. Augustine, *The City of God,* ed. Vernon J. Bourke (Garden City, N.Y.: Image Books, 1958). See especially the foreword by Etienne Gilson.

10. The same kind of parochialism was evident in efforts by some members of the U.S. Congress during the Clinton presidency to insist on a "reform" of the UN secretariat—eliminating positions and programs not in accord with those members' political goals—as a condition for authorizing payment of the United States' debt, which stood at more than $1 billion by 1997. These positions are outlined in Steven A. Dimoff, "U.S.-U.N. Arrears: What's the Deal?" *The Interdependent* 23, 1 (Spring 1997):5–6.

11. Stanley Hoffmann, "The Political Ethics of International Relations," Seventh Morgenthau Memorial Lecture on Ethics and Foreign Policy (New York: Carnegie Council on Ethics and International Affairs, 1988), p. 17.

12. The assertion that "law is the command of the sovereign" is that of the leading English Positivist writer on the law of the nineteenth century, John Austin. His strong emphasis on law as a system of subordination greatly influenced his contemporaries and many other writers down to the present day. The Austinian outlook tends to denigrate international patterns of order, which so seldom conform to the conception of law acting on subordinate subjects. Positivism is the jurisprudential philosophy that downplays or negates the place of natural law and thereby corresponds to the realist or materialist vision of politics more generally. For a brief discussion of Austin's work, see Charles G. Fenwick, *International Law,* 4th ed. (New York: Appleton-Century-Crofts, 1965), pp. 44–45.

13. See Richard A. Falk, "International Jurisdiction: Horizontal and Vertical Conceptions of Legal Order," *Temple Law Quarterly* 32, 3 (Spring 1959):295–320.

14. Case Concerning Military and Paramilitary Activities in and Against Nicaragua (*Nicaragua v. United States of America*). For a summary of the operative part of the Court's judgment, see *American Journal of International Law* 80, 3 (July 1986):785–807.

15. Functionalism constitutes one of the important theoretical explanations of how separate sovereigns become integrated over time. See David A. Mitrany, *The Progress of International Government* (New Haven, Conn.: Yale University Press, 1933) and *A Working Peace System* (Chicago: Quadrangle Books, 1966). For a clear interpretation of the functional approach, see Inis L. Claude Jr., *Swords into Plowshares,* 4th ed. rev. (New York: Random House, 1971), Chapter 17.

16. Two perceptive analyses written early in this century of the potentialities for this kind of functional growth of government outside the traditional institutions of government still are instructive today: Paul S. Reinsch, *Public International Unions* (Boston: Ginn, 1911), and J. A. Salter, *Allied Shipping Control* (Oxford: Clarendon, 1921).

17. As is made clear in a recent book that explores these issues: James N. Rosenau and Ernst-Otto Czempiel, eds., *Governance Without Government: Order and Change in World Politics* (Cambridge: Cambridge University Press, 1992).

18. For a discussion of this and other issues at Nuremberg, see Quincy Wright, "The Law of the Nuremberg Trial," *American Journal of International Law* 41 (1947):38–72.

19. See, for example, John Norton Moore, *Law and the Indo-China War* (Princeton, N.J.: Princeton University Press, 1972), and Richard A. Falk, ed., *The Vietnam War and International Law* (Princeton, N.J.: Princeton University Press, 1968).

20. Neighboring states have the greatest potential capability for military conflict simply because of their proximity, as well as the greater likelihood that they may hold competing claims to the same territory and resources. Traditionally, most states widely separated from each other (except for great powers) have interacted so little that the fact that their relations have been peaceful has meant little to the student of peaceful change on the part of socially interacting units.

21. Karl W. Deutsch et al., *Political Community and the North Atlantic Area* (Princeton, N.J.: Princeton University Press, 1957).

22. The founding members of the European Coal and Steel Community (ECSC) were Belgium, the Federal Republic of Germany, France, Italy, Luxembourg, and the Netherlands. For a brief summary of the development, organization, and powers of today's European Union from its beginnings in ECSC, see "The European Community," *The European Community and the Third World,* November 1977, Directorate-General for Information, Commission of the European Communities, Brussels, Belgium. Also see James Barber and Bruce Reed, eds., *European Community: Vision and Reality* (London: Croom Helm, 1973). For an analysis of current challenges to the EU, see Robin Niblett, "The European Disunion: Competing Visions of Integration," *The Washington Quarterly* 20, 1 (Winter 1997):91–108.

23. The Common Market (European Economic Community) was created by the Treaty of Rome on March 25, 1957. Among the most readable of the numerous studies of the integration process in Europe and its implications for the world is George Lichtheim, *The New Europe—Today and Tomorrow* (New York: Frederick A. Praeger, 1963). The European Union's original members were those of the ECSC. In 1973, Denmark, Ireland, and the United Kingdom were added. Greece joined in 1981, Portugal and Spain in 1986, and in 1995, Austria, Finland, and Sweden were added (when the name was changed from European Community to European Union). By 1998, new applications were either pending or expected from Bulgaria, Cyprus, Czech Republic, Estonia, Hungary, Latvia, Lithuania, Malta, Poland, Romania, Slovakia, Slovenia, Switzerland, and Turkey.

24. For a brief discussion of the origins and purposes of the EDC proposal and the reasons for its failure, see Robert E. Osgood, *NATO: The Entangling Alliance* (Chicago: University of Chicago Press, 1962), pp. 35–36, 91–96. Significantly, after another thirty-five years of cooperative practices within the European Community (EC) framework, the once impossible prospect of Franco-German military integration was realized—and went largely unnoticed by the public—in the creation of a joint military brigade.

25. Great Britain was the last of these imperialist powers to be persuaded of the new economic imperatives, and it refused to become an original member of the Common Market's Treaty of Rome in 1957 because of its special economic relationships with members of the Commonwealth. Eventually, those economic ties to its onetime colonies proved less compelling than the prospective gains from joining Europe. There followed a period in which Britain's applications to the EEC were vetoed by France, and then finally, after de Gaulle left office, its application was accepted. The United Kingdom entered the EEC along with Denmark and Ireland in January 1973.

26. See note 23 for the list of anticipated new members, which includes ten states from the former Soviet bloc. Others on this list would also challenge the EU's cultural homogeneity.

27. Robin Niblett, "The European Disunion," pp. 104–105.

28. For a related issue, see the discussion of NATO's altered mission since the end of the cold war in Chapter 5.

29. Jacques Santer, inaugural address to the European Parliament, Strasbourg, January 17, 1995. *Bulletin of the European Union, Supplement,* January 1995.

30. Although far greater wealth had become a fact of life throughout the EU, much of the discontent with EU goals in the late 1990s stemmed from high rates

of unemployment, particularly in France, where it stood at nearly 13 percent in the first half of 1997. There and in Britain, socialist governments came to power in 1997 (a socialist prime minister shared power with a conservative president in France) at least partly in reaction to the austerity policies that had been made a precondition for European monetary union.

Suggested Readings

Burton, John W., *World Society,* Cambridge: Cambridge University Press, 1972.

Carr, E. H., *The Twenty Years' Crises, 1919–1939,* London: Macmillan, 1946.

Cederman, Lars-Erik, *Emergent Actors in World Politics,* Princeton, N.J.: Princeton University Press, 1997.

Deutsch, Karl W., et al., *Political Community and the North Atlantic Area,* Princeton, N.J.: Princeton University Press, 1957.

Hoffmann, Stanley, "The Political Ethics of International Relations," Seventh Morgenthau Memorial Lecture on Ethics and Foreign Policy, New York: Carnegie Council on Ethics and International Affairs, 1988.

Johansen, Robert J., *The National Interest and the Human Interest,* Princeton, N.J.: Princeton University Press, 1980.

Keohane, Robert O., and Stanley Hoffmann, eds., *The New European Community: Decision-Making and Institutional Change,* Boulder, Colo.: Westview, 1991.

Klausen, Jytte, and Louise A. Tilly, eds., *European Integration in Social and Historical Perspective,* Lanham, Md.: Rowman and Littlefield, 1997.

Krasner, Stephen D., ed., *International Regimes,* Ithaca, N.Y.: Cornell University Press, 1983.

Leonardi, Robert, *Convergence, Cohesion, and Integration in the European Union,* New York: St. Martin's Press, 1995.

Lugo, Luis E., *Sovereignty at the Crossroad? Morality and International Politics in the Post–Cold War Era,* Lanham, Md.: Rowman and Littlefield, 1996.

Mitrany, David A., *A Working Peace System,* Chicago: Quadrangle Books, 1966.

Morgenthau, Hans J., *Politics Among Nations,* 4th ed., New York: Alfred A. Knopf, 1967.

Piening, Christopher, *Global Europe: The European Union in World Affairs,* Boulder, Colo.: Lynne Rienner, 1997.

Rosenau, James N., and Ernst-Otto Czempiel, eds., *Governance Without Government: Order and Change in World Politics,* Cambridge: Cambridge University Press, 1992.

Smith, Dale L., and James Lee Ray, eds., *The 1992 Project and the Future of Integration in Europe,* Armonk, N.Y.: M. E. Sharpe, 1992.

Smith, Michael, *Realist Thought from Weber to Kissinger,* Baton Rouge: Louisiana State University Press, 1987.

Soroos, Marvin S., *Beyond Sovereignty: The Challenge of Global Policy,* Columbia: University of South Carolina Press, 1986.

CHAPTER 5

Minimizing the Resort to Violence

> The underpinnings of logic that served historically to justify resort to war as the lesser of several evils have shifted or . . . quite disappeared. Victory has been deprived of its historical meaning.
>
> **—C. Vann Woodward, Address to the American Historical Association, 1959**

A central premise of this chapter is that historian C. Vann Woodward was (and is) correct when he spoke the words quoted above. In this century, victory in war has become extremely costly and increasingly hollow, for reasons that we are about to explore. When he spoke in 1959, Woodward almost certainly was thinking of the enormity of the costs, to winners as well as losers, of the two great world wars of the twentieth century. He probably also considered how little those conflicts had actually resolved. The "settlement" imposed by the victors of World War I set the stage for World War II only twenty years later, and that second global conflict resulted in the chilliest of outcomes—an unwaged war that for decades threatened millions with the prospect of a nuclear holocaust. Woodward may also have had in mind the inconclusive ending of the Korean conflict of the early 1950s or of any number of other "little" wars, both civil and colonial, that had marked the first six decades of the century.

Over three decades have elapsed since Woodward made this comment, and during that time many hundreds of thousands, if not millions, more human beings have died in warfare in many reaches of the globe. Why, if warfare is less "cost-effective" than it may once have been, does it still occur? What are the conditions under which it is most likely to break out? Least likely? What, if any, techniques are we developing either for inhibiting the resort to violence or, failing that, for regulating its conduct so as to bring it under fuller community control? Are we making any progress in moving away from an anarchical use of force, the results of which are essentially destructive, and moving toward using it as an incipient police power for the world at large?

After the Cold War: Anarchy or New World Order?

By the last decade of the twentieth century, the cold war was history. Its ending brought revolutionary change to world politics in many respects. Like all revolutions, perhaps, this one looked impossible not long before it happened; afterward, it assumed an air of inevitability. If one had to pick a benchmark year for this transformation of so much of the world, it would be 1989, which may one day rival the year 1648 in its importance for world politics. At the end of the 1980s two rival superpowers, along with their allies, were transformed from enemies into apparent friends. That change was largely the product of efforts for reform that were made throughout the former Soviet bloc and resulted in moves away from the rigid authoritarianism of centralized control toward greater democracy and economic freedom. Since these moves were at least generally in the direction of goals long espoused in the West, they represented what appeared to be a rapid convergence of high political values across most of the northern hemisphere, which had been enmeshed in conflict for more than forty years.

The ending of the cold war just as suddenly transformed the issue of nuclear weapons, which had long characterized the hostile standoff between the two superpowers. In summer 1991, U.S. and Soviet leaders signed the first Strategic Arms Reduction Treaty (START I), which called for cuts in their nuclear arsenals of a magnitude that both would have regarded as wildly unrealistic only a few years before. Yet at the moment that agreement was reached, it was already out of date, inasmuch as it had been built on the premise of a continuation of bipolarity and mutual deterrence through the threat of suicidal destruction that had characterized the cold war. Within another twelve months, Presidents Bush and Yeltsin had agreed to dramatic additional cuts of a type and scope designed to prevent either of their countries from launching a disabling first strike against the other (START II). When implemented, these cuts could finally end the fear of a nuclear conflagration that had threatened the lives of millions for more than a generation.

These events, combined with the nearly complete absence of violence in ending the authoritarian role of the Soviet empire in the world, no doubt gave rise to a surge of idealist thinking about the possibilities for progress such as the world had not experienced since early in the century. When

President Bush began to speak of how they might lead to "a new world order," his words may have led the naive to suppose that we soon would enter an era when major intergroup conflict itself would disappear.[1] But if such optimism existed, it was soon to be dashed. As in the case of other revolutions, the stunning changes that occurred as the initial upheavals of 1989 ended soon produced reactions that threatened to return us to the destructive ruts of the past. In parts of Eastern Europe and the former Soviet Union, conflicts erupted that were reminiscent of an earlier time. Death and destruction frequently reigned again in the collapse of effective order and the resulting resurgence of intercommunal conflict. Yugoslavia was torn apart in brutal fighting. Azeris and Armenians continued to battle each other for control of the enclave of Nagorno-Karabakh in the Caucasus. Even in Czechoslovakia, where violence was avoided, the idealism released by the Velvet Revolution of 1989 turned to a rather bitter realism as the country split at the end of 1992 into separate Czech and Slovak states. Vaclav Havel, the playwright and philosopher whose self-proclaimed "preposterous idealism" had led the anti-Communist forces in 1989 resigned as president of Czechoslovakia in July 1992. Early in 1993 he was elected president of the new Czech Republic.

Meanwhile, in the Persian Gulf region, there came another war. In summer 1990, Iraq attacked and attempted to annex its little neighbor, Kuwait, in what appeared to be an old-fashioned example of territorial aggression. Here too were many of the familiar elements that have so often led to violence in world affairs. Among these were greed, the temptation to increase one's capability at the expense of others, a sovereign leader's self-serving judgment of his own cause, and the expectation that a violation of fundamental norms would succeed if it were sufficiently ruthless and bold.

The initial revolutionary changes and the decidedly unrevolutionary reactions to them seemed another wry example of how we continue to live in the best and worst of times, even after our times have been so much altered. Events suggest that despite the reduction of the nuclear terror that so long afflicted us, we have regained the unfortunate freedom to kill each other, albeit in less species-threatening and more traditional ways. Are we removing one danger only to return in the next phase of our history to the kind of intercommunal violence and suffering that were so tragically a feature of our outmoded past?

Just as nothing was inevitable about the cold war's ending as it did, so we should not suppose that the next chapter in the world's political behavior must resemble what has gone before. The immediate aftermath of the cold war raised terrible possibilities in three areas of world politics: the potential spread of nuclear weapons, violent social disintegration, and armed aggression. Each of these issues posed fundamental dilemmas for political behavior, since our current condition clearly was fraught with prospects for destructive and retrogressive action on a massive scale. But each also contained the potential for creating unprecedented abilities to minimize humanity's resort to violence in the world of the future.

First, with the erstwhile cold war adversaries backing away from the nuclear brink, how should the world prevent further nuclear spread, blackmail, and possible future use of nuclear weapons on the part of any number of actors? Second, given the violent disintegration of a number of polities, how can the violence be stopped (or forestalled where it has not yet erupted) without at the same time stifling the self-determination sought in so many ethnic communities? Third, in light of renewed intrastate violence and the aggression of the Gulf War, how can we rein in such warfare in the future and, in the process, strengthen the peacekeeping and peacemaking capabilities of authoritative actors? Together, these questions raise two others that relate to the structure and agency of the next phase of world politics: Has the end of bipolarity revived Westphalian assumptions of greater anarchy, more self-help, and shifting coalitions in world politics? To what extent has the world become unipolar, with only one superpower remaining, and what should changes of that sort suggest to policymakers, especially in the United States?

Ending the Balance of Nuclear Terror

The atomic genie was first let out of the bottle in response to the Westphalian urge to win a military victory in World War II, although many of those best informed about its destructive potentialities from the beginning knew that it could not for long serve the traditional security interests of states. Rather, it undermined those interests by setting loose a destructive force against which there was no defense. The irony of the situation, particularly for Americans, is underlined in the plain words of a retired admiral of the U.S. Navy, Noel Gayler: "When we invented the atomic bomb, we invented the one thing that could place the United States at risk."[2] Even more poignant is the reported comment of Albert Einstein, whose great theoretical advances in physics made it possible to unlock the hidden power of the atom, to fellow scientist Linus Pauling not long before Einstein's death. The greatest mistake of his life, he told Pauling, was signing the letter to President Roosevelt that urged him to establish the Manhattan Project, which led to the first atomic bomb.

Until the cold war ended, we generally behaved as if thermonuclear instruments of destruction were simply the most advanced instruments of our security available. In fact, they cannot rationally be regarded as instruments of *protection* in any meaningful sense of the term, even though the structure and modes of thought inherent in the Westphalian system deluded millions into supposing that they did enhance our security, at least as long, and here was the incredible condition, as they were never used.

In Chapter 2 we saw that the rise of the Westphalian system more than three hundred years ago can be explained largely in terms of novel developments that permitted the defense of large territorial units through the military technologies of the day more successfully than had been possible for the preceding millennium in Europe. The rulers of the walled towns and citadels of the Middle Ages had little effective control outside them. The modern era produced nation-states whose sovereigns achieved that status principally through their ability to provide security for large groups of people, who in return gave them loyalty and fought to keep their homeland impermeable from without. Warfare retained a prominent place in that system simply because it remained the possible means of last resort for advancing or protecting socially important values of the community. In spite of the misery and destruction warfare produced, it was regarded as an occasionally necessary undertaking for fundamentally political purposes, its socially disruptive consequences outweighed by its political necessity. In particular, it could justifiably be used to maintain the overall Westphalian arrangement so that it would function in the future more or less as it had in the past. Since (in theory at least) it joined the military power of the state to its important security values, warfare was, in Clausewitz's classic definition, truly the continuation of politics by other means.[3]

Yet as the nuclear arsenals of the superpowers grew throughout the cold war, it became ever more difficult to imagine how they could enhance or even protect the important political values of either society. By about 1960, critics of nuclear politics were noting that the end result of even a limited nuclear exchange between the United States and the Soviet Union would produce so many millions of deaths in both societies that the original reason for releasing those weapons would become irrelevant. Each society would be so seriously dislocated that only the most basic concerns, hardly domination by a foreign power, would be all-important for the survivors. Both societies would lose control over so many of the higher values whose enhancement is the sovereign's chief raison d'être as probably to render meaningless our prenuclear preoccupations with such notions as sovereignty, independence, and freedom. Instead, survivors in both countries would face massive problems: disposing of millions of dead corpses, human and animal; assisting the millions more suffering from radiation burns; surviving in an environment in which food and water supplies were either poisoned or inaccessible, since much of the transportation and communication systems of both countries would have been destroyed.

As we have understood ever since Leibniz defined sovereignty at the beginning of the modern period, a state that cannot provide its people and territory with a reasonable assurance of security from without scarcely deserves to be called sovereign. It is little wonder that as early as 1948, Arnold Toynbee contended that the nation-state and the split atom could not coexist on the planet.[4]

Nonetheless, for more than half a century they have coexisted. How was that possible when our nuclear arsenals grew to the point by the mid-1980s that they held some 1.6 million times the destructive power of the bomb that had been dropped on Hiroshima, and so could easily have ended the lives of nations in a matter of hours? Toynbee's contention was confounded by the fact that these instruments of mass death were never employed after their first two uses, on August 6 and August 9, 1945. The mere *threat* to use them did not in itself destroy the state or states that played with these things. Still, it could be said that as long as the cold war lasted, the threat to engage in a nuclear war also provided some of us with an image of a postnuclear world that looked very different from the Westphalian arrangement of the past.[5]

Then, within a very short period, the elaborate and complex nuclear strategies of the two superpowers crumbled and their strategies became irrelevant even before much had changed with regard to the hardware in their arsenals. A brief review of how this occurred shows how inextricably ideas (in this case, ideas about who is the enemy and what values one is willing to die for) are attached to real capability (in this case, explosives capable of unprecedented destruction) in the formation of believable policy.

When Mikhail Gorbachev came to power in the Soviet Union early in 1985, the nuclear arms race was running at top speed. The foreign policy of Gorbachev's U.S. counterpart, President Reagan, was characterized by a huge military buildup. It was justified by a claim that the United States was vulnerable to the increased deployment of Soviet land-based missiles and by Reagan's oft-stated opposition to arms control negotiations, which had remained dead in the water throughout his first term. Finally, Reagan launched a massive research and development effort to create high-technology weapons systems meant to defend against offensive nuclear missiles, the Strategic Defense Initiative (SDI), better known as Star Wars. Reagan was in many respects more of a cold warrior than perhaps any U.S. president since Harry Truman.

Within short order, however, Gorbachev launched liberalizing policies that had dramatic and immediate impacts on world politics. What he denounced as Stalinism in international affairs was above all the pursuit of a reactionary military-strategic vision. It was his predecessors' efforts to achieve "absolute security" for the Soviets at the expense of others by imposing control and ideological orthodoxy through force. After four decades of Soviet rule, Gorbachev and those he led saw that effort as having brought exorbitant and wasteful costs, a spiraling arms race, and new insecurities. It also brought retrogression in the very material sectors of social life where exactly the reverse expectation was all that had given the ideology any power at all.[6]

After the false start of the Reykjavik summit between U.S. and Soviet leaders in 1986 (which foundered over Reagan's refusal to abandon Star Wars), a small step was taken toward the denuclearization of the super-power relationship in a decision to remove intermediate-range nuclear weapons from Europe. That INF agreement, reached at the end of 1987, eliminated a mere 3 percent of the nuclear arsenals of the superpowers. Yet it was of great *political* significance. It would bring about the actual destruction of a whole class of nuclear delivery systems for the first time in history. It would remove those that had seemed most destabilizing be-cause of their ability to rain down on enemy targets within minutes. It would require intermixing U.S. and Soviet inspectors to oversee disman-tling of these weapons in a way that revealed both a new mutual trust and a recognition of the actual interdependence of these nuclear adver-saries if nuclear reductions were to become a reality.[7]

The Soviet leader also launched impressive unilateral initiatives to defuse the military confrontations of the cold war. These included ending the Soviet intervention in the civil war in Afghanistan, a rapprochement with the government of China, the withdrawal of half a million troops from Eastern Europe, and a self-imposed ban on further nuclear testing. As a result, by the time Reagan left office early in 1989, negotiations were resumed between NATO and Warsaw Pact governments that were aimed at drastic reductions in their conventional forces in Europe (CFE). Negoti-ations between the United States and the Soviet Union were intended to slash the number of long-range missiles in their arsenals through the process of Strategic Arms Reduction Talks (START).

These developments were followed by the rapid dismemberment of what had been the Soviet bloc. Revolutionary change was driven from within the polities that made up that group of countries. When opposi-tion to Communist rule grew in Poland and other states of Eastern Eu-rope, Gorbachev's reformist pronouncements received their acid test. The leaders of the USSR refused to intervene to save Communist elites. That violated what had always been perhaps the most basic principle of cold war behavior on the Soviet side, namely, that Moscow would allow no popular movement or adversarial action to dislodge fellow Communists. With that practice ended, the cold war simply fizzled out.

The final chapter came after Gorbachev tried, with decreasing success over the next eighteen months, to sustain the unity of the Soviet Union it-self. The failed August 1991 coup against him by hard-line Communists unleashed a revolution of self-determination among the Soviet republics themselves. In dizzying succession, the operation of the Communist party was suspended, a new Commonwealth of Independent States was proclaimed, and the Soviet Union itself was abolished. Meanwhile, the formal end to the cold war perhaps had already come with the dissolution of the military structure of the old Soviet bloc, the Warsaw Pact, weeks before the coup.

Controlling Nuclear Weapons in a Post–Cold War World

While the cold war lasted, both superpowers solemnly maintained the traditional sovereigns' fiction that winning meant denying the other's goals. With the cold war behind us, we can see that the fiction actually masked a cooperative strategy of sorts. The superpowers in fact were partners in the nonuse of their nuclear weapons. The rhetoric of war between them was in fact largely that—rhetoric. For more than four decades they built a regime on nonuse of nuclear weapons, one that must be maintained and strengthened today for humanity's security. A troubling implication in the end of this odd cold war partnership is that the mutual refusal of the two antagonists to engage in a nuclear exchange was actually reinforced by the believability of their denial that such was their intent. If their threat of mutually assured destruction had not been credible at some primordial level, they might have relaxed and blundered into it. The threat of nuclear terror had much, if not all, to do with what kept the nuclear peace.

Now that the threat of mutual assured destruction is politically senseless, new and different (although surely less apocalyptic) nuclear dangers are arising. They include questions of who will have access to nuclear weapons as we enter a new century, to what extent their spread to other countries can be prevented, and how nuclear technology can be controlled and regulated in keeping with the security needs of the whole human population. Linking all of these is the central question of how to ensure that nuclear weapons will not be used in a world where far less fear exists that any use might lead to Armageddon.

Nor have old habits been entirely overcome. Nuclear arsenals have long symbolized a government's geopolitical swagger. The START II agreement signed by Presidents Bush and Yeltsin in June 1992 was intended to make unprecedented cuts in the nuclear arsenals of their two countries. It was meant to limit multiple, independently targeted warheads (MIRVs) so that neither country could attempt a disabling first strike against the other, each side being restricted to no more than 3,500 nuclear warheads. Yet, ratification of this agreement was delayed by the Russian government, the United States having ratified it in 1996. Opponents in the Duma charged that it would in effect cede nuclear superiority to the United States. The controversy reflected in part the unwillingness of many in the legislature, including many Communists, to accept the abandonment of what had been the Soviets' geopolitical interests in the world.

Nonetheless, President Yeltsin, meeting with President Clinton in March 1997, promised to submit START II for ratification. In exchange, the United States agreed to postpone until 2007 the deadline for destruction of all the missile silos and bombers called for under its terms. The two presidents also agreed to begin talks on START III, aimed at reducing the number of long-range warheads in the United States and Russia to 80 percent below peak levels that existed in 1991. What these events also reflected was more serious economic pressure on the Russian government than had been anticipated when START II was signed. For Russia, maintaining greater parity with the United States under the terms of START II would have meant building new single-warhead missiles to replace the MIRVed systems banned by START II. That, along with destroying silos and bombers, required funds badly needed for other priorities at home.

Meanwhile, U.S. and Russian leadership had taken the critical step in 1994 of no longer targeting their nuclear weapons at each other, a subtle change in the physical capability of each that nonetheless reflected an immense turnabout in the psychological (some might even say spiritual) dimension of their relationship. Doctrines of mutual assured destruction (MAD) and the like simply evaporated under exposure to the logic of the new era. It was not so much that the START agreements were ending the balance of terror as that they were helping to ratify what already had ended with little more than a whimper as the cold war came to a close.

Still, for years to come, the destructive capacity of the nuclear weapons that are *not* being thrown away will continue to surpass levels that existed when the Strategic Arms Limitation Talks (SALT) began in 1969. That fact—reflecting in part the immense structural lethargy still supporting the nuclear establishment—could serve to encourage nuclear proliferation, even though that is the very outcome post–cold war deterrence is meant to inhibit. One problem is that U.S. nuclear plans (and to lesser degrees, those of the other four self-acknowledged nuclear weapons states)[8] still try to square the circle that would prohibit nuclear use while threatening it under some circumstances. That dilemma is deepened by doubts over the security of nuclear materials today.

With the breakup of the Soviet Union, its nuclear weapons came under the control of four states—Russia, Ukraine, Belarus, and Kazakhstan—all of which eventually became signatories to the START II agreement. But concerns surfaced as to how well these materials were being protected from theft as well as about the effectiveness of governmental controls over the export of nuclear technology for much-needed hard currency. A 1997 report from the United States concluded that the dangers were actually growing as Russia scrapped thousands of nuclear warheads. According to the National Research Council, about fifteen tons of plutonium and forty-five tons of uranium are now being released from military control and turned over to relatively insecure civilian authorities each year. The report noted that "the challenge of controlling small amounts of nuclear material located in hundreds of buildings, including many in a poor state of repair, seems overwhelming."[9] Whatever the fears that flowed from the mutual nuclear deterrence of the erstwhile cold war enemies, their governments' strict control of their arsenals was at least more reassuring than the prospect today of even small quantities of plutonium or highly enriched uranium being spirited about the planet in suitcases.

The dangers inherent in letting go of nuclear weapons were almost entirely unanticipated in the years when nuclear arsenals grew. In today's world they may be minimized (if not eliminated) by the continued construction of antinuclear norms and regimes. Two treaty-making efforts have borne fruit within the past several years that continue that effort, if less than boldly. The Nonproliferation Treaty (NPT) was extended indefinitely in 1995. In 1996, after many years of effort, the Comprehensive Test Ban Treaty (CTBT) was completed and opened for signature.

The central problem of the NPT has always been that it divided the world into two groups: the five states that possessed nuclear weapons in 1967, when the treaty was being negotiated, and all of the other states that did not.[10] It assigned legitimacy to the first group's possessing these weapons while asking that the second group never acquire them. Some members of the nonnuclear club considered it an unequal treaty, particularly since it called for cutbacks in existing nuclear arsenals in a general way only. In fact, far from cutting back on their weapons, the principal nuclear powers added thousands more during the 1970s and 1980s in spite of their adherence to the NPT. India, Israel, and Pakistan all refused to join the NPT and became nuclear weapons states themselves. Moreover, Iraq and North Korea made considerable progress toward nuclear capability of their own in spite of the fact that they were signatories to the treaty. These issues resurfaced at the 1995 conference called to review the NPT. With the original nuclear countries still sometimes behaving as if possession of nuclear weapons added to their capability to coerce others, it was clear why some nonnuclear states resisted an indefinite extension of the treaty.

But 174 countries eventually did approve it (by consensus, to avoid revealing which governments would have voted no if a roll call had been taken). The result is the continuation of a weak set of norms against the proliferation of nuclear weapons beyond the original five. Coincidentally (or not) those five nations are the successors to the Big Five allied powers of World War II, who in 1945 made themselves the only permanent members of the UN Security Council. Thus the old issue, these states' insisting on the legitimacy of their possessing nuclear capability while denying it to others, still clouds the nonproliferation regime.

The United Nations produced a draft for a comprehensive test ban treaty at the beginning of the 1980s. In the cold war context of the time, it was argued that CTBT would inhibit the technologically induced spiral of the arms race. As it happened, the political incentive to ratchet the arms race up, not down, characterized Ronald Reagan's first term as president of the United States. As a result, the CTBT was put on hold while the United States resumed testing and drastically increased its military spending in the period before the cold war wound down as the 1980s drew to a close.

Several years had to elapse after the cold war ended before all the acknowledged nuclear powers could be induced to end their nuclear weapons tests. China and France both faced opprobrium when they engaged in nuclear testing as work on the CTBT was in its eleventh hour. President Clinton, who had ordered a halt to U.S. nuclear tests early in his term, threatened to resume them late in 1993 when China went ahead with its own weapons test. Finally the acknowledged nuclear powers agreed to a treaty in which they and all others who signed it were committed to halt all nuclear tests indefinitely. At the signing ceremony in September 1996, the one significant holdout was India, whose government objected that the treaty did not specify a date for the total elimination of nuclear weapons.[11] Although ratification of the treaty was not certain in the face of India's objections, the United States, Russia, France, and the United Kingdom had already halted production of fissile materials for weapons.

Together, the CTBT and the NPT can help ensure that the nuclear arms race does not resume. If all nuclear tests are convincingly ended for a considerable period, the nuclear arsenals that remain are certain to look increasingly irrelevant to real security needs. As that perception grows around the world, it should become more feasible to nourish in useful ways the antinuclear regime that is now emerging. But there are important caveats here.

One is the assumption that treaty signatories are confident that neither holdouts nor would-be violators of these treaties pose a threat to them through nuclear development that the signatories have tried to freeze in place by creating norms against further testing and new weapons acquisition. A second is the assumed acquiescence in the view of the government of the United States that it—and, presumably, any other nuclear-state signatory—is permitted under the terms of the CTBT to conduct periodic checks on the reliability of its aging stockpile without actually conducting nuclear explosions to do so. The U.S. interpretation is that it must periodically engage in "subcritical experiments" on the plutonium and other components of its nuclear weapons to be assured that they still work.[12] With reciprocal permission tacitly extended to the other declared nuclear powers party to the CTBT and the NPT to maintain the reliability of their own weapons as well, the result remains a case of attempting to square the circle that prohibits nuclear use, on the one hand, while maintaining a credible deterrent on the other on the part of governments that form a nuclear elite.

This dilemma may have to be tolerated for the foreseeable future while we work to end it. Until then, we must hope not to have to test whether would-be nuclear terrorists can be deterred by the threat or the use of nuclear weapons directed at them. To break out of this dilemma over the longer term, however, the world's goal should be to ban completely the unregulated possession of nuclear materials—let alone nuclear use—by all states as well as by substate actors. This entails exploring avenues for the eventual supranational control of nuclear capability. No serious thinking about such a structure has been done since the first years of the atomic age, when the U.S. government proposed to bring its monopoly of atomic technology under international control. The Baruch plan of 1946 was crippled by cold war politics and never saw the light of day.[13] It may now be time to revisit that proposal in order to learn from the mistakes that surrounded its presentation and to give serious attention once more to building a supranational authority that is capable of maintaining effective, worldwide controls over nuclear technology. The International Atomic Energy Agency (IAEA) already possesses the appropriate institutional framework, but its power and authority need to be significantly enhanced if it is to assume truly governmental power in this area.

A shift toward more supranational authority in the nuclear field might also include creating an internationalized framework for antimissile defense. The goal would be to ensure that both the production and the resulting benefits of defensive technologies would be shared, thereby making them instruments of world community defense. The Clinton administration revamped and scaled back the SDI program, ending research programs on weapons in space while continuing to work on ground-based antimissile weapons. As a result, the program became an arena of conflict between the Democratic president and the Republican Congress. Instead of internationalizing research on antimissile defense, as President Yeltsin proposed in 1992,[14] Congress each year lavished billions of dollars more on America's own program than its president asked for.[15]

The National Academy of Sciences, created by the U.S. Congress to advise its government on scientific issues, has made important suggestions for enhancing antinuclear norms and regimes in the years ahead. In its June 1997 report the Academy urged the United States and Russia to reduce their arsenals to as few as three hundred warheads each. It called for the U.S. government to renounce the first use of nuclear weapons and to make plain that they would only ever be used to deter a nuclear attack. The scientists' rationale was that "continued actions by the United States and Russia to reduce their nuclear arsenals—and to reduce the roles assigned to those arsenals—are needed to help bring the other declared and undeclared nuclear weapons states into the arms reduction process and to strengthen the global nonproliferation regime."[16] Actions of this magnitude could diminish the world's perverse fascination with these instruments of mass destruction.

The Revival of Ethnic Violence

The end of the cold war exerted a positive and a negative impact on group violence in a number of places in the world. Clearly, the Westphalian order continues to make international action far more likely where the cause of the conflict is external intervention than where it is rooted within the sovereign state itself. But what is new in the post–cold war world is the end of superpower competition in support of rival antagonists and the continuation of their client-protector relationships.

In the horn of Africa, for example, increased anarchy in Somalia resulted partly from the fact that its government no longer found support and protection from one or the other of the superpowers. Civil conflict produced massive numbers of refugees, as well as famine that threatened more than a million people with starvation. In summer 1992 the United Nations authorized only a humanitarian relief effort. By the autumn of 1993, however, forces participating in that operation had found themselves drawn into the conflict between rival Somali factions. What began as a humanitarian mission soon became an effort at peacekeeping. When it became apparent that no real peace existed to be kept, U.S.-led forces of the United Nations attempted to capture a local warlord, and when that failed, to appease him. Finally, the UN mandate ("an awkward combination of traditional peacekeeping, enforcement, humanitarian relief, and nation building," in the words of a veteran observer[17]) so crippled the operation that it was ended in 1995 without having restored political stability.

Elsewhere, however, the changed international order allowed some armed struggles to be addressed that had festered for years because of cold war competition. Among these were conflicts in El Salvador, in Namibia and Mozambique, and in Cambodia. Even beyond these situations, in which settlements to long-standing conflicts were concluded in the 1990s, peace initiatives in the Middle East also owed new life to the altered structure of the post–cold war world. Talks that began in 1991 over the Palestinian issue produced a dramatic breakthrough on the part of Israel and the Palestine Liberation Organization (PLO) in September 1993. From that date, in spite of periodic setbacks, particularly after a hard-line government came to power in Israel in 1996, some form of Palestinian autonomy became the stated goal of both parties.

The most terrible paradox of the early 1990s juxtaposed intercommunal violence, which saw the disintegration of old state structures, against the peaceful integration of nation-states across much of the rest of the north-ern hemisphere. The violent disintegration and the peaceful integration were in many respects the disparate legacies of the cold war, too. Where the authoritarian rule of the Soviet empire collapsed, long pent-up forces of nationalism were fed by economic decline, which they then served to hasten. Further to the west, the European Union's structure for the inte-gration of nation-states produced such generally successful results that it boded well to survive what had given it impetus at the beginning of the cold war—the determination not to be ground to bits by the far greater economic and political power of the United States and the Soviet Union.

On the whole, the disintegration of the Communist bloc was peaceful. Nonetheless, the process revealed dramatically how much ethnic conflict had been frozen in this part of the world through decades of authoritarian rule. As the Soviet Union fragmented, the continuing size and importance of Russia, where democratic forces were in the ascendant, frequently gave that "new" country a leading role in regional conflict management. Still, the Russian government was beset by so many problems, especially in connection with its effort to transform its country's economic system, that it could by no means act as an effective police power throughout the vast region. More ominous was the fact that after the end of 1991, millions of Russians found themselves living in neighboring republics where major-ity populations frequently were hostile to them. For example, Russians constituted 28 percent of the population in Estonia, 13 percent in Moldova, and 10 percent in Tajikistan, where their presence raised the specter of ethnic conflict or irredentist politics for years to come.

By 1993 the intercommunal warfare that raged across much of the for-mer Yugoslav federation, especially Bosnia-Herzegovina, had produced conditions tragically reminiscent of those associated with the Nazis. Civilians were besieged in their cities or corralled into prison camps where they were tortured, shot, or allowed to starve. Hundreds of thou-sands became refugees as they were driven from their homes by forces seeking the "ethnic cleansing" of what had been multiethnic territories. As in Croatia months earlier, violence spread unchecked thanks to a lethal combination of political forces. Newly independent republican govern-ments faced a rump federal army dominated by Serbia, and these "au-thorities"—republic and federal—were either unwilling or unable to con-trol irregular armies battling in their name.

The principal victims were the very segments of the population most willing to continue to live peacefully in multiethnic communities. Indeed, an independent Bosnia-Herzegovina was necessarily conceived as a state where citizenship would supersede nationality, thanks to the way in which its main ethnic communities of Muslim Slavs (44 percent of the to-tal population when the conflict began), Serbs (31 percent), and Croats (17 percent) were intermixed throughout the territory. Yet the initial result of the warfare was to carve the republic into ethnic enclaves. Bosnian Serbs had the initial advantage, thanks to armed support they received from neighboring Serb-dominated Yugoslavia. Not until 1995 did the Bosnian army, with help from Croatia, begin to redress the military balance.

Meanwhile, the world community failed repeatedly to take effective action to end the conflict. The United States and leaders of the European Community each looked to the other to take the lead. Periodically, they brokered cease-fires that were immediately broken. These countries did push for a UN trade embargo of Yugoslavia (by then reduced to Serbia and Montenegro) in 1992. The embargo emphasized that Serbia had become an international pariah, but it took some three years for the effect of those sanctions, combined with loss of territory previously conquered by Bosnian Serbs, to induce Yugoslavia's leaders to push its Bosnian surrogates toward peace.

Then came the ill-fated effort to turn the UN Protection Force (UNPROFOR), created to police the earlier armistice in Croatia, into a force that could keep the peace in Bosnia. As the operation was redeployed there starting in 1992, it became increasingly evident that the combatants were not yet interested in laying down their arms. On occasion, NATO warplanes, acting at the behest of the United Nations, bombed Bosnian Serb targets in retaliation for action by Serb militias against peacekeepers. In May 1995, Serbian soldiers seized several hundred peacekeeping troops in UN-designated "safe areas" and held them hostage; that effectively thwarted further NATO air strikes at Serb positions while making clear that for the Serbian side, at least, UN peacekeepers were the enemy. Once they viewed UNPROFOR not as neutral but as an impediment to achieving their goals through force of arms, Serbs made victims of the peacekeepers.

More than three years of carnage elapsed before a more effective effort was made to stop the war in Bosnia. NATO allies were persuaded to agree to a more sustained bombing campaign against Serb targets outside UN control. Then, as Bosnian Serb forces began to lose ground they had previously won, President Clinton stepped up the pressure to achieve a negotiated peace. That came to fruition at the end of 1995 in the Dayton accords. Bosnia was preserved, at least in theory, as a single state. But it was divided into a Muslim-Croat federation controlling 51 percent of the territory and a Serb republic in charge of the remainder. A much larger and more heavily armed NATO force (IFOR)—one composed of 60,000 soldiers—replaced UNPROFOR to police the new arrangement. One-third of IFOR troops were furnished by the United States (which had provided none to UNPROFOR), with the rest supplied by other NATO members and (for the first time) Russia. Two years after Dayton an uneasy peace still held, although it was far from clear that it would last much beyond the scheduled departure of U.S. troops in mid-1998.

These post–cold war conflicts (especially the conflict in the former Yugoslavia) taught the world several lessons. First, they demanded remedies that differed from those of cold war–era peacekeeping, whose success had been promoted by fear of a general war between the superpowers if local wars were not quickly frozen in place. With the threat of a possible global conflagration lifted, major powers find it difficult to expend much blood and treasure on conflicts that seem less threatening to what appear to be their immediate interests. And by hiding behind the more comfortable (because less costly) excuse that a small and neutral peacekeeping contingent will fill the bill, these states risk making hostages of the very troops who now cannot protect the peace but rather need to be protected, vitiating their mission.

Second, little agreement had been reached on the appropriate instrumentalities for policing conflict after the cold war. Decades earlier the United Nations had invented the techniques of peacekeeping as a response to the dangers of bipolar competition in regions beyond either superpower's sphere of interest. Its success was predicated on the willingness of combatants to stop fighting so that a small international force could be interposed between them to monitor a cease-fire.[18] In the late 1980s and early 1990s, however, many new "peacekeeping" operations were being created for situations where these conditions did not apply—Somalia and former Yugoslavia were the clearest such departures—and so were almost doomed to fail at their missions. Then came conflicts over the effort to coordinate UN directives with NATO's participation in the Bosnian operation. Above all, these revealed how little essential planning had gone into ensuring the success of such an unprecedented undertaking.

Third, no overarching structure for cooperative security had been put in place or had been seriously planned during the first decade of the post–cold war era.[19] Plans and suggestions abounded for strengthening particular pieces of a collective policing capability in the world. Those that look most viable will be considered later in this chapter. But the evidence to date is that would-be leaders of such an effort—most notably, the United States—prefer to "muddle through" from case to case, reacting to security challenges as they arise rather than working to devise more institutionalized procedures for minimizing violence.

The Gulf War and Collective Security

The Gulf crisis and Gulf War of 1990–1991 stood apart from the other conflicts of the immediate post–cold war period in three respects: their origins, the international community's responses to them, and the implications that those responses held for an evolving police power for the world. What occurred amounted to a form of collective security through the United Nations such as we had not witnessed before.[20] Woodrow Wilson had tried to create just such a kernel of a police power early in the century through the League of Nations; seldom until 1991, however, did we seriously confront implementation of the principle. Nonetheless, the 1990–1991 action against Iraq was unrefined and even distorted as an example of what the Charter called for because no real collective security system had been put in place forty-five years after the terms for it were laid down in Chapter VII of the Charter. Between August 2 and November 29, 1990, the Security Council adopted twelve resolutions on a number of aspects of the Kuwait crisis. These imposed economic sanctions and a trade embargo, finally authorizing the use of force by member states if Iraq did not comply with its resolutions by January 15, 1991. But these agreements ignored the letter, if not the spirit, of Chapter VII, which states that enforcement measures are to come under the control of the Security Council's Military Staff Committee (MSC). There, the chiefs of staff of all five permanent members were to share in developing plans for the collective use of force. Because those expectations were an early victim of the cold war, no such arrangements were in place in 1990. Thus Resolution 678 of November 29, authorizing the use of force, simply granted that right to "member states cooperating with the government of Kuwait" to end the Iraqi aggression.

It was clear that the use of force, when it came, would be directed by the United States, not by the MSC, and, therefore, not by the Security Council, although the Council had authorized all twelve resolutions and so was at least symbolically in charge. But by the time Resolution 678 was adopted, the United States was well on the way to deploying 500,000 troops in Saudi Arabia on the grounds that this buildup was required to prepare for the inherent right of collective self-defense allowed in Article 51 of the Charter. That action not only turned attention from (and underlined U.S. impatience with) the collective economic sanctions imposed earlier but also inexorably transformed the self-defense justification into an argument for forcible collective security. Thus sheer numbers of troops moved the argument from collective *defense* to incipient *offense*, although, as the principal agent of Security Council resolutions, the United States did not draw attention to how its Article 51 argument had become the basis for Article 42–style military action.[21]

Clearly the desuetude of the MSC through the cold war years explained the primitive UN response in the Gulf, as well as the ease with which self-defense and collective military action could be fused. But we saw in the Gulf, as never before, that effective collective security waged against a determined aggressor could, quite simply, produce a major world war. Hitherto, the focus of most criticism had been fear that sanctions would be too weak to curb an offense against world order, not that their very potency might produce worse human suffering than the original crime.

But even the massive cost of the collective military effort in the Persian Gulf proved largely incapable of more than minimal redress. Kuwait was liberated at unprecedented cost to its own resources and the region's environment, with enormous suffering and loss of life on the Iraqi side. But Saddam went free and went back to slaughtering his Kurdish and Shiite citizens. The social and political problems of both Iraq and Kuwait persisted unchanged. The collective military action also created a crucible (as war always does) for inhumane acts by the police, leaving many to wonder how the legitimacy of the collective security principle could be upheld where the outcome was characterized by moral ambiguity.[22]

In the prewar stages of the Gulf conflict, the arguments over the effectiveness of economic sanctions also called attention to the clumsiness of collective security as an instrument of law enforcement. Critics noted that such measures would take an unconscionably long time to produce desired results. Their hurtful impact would be borne primarily by the most victimized members of the Iraqi community, not its elite. Therefore, sanctions should be regarded as an inadequate or a misguided instrument for redressing Saddam's aggression. Enduring memories of the League of Nation's failure in the 1920s to end Mussolini's aggression against Ethiopia through economic sanctions no doubt reminded some why the UN Charter had been written to permit the much fuller marshaling of military force in the name of collective security.

To summarize, there were several important imperfections in the collective security application to the Persian Gulf War. First, it produced frustrations at the delayed and unclear impact of economic sanctions on the target state. Second, it muddled self-defense and enforcement action in a way that paradoxically justified the massive use of force. Third, it demonstrated that even the massive use of force was unable to produce more than the most basic goal of liberating Kuwait. Fourth, thanks to the nonimplementation of Chapter VII of the UN Charter through the cold war era, it revealed how dependent collective action was on the unipolar leadership of the United States, which in turn suggested that the United States would only assert its leadership when it saw a strong and direct self-interest in corrective action.

These imperfections in the collective action against Iraq remained evident for years. Early in 1998, the Clinton administration found it difficult to win support from many members of the 1991 coalition for possible air attacks on Iraqi facilities where, it was feared, illegal chemical and bacteriological arms were being manufactured. If such an attack should be sufficiently surgical to make a convincing case for its proportionality—so that undue suffering would not befall the innocent—it would fail to solve the challenge that Saddam's presence continued to pose to the world community. Such doubts mattered, inasmuch as if the United States were to act convincingly as the world's police agent in Iraq, considerable collective legitimation of its action was essential.

Above all, the Gulf conflict and its aftermath were a reminder that collective security action employing military force will only be considered when the world community is faced with aggression as clear-cut as that directed by Saddam Hussein against Kuwait in 1990. Ironically, the attack on Kuwait was a sort of throwback to the kind of foreign policy behavior that we thought had become outmoded, since territorial aggression has been so clearly outlawed in our time. In contrast, the civil war that raged across the former Yugoslavia did not begin to elicit a collective response from the outside world until August 1992, when forces with ties to Serbia increasingly were viewed as the chief perpetrators of aggressive action.[23] Yet not even that perception made the collective response effectively forcible, perhaps because no single enemy there could be repelled with the quick and surgical military action that had been possible in the Gulf. The aim of real collective action is to punish a wrong done (typically, aggression), which logically requires action that truly punishes the lawbreaker instead of simply assisting the wrongdoer's innocent victims.

Security Through Multilateralism: Prospects and Possibilities

After the cold war ended, confidence prevailed that the time was at hand for improving the efficacy of the security functions of the United Nations. Newfound harmony in the Security Council had brought a huge leap in the number and complexity of peacekeeping operations it authorized and a sense of bold accomplishment over success in the Gulf. When the Council met for the first time in its history at the level of heads of state, early in 1992, it asked the secretary-general for "analysis and recommendations on ways of strengthening and making more efficient . . . the capacity of the United Nations for preventive diplomacy, for peace-making and for peace-keeping."[24] Some months later, the secretary-general responded with a thoughtful monograph that proposed a number of new initiatives.[25] In a campaign speech in 1992, presidential candidate Bill Clinton suggested support for a rapid deployment force under UN authority that could be used for purposes "such as standing guard at the borders of countries threatened by aggression or preventing mass violence against civilian populations."[26]

Second thoughts came soon, however. It became apparent that peacekeeping operations were in danger of overwhelming the limited capabilities of the United Nations at the same time that member states could not agree on the kinds of institutional reform that would make them more efficient and would assure their financial support. The secretary-general's analysis was largely ignored by the very governments that had asked him for it. Not long into his first term, President Clinton largely abandoned the idea of "assertive multilateralism" as his administration's preferred approach to international conflict management. At a moment when the United States owed the United Nations some $1.7 billion, effectively crippling the organization's ability to fulfill much of its mandate, it also vetoed the reelection of the secretary-general who had been most closely identified with the effort to articulate new peacemaking capabilities for the UN.

After President Clinton won reelection in 1996, he made the expansion of NATO into Eastern Europe a priority. In July 1997, the Czech Republic, Hungary, and Poland were approved for membership. It was acknowledged at the time that other states in the region—such as Romania, Slovenia, Ukraine, and the Baltic states—were likely candidates for future membership. Russia's objections to the chief Western cold war alliance's extending toward its borders were only partially overcome when President Yeltsin signed an agreement giving Russia a consultative role—but no veto—in the enlarged NATO.

Proponents of the extension viewed it as a way to transform NATO into an appropriate instrument for the post–cold war security of all of Europe. The agreement with Russia eliminated "the last remnants of the cold war," in the words of French president Jacques Chirac. President Clinton saw it as joining the NATO countries with Russia in the quest "for a long-sought but never before realized goal—a peaceful, democratic, undivided Europe."[27] According to this vision, a reconfigured NATO would tie its new members firmly to the political culture of the West while building on its experience policing the Dayton accords in Bosnia to provide a security system that could be called on wherever democratic processes were threatened on the continent.

Critics generally argue that NATO's cold war identity (indeed, the mere fact that it remains essentially a military alliance) provokes Russia and renders NATO ill suited to advancing democracy in Eastern Europe. They worry that it could give Russian nationalists an appealing argument against further arms control agreements with the West. In the words of a number of lawmakers from the former Soviet republics of Russia, Belarus, and Ukraine, the expansion represents a decision "to consider force or threat of force as the main factor in international relations."[28] Some argue that the Organization for Security and Cooperation in Europe (OSCE), because it includes all the members of the former Soviet bloc as well as the NATO countries, would constitute a more logical framework on which to build an effective post–cold war security structure for much of the northern hemisphere. Many insist that membership in the European Union would be the better way to ensure the democratization of states formerly within the Soviet sphere.[29]

These disagreements and confusions, which pertain to both the organization meant to police the world and to a large and important region, reflect the difficulty of inventing security arrangements appropriate to the needs of the new era. It is by no means clear in the waning years of the century that there is significant agreement among government officials on how to respond to the security challenges they can anticipate. And as more governments become involved in such decisions, the chances for unity become even slimmer. That partly explains the sense of retrenchment that characterizes the reformation of UN security functions today. That sense is also due to the unwillingness of the era's dominant military power, the United States, to forgo its ability to decide unilaterally and case by case when and where it will exercise that power.[30] From this standpoint, the United States has more control over (and, many would argue, interest in) its military options in Europe than it does where it must share decisionmaking more widely in the United Nations.

Considering these issues just as NATO's expansion has been authorized but not yet implemented, one can only hope that the most positive vision of this move, which sees it as a way of transforming our very basis for building security in much of the North, will be borne out in years to come. Because any number of factors could work against that end, it is critically important that the vision, not loyalty to a particular instrumentality (i.e., NATO), guide our action. That means in part that Russia's role in such a security system should evolve and grow along with an intraregional capability to foster peace and democratic processes.

To date, the progress that has been made toward improving the ability of the United Nations to maintain or restore the peace has been feeble. Nevertheless, the United Nations will, in Brian Urquhart's words, "be called on again and again, because there is no other global institution, because there is a severe limit to what even the strongest powers wish to take on themselves, and because inaction and apathy toward human misery or about the future of the human race, are unacceptable."[31] For those who wish to make true security for people everywhere the only purpose of military might, it is only good sense to consider how the UN's rudimentary capability can be strengthened.

Chapter VII of the UN Charter provides a sensible framework for maintaining peace with justice in the world. One specific goal of a more effective United Nations should be to institutionalize a structure for collective military action, as opposed to relying on ad hoc—and partisan—willingness of a single great power to undertake the use of force. Even so, as the Gulf War showed, collective enforcement in the terms of Chapter VII will remain a last resort, costly in all respects and unrefined in its impact.

It is therefore critical that it be built on the peacekeeping system that has evolved through the practice of the United Nations, although that system was not clearly articulated in Charter provisions. Peacekeeping must address the conditions and assumptions that accompany much of the intergroup violence that the world witnesses, most importantly, the frequent need to interpose a police force between warring parties rather than name an outlaw state and mount a punishing offensive action against it. The inability (or unwillingness) of policing states to determine the rights and wrongs that underlie a clash of arms will surely continue to be the rule rather than the exception in the contemporary world.

The actions of a revived Military Staff Committee should complement and assist, not replace, the peacekeeping system. The MSC should help to develop and refine peacekeeping, for example, by encouraging the training and earmarking of forces for peacekeeping service or by assisting in developing effective, UN-based diplomacy to accompany peacekeeping initiatives. Nothing should prevent a revived MSC from inviting additional governments to participate in its planning functions. That would demonstrate seriousness about restoring the MSC while, in the spirit of newfound cooperation in the Security Council, getting around some of the Charter's constraints regarding permanent membership and the like without entering into the formidable process of Charter amendment.[32] A revised and expanded MSC could attend seriously to all the implications of its Charter responsibilities, including provisions calling for the Security Council to utilize regional arrangements to carry out its mandates. Those provisions were generally misconstrued (if not entirely ignored) in cold war conflicts that periodically confronted the OAS, NATO, or the Warsaw Pact. It is little wonder that their unclear authority added to the confusion in 1992 as to which regional organizations had what kinds of responsibilities for helping bring peace to the former Yugoslavia. Nonetheless, the Charter contains sensible guidelines for creating lines of authority that seem entirely appropriate to the more fully developed security system possible in the near future; these should include clear lines of authority with regional arrangements.

The idea of a small standing force under UN auspices, perhaps composed of volunteers, is generating considerable support today on the part of thoughtful individuals, including some governmental officials.[33] Such proposals recognize the need for the Security Council to insert a police presence before an erupting conflict grows unmanageably large. Without such a force (and in the absence of a built-in military structure, contingency funds) or an ability to plan security operations in advance, the United Nations still must create every peacekeeping operation from the ground up. The result is that the deployment of forces is agonizingly delayed while the conflict worsens. Then the command and control of those

forces are confused and complex, and their logistic support is typically weak.

It has been suggested that the costs of a strengthened UN system would make such reform prohibitive. Put in proper perspective, however, that issue is less than formidable. "From the comments of the press and national legislators, one might conclude that the UN and its operations are an unbearable financial burden. In fact, in 1992 (nearly the high point to date for peacekeeping) the UN and all its peace-keeping operations throughout the world cost $2.4 billion—less than the cost of two days of Desert Storm or two Stealth bombers. The average ratio of UN peace-keeping assessments to national defense expenditures is of the order of one dollar to one thousand dollars."[34]

We have considered only a few of the many proposals that reveal a lively interest in strengthening multilateral security measures today. In the current context, they are all meant to encourage a peacemaking system in which the United States is not left as the sole agent of action. To act as such is not cost-effective for the United States in narrowly realist terms. The European governments' reluctance to intervene in the Yugoslav conflict revealed that this freedom to choose when and on what terms to make a commitment to police action can carry a heavy price. It may be opprobrium for inaction and the greater violence and anarchy that may result, or it may be an expensive commitment in the lives and treasure of a single nation from which many others benefit without sharing in the cost. A more coherent ordering structure for the world would try to ensure effective and proportionate responses among appropriate actors at appropriate levels.

Early in this century Woodrow Wilson argued against returning to the pattern of self-serving alliances that was characteristic of the international state of nature in his day. Today's world differs from Wilson's as a result of essentially three developments. First is the post–World War II invention of and experience with UN-style peacekeeping, which can be described as action where self-serving interest is circumscribed by the constraints of global community authority. As a response to the power balancing of much of traditional Westphalian politics, it is more objective than the unilateral actions that states took before the era of peacekeeping and is therefore more supportive of an ordering consensus. Second is the still tentative prospect that we can actually make Chapter VII of the UN Charter mean what it says. That would both institutionalize collective security planning and bring regional arrangements under the authority of the Charter in a way that would rationalize, develop, and, we hope, improve the centrally directed security system for the world. Third, and of potentially the greatest importance by far, is the emergence of a world in which all of the most economically advanced societies recognize that their real security lies in protecting the mutually shared, law-governed

values that permit human beings to prosper in a common peace, not in a geopolitical game of winning land and treasure at the expense of others.

Finally, to advance reform in building a more reliable system of peaceful conflict resolution will also require a heretofore unprecedented involvement of nongovernmental interests and committed citizens. It will require strong commitments on the part of many in both the private and the public realms to enhance the abilities of peacemaking processes to govern the life of the world community. As always where Westphalian structures are involved, governmental officials have less freedom than has an informed public to press for the effective development of authoritative peacemaking capabilities beyond their states. Without real effort from the public, governments may dither and fail to improve the machinery the world now needs for minimizing violence. They may wait until they are forced to go to war to resolve what might have been resolved with far less blood and treasure at an earlier stage of the conflict.

Toward Civilian-Based Defense

Much of the previous discussion has been oriented toward the prospects for, as well as the limitations on, the contemporary international system's capacity to provide a police power for the world of the future. Now we shall consider a security potential that is essentially inherent in the nation-state, a capability that can be developed as a complement to a more centrally guided police power at the world level.

True realism in international politics recognizes the principle that genuine security in the Westphalian system is rather modestly tied to the needs of the individual state. A noninterventionist orientation to the world respects the tolerance for diversity that is a hallmark of the international system and simultaneously encourages the adoption of nonthreatening security techniques for maintaining state interests. Nonthreatening security techniques must demonstrate by their very application that they cannot threaten the legitimate security interests of others but will defend against illegitimate incursions of outside power.

Switzerland's posture has served as one model of this kind for many years. Switzerland has never sought security through the costly and probably vain attempt to match its great power neighbors militarily. Rather, Swiss policy has been to show any would-be aggressor that the Swiss people will fight to defend their society, making the costs of conquest very high indeed. All Swiss males undergo training in the specific military techniques that support such a policy. They learn to use their rugged terrain as a natural fortress and to thwart invasions by demolishing bridges and other roadways. They maintain a state of military readiness that is adequate to make any would-be attacker think more than twice.

The Swiss model cannot be duplicated exactly, since no other country shares Switzerland's unique terrain. But the Swiss example demonstrates that the costs of providing for the safety and well-being of a country's citizens at home are low. And if a country's well-being is measured by its citizens' standard of living, the Swiss approach has served its citizens very well indeed. The crucial point is that the state's capability must be truly defensive and must be perceived as such by potential adversaries. As soon as it can be interpreted as provocative, whether or not its creators intend it to be, it encourages the adversary to take exactly the kind of action that is not wanted.

A truly defensive capability is a civilian-based defense (CBD). Its purpose is to prepare an entire society, not just its military arm, in the myriad techniques of resistance against an invader or would-be usurper of power. It is meant to create an ability "to make effective domination and control impossible by both massive and selective nonviolent noncooperation and defiance by the population and its institutions."[35] CBD techniques are essentially nonmilitary but vary for different groups within the society. For example, workers and managers might resist exploitation of the economy by an occupier through selective strikes, delays, and so on, whereas teachers could refuse to teach whatever "new line" was demanded by the invaders. Other groups would develop particular techniques of resistance and defiance suited to their social roles.

Many of the likely techniques of CBD have been tested successfully in political conflicts from ancient times to the present. Gandhi's successful use of satyagraha to free India from British colonial rule is a dramatic recent example. Aspects of various European resistance movements to Nazi occupation are also pertinent. Lacking in virtually all these historical examples, however, has been conscious, society-wide consideration of and training for civilian-based defense *prior to* the actual domination of that society by an unwelcome power. Resistance had to be improvised after the fact, when it was most difficult to make an already demoralized and frightened population—understand its own potential power over the conqueror through concrete forms of resistance. Advocates of CBD suggest that advance planning offers virtually limitless resistance techniques that could deter attempts at conquest.

CBD can reduce the incidence of military interventionism in several ways. First, it seeks to realign a state's policy with its basic purpose—providing security to its population—in a tangible, more effective, and more normatively acceptable way than is possible through interventionism. Second, it enormously and visibly raises the cost of conquest and occupation by a foreign sovereign, thereby providing a deterrent force that is at least as real (and very much less dangerous) as nuclear capability. Third, it strongly supports democratic values and by its example can undermine the legitimacy of authoritarian control, since participation in civilian-based defense must be voluntary to be reliable in time of crisis and the determination to defend the society must be widely shared. Fourth, thanks to its reliance on nonviolent means, it can reduce violence and destruction and could conceivably have a snowballing effect in delegitimizing traditional military applications of power.

CBD is not a panacea for all the ills that have brought violence to the world in this century. Yet had it been well developed in, say, Poland in 1939 or Kuwait in 1990, the history of the twentieth century might have been quite different. The various communities of the former Yugoslavia might have experienced a more just outcome if there had been a prior opportunity for broad education in civilian-based defense, since it might at least have provided a counterweight to domination by those with the greatest numbers of guns.

Civilian-based defense is no doubt too radical a departure from what states—and particularly great powers—have traditionally thought about their security needs to suppose that many governments will take the initiative in putting its premises into strategic doctrine. Immediate candidates are probably restricted to several of the small, advanced democracies of Europe that have long eschewed militarized foreign policies and consequently know how great have been the resulting benefits. We should not expect any but perhaps the very smallest countries to dismantle their military capabilities while adopting civilian-based programs. Such programs would have to be seen as adjuncts to the military, perhaps for a very long time. Once civilian-based programs were actually in place in several countries, however, confidence in their ability to deter and defend would naturally grow, thereby increasing support for them and, perhaps, decreasing support for the military component.

Toward the Legitimate Use of Force

The war system survives today not only because it is encouraged by the Westphalian structure of decentralized states but also because it still is seen as the ultimate alternative to impotence in the face of unacceptable threats to a society.[36] If the citizens of a state come to view it as illegitimate, the world community is ill equipped to deal with the resulting warfare, which takes the form of civil strife. Different sources of large-scale intergroup violence require different responses.

What has often seemed the hardest for the international community is to cure the last of these ills, civil war that results from internal disagreement over the legitimacy of a particular state. It has been hard to cure because the effort to do so runs most directly counter to the Westphalian premise that a state's internal and external politics are (and should be) separate. Although the principles of nonintervention and self-help remain sensible up to a point, the world community has concluded in this century that a collective police power is increasingly needed if justice and order are now to be advanced. The development of that police power postponed any serious attention to what role or roles it might have in civil conflict. Only in the 1990s has serious attention been devoted to making humanitarian intervention advance world order by making it helpful to people threatened by the collapse or misuse of sovereign authority. The unfortunate growth in civil conflict since the cold war is of course responsible for these developments in our peacemaking norms and practices. Although we are far from having a clear set of operable doctrines for marshaling community force to save lives within states torn by civil strife, we may at last be seriously addressing one of the problems inherent in Westphalianism.[37]

Meanwhile, what stable communities can develop individually is an understanding of and a preparation for civilian-based defense. CBD would enable those most desirous of living in peace to defend their way of life against those who have the guns. Clearly, if every state's population were contented with each other and with the world around them, then war itself would vanish. But we rightly regard such a prospect as utopian. Even where internal social conflicts can be resolved in peace, too many societies are ruled by oppressive elites who maintain themselves, sometimes precariously, through the threat and use of force against their own people. Such governments need to command their own military forces to maintain themselves in power. Some will pursue interventionist policies against their neighbors to help maintain their control at home. None of them is in a position to support civilian-based defense programs, which, of course, would be used to undermine their own unpopular control. For these reasons too it is necessary to complement what are essentially the self-help strategies of noninterventionism and civilian-based defense with a greater global capability to use force as a sanction against unacceptable behavior by such actors.

Recognition of the need to restrain unacceptable behavior has motivated all the efforts to create global collective security, peacekeeping, or other peacemaking approaches in the modern period. Even though the twentieth century has produced novel efforts of this kind, they have so far proved to be less than adequate solutions to the complex causes of intergroup violence. The ending of the cold war almost immediately produced an unprecedented example of international police action in the Persian Gulf, which clearly enforced the world's ban against aggression. But the very success of that example revealed the rudimentary nature of the global collective security system that has been developed to date. It may also have provided the opportunity to build on that system, thanks to the interest focused on the United Nations and the relevant provisions of its Charter. For the first time since 1945, plans to flesh out those provisions of Chapter VII assumed an air of realism.

The internal upheavals produced by the ending of the cold war demonstrated the limited and inadequate nature of the world's ability to interpose a police power in a civil conflict. But at the same time, these events revealed that any number of intergovernmental arrangements have been created that have the potential, though not yet the clear constitutional mission, for acting as effective agents of the kinds of peacemaking that could be applicable here. The coming years should see widespread and systematic efforts to provide those various constitutional missions in whatever organizational structures are appropriate. It was instructive, for example, that NATO did not die once its cold war mission was complete. Rather, it began to develop a new if rather different life, including expanded peacekeeping functions for the Europe of the twenty-first century.

It is commonly assumed that the post–cold war world faces more conflicts than the bipolar past did. That is nonsense. If it seems so, it is because myriad small wars now gain our attention, whereas in the past the superpowers were "obsessively preoccupied by the constant demands of managing containment. The only small wars that did not escape their notice were those fought between pro-Western and pro-Soviet antagonists." What is different today "about the tragedy of small, localized wars is not that they exist but that we now see them, are moved by them, and want to do something about them."[38] The something we want to do and the techniques we ought to use to do it are much in dispute today. For the first time in history, we sense that it may be realistic to bring collective power to bear in an attempt to enhance the security and welfare of others.

Creating institutions that can function effectively as an agent of international police power probably is beyond our reach, at least in our lifetime. Every successful effort in that direction inevitably raises divergent questions such as, Power for whom? In support of what social values? In opposition to what legitimate wants and needs of which groups? We need only imagine a world in which the UN Security Council as presently constituted could function exactly as the Charter prescribes, with perfect harmony among the permanent members and their complete agreement on action needed to maintain the peace. Such a world would unquestionably be a more peaceful place, although many groups within it would not find it more just.

It is therefore important to understand and encourage informal patterns of behavior that support the acceptable uses of force in the world. Clearly, formal and informal approaches, as well as institutional and behavioral approaches, can and should be made to complement each other. The first will necessarily emphasize ideal solutions, and the second, real ones, and each must be made to enhance the other. Balancing power has been the most durable of the latter techniques in the decentralized international system, and to the extent that the system remains decentralized, it will continue to play an important role. Yet historically, balancing power has proved to be far from adequate for legitimizing the use of force. It leaves all responsibility for measuring capabilities and determining motives in the hands of those who must always base their calculations on very imperfect information and who are, to a very great extent, judges in their own causes.

Two basic and recurring kinds of risks result. First, the complacent or satisfied actor may project similar motivations onto the policies of other governments that in fact have revisionist intentions. For example, the European democracies in the early 1930s concluded that Hitler was a reasonable statesman whose reasonable demands should be met. Before Saddam Hussein attacked Kuwait in 1990, the governments that finally opposed his aggression were helping make it possible by giving him military support in his war against Iran. Second, the anxious actor may be convinced that its opponents have limitlessly revisionist designs on the world. This was the characteristic risk of the cold war. Every disturbance of the status quo was seen as the product of the enemy's machinations, calling for a provocative response. Our survey of the modern period suggests that when actors incorrectly view their fellow sovereigns in either of these ways, the overall configuration of world power is almost sure to be disrupted rather than stabilized, even though the disruption takes place in the name of maintaining or reestablishing a power balance.

But if we apply this approach to all political life, not just that between states, we note something else that is characteristic. Balancing power is an inherent function of life in pluralistic societies, and it is manifested in a number of ways, for example, in tolerating values and behavior different from one's own. It is nourished by expectations of the peaceful resolution of one's conflicts with others. It assumes a willingness to live with dominant policies that are not necessarily your own because the pluralistic bargain is that your own goals can compete with them in the marketplace of ideas, perhaps to replace them as the balance shifts. Seen in this light, patterns of behavior that lead to balances of power are essential to what is loosely associated with democratic pluralism. Beyond the nation-state, the encouragement of comparable arrangements is helpful to world order when a conscious policy of balancing power can help protect diverse values and interests that are in conflict.

Such a conscious policy, in fact, is apparent in the evolution of peacekeeping within the United Nations. The purpose of peacekeeping is to renew or to maintain a balancing of rights and power in situations in which no judgment is made as to the rightfulness of disputed claims. It is an alternative to collective security in the sense that the conflicts to which it responds do not include authoritatively identified lawbreakers and victims. Peacekeeping amounts to a somewhat idealized design of an observed behavioral pattern. Where it is successful, it helps to strengthen the growth of a pluralistic and more peaceful world order.

The vast and complex effort to reduce the threat of violence in international affairs has been reduced to its bare outlines here. First, this discussion considered dizzying alterations that have occurred recently in regard to the place of instruments of mass destruction in the military plans of sovereign states. A fundamental change in the world's political alignments produced a fundamental change in our perception of these species-threatening explosives. The task now is to prevent them from reemerging as the vaunted capabilities of separate sovereigns. That will require a determination on the part of all who still possess the weapons to work consistently for their elimination, which ultimately requires a willingness to detach their use as a deterrent from the unilateral policy of individual nuclear states.

Second, the discussion examined problems and prospects surrounding intergroup violence in the sudden shifts and realignments that have accompanied the end of the cold war. Among the most serious problems has been the unleashing of a violent ethnic tribalism in some quarters, for which the world had developed very little peacemaking capability. Among the most reassuring prospects has been the comparatively peaceful rearrangement of large sections of the world's political map, by way of the dissolution of outmoded state structures and the integration of other national communities.

The reaction to all these complex changes reveals an unprecedented attention to how the world community can improve its ability to minimize large-scale violence. Both collective security and peacekeeping have gained new prominence as a result. But the world has been so unwilling to provide these activities with well-defined constitutional structures or effective funding that much of the current work has been ad hoc and piecemeal, depending on whatever political bargain can be struck by leading governments.

Since, in the words of the famous aphorism, absolute power tends to corrupt absolutely, constitutional restraints on the exercise of force are essential to its legitimate use at any level of society. That effort has produced generally satisfactory results in democratic societies. But comparable progress has not yet been reached at the world level. Formal, or constitutional, reforms still show some promise of being carried out today, although hopes for reforms comparable to those in the immediate aftermath of World War II are fading. The world is still so little integrated on the issue of the legitimate social ends force can serve that a dilemma results: If such plans are modest enough to be acceptable to governments, they are probably too modest to do the job; if they are comprehensive enough to embody an effective global police power, they are probably not acceptable to states.

To resolve this dilemma, we must proceed simultaneously on a number of fronts. One front draws attention to the dangers to democratic values posed by overrelying on force in foreign affairs. Another front encourages the development of unambiguously defensive strategies in foreign policy, such as civilian-based defense. Another supports the widest possible international sharing of any decision to use force in an interventionary way, recognizing that what is possible in one context may not be so everywhere. Another seeks the kinds of concrete actions from antagonists that can work to minimize their mutual hostility and build more harmonious relationships.

There are still other fronts, of course, all of which extend from the conscious effort to promote development of community at a global level. Some of these will be discussed in the next several chapters.

Notes

1. That assumption probably was not widespread outside the United States, even in 1989, however. It was, after all, the leader of the one remaining superpower who first used the phrase, no doubt suggesting to some Americans that their country's presumed new ability to lead the world could be equated with an end to conflict. For a widely cited—and much criticized—version of this view, see Francis Fukuyama, "The End of History?" *National Interest,* Summer 1989, pp. 3-18.

2. "Opposition to Nuclear Armament," *Annals* (American Academy of Political and Social Science) 469 (September 1983):14.

3. Karl von Clausewitz, *On War,* trans. J. J. Graham, rev. ed. (London: Routledge and Kegan Paul, 1966).

4. As cited by Paul Kennedy, "Why We Can't Give Up the Bomb," *The Atlantic* 262, 2 (August 1988):77.

5. A sampling of the fiction that portrays the radically altered human condition after a nuclear war includes Margot Bennett, *The Long Way Back* (London: Bodley Head, 1954); Alfred Coppel, *Dark December* (Greenwich, Conn.: Fawcett, 1960); Russell Hoban, *Riddley Walker* (London: Cape, 1980); Daniel F. Galouye, *Dark Universe* (New York: Bantam, 1961); Hans H. Kirst, *The Seventh Day* (Garden City, N.Y.: Doubleday, 1959); Ibuse Masuji, *Black Rain* (Tokyo: Kodansha International, 1969); Walter M. Miller Jr., *A Canticle for Leibowitz* (New York: Lippincott, 1959); Nevil Shute, *On the Beach* (London: Heinemann, 1957); and Herman Wouk, *The Lomokens Papers* (New York: Pocket Books, 1968).

6. These and other aspects of Gorbachev's thinking on foreign policy were set out in his book *Perestroika* (New York: Harper and Row, 1987).

7. The INF Treaty's official title is Treaty on the Elimination of Intermediate-range and Shorter-range Missiles. It required the United States to remove a total

of 429 Pershing II and Ground Launched Cruise Missiles carrying 429 warheads. Soviet missiles removed totaled 857 SS-20s, SS-4s, SS-12s, and SS-23s carrying a total of 1,667 warheads. The treaty also called for the destruction of 1,417 nonoperational missiles previously used for training and testing.

8. The five states were those with a nuclear capability and defined as such as of January 1, 1967, when the Treaty on the Non-Proliferation of Nuclear Weapons was being negotiated. They are China, France, Russia (Soviet Union in 1967), the United Kingdom, and the United States. Not until 1991 did both France and China agree to ratify the Nonproliferation Treaty.

9. As quoted by Robert S. Boyd, *Philadelphia Inquirer,* April 18, 1997, A28.

10. See note 8.

11. The Comprehensive Test Ban Treaty was signed by officials of the five declared nuclear weapons states at the opening of the Fifty-first General Assembly of the United Nations, September 24, 1996.

12. The first such experiments, conducted in the summer of 1997, were on plutonium. According to an Associated Press account, scientists placed pieces of plutonium about the size and shape of a silver dollar inside steel canisters and then smashed them with a blast of conventional explosives. The result, which did not produce chain reactions, showed whether any breaking down of the plutonium had occurred. Robert Macy, *Philadelphia Inquirer,* June 15, 1997, A7.

13. For a work appearing at the end of the cold war that analyzed the Baruch plan, including the political factors that made it unacceptable to the Soviets, see Elliott L. Meyrowitz, *Prohibition of Nuclear Weapons: The Relevance of International Law* (New York: Transnational, 1990).

14. Early in 1992, Russian president Boris Yeltsin offered his suggestion for replacing SDI with a joint U.S.-Russian program. He proposed that the two countries create a global antimissile shield to safeguard against accidental and unauthorized launching and to assist in nonproliferation. He acknowledged that one benefit of such a plan would be to provide work for Russia's unemployed nuclear scientists, stopping them from "drifting abroad and spreading dangerous technologies." *New York Times,* February 1, 1992, 5A.

15. The U.S. defense budget proposed by President Clinton for 1997, for example, included $2.5 billion for antimissile research and development. The bill that Congress passed in September 1996 was for $9.4 billion more than Clinton asked for, including $3.7 billion in addition for antimissile defense. The total authorization that year came to $244 billion.

16. "U.S., Russia Urged to Cut Nuclear Arms," *Philadelphia Inquirer,* June 19, 1997, A8.

17. Brian Urquhart, "Who Can Police the World?" *New York Review of Books,* May 12, 1994, p. 32.

18. Urquhart provides a summary of the origins of peacekeeping. Ibid., p. 30.

19. "Cooperative security" is the goal of the Institute for Defense and Disarmament Studies. See Randall Forsberg and Alexei Arbatov, "Cooperative Security: The Military Problem," *Boston Review* 19, 2 (April/May 1994).

20. The Korean action that began in 1950 was in some respects a collective security action through the United Nations. But in the cold war context, its aftermath was not the implementation of the UN Charter's Chapter VII, but a tacit agree-

ment that it could not be implemented as long as bipolar rivalry dominated the international system. The end of the cold war forty years later marks the first time that the Charter's presuppositions of great power harmony were realistic in a way they demonstrably were not in summer 1950. See also the discussion of collective security in Chapter 3.

21. Article 42 states that "should the Security Council consider that measures provided for in Article 41 nonmilitary sanctions would be inadequate or have proved to be inadequate, it may take such action by air, sea, or land forces as may be necessary to maintain or restore international peace and security. Such action may include demonstrations, blockade, and other operations by air, sea, or land forces of Members of the United Nations."

22. Months after Operation Desert Storm was concluded, it was reported that U.S. forces had buried alive "scores" of Iraqi soldiers entrenched along the Saudi-Iraqi border during the first hours of the ground offensive. These burials took place when tank battalions equipped with plows and earth-moving equipment attacked a ten-mile-long section of Iraqi fortifications, pushing tons of sand and earth into the trenches (*New York Times*, September 12, 1991, A1).

23. A Security Council resolution of August 13, 1992, approved the use of military force as a last resort to ensure delivery of food, medicine, and other humanitarian aid to the residents of Bosnia-Herzegovina. However, Council members did not proceed with plans for military intervention, not even for the purpose of ensuring aid deliveries. As a result, the resolution was no more than a tentative step toward defining collective action. Bosnian officials criticized it as treating symptoms rather than causes, which, they insisted, stemmed from Serbian aggression.

24. UN document S/23500, 115, January 31, 1992.

25. Boutros Boutros-Ghali, *An Agenda for Peace*, 2d ed. (New York: United Nations, 1995).

26. As quoted by Alison Mitchell, "Clinton's Pre-emptive Strike," *New York Times*, September 24, 1996, A8.

27. *Philadelphia Inquirer*, May 28, 1997, A15.

28. Ibid., July 9, 1997, A10.

29. See the discussion of potential new members from this region in Chapter 4, "Pluralistic Integration in Europe."

30. In 1997, the United States was still spending nearly 90 percent of its average cold war funding on its military sector while Russia's military sector had dropped by two-thirds from that of the Soviet Union a decade earlier. The United States was spending more on its military than were the next fifteen nations combined (Matthew Miller, *Philadelphia Inquirer*, May 29, 1997, A18).

31. Urquhart, "Who Can Police the Gulf," p. 33.

32. Brian Urquhart, "Learning from the Gulf," *New York Review*, March 7, 1991, p. 37. Additional participation is entirely consistent with the terms of Article 47(2): "Any Member of the United Nations not permanently represented on the Military Staff Committee shall be invited by the Committee to be associated with it when the efficient discharge of the Committee's responsibilities requires the participation of the Member in its work."

33. Sir Brian Urquhart elaborated on then secretary-general Boutros-Ghali's suggestion for such a force in an article in *The New York Review of Books*, June 10,

1993, pp. 3–4. That stimulated generally supportive responses from a number of writers. See ibid., June 24, 1993, pp. 58–60; and July 15, 1993, pp. 52–56.

34. Urquhart, "Who Can Police the World?" p. 33.

35. Gene Sharp, *Making the Abolition of War a Realistic Goal* (New York: Institute for World Order, 1980), p. 9. This prize-winning essay explores many of the possibilities for civilian-based defense in realistic terms.

36. The description of war as the alternative to impotence is that of Sharp, *Making the Abolition of War a Realistic Goal*, p. 4.

37. See, for example, Stanley Hoffmann, "Out of the Cold: Humanitarian Intervention in the 1990s," *Harvard International Review* 16 (1993); Samuel M. Makinda, *Seeking Peace from Chaos: Humanitarian Intervention in Somalia*, International Peace Academy: Occasional Paper Series (Boulder, Colo.: Lynne Rienner, 1993); and Robert L. Phillips and Duane L. Cady, *Humanitarian Intervention: Just War vs. Pacifism* (Lanham, Md.: Rowman and Littlefield, 1995).

38. Elliot L. Richardson, "The Problems and Pitfalls of Peace-Enforcement," *The Interdependent* 22, 1 (Spring 1996):4.

Suggested Readings

Boulding, Kenneth E., *Three Faces of Power*, Newbury Park, Calif.: Sage, 1989.

Burrowes, Robert J., *The Strategy of Nonviolent Defense*, Albany: The State University of New York Press, 1996.

Dinstein, Yoram, *War, Aggression and Self-Defence*, Cambridge, U.K.: Grotius, 1988.

Ericson, Eric H., *Gandhi's Truth: On the Origins of Militant Non-Violence*, New York: W. W. Norton, 1969.

Falk, Richard A., Robert C. Johansen, and Samuel S. Kim, eds., *The Constitutional Foundations of World Peace*, Albany: The State University of New York Press, 1995.

Fischer, Dietrich, Wilhelm Nolte, and Jan Oberg, *Winning Peace: Strategies and Ethics for a Nuclear-Free World*, New York: Crane, Russack, 1989.

Forsberg, Randall S., and Rob Leavitt, *Alternative Defense: A New Approach to Building a Stable Peace*, Brookline, Mass.: Institute for Defense and Disarmament Studies, 1988.

Glasstone, Samuel, and Philip J. Dolan, eds., *The Effects of Nuclear Weapons*, Washington, D.C.: Government Printing Office, 1962.

Isard, Walter, *Arms Races, Arms Control, and Conflict Analysis: Contributions from Peace Science and Peace Economics*, New York: Cambridge University Press, 1989.

Kennan, George F., *Nuclear Delusion: Soviet-American Relations in the Atomic Age*, New York: Pantheon Books, 1982.

Krause, Keith, and W. Andy Knight, *State, Society, and the UN System: Changing Perspectives on Multilateralism*, Tokyo: United Nations University Press, 1995.

Rochester, J. Martin, *Waiting for the Millennium: The United Nations and the Future of World Order*, Columbia: University of South Carolina Press, 1993.

Rosenau, James N., *The United Nations in a Turbulent World*, Boulder, Colo.: Lynne Rienner, 1992.

Ruggie, John Gerard, ed., *Multilateralism Matters: The Theory and Praxis of an Institutional Form*, New York: Columbia University Press, 1993.

Schmookler, Andrew Bard, *Out of Weakness: Healing the Wounds That Drive Us to War*, New York: Bantam Books, 1988.

Sharp, Gene, *Making Europe Unconquerable: The Potential of Civilian-Based Deterrence and Defense*, Philadelphia: Taylor and Francis, 1985.

Simai, Mihaly, *The Future of Global Governance: Managing Risk and Change in the International System*, Washington, D.C.: U.S. Institute of Peace Press, 1994.

Teson, Fernando R., *Humanitarian Intervention: An Inquiry into Law and Morality*, Irvington, N.Y.: Transnational, 1996.

Weiss, Thomas G., ed., *Collective Security in a Changing World*, Boulder, Colo.: Lynne Rienner, 1993.

CHAPTER 6

The Search for Economic Well-Being

> Our first concern is to redefine the whole purpose of development. This should not be to develop things but to develop man.
> **—The Cocoyoc Declaration, October 12, 1974**

The term "developing nations" came into fashion in the 1950s, reflecting the somewhat optimistic view of the time that the problems of widespread poverty in traditional societies could be corrected through industrial development. Although two developmental models competed for favor during the cold war years—those of laissez-faire capitalism and Leninist-style centralized planning—political economists in the East and West nonetheless were largely united in their view that the industrialization that had served to enrich their own societies would also allow the so-called third world to emerge from poverty.[1]

By the 1990s, a few states had indeed made remarkable economic strides, and the Leninist model for development had been almost completely discredited. Even though the ideology of capitalism seemed to triumph in most of the world, skepticism remained as to its implications for economic development. The world was even more highly stratified than it had been a generation earlier, with much of the South strapped by the debt it owed to lending institutions in the North—debt that was itself the direct product of the development effort. From 1974 to 1984, that debt had increased tenfold, from $70 billion to nearly $700 billion, as the result of the North's high interest rates, deep recession, and sharp drop in trade with third world countries during that period. In spite of the restructuring of much of that debt early in the 1990s on terms more favorable to the South, it nearly tripled again in the decade between 1984 and 1994, to about $1.9 trillion.

Oil shocks in the 1970s had provided a dramatic foretaste of how the interdependence that is an increasing feature of advanced economic life can produce unprecedented stress for seemingly innocent citizens in many parts of the world and thus political problems for their governments. In the 1970s, the decisions of oil sheiks made Americans wait in line for gasoline. In the 1980s, the falling price of oil helped trigger riots in Venezuela, which in turn forced that government to suspend its debt repayment to banks in New York and London. In the 1990s, Iraq's seizure of Kuwait's oil fields was met with a combined and overwhelming show of force led by those whose economic lives might have been seriously damaged had that conquest been allowed to stand. When the retreating Iraqi army set Kuwait's oil fields ablaze, the ecological disaster that resulted was a sobering reminder of the unacceptably high cost that accompanies the way in which much contemporary economic development is fueled.

Ironically, during the 1980s, when many less developed nations were shunned by wary lending institutions, the United States became the greatest debtor nation in the world. Yet that nation continued on a wave of prosperity thanks to a huge increase in foreign investment in the United States, investment prompted by a sharp decline in the value of the dollar. Today, as the centuries-old habits of Westphalia confront the dynamics of late-twentieth-century economic imperatives, the resulting clashes are rapidly reshaping much of the agenda of world politics. States find their traditional freedom in economic policy making constrained by globalization, and their authority in domestic arenas challenged by private actors as never before in the modern period.[2]

Westphalia and the Industrial Revolution

Probably no aspect of human life has remained as constant for many centuries or has changed at such a dramatically accelerated pace in modern times as its economic base. From the origins of the earliest known societies until well past the emergence of the Westphalian international system, economic life for most people in all parts of the globe meant little more than bare subsistence. The small farmer of Elizabethan England was like his or her Celtic or Anglo-Saxon ancestor a thousand years before in that both were concerned primarily with sustaining themselves and their families through the fruit of their labor on the land. Like their counterparts over as many centuries in Mexico or Egypt, the greatest economic reward they could expect from hard work was to fulfill their basic survival needs—food, shelter, and clothing, most of which they and their families produced for themselves. When there was a tiny surplus, it could be bartered or sold for some amenity beyond their means of production, but they mostly remained poor for countless generations, malnourished, illiterate, and with a life expectancy not much beyond thirty years.

The two most compelling facts about this traditional way of life are, first, that it was everywhere accepted as the inevitable and unchanging condition for most of humanity (the rich 1 percent of the population was viewed as naturally entitled to its more exalted state), and, second, that the kinds of economic organization it produced were comparatively small scale, self-contained at local levels, and demanded very little interchange with other societies. Just as the milkmaid of Europe typically lived her whole life within sight of her village's church steeple, so her economic needs were sustained by that same tiny society, which alone knew the fruit of her labor.

By the time of the European Renaissance, larger units of economic organization began to emerge from the combination of the myriad local markets of earlier times. Greater centralization and control of economic activity from the capital became one of the fundamental features in the evolution of modern nation-states; yet the only real novelty at first was the scale of the new economic units. For the great mass of the population, material well-being still improved imperceptibly. Nonetheless, the emergence of the Westphalian system laid the foundation for profound changes in traditional economic life by creating nearly self-contained units large enough to encourage intrastate economic activity of a scope and a complexity never achievable while the Middle Ages' hatchwork of barriers to economic exchange persisted.

For at least a century and a half after 1648, Westphalia served mainly to legitimize the development of separate, state-based economies. The new normative order had to treat economic exchanges across state lines and to lay down rules for the exploitation of the sea's resources, that community property of all nation-states, but these remained insignificant activities compared to those that grew within each territorial unit. The Westphalian dynamic moved states in the direction of national self-sufficiency, the economic condition of autarky, although not every state had a large enough territory or population base or the diversity of resources to make such a goal possible. Nonetheless, the political principle of laissez-faire on which the new international system was built encouraged states to focus most of their economic and other energies on internal development and to relegate most interstate economic activity to secondary importance.[3] Thus economic developments in early modern Europe, like those in the political sphere, tended to reinforce the construction of comparatively impermeable or "hard-shelled" national units.

Then, at the end of the eighteenth century, the industrial revolution began in Western Europe. It was from the first a social revolution that altered the traditional economic relationships of individuals, attracting huge numbers of people from the land to work for wages in city factories, demanding ever larger manufacturing enterprises, fueling the creation of an entrepreneurial class, and growing insatiable in its demands for new energy resources to drive the new modes of production. Within a few decades, industrialization also began to increase the overall wealth of a number of Western nations as they pulled away from traditional societies. It is estimated that as early as 1850, the ratio between incomes in the industrializing societies and those elsewhere may already have been about two to one—a dramatic portent of the gap between rich and poor that would widen to the present day.

As the incomes of people living in industrialized nations noticeably increased, an expectation took root for the first time in history that ever greater economic growth and wealth was natural. However grim the working conditions in early industrial England may look to us today, most laborers viewed their own material prospects as better than they had ever been before. In fact, as average per capita income slowly rose, each generation came to expect and demand an improvement in its own economic situation over that of its predecessor, a phenomenon that has accompanied industrialization ever since.

Expectations of growth clearly create a beast with an enormous appetite. To be satisfied, it must be fed with ever greater resources, including capital and labor, which in turn help create ever larger enterprises that gain strength and generate more wealth through economies of scale. From the beginning, the industrial revolution most enhanced the place in the world of those states large enough to create formidable, diversified industrial economies. England and France led the way, followed before the end of the nineteenth century by the United States and a newly united Germany. The growth appetite could be most readily fed in states like these that commanded large and diverse resources, whether, as in the United States, in their own, largely undeveloped backyards or, as in Britain and France, in overseas territories that could supply many of the resources not available at home. The nineteenth-century period of imperialist competition was driven above all by the growth ideology. The prospect of ever greater wealth was perhaps motivation enough for many entrepreneurs, but it also carried with it greater power on the global stage than could have been imagined by earlier leaders of states.

The Westphalian order adjusted to the imperialist drive, as we have seen, by creating a double standard in which huge sections of the globe simply were not deemed to be full participants in the international system. Such territories were fair game for the kind of conquest and exploitation denied the nation-states of Europe when they interacted on their home continent. Once attached to the flag of a European power, their presumed interests then were expressed for them in the distant capital. This double standard created a situation that has come to be regarded today as unjust. But as a legal fiction, it served to perpetuate the laissez-faire thrust behind the international order: Hands-off principles applied only to full-fledged sovereign states. Very different principles of behavior were accepted vis-à-vis those that, by definition, were not sovereign. As a result, colonialism could rationalize the creation of larger and larger units in keeping with the new economic imperatives as long as the core territory of the original European actors was not swallowed up in the process.

Had the world at the beginning of the nineteenth century not been essentially defenseless against the more powerful industrializing countries of Europe and North America, Westphalia's impact on economic organization probably would have placed much greater restraints on the development of great industrial powers, for the growth ideology is not stopped by a sign at the nation's edge that reads "hands off." Colonialism in effect successfully masked for a century and more the artificiality of state borders from the standpoint of industrial capitalism's constant need for growth and expansion.

In addition, nineteenth-century colonialism had important economic consequences on the colonized world. The most long-lasting of these stems from the universal imperial practice of treating the overseas territories and their populations as valuable only for the supporting role they could play in feeding the growth machine at the imperial center. Thus, colonies were typically suppliers of raw materials and providers of an agricultural base to the mother country. Theories of comparative advantage were created to explain why, say, Africa's Gold Coast should grow cocoa to be produced into fine chocolate in London or Edinburgh, or why Vietnamese peasants should labor on rubber plantations so that workers at a Michelin factory in France could produce tires for Peugeots. Economic growth became a basic fact of life at the imperial center; in the colonized periphery, life remained largely at the age-old subsistence level.

The real legacy of that practice has been its persistence even after the end of colonialism. Independence for colonized territories has not yet let them overcome, with few exceptions, their historic poverty and dependence on the North. Put slightly differently, the first industrial societies had advanced by the mid-twentieth century to the point that they were able generally to maintain a momentum in their growth that has not yet appeared in most of the once-colonized world. The 1850 income gap of about two to one, dividing industrializing Europe from the rest of the world, grew to ten to one by 1950. A decade later, the ratio had increased to about fifteen to one. It has continued to widen in the decades since then, if not quite as rapidly. This begins to explain the principal force underlying many current global problems and the enormous increase in attention to issues of economic development on the world's political agenda.

The Northern Approach to International Economic Development

The global upheavals between the two world wars were marked in the economic sphere by the Great Depression. As one advanced industrial country after another experienced the devastating effects of widespread unemployment and the collapse of capital, their governments turned to strictly protectionist policies in the effort to save their own societies. Even though the members of these governments had long shared the view that economic liberalism in the international marketplace served their mutual interests in continued growth, suddenly they had to respond to the desperate conditions of their own national constituencies. The governmental response was to ignore, regardless of the consequences, the interests of other publics as they sought to seal their own economies off from the rest of the world to save themselves.[4] Most industrialized countries adopted protectionist measures reluctantly, regarding them as short-term palliatives. They almost certainly made recovery more difficult by choking back international trade instead of encouraging it.

These developments remain a classic example of an ongoing dilemma in all considerations of world order. State actors, obligated to their own populations in ways they are not to the rest of the world, will always respond first to demands arising from within. If those demands are insistent or desperate enough, as they were during the Depression, it matters little that they may run counter to the interests of global society, which include the long-term interests of the local society as well, even though when basic values are at stake, these tend to be blocked from sight altogether. It is again a case of the hunters losing the stag when one of them grabs for smaller game in the hope he will thereby satisfy himself.

Although protectionist measures generally hindered economic recovery in the 1930s, the different and more complex cure of national economic planning seemed to many in industrialized societies to produce a positive alternative to renewed growth. When the world's economy had to be rebuilt at the end of World War II, many argued in favor of international economic institutions that would allow considerable national regulation of interstate economic relations while at the same time working to minimize conflicts between and among national regulations.

But that view lost out, and the postwar world instead was built on the dominant U.S. vision of a return to international liberalism. Specifically, "the most significant American policy makers imagined postwar economic institutions as agencies that would aim to abolish national restrictions on the international economy rather than merely regulate them."[5] That vision guided most international policy for the next several decades. For example, the new international financial system created at Bretton Woods in 1945 made the U.S. dollar a kind of international currency to stabilize and facilitate investment and trade throughout the world. One can read the motivation behind the U.S. Marshall Plan in the same light. Because it gave the previously rich market states of Western Europe the opportunity to reconstruct their economies, it in effect ensured a more liberalized international (Western) system of work, expansion, and growth.

A continuing example was the long-term effort to increase trade through the gradual reduction of restrictive tariffs. To this end, the industrialized countries of the North in the 1950s formed the General Agreement on Tariffs and Trade (GATT) to work toward the gradual reduction of protectionist measures on a reciprocal basis. In the 1960s, 1970s, and 1980s they engaged in the protracted negotiations of the so-called Kennedy, Tokyo, and Uruguay Rounds that were aimed at further liberalizing trade relations. In the 1990s, the liberal international model gained its fullest expression to date in the creation of a World Trade Organization (WTO) that superseded GATT, providing an authoritative agency to reconcile the differing trade regulations of its members.

In these and other manifestations of the liberal economic ideology, the Soviet Union and other socialist states were left largely on the sidelines. As centrally planned economies, rigorously controlled from the top, they rejected the liberal premise in both its national and international guises. They relied on neither the marketplace to determine the form and shape of their domestic economies nor the free exchange of goods and money with the West to form economic links with the outside world that might grow to become unresponsive to political control from within. As one of the two dominant powers in the world system between 1945 and 1990, the Soviets did engage in economic politics as an aspect of their foreign policy. That is, they followed the example of the United States in offering foreign assistance for development projects in a number of third world countries. They also assisted selected friendly governments with large capital outlays, much as the United States did.[6] But throughout the development debate of the cold war the Soviets were largely sealed off from important participation in the international economic arena. Now that the successor states of the Soviet Union have turned to free-market economics, a dual irony has followed: The old ideological divide at last has disappeared, but so has the ability of these successor states to encourage development in the South. Indeed, most have become more like third world states themselves, particularly in their need to import rather than export capital.

The international economic regime established after World War II did not exactly turn its back on the problems of what later was to be called the South, with its legacy of poverty and lack of development and the consequent growing disparity in well-being between its enormous population and that of the increasingly rich world of the North. Rather, the international system was built on several general assumptions, often more implicit than explicit, in keeping with the precepts of laissez-faire liberalism.

The first assumption was that development in the poor countries would follow the revitalization of the rich, since growing demand in the North presumably would stimulate increased production in the South. Another was that states had to come to their own industrial revolutions in their own natural course, just as had occurred in nineteenth-century Europe. That assumption raised certain dilemmas: Although traditional societies were encouraged to rely on the marketplace for the stimulation of capital for investment, they were also advised to take governmental action in sectors where private capital is least likely to flow. These included specifically improving the agricultural base to ensure the kinds of crop surpluses for capital that could fuel investment in industry as a second step, and increasing education, since illiterate peasants never have made successful capitalist entrepreneurs. Still another assumption stemmed from the theory of comparative advantage, suggesting that at least some poor nations—those without the resources to build diversified, self-sufficient economies on the model of the large Northern states—should expect to improve their lot by concentrating on the production of the one or two commodities they were particularly well suited to produce. In all of these assumptions, economic development throughout the South was assumed to be a positive good for everyone, but it should not be hurried for fear traumatic social upheaval would result. Nor should it be skewed through massive national planning to the detriment of the overall interests of the global economy—one integrated, that is, through liberal economic policies.

This slow-going approach to the problems of economic underdevelopment is reflected in the creation of relevant formal arrangements in the international system in the early postwar years. The International Bank for Reconstruction and Development (the World Bank) concentrated on the first rather than the second of its purposes in the immediate aftermath of World War II and played an important role in financing the recovery of the war-torn but already industrialized countries. Its weighted-voting scheme ensured that the Western states, which contributed most to its assets, would have the dominant voice in its lending policies. Since it typically made loans at conventional rates of interest, third world governments were quick to assert that it was ill equipped to deal with what they saw as their massive needs for development assistance.

As the result of continuous pressure from the underdeveloped world, new institutional arrangements and more development-oriented policies gradually were adopted over the next twenty years. In 1956, the International Finance Corporation (IFC) came into being as a World Bank affiliate to promote the growth of the private sector in third world countries; that is, it largely embodied the traditional economic views of the dominant ideology while stimulating a greater flow of private capital for development purposes. In 1960, the International Development Authority was added as the "soft-loan" affiliate of the World Bank in a move that finally acknowledged the need to grant to many loan recipients the kind of concessions in interest rates and pay-back schedules unavailable before. After Robert S. McNamara assumed its presidency in 1968, the World Bank expanded its lending more than twelvefold and explicitly redirected many of its resources toward combating world poverty.[7] Even so, many of the problems of underdevelopment remained so intractable—particularly in light of the ever deepening gap between rich and poor—that the Western approach to development and the economic system it had created came under increasing attack through much of the world. That development in turn had its origins in the vast expansion of the state system after World War II.

The Rising Voice of the South

Rapid decolonization in the 1950s and 1960s brought increasing numbers of peoples who had always been voiceless in the councils of international politics into formal participation in the global system. When the United Nations was created in 1945, slightly more than half its original fifty-one members were what the United Nations later would describe euphemistically as less developed countries. Almost none of that group of between twenty-five and thirty had more than the bare beginnings of an industrial base. Twenty years later, UN membership had more than doubled (to 118 in 1966), and almost all the new members were former colonies that fell into that category. After that date they could outvote the industrialized North in such forums as the General Assembly—a formal power that, as all would learn, could be frustratingly empty if it did not command the real financial resources of the rich minority. But their participation inevitably gave them a growing voice and helped, for a time, to tilt the international agenda increasingly away from the more traditional concerns of the old states.

New voices, new forums for discussions, and an ever widening gap between rich and poor formed an ideology that challenged the liberal vision of international economic development as outmoded and discredited by its impact on the poor. Before examining some of its specific components, it is worth noting how the global political system itself served as a kind of catalyst in creating by the 1970s what can be called the New International Economic Order (NIEO) ideology.[8]

One of the early decisions of the UN Economic and Social Council (ECOSOC) was to create a number of permanently functioning regional economic commissions, which, it was thought, could attend to the economic problems of particular geographical areas of the world in ways that ECOSOC as a whole could not. On one of these, the Economic Commission for Latin America (ECLA), sat an economist whose experience there led him to develop a deep and far-ranging critique of the impact of the world's economic system on the underdeveloped countries of Latin America. In 1950, Raul Prebisch published a major work setting forth his views, which argued essentially that the international economic system was structurally biased in favor of the industrialized states and worked against the development interests of the South. The effect of economic liberalism was to maintain and strengthen the positions of the dominant industrialized countries, those at the core of the system, and to perpetuate the dependency of the underdeveloped world on their policies.[9] Prebisch's views struck responsive chords in increasing numbers of third world leaders, who by the 1960s were in widespread agreement with him as to what was wrong with the international economic system. Just as important, third world governments were developing increasingly powerful political attacks on it.

But the newly formed third world position first was most dramatically expressed in another international forum. In 1964, the first UN Conference on Trade and Development (UNCTAD I) saw the participating bloc of seventy-seven underdeveloped countries caucusing and voting as a unit, with the result that they succeeded through the weight of their numbers in getting many of their resolutions passed in opposition to the longstanding policies of the North. The Group of 77 (as they are still called, even though their number has nearly doubled), acting on the basis of their only strength—voting power—thus learned the importance of their own unity in the effort to implement their views. The very form of their participation in the international institutional framework encouraged the evolution of the NIEO outlook.

The NIEO Response to Economic Liberalism

The core assumption in the NIEO critique is that the established approach to development has not succeeded (and can never succeed) in eliminating the dependency of third world economies on those of the North. It does not deny that in many parts of the underdeveloped world, industrialization has taken root and grown or that increases in gross domestic products have raised living standards in a number of countries. But it asserts that the underlying condition of dependence on economic decisions taken in the North remains and that, in effect, as a solution to one part of the problem of underdevelopment appears, a new problem arises and dependence remains. This assumption is best examined by looking briefly at several of the components in the international economic situation today.

Trade is particularly vital to developing countries as a potential source of investment capital, yet their principal trade commodities are primary products sold to industrialized countries for processing and manufacture, which may then be sold back to the developing countries as finished goods. This process presumably exemplifies notions of comparative advantage (the production of primary products—food crops, mineral extraction—is typically labor intensive, whereas that of manufactured goods, particularly those requiring high technology, is much more capital intensive). Nonetheless, it is harmful to poor countries in several ways.

First, it is self-perpetuating, particularly in a world economic system dominated by private investment rather than centralized planning, for if good-quality peanuts can be grown more cheaply in Gambia than anywhere else, it will encourage the growing of peanuts there ad infinitum, regardless of the fact that virtually the entire crop must be exported for the survival of Gambia.

Second, this dependence maintains and perhaps even increases the relative poverty of the exporting nation because of marketplace factors. In the 1980s, the demand for oil fell, along with its price, and countries such as Venezuela were suddenly faced with dwindling foreign exchange and inexorably mounting debt payments. Economic growth was choked off as the Venezuelan government was forced to impose austerity measures to try to meet its debt payments. Whatever the long-term effects on creditors in the North, the immediate and most volatile political effects were felt within Venezuela when violence erupted there in 1989. Such developments are inevitable, in the view of the NIEO critique of economic liberalism, because of the ongoing tendency of the world's economic system to maintain negative terms of trade for the producers of primary products.

A third negative effect has become apparent in recent years. Northern countries have developed increasing numbers of synthetics and other substitutes for the primary products they used to import from the South and they continue to discover exploitable raw materials within their own domains. Thus they have less need for the resources that the South has traditionally supplied.

A closely related assumption is the view that major inflationary or deflationary swings in the global economy have their root cause in the practices of the industrialized countries. Wages rise in the North and the prices of goods produced there increase, making them more costly for poor countries to buy. As the purchasing power of these countries is reduced, they soon find themselves forced to enter the inflationary path themselves by raising the price of their exports in the effort to redress the growing imbalance. Northerners with memories of the leaping prices in oil exported by OPEC during the 1970s may explain the situation as an example of worldwide inflation fueled from the South. Although Northern officials worked assiduously at the time to convince poor countries of the treachery of their oil-exporting fellow governments, few third world governments were persuaded. Rather, they insisted that the artificially low price of oil prior to the first OPEC action—a condition produced by the decisive power of transnational oil companies—had in fact amounted to an ongoing subsidy by oil producers of the economic growth of the industrialized countries, where that precious resource had been used profligately. Moreover, as the North exported its inflation, oil-producing countries were forced by their declining purchasing power to correct the situation.[10]

Conversely, as we learned in the early 1980s, when the industrialized nations take drastic domestic action, such as encouraging widespread unemployment to curb their inflation, they also export their resulting recession to the rest of the world. Starting in 1982, the plight of third world debtor states grew ever worse, lasting long past the end of the North's recession, when growth and a fragile prosperity once again were the order of the day for rich countries.[11] By the end of the decade, developing countries were making more interest and capital payments to the World Bank than they were receiving from it in development assistance.

Critics of the existing economic system also observe that dependency ordinarily does not end once industrialization and diversification of a poor country's economy get under way. Societies that traditionally have been able to feed their own people, if only at subsistence levels, increasingly become food importers as their populations are drawn away from traditional agricultural practices into the cities and factories. The subsistence economy is self-sufficient; advanced industrial economies typically are much less so. Even though that may explain a good deal about the development of liberal trade attitudes in advanced societies, for the country in transition today from a traditional to a modern economy, one form of dependence is being exchanged for another.[12] The new dependence presents quite different problems, psychologically at least, from those faced by Europeans in the nineteenth century as they moved from the self-sufficiency of subsistence into the industrial revolution. For them, unlike third world populations today, it would be a century or more before international dependence or interdependence would become a meaningful concept.

There are many other factors in the NIEO critique. These include what is known as the transfer of technology problem, that is, the fact that most of the essential technology for development remains in the private hands of Northern entrepreneurs and managers, and so is inaccessible to those in third world countries who need it for their independent development. A related issue is that of the brain drain, which attracts intellectuals from developing countries to the better-paying jobs and higher standards of living in the North, a phenomenon that "really constitutes gratuitous and inverse transfer of technology" in the wrong direction.[13] In addition, the international monetary system and multilateral financing agencies are seen to be slanted in favor of the interests of the highly developed countries to the disadvantage of the poor. For evidence, critics note that the World Bank's loan terms are about as stringent as those from private banks, the IFC has always been much underfunded, and the austerity policies demanded by the IMF in return for its assistance may exacerbate unemployment and otherwise pinch consumers in the target country.

All of these are viewed as symptoms of the third world's continuing dependency on the core industrial states, which is to say that the cause of underdevelopment problems is thought to be the system itself. As a result, NIEO advocates argue that basic structural changes are needed. More development capital, more technical assistance, and more extensive use of soft loans with low interest rates will not in themselves change the underlying condition. Although no exact blueprint exists for all the needed reforms, advocates of systemic change generally agree on certain principles that should guide the effort.[14]

These principles flow from what are regarded as the inherent rights and duties of states in the modern world. The thrust of these arguments permits confrontation with the main dynamic of modern capitalism, especially in its postindustrial phase: It is not limited by state boundaries. The invisible hand that drives laissez-faire practice cannot justifiably be limited in its operation by the artificial constraints of national borders. If the most profitable investments are halfway around the globe, capital will flow there if allowed to. If a particularly valuable resource, such as copper, exists in plentiful supply in Chile, then Chilean copper should be mined to fuel the industrial machine of the rest of the world. Free market economics does not concern itself with the effects of these practices on local polities—or rather it *would* not in a world free from pluralistic political interests and values.

In response to this tendency, the NIEO outlook places great stress on some of the traditional attributes of membership in the Westphalian political system. State sovereignty implies the inherent right of the sovereign to say yea or nay to any economic activity taking place within its borders. Not the invisible hand of the international marketplace but the very visible hand of the local government should determine the direction of its economy. No advanced industrial country can counter with a commanding argument about that principle, since all have turned, and still do, to the logic of sovereignty to justify their own repeated interventions in the marketplace. Liberalism, after all, has simply been one, usually dominant, impulse powering Western economic growth. It has been tempered by increased governmental interventions to alleviate the worst effects of the marketplace at home. Third world leaders who argue that their own infant industries need protection to face the competition of the mature industrial sector of the North need only point to U.S. practice throughout the nineteenth century to support their case. Alexander Hamilton convinced his compatriots of the need to protect U.S. industrial development two hundred years ago. Some Americans remained persuaded of that need well into the twentieth century, when those infant industries had become the giants of the world.

But lines tend to be drawn when sovereignty justifications for antiliberal policies go beyond any presumably encountered by Northern societies as they were developed themselves. Such is the case in the South's claim to permanent sovereignty over its own resources, which hold great potential wealth, increase in value over the long term (in spite of short-term fluctuations in the price of, say, oil) because of the continuing demand for them in advanced societies, and cannot be replaced once they have been exploited. The NIEO position makes clear the potential power of the third world in this principle: "The exercise of full and effective permanent sovereignty and control over natural and other commodities and raw materials is a way to eliminate unequal exchange, the exercise of control over foreign capital and over the actions of transnational corporations."[15]

At least part of the reason for this focus on the rights and duties of states, then, is a quest for greater third world political power over the economic life of the world. One of the important component arguments of the Westphalian system is that more of the binding international decisions should be made democratically, that is, on the basic principle that every state should have but one vote.[16] Some international institutions, including the General Assembly of the United Nations, operate on this principle, but the Assembly's resolutions are specifically described in the Charter as nonbinding recommendations. Institutions with true "legislative" power to command resources in the economic sphere, such as the World Bank, are exactly those whose votes are weighted in favor of the Northern countries. The democratization argument received its first major boost at UNCTAD I, which operated on the one-state, one-vote principle and saw the Group of 77 vote its policies into effect over the opposition of the developed countries. In the years since, that voting power has continued to enable the Group of 77 to advance its views through their formal adoption in such forums as the General Assembly, although in general the outvoted minority of Northern states still refuses to acknowledge any obligation to acquiesce in the majority will.

New Problems, Strategies, and Goals

The NIEO received its most serious attention as a cohesive set of agenda items in the 1970s. In that decade, when Northern commitments to development assistance remained comparatively strong, the Group of 77 presented a coherent program across a wide spectrum of economic issues. In the years since, that conjunction of forces has tended to split apart. Governments of several major capital-exporting states moved to the right in the 1980s, refusing to treat the NIEO agenda with sympathy. Effort also had to be devoted to putting out fires in the existing structure (as in the case with the debt crisis) instead of attempting to build a new one. Then came the "cold water plunge" of former Soviet bloc states into market economics, with the initial result of pushing the NIEO agenda farther into the background. Whatever the economic adjustments involved (and for many they were seriously destabilizing), these former Soviet bloc states were generally industrialized but sclerotic countries whose economic problems would complicate the search for greater economic well-being worldwide.

By the mid-1990s, some discerned a "new paradigm" for development, which, with its renewed emphasis on privatization and the relaxation of trade and capital controls, looked very much like the dominant model of half a century earlier. Its proponents saw in it greater agreement between North and South on the value of political and economic stability, participation, and reliance on market forces combined with growing environmental awareness.[17] Yet even if a consensus is forming around such a paradigm, it is unclear how well—or even if—it can address many of the issues with which NIEO advocates have been concerned. A number of these issues continue to trouble the world's agenda. As a result of these and other factors—some the result of longer-term trends—new debates have arisen, sometimes bringing to the fore new values that are altering much of the substance of development strategies.

Curbing Population Growth

Solutions to the world's problems of poverty and underdevelopment have been made increasingly difficult over the past several decades as the result of the zooming growth in populations throughout much of the third world. In fact, it may not be so much that established development policy has failed as that the resulting overpopulation has not been adequately addressed. It took 2 million years and more before Homo sapiens numbered about 1 billion, which was the figure attained early in the nineteenth century at about the time the industrial revolution began. Little more than a century later, by about 1930, a second billion had been added. Forty-five years after that, global population had again doubled, to 4 billion, and was headed for more than 6 billion living human beings by the end of the century. Clearly, the doubling of our population in ever more telescoped periods has thrust us very far along a collision course with the planet's finite capacity to sustain human life.

Since World War II, most of this explosive growth has been in poor countries, as attention to the problems of poverty focused on the kinds of basic health and sanitation measures that can reduce the death rate. Meanwhile, as deaths per thousand persons dropped radically throughout the underdeveloped world, patterns of fertility remained at traditionally high levels. The economic output of societies caught in explosive population growth must be stretched ever farther just to feed and support their huge sector of dependent children. Like Alice, these societies must run ever faster just to stay in the same place. This phenomenon, much greater in scale and scope than anything the Northern countries had to face a century and more ago as their economic growth took off, accounts for the fact that even though productivity has increased (in many cases more than doubling) throughout the third world since World War II, it frequently has been offset by comparable growth in the population.

Although serious efforts to address the problem of high birthrates have been undertaken in a number of countries, they have been both agonizingly slow to produce the desired results—although results now are beginning to be seen[18]—and often Draconian in their implications for the authoritarian control of governments over personal and family life. The late Sanjay Gandhi, the son and brother of two of India's prime ministers, became a very controversial figure in the 1970s for directing alleged forced sterilization and contraception programs throughout the country. In China, which with India accounted for nearly 40 percent of the world's annual population growth before the end of the 1970s, Mao Tse-tung's successors sought to achieve negative population growth through a system of increasingly severe punishments for couples who produce more than one child. Two children are permitted. Couples who produce a third child must undergo a socially embarrassing reeducation program. Any additional children mean a forced *reduction* to the family of certain essential goods. Such drastic measures to curb population growth, however necessary they may be to the well-being of the local society immediately and the future of the entire species over the longer run, are not exactly conducive to the development of free, nonauthoritarian societies. Indeed, some Chinese couples reportedly were abandoning, even murdering, their young daughters when faced with the prospect that they would not be allowed to try to have a son.

It is tempting for the members of rich societies to blame population problems on poor nations whose numbers are increasing rapidly, forgetting that such increase is produced by the first steps of the modernization process. In its most extreme form, this kind of thinking has suggested curtailing international assistance programs to such countries until famine, disease, and wholesale death have occurred on a scale massive enough to reduce substantially such populations, thus solving the problems of an increasingly crowded planet.[19] According to this view, only the rich members of the species have a right to places in the economic lifeboat. The poor, because of their failure to control their growing numbers, deserve to be consigned to the sea.

Some spokespersons for developing countries have turned that metaphor around by noting that the rich societies, not the poor ones, are straining the earth's carrying capacity to its limits. Infants born in the United States will consume some fifteen to twenty times more of the globe's economic output over the course of their lifetimes than will those of their generation who happen to be born in Mauritania or Sri Lanka.

The United States as a whole, with only 4 percent of the world's population, accounts for more than 30 percent of its consumption annually. So the typical American is a much more burdensome passenger in the economic lifeboat than his or her third world counterpart. The boat obviously can support a dozen of the world's poor more easily than it can the weight of a single North American.[20]

Disturbing though the lifeboat metaphor may be, whoever its occupants, it is a vivid illustration of why the income gap cannot possibly be closed by increasing the wealth of the poor to something like U.S. levels, the supposition that has seemed to underlie most of the traditional efforts at development. That supposition would mean an approximately sixfold increase in the gross global economy from its current level, with none of the increase going to today's wealthiest societies. Such a goal is wrong both practically and morally. No one supposes that existing economic and political realities permit its achievement, but if it could be done, the result would be catastrophic for the biosphere. It would be a self-defeating goal for the species.

Transnational Corporations

Meanwhile, technological momentum relevant to production has brought sweeping change in the world's economic structure. In the past thirty or forty years, transnational corporations (TNCs) have emerged as powerful global actors. Thanks to technological advances in communication, transportation, and management, production has been internationalized wherever these corporations have arisen. That is, TNCs operate by drawing the components necessary for modern production from more than one country. This typically means combining capital, management, and technology from an advanced industrial society and labor and raw materials from a poor country.

This internationalization of production is the essential and novel feature of TNCs, for it is no longer possible to say that the goods they produce were made in the United States, Japan, or Mexico. They may have received essential components from all three. This point bears emphasis because it is tempting to view TNCs as simply the huge offspring of the already large national corporations of an earlier day whose names they still bear. True, internationalization began when national corporations organized divisions to coordinate their overseas operations, which at first were marginal. But as the overseas component grew in size and complexity, national organization no longer was adequate. As a result, the transnational corporation "is now moving toward a global corporate structure, organizing along functional lines—production, R&D and marketing—rather than along geographic lines. Corporate strategies are be-

ing formulated increasingly on a global scale in terms of utilizing R&D results, selection of production sites, procurement of raw materials, and
marketing of products."[21]

The size of TNCs is staggering, suggesting their economic impact on
the world. The gross annual sales of many are larger than the gross national products of a great many states. In 1994, the annual product of Mit-
subishi was larger than that of all but the twenty-one richest nation-
states, and ten of the top forty economic actors were corporations, not
states.[22]

Some of the implications of these developments are evident, whereas
others are debatable. It is clear from the kind of rank ordering mentioned
above that the impact of transnational activities on the development
strategies of many third world countries is enormous. Some economies
may be penetrated to the point of being overwhelmed by TNC operations
within them. That situation is obvious where a largely subsistence economy becomes the locale for the production of a primary product such as
coffee by a transnational corporation making use of the nation's comparative advantage in growing conditions and its inexpensive labor. A huge
portion of the available land and workforce fall under the company's domain. Although the standard of living may rise as a result, so will all the
signs of increased dependence on management and investment decisions
made elsewhere. Moreover, the once self-sufficient society may be forced
to import basic foodstuffs, thereby creating a new foreign exchange problem for its government. In the long run, some local workers may advance
into management positions. Conceivably, as the skills of that workforce
grow, some aspects of coffee processing may be relocated into the territory, providing new jobs for more highly skilled workers. Yet short of a
controlling interest from the local population in investment and corporate
decisionmaking, it is difficult to detect a noticeable decrease in its dependency on external economic forces.

This kind of situation also contributes to an increasingly apparent fact
of global economic life—the economic gap *within* developing countries is
widening, as is the gap *between* North and South generally. A comparatively skilled, consumption-oriented, and increasingly affluent class is
emerging worldwide. Its members have developed lifestyles that resemble those of their counterparts in North America or Europe more than
those of most of their fellow citizens in Pakistan, Peru, or Yemen. Although this class is increasingly cosmopolitan (a fact that may cheer those
who see it as a sign of increasing global integration), its development
heightens evidence of distributive injustice, which may further feed the
flames of resentment among the still impoverished masses and thereby
spread the revolution of rising expectations. Moreover, the culture of materialism and wasteful consumption spawned by this new affluence of a

global class raises a growing number of questions about its moral and political acceptability in a world that must confront both profound economic inequities and the long-term effects of unbridled materialism.
Transnational corporations are both the products and the agents of that
culture, which is rapidly spreading throughout the globe.

The debate about the impact of TNCs on global integration extends beyond these concerns. Those who view them as a positive force for integration emphasize that in cutting across state lines to do their work, they encourage the creation of a peaceful international environment, which is the
sine qua non of their successful operation. In this view the TNC "is by far
the most effective agent yet devised for disseminating technology across
national borders, dwarfing in its effectiveness other types of institutions
such as the UN Special Agencies, international professional societies, private consulting firms or bilateral assistance agencies."[23] Some even argue
that "by breaking the monopoly of the nation-state over international economic relations the multinational corporation has . . . altered the very nature of international relations,"[24] breaking down Westphalian barriers to
global interaction.

A more negative assessment emphasizes how TNCs further strengthen
dominant economic groups, through the stratification process already
mentioned and through the fact that the managerial and high-tech aspects of their work tend to take place only in the rich societies of the
North. Although they do indeed disseminate technology across national
borders, by far the greatest amount of this transnational flow occurs only
among the rich countries. Because they also are products of the Westphalian system, they can exacerbate its most divisive, antiglobal features.
Too often they act as instruments in the foreign policy of their home governments abroad, as when, for example, the U.S. government required
overseas subsidiaries of U.S.-based firms to avoid trade with centrally
planned economies. Too often their powerful ability to lobby in their own
interests misdirects foreign policy away from its larger public purpose, as
when U.S.-based firms persuaded Congress in 1972 to violate the UN
boycott of Rhodesian chromium ore.

Too often their apolitical thrust works against the protection and extension of important world order values, as when profit motives alone persuade them to do business in societies with repressive or racist regimes or
to sell products with little regard for whether they may be disastrously
misused, as occurred when Nestlé marketed infant formula in a number
of third world countries. Misuse of the formula led to markedly increased
malnutrition and morbidity rates for babies. (The ending of the Nestlé
story is, nonetheless, an example of the power of world order tendencies
in the contemporary world. Once the impact of the corporation's marketing practices on third world infants became known, a worldwide con-

sumer boycott of the company's products was instituted in 1977. After seven years, that action finally led the Nestlé corporation to agree to implement an international code of marketing of breast milk substitutes.[25])

The Limits of Growth and Sustainable Development

Not surprisingly in light of this history, thoughtful analysts throughout the world are viewing with increased alarm the effects of the growth imperative on all of us. Although occasional voices have objected to its moral effect on our values and priorities in the past, only within recent memory has it become apparent that the growth appetite must be curbed. Nature will do it for us if we do not take more effective steps than we have to date to bring it under control ourselves. Today's environmental crisis is almost entirely the result of our failure to control the ravages of greater and greater economic development on the planet's finite resources. That realization is only beginning to have profound implications on development strategies for poor countries.

Knowing that the traditional Northern model of industrialization and development is an ecological threat, we can grasp its irrelevance to many of the situations confronting underdeveloped societies. That model demands large infusions of capital, advanced technology, and a skilled and highly paid workforce—all of which are in short supply in the South. When massive amounts of capital are borrowed from abroad, development may be stifled under a mound of debt, as the 1980s demonstrated. But there are other grounds for questioning whether development should blindly follow the example of the most highly developed societies. Not only is it very costly to teach farmers on the northern Chinese plain how to use a U.S. wheat-harvesting combine but the combine is probably inappropriate to the scale of the Chinese wheat field. Adopting it would displace the jobs of several dozen harvesters, which in the aggregate causes widespread social disruption.

Similarly, the destruction of traditional cottage craft industries in favor of huge manufacturing plants obviously disrupts social life, drawing millions from the land into already overcrowded cities. It may also prove counterproductive if transportation systems are inadequate to move the new manufactured products throughout the country or if housing is not available for the influx of workers at the new plant. In addition, there may be a host of other reasons that project planners have overlooked. Modern industrial enterprises typically operate on a scale that increasingly is seen as wrong for the well-being of society, including its relationship to the natural environment.

In concrete terms, appropriate technologies need to be applied to the existing economic and social situations of poor societies. To determine appropriateness entails considerably more soul-searching about the meaning of work and production in human terms, including a concern with humankind's relationship to the natural world, than it typically receives in the more orthodox discussions of development needs and problems. One of the most influential advocates of appropriate technology, E. F. Schumacher, proposed four essential guidelines for overcoming the evils of large-scale industrial development:

> First, that workplaces have to be created in the areas where the people are living now, and not primarily in metropolitan areas into which they tend to migrate.
>
> Second, that these workplaces must be, on average, cheap enough so that they can be created in large numbers without this calling for an unattainable level of capital formation and imports.
>
> Third, that the production methods employed must be relatively simple so that the demands for high skills are minimized, not only in the production process itself but also in matters of organization, raw material supply, financing, marketing, and so forth.
>
> Fourth, that production should be mainly from local materials and mainly for local use.[26]

Clearly, Schumacher wished to conserve what is soundest in the value systems of traditional societies while encouraging the development of an ability to provide greater economic well-being than they have ever known before. This concern is the common thread visible in all the counterestablishment development literature, whether criticizing the practices of advanced or postindustrial societies or the strategies for development that seek to copy them.

One not untypical result of such thinking led, for example, to the experiments with rice farming undertaken by the Japanese philosopher-farmer, Masanobu Fukuoka. Motivated by a deep reverence for nature and a conviction that modern rice-farming techniques violated nature's order far more than was necessary, he successfully attempted to grow rice without engaging in the kinds of backbreaking labor and extensive fertilization procedures that had been thought necessary for centuries. He refused to flood or weed his fields. Instead, he provided weed control as well as nutrients by scattering various kinds of grass seed among the plants. His experiment with natural farming succeeded, he is convinced, because it was in accordance with nature's own principles. As an admiring commentator noted, "humans work best when they work for human good, not for the 'higher production' or 'increased efficiency' which have been the nearly exclusive goals of industrial agriculture. 'The ultimate goal of farming,' Mr. Fukuoka says, 'is not the growing of crops but the cultivation and perfection of human beings.'"[27]

Since the 1992 Earth Summit in Rio de Janeiro, the catchphrase "sustainable development" has suggested the world's acceptance of a new paradigm, one where technologies are employed that are appropriate to the human and nonhuman environment. But five years after the summit, there was little serious renewal of development strategies in keeping with that idea. At Rio, the goal was set for rich countries to devote 0.7 percent of their GDP to development assistance annually. But instead of rising, aid fell from an average of 0.33 percent of GDP in 1992 to 0.27 percent in 1995. The United States devoted only 0.1 percent in that year, the lowest among donor states. To many in the South, the new emphasis seemed a kind of "green colonialism" meant to justify a perpetuation of the economic gap between North and South.[28]

Aid and investment flows from the North did not surge toward the goals of sustainable development. Westphalian shibboleths were raised here too. Some governments in the South claimed sovereignty rights as their justification for exploiting whatever resources they commanded for their own development. Those in the North argued that the proposal for an international tax to be used for sustainable development would infringe on their own sovereign prerogatives. The United States, meanwhile, found that it was unable to meet the goals for carbon dioxide emissions that had been set at Rio, which was tantamount to admitting that its own development, driven by the burning of irreplaceable fossil fuels, was not sustainable.[29]

Now that the greenhouse effect is becoming a widely recognized phenomenon, the mass planting of trees is frequently touted as a simple way of countering rising temperatures and increasing levels of carbon dioxide in the atmosphere. Large-scale tree cultivation may also be seen as an appropriate technology for improving economic well-being on much of the planet. It is cheap to undertake and is labor intensive, with long-term returns that include (in addition to cooling shade) providing populations with food, building materials, water, and topsoil that remains in place for growing and grazing.[30]

Fulfilling Basic Needs

In some respects, the concern with sustainable development is the 1990s variant on a strategy that received its greatest attention some twenty years earlier, which identified fulfillment of people's basic needs as a development strategy. The basic needs approach deliberately relegates the process of large-scale industrialization and development of agribusiness to the background. Its first priority is to provide poor societies with adequate food, shelter, health care, and education. It responds to the problem of dependency by attempting to restore the food independence of many societies where it has been lost thanks to global specialization and the growth of transnational corporations. It is sympathetic, therefore, to demands for greater self-reliance, although in another sense it is more modest in its goals than the schemes for autarkic development of highly diverse industrial economies. Many people associated with this approach call for an agrarian revolution oriented to home consumption, which, they think, can provide the society's basic needs and thus a platform from which to seek higher economic values.[31]

Under Robert McNamara's direction, the World Bank in the 1970s began to associate itself with basic needs strategies, if not to the exclusion of more traditional, capitalist-oriented policies. More attention to subsistence agriculture was meant to help reverse the slide of the world's poorest countries into ever greater dependency on the vagaries of the world market. Yet after a decade of this increased orientation, both inside and outside the World Bank, obvious success stories were hard to find. Overall, the gap between the richest and the poorest societies continued to widen. Two third world countries whose governments had gone farthest to cut their ties to the international economic system—Tanzania and Burma—appeared to suffer much greater impoverishment than countries that did not go so far. During the 1980s, Tanzania took halting steps to reestablish greater economic ties to the outside world while Burma's decline contributed to a cycle of civil unrest and ruthless political repression that further worsened the plight of its citizens. Also during the 1980s, the World Bank shifted its emphasis back to stimulating the private sector through its new development loans, which represented a return to more traditional liberal economic policies.

Even as the basic needs approach was receiving its widest hearing, many criticized its goals. They argued that in addressing the issue of dependence and skewed efforts at industrialization, the approach was really little more than a design for keeping poor nations relatively poor. If one of its principal goals was the reinvigoration of subsistence agriculture, then the dramatic increases in living standards that accompany Western-style growth would be deferred forever. Even if basic needs strategies were to succeed, so this argument went, the result still would not be the enrichment of societies much beyond the level they had attained in the past. The gap between North and South would remain. But it would become not only one of wealth but also one separating two worlds: one rich, highly skilled, and increasingly integrated, and the other still poor, backward, and perpetually divided within itself.

This record suggests why the idea of sustainable development is largely replacing the basic needs approach, at least as a rhetorical strategy, at present. Both purport to address at least two problems that remain intractable, namely, how to reinstate a measure of self-sufficiency to a society that has become dependent on economic decisions made from afar, and how to avoid the dislocations, injustices, and environmental threats that have accompanied Northern-style development even in some countries where that effort may be counted a success (as we shall see next).

Given the current absence of solutions to these problems, it is doubtful that we have yet heard the last of developmental policies oriented toward avoiding, if not resolving, these problems.

New Industrialization in the South

In recent decades, development has taken off for a few countries in ways that seem to defy developmental pessimists. Newly industrialized countries (NICs) have emerged from the ranks of the chronically poor. Hong Kong, Singapore, South Korea, Taiwan, Brazil, and Mexico achieved NIC status in the 1970s, although the latter two countries were badly caught up in debt and balance-of-payments problems in the 1980s. By the 1990s, many analysts added China, Indonesia, Malaysia, and Thailand to this list.[32] By 1998, however, several of these Asian states had experienced severe reversals, including the flight of investment capital, that threatened to infect the global economy after choking off their own rapid growth. For most of the previous decade, nonetheless, all of these states had seen their gross national products and exports grow at unprecedented rates. Still, their paths out of poverty were varied and often troublesome when examined in terms of their domestic social impact. Where per capita income has grown through the application of more or less orthodox development strategies, as in the Latin American nations, the flight to the cities has created new social problems—overcrowding and greater stratification—even as it has heightened the country's sensitivity to the growth and recession cycles of Northern economies and to the whims of foreign investment. The near collapse of Mexico's peso in December 1994 was triggered by the rush of foreign investors to sell their holdings out of distrust of the new government's monetary policies. Where labor-intensive industrial development produced dramatic results, as in several Asian countries, it was made possible through the control and, as 1998's crises proved, sometimes the corruption of centralized and authoritarian government policy.

The experiences of the NICs provide late-twentieth-century examples of the kinds of experiences a number of European states underwent in their own rapid development of about a century ago.[33] We should be heartened to note that the sharp inequalities and injustices that often accompanied developmental takeoff in Europe have been much reduced in the decades since. Nonetheless, for a number of the NICs today, it is the old lesson that is evident in the pains that are accompanying economic development: Solutions to some of the problems of poverty do not solve all problems of human well-being and in fact may create new ones. The search for convergent solutions to social problems continues even when the stakes and the problems themselves change.

For one example, recently arrived laborers in Mexico City may enjoy twice the income they had in the countryside. But their new environment may leave them isolated and bereft of the kind of social support they once had from their villages. They may be subjected to increased health hazards from the capital's pollution and may not be able to find adequate nourishment and housing in a city that grew too fast to meet everyone's needs for food and shelter. Or this: Indian communities of the Amazon are being threatened by Brazil's determination to exploit the vast natural resources of the basin, which include gold, silver, oil, iron ore, and bauxite. Logging and burning in the Amazon rain forest, the largest rain forest in the world and a vital source of oxygen for the planet, are encouraged at a rate that will transform this region into a desert within thirty years. Yet the immediate economic development imperatives are so great that the Brazilian government has refused offers for international protection of its environment in return for reducing repayment of its foreign debt, which in 1989 stood at more than $110 billion.

As other countries try to emulate the NICs, their successes will spawn comparable side effects, which include extending economic stratification across the globe. The growing wealth of the Asian NICs, in particular, has drawn them further into the dominant economic system of the North and away from a unity of interests with the poorest nations of the world. These relatively wealthy countries are able to obtain the private investment capital of the North, whereas the poor have virtually no access to commercial credit. Meanwhile a number of states—members of the Organization of Petroleum Exporting Countries (OPEC) being the prime examples—that looked as if they were enriching themselves dramatically in the 1970s fell back in the next decade along with declining oil prices. In the same period, and in spite of enormous efforts to copy the success of the NICs, no other nation succeeded in joining their ranks.[34] The number of NICs did grow again in the recovery years of the 1990s. Yet many were doubtful that the list could continue to expand very greatly. Long-term changes in the global economy still worked against countries unable to diversify their exports, and the consumption demands of the fastest-growing economies were too great to be sustainable indefinitely into the future. These and interrelated factors should cause some skepticism about the easy or inexorable emergence from poverty of much of the third world in the years ahead.

New solutions create new problems, which are becoming the thorny legacy of development today. Yet development, defined as the escape of more and more human beings from the inhuman poverty to which their ancestors have always been subjected, is and must remain a central world order goal.

North-South Investment and Trade

The globalization of economic life that is so much a part of our present is deeply rooted in the past. One reflection of this long-standing trend has been the enormous twentieth-century increase in the amount of foreign direct investment (FDI)—that of the private sector—moving from country to country. In spite of that trend, the poorer societies of the South have experienced a continual *decrease* over most of the century in the percentage of FDI they have received from the North. In 1914, FDI in less developed countries amounted to 60 percent of the total investment worldwide; by the 1960s, it was reduced to 30 percent of the total; in the mid-1980s, it was down to one-quarter of total foreign investments.[35] In the 1990s, that long pattern of decline at last began to be reversed, heartening those who saw a new post–cold war paradigm for development (albeit one shaped far more by the profit motive than by reasoned social policy). FDI from North to South stood at $26 billion in 1989. It more than tripled during the first half of the 1990s.

Nonetheless, that trend was perhaps not as positive as these figures might suggest, for two reasons. One was that official development assistance (ODA; assistance from governments) was in gradual decline during that same period. FDI surpassed ODA in 1991. By 1995, 72 percent of the capital invested in developing countries came from the private sector. The other reason was that the ten largest developing country recipients of FDI in this period were states that were already counted as NICs or were close to entering that select company. Among them were China, the largest recipient of FDI in this group, followed by Singapore and Mexico, with Indonesia in tenth place.[36] These countries experienced some of the most rapid rates of growth in the world. A number of them were under authoritarian rule.

The countries of sub-Saharan Africa, whose economies were least likely to attract FDI, were left almost entirely out of this rise in investment. Consequently they were dependent on ODA for, in some cases, their survival. This region, excluding South Africa, had a collective debt of $180 billion in 1994, triple the 1980 total and actually exceeding its annual output of goods and services by 10 percent. The debt service payments of these countries came to about $10 billion annually, which, as one analyst noted, is "about four times what the region spends on health and education combined."[37]

World trade too has increased dramatically in this century (with the exception of the 1930s, when trade sharply declined). World exports as a percentage of global GNP increased from 8 percent in 1950 to nearly 20 percent in 1992.[38] As we have seen, the rise of the NICs is largely explained by the huge increases in their export earnings as they stepped up their share of world trade. But the story has been quite different for the poorer countries of the South. Their raw materials, which were once so essential to the industrial machine of the North, tend to be less so as synthetics are developed. Moreover, these nations constitute a shrinking market for the products of the North. In 1950, more than 30 percent of the

North's exports were to less developed states; by the late 1960s, that share had declined to less than 20 percent. There it stayed until the early 1990s, when it once again increased, to just over 20 percent.

More hopeful signs appeared in the generally prosperous mid-1990s. In 1994 and 1995, the forty-eight poorest countries—those classified as "least developed" by the United Nations—saw their gross domestic products grow by some 3 percent. That growth was due to a renewed upturn in commodity prices, greater stability for some of these countries, and cooperative weather.[39] It is too soon to say whether or not these positive but slight indicators suggest that the endemic problems of poverty in Southern societies are beginning to be overcome.

The Economic Development of the North

Most of the dialogue about economic development since the end of World War II seems to have been predicated on the assumption that the globe was divided between a rich Northern sector, which had already "arrived" at its developmental goals, and a poor South, which had not. That depiction of reality has always been much too simple for a variety of reasons, some of which have been alluded to earlier in this chapter. But even after we have noted the enormous and growing gap between rich and poor, even after we have acknowledged that the problems of value realization faced by the truly destitute are of an entirely different order from those of the rich, it is still the case that no Northern society is immune from "developmental" problems of its own. In an increasingly interdependent world, those problems too affect the well-being of many persons both within and beyond the borders of Northern countries.

This is a matter that Americans began to see in the 1980s with regard to their own nation. The prosperity of the United States in that decade was made possible by deficit financing and the increased ownership of the U.S. economy by foreign investors. Both trends eroded the freedom of U.S. decisionmakers, for they made it ever more difficult to initiate the kinds of bold (and expensive) programs associated with great power leadership and to maintain broad influence over the policies of others. By 1992, the United States faced a national debt of $3.8 trillion—approximately four times that of ten years earlier—and a budget deficit of $290 billion. Interest payments on the debt were claiming an ever larger share of tax dollars, which, along with the growing political imperative to reduce the deficit, forced cutbacks in federal programs throughout the Clinton years. By 1997, governmental costs—and therefore, spending—constituted a smaller percentage of GDP than they had averaged during the Reagan-Bush administrations, and major new federal initiatives were a thing of the past.[40]

The sluggish growth and high unemployment of the early 1990s plunged the United States into its deepest recession since the Great Depression. Even with recovery and a substantial reduction in unemployment by mid-decade, the disparities in the extremes of wealth and poverty remained. Conditions in the United States increasingly resembled some of the worst poverty of the third world. If homelessness was not yet as great a problem as in Calcutta or Dacca, the potential violence of U.S. ghettos, the waste of lives in drug addiction, and the despair of the inner cities were often worse than anything that existed in Lagos or Manila. The bottom strata of U.S. society lived in a separate world (if frequently only a street or two distant) from the high-rise office buildings, banks, and hotels of the middle and upper classes.

The collapse of the Soviet Union both magnified that late superpower's enormous economic problems and added huge new economic burdens to the successor republics. From Eastern Europe to the Bering Strait, governments wrestled with the unprecedented puzzle of how to turn economies that had long run at the command of government planners into systems responsive to the millions of largely self-interested economic decisions where profit motives are the rule. But the very fragmentation of the old Soviet system also crippled (where it did not completely stifle) the free movement of many goods and services that had helped to build and sustain what had been a leading industrial region. Among the results in the early 1990s were runaway inflation that sent prices for such necessities as food soaring almost out of reach for millions, a thriving black market, and the encouragement of a kind of "mafia economy" beyond governmental control that offered riches to those willing to make a living through illegal actions.

By the mid-1990s, the countries of the former Soviet bloc were having varied experiences in overcoming the problems that accompanied their transition from communism to capitalism. Some, such as Russia, had achieved considerable privatization, but at the expense of growth (minus 4 percent in 1995) and inflation (140 percent). Others—in particular, the Czech Republic, Hungary, Poland, and Slovakia—all had much more vigorous rates of growth and led the way in generally successful transitions. These same countries had no doubt been helped by the association agreements they had held with the EU since 1991, which greatly increased their trade with Western Europe. States that had refrained from major reforms, such as Belarus and Ukraine, tended to have the poorest economic records, whereas the newly independent republics in the Caucasus all suffered economic losses from periodic or continuing warfare. As a whole, the transitioning economies grew more strongly each year from 1996 through 1998. If IMF projections were met, their anticipated rates of growth—some 4.8 percent in 1998—would somewhat surpass those of the OECD countries by that year.[41]

Russia, meanwhile, was gradually securing its seat with the largest industrial democracies. The press began to refer to the group, which convened its 1997 summit in Denver, as the G-8 instead of the G-7. Earlier that year, the IMF had agreed to disburse two delayed payments to Russia, totaling $647.2 million, of its three-year, $10.2 billion loan. While Russia's GDP continued to fall slightly, its foreign trade in 1996 marked a 5 percent increase over the previous year. At Denver, President Clinton pledged to work for Russian membership in the WTO by 1998, and for greatly increased FDI from U.S. investors in Russia during the same period.

At a time when Russia was preoccupied with its nearly desperate economic situation and the United States had its own economic difficulties, other actors were moving to the fore. Japan's growth was most dramatic until the early 1990s, raising that country to the rank of economic superpower. From 1985 to 1987, Japan's total national assets more than doubled, leaping in value from $19.6 trillion to $43.7 trillion. By the latter date, Japanese wealth exceeded that of the United States—a country with more than double Japan's population. During the same three-year period, the total national assets of the United States increased only by some 20 percent, climbing from $30.6 trillion to $36.2 trillion.[42] A decade later, that bubble had largely burst as the Japanese economy retrenched and that of the United States picked up steam. By late 1997, reverberations from Japan's economic problems began to be felt elsewhere in Asia, threatening to shake healthier economies in the West.

With all of these developments, the U.S.-Japanese trade and investment relationship grew increasingly complex. The U.S. economic expansion of the 1980s was heavily fueled by capital investment from Japan (and West Germany). After Tokyo's stock market crashed in 1990, that investment plummeted. Then many who had feared an "invasion" of the United States by Japanese capital longed for more of that capital to help pull the country out of its recession and to continue to finance the U.S. debt. A persistent imbalance in trade between the two nations produced a $66 billion deficit for the United States by 1995, which in turn fueled protectionist sentiments and charges against Japan of "dumping" and other unfair practices to undercut domestic competition. Yet as the opponents of protectionism noted, the lines between foreign and domestic production were becoming increasingly blurred in the U.S.-Japanese economic relationship; for example, Japanese automakers had invested roughly $9 billion in their U.S. automobile plants by the early 1990s, helping to create more than 110,000 U.S. jobs in the process.[43] Throughout the recession that hit Japan in the 1990s, the U.S.-Japanese trade relationship was frequently acrimonious. U.S. officials drew headlines with their charges of unfair Japanese practices that inhibited the sale of U.S. exports in Japan. Meanwhile, the Japanese trade surplus with the United States continued to grow. At a minimum, the relationship was expected to test the dispute settlement procedures of the new World Trade Organization.

The complex interdependence that existed between the United States and Japan increasingly characterized the economic life of all of the world's richer countries. In a relentless quest for ever larger unrestricted markets, a number of Northern states were forming regional trade blocs, both among themselves and with less developed countries. The success of the European Union perhaps served as the inspiration. With the transition of the EU to a single market by 1993, its 345 million people replaced the United States as the world's largest consumer market. At the same time that the EU was completing this final phase of its economic integration, it was opening its borders, as we have seen, to new members and new forms of association. It remains to be seen how that enlargement, combined with integrative action moving at different speeds for older and newer members, will shape the EU over the long run and affect the development of Europe and, indirectly, the world.[44]

Meanwhile, the North American Free Trade Agreement (NAFTA) was being formed. It started in 1989 as an association of the United States and Canada (each of which was already the other's most important trading partner), and Mexico was added in 1993 as the third partner. Within three years, Mexico had become the third-largest trading partner of the United States, with Japan in second place after Canada. The Clinton administration's goal was to expand the trade pact further with other nations in the Americas. Mexico's peso crisis, occurring less than a year after NAFTA took effect, caused that prospect to cool for a time. A mid-1997 report on NAFTA's comparatively modest success in generating jobs and incomes did not encourage those eager to add Chile to the grouping. Chile also considered joining Mercosur, an association that included Argentina, Brazil, Paraguay, and Uruguay. Since the mid-1980s Mercosur has evolved from a free trade association into a customs union. The march toward free trade in the Americas was still moving forward in the late 1990s, although often in fits and starts.

Regional trade arrangements also have made strides in Asia, largely on two fronts. First, starting in 1992, the Association of Southeast Asian Nations (ASEAN) agreed to move toward integration of its economies. Its nine members—Brunei, Burma, Indonesia, Laos, Malaysia, the Philippines, Singapore, Thailand, and Vietnam—are a mix of vigorous NICs and less industrialized countries. The plan calls for the gradual reduction of tariffs among the members to no more than 5 percent by the year 2008. The 1997 admission into ASEAN of Burma, whose government was an illicit military dictatorship, seemed designed to test one of the burning questions of our time: How far can economic modernization proceed in the absence of even minimal political participation? Second, the Asia Pacific Economic Cooperation forum (APEC) has increased in importance since President Clinton made it a cornerstone of his trade policy with the Pacific Rim. Its eighteen members have approved specific measures for freer trade. They agreed in 1994 to remove all trade barriers among them by 2010 for industrialized members and by 2020 for those classed as developing economies.

Much of the impulse that underlies the formation of these regional trade zones is the presumed triumph of economic liberalism in the closing years of the century. But the word "presumed" is an important modifier because of the challenges for resolving divergent problems posed by these developments.

First, the wild dislocations and economic hardships that developed in Russia and elsewhere in the former Soviet system after that system's collapse serve as a reminder that to create a free market where none has existed is a daunting and difficult task. That suggests, second, that these very hardships still could produce reactions that again would impose control from an authoritarian center in the effort to end the anarchy produced by the myriad self-interested choices of individuals. Third, even where long-established free market systems are at the core of emerging free trade areas, the history of liberalism indicates that, just as they have not been panaceas for all those citizens previously included in them, it would be naive to suppose that they will produce unmixed blessings for the less developed countries now to be brought within their compass. Finally, regional trade zones could themselves develop into closed economic systems, competing with each other and thereby dividing up the global market in ways that could reduce the worldwide flow of trade. That could scarcely be counted a triumph for the doctrine of laissez-faire liberalism.

The Dialectics of Global Economics

No aspect of human life seems more fraught with dialectical tensions at every turn than the effort to provide economic well-being for all the world's people. Every set of priorities and every preferred strategy for dealing with global scarcity gives rise to its contradictory opposite. Only dimly do we yet see paths toward reconciling these opposing needs and values in ways that could help minimize the world's distributive injustice. However, a closer look at two of the conflicting configurations apparent in this chapter may reveal some of the signposts pointing to their eventual synthesis.

The first of these centers on the growth in global economic interdependence on the one hand versus resistance to it through national regulatory control on the other. The substantial growth in interdependence in recent decades is largely the product of the ideology and practices of the dominant free enterprise economic system of the North, which in this period has increasingly permitted the invisible hand of laissez-faire to move about the globe far more widely than Adam Smith could have imagined. In the last decade of the century, it was, for the first time, being given scope to operate in all but a comparative handful of states. Yet the very power of globalization adds allure to doctrines of economic nationalism in many quarters, not just the capitals of the southern hemisphere where the NIEO ideology drew most of its support.

The implications of the development debate that dominated most of the past half-century were that the highly developed states of the North supported a global economic ideology cutting right through Westphalian divisions, whereas the less developed countries of the South took strength from the rights and duties Westphalia provided them. It is no contradiction to note that the latter have been strongest at the formal or institutional level of global politics, which gives fullest application to the Westphalian logic of the sovereign equality of states. On the other side, the free market industrialized states have built their economic power essentially by ignoring the logic of Westphalia, which is diametrically opposed to the creation of a global economic system. In this sense transnational corporations are viewed by some proponents of economic liberalism as potentially revolutionary actors in world politics, successfully challenging the economic power of sovereign governments and capable, therefore, of altering the basic nature of international relations.

These highly generalized descriptions suggest that the international economic life of the North, which has become so ascendant since the cold war's end, is therefore revolutionary in its impact on the Westphalian system, whereas the policies of the South, like those of the erstwhile centrally planned economies, have been conservative or even reactionary. If that conclusion seems peculiar, it is because we have not yet brought any questions regarding the *purposes* of economic activity into the equation. They all have to do with the struggle to provide greater material well-being to people; that, in turn, instantly raises issues of relative equity in the distribution of the world's material goods. These are, in short, questions of justice.

The principal argument against laissez-faire economics has always and everywhere been that its effects are unjust in two ways. First, it typically increases the wealth of those who already have more to begin with (ordinarily, those with some form of property) so that even if the energies released by economic activity at the top of the society do eventually trickle down to benefit those at the bottom, they remain relatively no better (and are probably worse) off, whereas the incomes of those at the top continue to soar. Second, its profit motive ensures production of salable goods for consumption but leads to deficiencies in the supply of needed public goods—health, education, public safety, and environmentally sound production policies. As a result, the phenomenon of "private affluence and public squalor" is inherent in any economic system that gives free rein to the laissez-faire impulse.[45] These issues clearly underlay the NIEO critique of the contemporary world economic system, if not that of every economic nationalist. The argument has been fueled by evidence of a continually widening North-South gap in spite of the efforts to close it—always with the policies permitted by the dominant ideology, such as insistence on voluntarism by donor countries, emphasis on the role of private capital, nonpreferential treatment of poor countries in international trade, and so on.

As the inequities widened, the Group of 77 emerged in the 1960s to press for greater distributive justice with the only arrow they could find in their quiver—their formal equality in a system in which they were so materially unequal. In forums like the General Assembly and UNCTAD, the poor have been enfranchised. That at least seems to be the point of the rules for participation in those institutions, and the Group of 77 has pressed that point in its demands on the rich minority. Yet their enfranchisement is not as real as it appears, for these international institutions have been carefully constructed to deprive them of truly legislative power over global society. At this point the rich and powerful minority of states takes refuge in the logic of Westphalia: Their sovereignty cannot be bridged by the votes of other sovereigns; formal participation in the international institution does not confer equal rights to command the world's economic resources. By a historical and natural accident, in this view, some sovereigns are able to command more economic resources than others, but nothing in the Westphalia tradition alone can alter that fact. Rather, Westphalia serves to maintain it.

If we were to imagine a world in which, say, the UN General Assembly had true legislative power, in which majority votes somehow were translated into world law, what would make its authoritative power legitimate in our eyes? For those of us from democratic political cultures, the most important would no doubt be some assurance that it functioned more or less responsively to the needs of the global population. Legitimacy in any representative institution always flows in part from a sense that it truly represents a variety of interests. We are often told that one of the chief flaws in the constitution of the General Assembly, and presumably the main reason for resisting growth in its quasi-legislative power, is the very great inequality in the size and representativeness of the states that sit there. Even apart from considerations of how popular particular governments may be with their own people, we should be leery of legislative power accruing to an institution in which Maldives has a vote equal to that of India, China, or the United States.

Yet that argument ignores the fact that the General Assembly has long since witnessed the emergence of considerable bloc caucusing and voting, one result of which can be seen in the emergence of the Group of 77. Bloc votes typically come far closer to being representative of real populations and their diverse interests than is suggested by the one-state, one-vote formula. To take only the most obvious divisions, which happen to be those that hold most generally in international economic matters, Southern states now number about 130 in the General Assembly, with as many votes. Northern states, including the "transitioning economies" of the former Soviet bloc, have some fifty seats, depending on how all of the latter states from Europe to central Asia are counted. The total population of the South now comes to more than 4 billion, and that of the North, some 1.7 billion. Simple division reveals that every vote cast by the South *as a bloc* may be made to stand for some 31 million people. By the same measure, each Northern vote reflects about 34 million people.

If, as democratic theory suggests, votes in governmental institutions are meant to represent human beings and not land or trees or money, then the insistence of many poor states on democratizing international economic politics takes on meaning beyond the reactionary retreat into an outmoded nationalism such as the champions of interdependence are inclined to assign it. Voting by this measure is far less biased toward the South than the one-state, one-vote analysis alone suggests. This is not to say that the General Assembly as currently structured would make a model international parliament—it still makes the vote of San Marino, with a population of 25,000, the equivalent of China's, with a population exceeding 1 billion. It simply suggests that the third world's demand for greater participation in the effective decisions about allocation of scarce resources supports in general terms notions of how a pluralistic community might be advanced at the global level.

The second major configuration of conflict is that between the growth imperative and the limits of growth. It does not break down as clearly as a debate between North and South, although unquestionably the effects of the growth reached by highly industrialized societies and the voracious appetites of those now joining their ranks have forced us to question its limits. At the moment, the forces appear to be very unequal in that the growth dynamic is still what motors virtually all development efforts, whether in the ever expanding postindustrial economies of the North, in the effort of other Northern states where central planning was recently the rule to increase the production of consumer goods, or in the effort throughout much of the South to emulate the NICs. Yet it is absolutely certain that the limits to growth imposed by nature itself increasingly will shift the balance to the other side, for limitless growth is quite literally unnatural.[46] Our economic activities have not forced us to consider that fact before the recent past, for the simple reason that they did not come close to testing nature's limits.

To the extent that we are now discussing the limits of growth, rich and poor alike still seem to suppose that it is not their own growth but that of the other group that has to be constrained. At least many of the world's poor view with suspicion any arguments from the rich to the effect that the biosphere cannot now support the kinds of wasteful and destructive industrialization processes in the South that the North itself engaged in. If the economic pie is finite, they argue, that does not alter the need of poor countries to have a relatively larger piece of it than they now enjoy. From rich societies, the moral force of this argument for greater equity is not so much denied as ignored because of its implications for their own aspirations for still more. What Ward and Dubos noted a quarter century ago remains true today:

> Whatever their good will, most developed peoples are still affected with one type of "tunnel vision." Although they make up no more than a third of the human race, they find it exceptionally difficult to focus their minds on the two-thirds of humanity with whom they share the biosphere. Like the elephants round the water hole, they not only do not notice the other thirsty animals. It hardly crosses their minds that they may be trampling the place to ruin.[47]

Nothing in human life may be much harder than for people to curb, voluntarily and rationally, their appetites for more of the world's material goods. No society known has yet voluntarily set out to reduce its standard of living. Since any of us will naturally resist the effort to rob us of those things that we enjoy—particularly those that, through technology, provide us with a power over our personal environment such as our primitive ancestors never knew—resistance will no doubt be fierce to any antigrowth tendencies that do not provide us with alternative economic value systems to those of ever greater consumption. In short, the challenge to the affluent today is to find the means to live better with less. That does not need to mean enjoying our lives less. It does mean learning that not every artifact produced by our technology provides greater happiness. The critical point is that if we begin seriously to think about what it means to live in greater harmony with nature's rules, we will find new ideas and relevant values. Once that has happened, the way will be much more clearly pointed toward finding the kinds of changes needed in our economic lives.

We do not begin that effort with an absolutely blank slate, for the traditional economic lives of societies and the increasingly insistent voice of nature already provide us with nonthreatening lessons. Our sternest critics of the growth ideology have understood since early in the industrial age that the kind of power our machine age has given us also has alienated us from nature with dehumanizing effects. The devastation of the environment of Eastern Europe through forty years of Communist rule has been an alarming recent case in point. When we say that the huge scale of much of our economic activity works against nature's demands, we also understand why it is dehumanizing for those caught up in it, for we are part of the natural order. From that starting point we can learn to develop technologies that have a gentler impact on the ecosystem; culti-vate renewable, nonpolluting energy sources, such as wind and solar power; and learn to find greater fulfillment in the free gifts of nature that increasingly are obscured from the view of modern, highly urbanized so-cieties. There is nothing romantic in such views, as suggested by the ad-vocates of unchecked growth, for those who hold them do not advocate turning the clock back to a presumably simpler time. Rather, they strive, in learning from the economic lessons of our premodern history, to har-ness our modern technological skills in ways that can make them work for the development of people, a development that is in harmony with nature.

Toward Greater Global Welfare

Growing awareness of the limits to the kind and scale of growth charac-teristic of the industrial age can gradually build a bridge across the North-South gulf. In fact, its sketch is already being drawn from the in-creasingly complex facts of international economic life today.

The mere fact that opposing visions of economic development grew to shape the international agenda is in one sense merely an indication that development concerns have received attention on a global scale in recent decades for the first time in history. The attention and resulting conflicts have been the first steps toward more effective treatment of our ills. We would do well to remember that when we long for the good old days be-fore these issues loomed so large in international politics. Where new po-litical conflicts come into being, social injustice at last is finding expres-sion through the political system. The interests of particular oppressed groups—whether slaves, untouchables, homosexuals, or women—are not politically relevant as long as their oppression goes unchallenged within the social order (usually meaning unchallenged by the oppressed groups themselves). Once significant challenges arise, what had been out of bounds to political inquiry and adjustment, perhaps for centuries, sud-denly finds its place on the political agenda. What follows is typically a period of struggle between the oppressed and the dominant that gives every indication to many that the community itself is disintegrating. Cer-tainly, a struggle is required to change the traditional social consensus about how some of its members are treated. Certainly, too, the struggle may result in bloodshed, more repression, or a revolution that brings those previously oppressed into the newly dominant position.

To say that a particular social issue, such as the impoverishment of two-thirds of the world's population, has made its way to the world's political agenda is, as we have seen, by no means to guarantee its quick and peaceful resolution. Conflicts no doubt will continue well into the future while some groups rise out of poverty and the plight of others of the world's poor worsens. Resistance to the entreaties of the poor probably will continue from the rich. Yet when we take the long view of this subject, there may be more reasons for hope than despair.

First, with the rapid decolonization of the non-European world after World War II, the Westphalian system was opened up in a way that gave the impoverished a new voice. Although the relevant international institutions through which these voices were heard equally did not grant them equivalent decisionmaking power, their growing insistence that it be given to them probably cannot be resisted forever. Increased interdependence at a multiplicity of levels all combines to make a wider sharing of economic decisions increasingly imperative. Furthermore, the quasi-parliamentary appearance of the international institutions in which economic discussions take place may itself gradually support their evolution into more truly legislative bodies. We live in a world in which most of the states of the globe have long since taken on the trappings—and increasingly, it seems, even the substance—of representative government. In this sense, most of the world lives in a political culture in which such forms of government are perceived as the norm. We may find it increasingly illogical that such comparable forms at the world level should not take on more decisionmaking power.

Second, the presumed triumph of liberalism after the collapse of communism should not hide the fact that even the leading capitalist states have for many decades supported widespread government intervention in their own economies to provide greater distributive justice. Even though in some of them the welfare state has been under attack in recent years, they have scarcely taken up completely laissez-faire policies. The social necessity of governmental intervention to provide greater distributive justice at home is now so widely accepted throughout the North that there is no very good reason why the logic that supports it should not extend to the larger social system of the world. In fact, much of the NIEO program stemmed from exactly such a vision. It called for establishment of the principle of the graduated income tax at a world level in asking for official development assistance commitments from the rich based on percentages of their GNP. Furthermore, as the formerly socialist world is integrated more fully into the global economy—which is occurring rapidly in the 1990s—it is inevitably joining and altering the global dialogue about development. It may not be far-fetched to suppose, in fact, that the addition of these states to the development equation may serve as a catalyst that could help produce a synthesis of accommodation and new understanding.

Third, the pace and power of globalization today is shattering the (never total) ability of governments to control economic life. While that is unsettling for economic statecraft—indeed, unsettling for all those left unprotected from the currently ascendant market forces—it can, with effort, be made to serve many of the larger human interests in two (divergent) respects. On the one hand, it should be possible to make the pluralism of economic decisionmaking that results more responsive to real human needs and imperatives than are those more closely under the control of the state. Governments are partly under siege today because of the ability of the private sector and nongovernmental organizations to provide more efficient and less costly services to people than did governmental bureaucracies. On the other hand, governments must be nudged to concentrate on providing the regulatory protections that enhance social well-being, reining in the injustices of the market so that both sectors—public and private—thrive. Health in both, it seems, will come from a healthy tension between them as coequal contributors to our material happiness.

In the final analysis, the effort to improve economic well-being is mutually enriching in far more than the material sense. Looked at negatively, societies that fail to advance economically or, worse still, fall back while others are making gains are potentially the most dangerous threats to world order values. They are prime candidates for military takeover and harsh repression and, in extreme cases, for violent efforts to improve their situation by attempting to conquer others. That is surely the most potent reason well-to-do societies have for promoting the greater economic welfare of the rest of the world. On the other side of the scale, it is increasingly apparent that the most highly developed societies of the modern age are those least likely to be well served by policies of militarism and territorial conquest. The welfare of postindustrial states hangs on their economic interdependence, that is, on their ability to trade and to provide a wide array of goods and services throughout an ever expanding global market. Some observers go so far as to posit the coming end of war as the result of such development:

> Developed states are unlikely to engage in a modern war with each other directly. The mutually reinforcing reasons are that their wars are too costly and that they need each other for the fulfillment of important interests which can be most adequately achieved by nonviolent methods. Once the developing states reach a sufficiently high level of intensity and diversification of interests, they too will experience similar constraints upon the conducting of wars.[48]

These words form an even more prescient argument as it relates to the current era than they did when written, at the start of the 1980s. The cold war was undermined in large part by the economic imperatives that confronted the creaking and antiquated command system of the Soviets. Those imperatives in a real sense created the conditions that first made possible *perestroika*, with its greater openness to the rest of the world, and then the collapse of the command system itself. Economic modernization for the former Soviet republics must be accompanied by democratization if it is to succeed. Sixty years ago, the Stalinist police could point a gun at a laborer's head and shout, "Dig that canal, comrade!" With that, the country's economic modernization was under way. Today, however, the Russian computer operator cannot be made to do her job with a gun at her back, for she can easily destroy a crucial network of the modern economic system with an unseen act of computer dissidence. The state had better win her voluntary loyalty.[49]

We are still far from the point at which most states have achieved such levels of development that they feel the constraints against repression and violence suggested above. Today, the political conflicts inherent in development problems and strategies are still paramount. These conflicts increasingly will be overcome if we can focus on the appalling consequences of distributive injustice and the gains for other world order values of economic well-being.

Notes

1. The term "third world" reportedly was first used in the 1950s by Alfred Sauvy, who related it to the third estate of the French Revolution, which sought the same rights and privileges as the first (aristocratic) and second (clerical) estates. By analogy, during the cold war period, the United States led the "first world" and the Soviet Union led the "second." See John D. Hamilton, *Entangling Alliances: How the Third World Shapes Our Lives* (Cabin John, Md.: Seven Locks, 1990), p. 7. Today, seeking more value-neutral terms, many refer to the major industrialized states as the "North" and to the less developed countries collectively as the "South," since most of the former are in the northern hemisphere and many of the latter are situated south of the equator. This distinction still amounts to a gross oversimplification, however, since the states of the South today can be divided into several categories depending on their level and type of economic development. One writer describes five separate types of developing countries: (1) high-income oil-exporting countries, such as Saudi Arabia; (2) industrializing economies where statism is strong and indebtedness at relatively low levels (Taiwan, etc.); (3) industrializing economies where the state apparatus is under challenge and/or debt problems are severe (Argentina, Poland); (4) potential new industrializing countries (Malaysia, Thailand); (5) primary commodity producers (sub-Saharan Africa, Central America). See J. Ravenhill, "The North-South Balance of Power," *International Affairs* 66, 4 (1990):745–746.

2. World Bank, *World Development Report 1997* (New York: Oxford University Press, 1997).

3. This is not to say that the new Westphalian order was solely or even primarily responsible for the development of laissez-faire economics, although a number of connections are no doubt likely. As we saw in Chapter 2, the term "laissez-faire" is just as appropriate to describe an international political system built on the absence of a central regulatory authority as it is to label the identical ordering principle of laissez-faire economics. Nonetheless, the principle has acted on conceptually distinct spheres of social life with different consequences at different times. Until the time of Adam Smith and the beginning of the industrial revolution, the chief *economic* thrust of laissez-faire in international *politics* was to bring to the fore mercantilist policies for the encouragement of autarky on a state-by-state basis in Europe. Smith's *Wealth of Nations* was mainly concerned with showing how intrastate economic development could be better fostered by eliminating such governmental regulations in favor of marketplace forces. But the logic of capitalism's "invisible hand" premise clearly has extended beyond national boundaries for highly developed societies. The theory of international liberalism with its espousal of free trade arose in response to that logic once intrastate development had reached a certain level in industrial societies. Today the impulse toward international laissez-faire confronts more autarkic imperatives in less advanced countries for the first time on a global level.

4. The irony of that response is apparent in the following observation: "Nationalism was in fact strengthened by the reformist orientation of modern politics: Franklin Roosevelt, a domestic reformer who tried to put the United States on the road to economic recovery after the Depression, did so at the expense of the international economic and, to some extent, political system. When governments are expected to regulate the economy to obtain maximum welfare for their citizens, they must often slight the interests of economic and political partners" (Richard Rosecrance and Arthur Stein, "Interdependence: Myth and Reality," *World Politics* 26, 1 [October 1973]:4–5).

5. Craig N. Murphy, "What the Third World Wants: An Interpretation of the Development and Meaning of the New International Economic Order Ideology," *International Studies Quarterly* 27, 1 (March 1983):6.

6. Presumably the largest of these for many years was to the Cuban government, by 1983 reportedly amounting to some $4 billion annually. See *New York Times*, August 7, 1983, sec. 4, p. 1.

7. *New York Times*, June 21, 1981, A1.

8. The term "new international economic order" did not come into general usage until the Sixth Special Session of the General Assembly in 1974 when that name was attached to the program of economic reform supported by the third world, parts of which predated that session. See the Declaration of the Establishment of a New International Economic Order (A/Res/3201 [S-VI]) and the Programme of Action on the Establishment of a New International Economic Order (A/Res/3203 [S-VI]).

9. For a sense of Prebisch's contribution, see Luis Eugenio di Marco, ed., *International Economics and Development: Essays in Honor of Raul Prebisch* (New York: Academic, 1972).

10. Non-Aligned Conference, NAC/CONF.6/C.2/Doc. 1/Rev. 3, p. 111.

11. U.S. prosperity was itself made possible largely by foreign investment in its economy during the 1980s. That produced serious new problems for U.S. economic planning; yet, even as the United States became the world's greatest debtor nation, its resulting constraints were generally not comparable to those on third world debtor countries, a fact that seemed further evidence of the central NIEO charge that the existing international economic system was structurally biased in favor of the most highly developed states.

12. Great Britain has not been self-sufficient in food production since it became the first great industrial power, nor are other advanced European countries independent of the need to import food and essential raw materials. The United States has retained a greater measure of self-sufficiency because of its vast size and diversity of resources—the United States and Canada among major industrial powers are also principal exporters of food—although the question of self-sufficiency versus dependence is no doubt more complex than these remarks suggest. On the one hand, the diversification of the economic sector that accompanies industrialization tends to produce greater self-sufficiency in the sense that the generation of wealth is no longer entirely dependent on one or a few economic activities. But on the other hand, advanced industrial countries can maintain their growth only through wider markets, increased consumption, and the search for ever more precious and far-flung resources, all of which make them increasingly dependent on access to the outside world. The United States, for example, did not become dependent on foreign production of oil until the 1970s. By the 1990s, that dependence was vital to the American economy. Without it, the proven oil reserves remaining in the United States—about 35 billion barrels—would scarcely sustain U.S. needs past the end of the century. See Lester R. Brown and Sandra Postel, "Thresholds of Change," in *State of the World: 1987,* ed. Lester R. Brown et al. (New York: W. W. Norton, 1987), pp. 11–12.

13. Non-Aligned Conference, p. 133.

14. The most fully elaborated set of such principles and policies is found in the UN Charter of Economic Rights and Duties of States, which was adopted by the General Assembly in 1974. A/Res./3281 (29).

15. Non-Aligned Conference, p. 118.

16. Murphy, "What the Third World Wants," p. 65. See also Stephen D. Krasner, *Structural Conflict: The Third World Against Global Liberalism* (Berkeley: University of California Press, 1985).

17. According to James H. Michel, chair of the OECD's Development Assistance Committee, the new paradigm meant that "distinctions between East and West, North and South, donor and recipient should become less significant." Quoted in George H. Mitchell Jr., "Economics and Development," in *A Global Agenda: Issues before the 50th General Assembly of the United Nations,* ed. John Tessitore and Susan Woolfson (Lanham, Md.: University Press of America, 1995), p. 114.

18. The note of hope in recent demographic trends was that the rate of population growth was leveling off somewhat in the final decades of the twentieth century. It now might take slightly longer (by 10 to 20 years) for the 4 billion population figure of 1975 to double to 8 billion (early in the twenty-first century) than the 45 years required for the 1930s' 2 billion to double to 4 billion.

19. That proposal is familiar to medical personnel on the battlefield whose limited resources prevent them from treating all casualties effectively. Acting on the principle of triage, they may divide the wounded into three categories: first, those beyond help who must be left to die, ideally with a palliative to ease their suffering; second, those who should survive and recover with the medical assistance available; and third, those who can safely be ignored on grounds their injuries are such that they will recover even without medical attention. Thirty years ago, U.S. writers William and Paul Paddock suggested the triage concept as a policy guide to a U.S. government faced with the prospect of famine in much of the third world. See their *Famine 1975! America's Decision: Who Will Survive* (Boston: Little, Brown, 1967), Chapter 9.

20. The U.S. Department of Agriculture released a study in July 1997 documenting the enormous waste of food—up to one-fourth of the U.S. food supply—annually. The report estimated that in 1995, 27 percent, or 96 billion pounds of food, had been wasted in the United States. *Philadelphia Inquirer*, July 2, 1997, p. A24.

21. Lester R. Brown, *World Without Borders* (New York: Random House, 1972), p. 213.

22. *Fortune*, August 7, 1995, p. E1.

23. Brown, *World Without Borders*, p. 20.

24. Robert Gilpin, "The Politics of Transnational Economic Relations," in *Transnational Relations and World Politics*, ed. Robert O. Keohane and Joseph S. Nye Jr. (Cambridge, Mass.: Harvard University Press, 1970), p. 418. Gilpin himself does not support such a view.

25. See Kathryn Sikkink, "Codes of Conduct for Transnational Corporations: The Case of the WHO/UNICEF Code," *International Organization* 40, 4 (Autumn 1986):815–840.

26. E. F. Schumacher, *Small Is Beautiful* (New York: Harper and Row, 1973), pp. 175–176.

27. Masanobu Fukuoka, *The One-Straw Revolution: An Introduction to Natural Farming* (Emmaus, Pa.: Rodale, 1978). The quotation is from the introduction, by Wendell Berry, p. xii.

28. Gail V. Karlsson, "Environment and Sustainable Development," in *A Global Agenda*, p. 131.

29. In an address to the UN follow-up conference to Rio, on June 26, 1997, President Clinton noted, "Here in the United States, we must do better. With 4 percent of the world's population, we already produce more than 20 percent of the greenhouse gases." *New York Times*, June 27, 1997, A11. He then postponed setting a limit for curbing these gases until the end of the year, when international negotiations on global warming were scheduled to culminate in Kyoto, Japan.

30. Schumacher, *Small Is Beautiful*, pp. 219–220.

31. See Samir Amin, "Self-Reliance and the NIEO," *Monthly Review* 29, 3 (August 1977):1–21, and Johan Galtung, "The NIEO and the Basic Needs Approach," *Alternatives* 4, 4 (March 1979):455–476.

32. Hong Kong achieved its NIC status several decades before it was reincorporated into China in 1997. Taiwan, still officially a province of China, also grew dramatically as a de facto separate economy.

33. As Richard Rosecrance noted in the 1980s, "Nineteenth-century Great Britain and 1930s Sweden did not have quite as much disparity in income before

taxes as contemporary Brazil, but they had more than Argentina, India, and Mexico have today. . . . It was taken for granted in the nineteenth century that the developmental process was one in which the income pyramid temporarily narrowed at the top, at least until income taxes were applied to equalize the differences. It will then be said that many contemporary Third World governments are authoritarian and will not apply such remedies. But nineteenth-century Japan and Germany—to say nothing of Russia and the Austro-Hungarian Empire—were also authoritarian having a small class of landowners and wealthy capitalists controlling politics" (*The Rise of the Trading State* [New York: Basic Books, 1986], p. 52).

34. Robin Broad and John Cavanaugh, "No More NICs," *Foreign Policy* 72 (Fall 1988):81–103. In their words, "The answer lies in far-reaching changes in the global economy—from synthetic substitutes for commodity exports to unsustainable levels of external debt—that have created a glut economy offering little room for new entrants."

35. Rhys Jenkins, *Transnational Corporations and Uneven Development: The Internationalization of Capital and the Third World* (New York: Methuen, 1987), pp. 5, 13.

36. UNCTAD, "Trends in Direct Investment," TD/B/ITNC/2, February 18, 1994, Figure 1.

37. Gary Gardner, "Third World Debt Still Growing," in *Vital Signs: 1995*, ed. Lester R. Brown, Nicholas Lenssen, and Hal Kane (New York: W. W. Norton, 1995), p. 72.

38. Stephen D. Krasner, "Economic Interdependence and Statehood," in *States in a Changing World*, ed. Robert H. Jackson and Alan James (Oxford: Clarendon, 1993), p. 311.

39. UNCTAD, *The Least Developed Countries 1996 Report*, TD/B/42/(2)/11.

40. Senator Daniel P. Moynihan liked to argue that the Reagan-era deficit had been deliberately inspired to thwart the government from initiating new social programs.

41. International Monetary Fund, *World Economic Outlook*, April 23, 1997.

42. Alexander King and Bertrand Schneider, *The First Global Revolution*, A Report by the Council of the Club of Rome (New York: Pantheon Books, 1991), pp. 79–80.

43. Foreign Policy Association, *Election 1992: Guide to U.S. Foreign Policy Issues* (New York: Foreign Policy Association, 1992), p. 36.

44. Within this century, Europeans have gone from controlling more than 84 percent of the earth's land surface to less than 10 percent. Yet most are clearly richer today than at the beginning of this century. That is, at least, a remarkable indication of the change in this period that has moved from pre- to postindustrialism in what accounts for and generates wealth.

45. Barbara Ward and René Dubos, *Only One Earth* (New York: W. W. Norton, 1972), p. 20.

46. In the words of E. F. Schumacher, "Technology recognizes no self-limited principle—in terms, for instance, of size, speed, or violence. It therefore does not possess the virtues of being self-balancing, self-adjusting, and self-cleansing. In the subtle system of nature, technology, and in particular the super-technology of the modern world, acts like a foreign body, and there are now numerous signs of rejection" (*Small Is Beautiful*, p. 147).

47. Ward and Dubos, *Only One Earth*, p. 145.

48. Werner Levi, *The Coming End of War* (Beverly Hills, Calif.: Sage, 1981), p. 15. Rosecrance's *The Rise of the Trading State* is a particularly important contribution to the growing literature on this theme. See also J. M. Owen, "How Liberalism Produces Democratic Peace," *International Security* 19 (1994):87–125.

49. This paraphrases a point made by Michael Harrington in a lecture at Temple University on February 16, 1989.

Suggested Readings

Chan, Steve, ed., *Foreign Direct Investment in a Changing Global Political Economy*, New York: St. Martin's Press, 1995.

Dowd, Douglas, *The Waste of Nations: Dysfunction in the World Economy*, Boulder, Colo.: Westview, 1988.

Gilpin, Robert, *The Political Economy of International Relations*, Princeton, N.J.: Princeton University Press, 1987.

Isaak, Robert A., *Managing World Economic Change*, 2d ed., Englewood Cliffs, N.J.: Prentice-Hall, 1995.

Jenkins, Rhys, *Transnational Corporations and Uneven Development: The Internationalization of Capital and the Third World*, London: Methuen, 1987.

Kapstein, Ethan B., *Governing the Global Economy: International Finance and the State*, Cambridge, Mass.: Harvard University Press, 1994.

Keohane, Robert O., *After Hegemony: Cooperation and Discord in the World Political Economy*, Princeton, N.J.: Princeton University Press, 1984.

Krasner, Stephen D., *Structural Conflict: The Third World Against Global Liberalism*, Berkeley: University of California Press, 1985.

Lenski, Gerhard E., *Power and Privilege: A Theory of Social Stratification*, New York: McGraw-Hill, 1966.

Lipietz, Alain, *Towards a New Economic Order*, New York: Oxford University Press, 1993.

North, Douglass C., *Structure and Change in Economic History*, New York: W. W. Norton, 1981.

Oxenham, John, *Education and Values in Developing Nations*, New York: Paragon House, 1988.

Rubenstein, Richard L., ed., *Modernization: The Humanist Response to Its Promise and Problems*, New York: Paragon House, 1985.

Schaeffer, Robert K., *Understanding Globalization*, Lanham, Md.: Rowman and Littlefield, 1996.

Stiles, Kendall W., and Tsuneo Akaha, *International Political Economy*, New York: HarperCollins, 1991.

Tucker, Robert W., *The Inequality of Nations*, New York: Basic Books, 1977.

Wallerstein, Immanuel, *The Capitalist World-Economy*, Cambridge: Cambridge University Press, 1979.

Weiner, Myron, and Samuel P. Huntington, eds., *Understanding Political Development*, Boston: Little, Brown, 1987.

Weisband, Edward, ed., *Poverty Amidst Plenty: World Political Economy and Distributive Justice*, Boulder, Colo.: Westview, 1989.

CHAPTER 7

The Enhancement of Human Dignity

All human beings are born free and equal in dignity and rights. They are endowed with reason and conscience and should act towards one another in a spirit of brotherhood.

—Universal Declaration of Human Rights, Article 1

The logic of Westphalia suggests that the nation-state is principally what determines whether or not human beings live in dignity and justice. Since the state is by far the most important locus of political power in the world, it must provide security from without and security—in all its implications for the realization of human values beyond the basic one of mere survival—to the members of the society within it. If civilized life requires the protections afforded by the state, then the state must help humanity realize its higher needs and aspirations. Nation-states can have no other justification for their existence.

But this fundamental premise has always been built on a disturbing foundation of wishful thinking. Although it assumes that the state *ought* to enhance the rights of human beings in its jurisdiction, it does not ensure that the state *will* do so. Worse, it fails entirely to address the possibility (indeed, the likelihood, as modern history has shown) that governments may become the greatest violators of the rights of individuals within their control, even to the point of denying many of them the right to life itself. What is justified for its presumed ability to advance human welfare can become the most dangerous enemy of humanity's well-being.

Yet throughout much of the Westphalian period, this wishful thinking could be largely overlooked, for more often than not, people were less repressed by their own governments than they were protected by them.

Their human potential seemed better fulfilled by life within the sovereign state than by a struggle for survival in the hypothetical jungle outside an advanced and organized polity. Had this not been so, the nation-state system probably would not have flourished for more than three hundred years. Material realities and normative standards combined to provide a measure of well-being for individuals within the sovereign state in most times and places.

At the *material* level, even the most autocratic governments of the past did not for the most part have the capacity to terrorize whole populations, to choke off food supplies on a scale to make mass starvation an instrument of policy, or to peer into and control the private lives of most of their citizens. These capabilities have been made available to twentieth-century tyrants as the result of the insidious power available to them from various modern technologies. At the *normative* level, the growth of the nation-state system was accompanied by continual and, in many cases, increasingly successful efforts to create domestic legal systems under which the ruler was made accountable to the ruled. The end result of that process is summed up in the postulate of democratic theory that says that sovereignty in fact resides in the people rather than in the governing elite.[1] That postulate is intended, above all, to ensure that governments shall be the servants of society rather than its capricious masters.

Yet the potential danger to human well-being has always lurked behind all claims to the absolute sovereignty of the state, as finally became abundantly clear in the terroristic and genocidal behavior of twentieth-century governments. The Nazis of Hitler's Third Reich exterminated millions of Jews and other "non-Aryan" peoples legally, that is, through the directives of those authorized to govern the state. The Soviet Union under Stalin institutionalized rule by terror, particularly over those members of the political elite most threatening to Stalin's rule, through political trials and the gulag system. Italian fascism produced a philosophical argument for the state's unlimited power over the individual that theoretically left *all* possibilities for realizing human potential at the whim of the state itself.[2] Out of such experiences was born totalitarianism, the most monstrous challenge to the autonomy of individual persons the world had ever seen.

The Development of International Human Rights Standards

Finally a horrified reaction arose throughout the world to atrocities committed by states that actually attempted to justify such behavior through theories of state absolutism. By the close of World War II, the Allied powers had agreed that a first order of business should be the prosecution of alleged war criminals in Germany and Japan for their violations of international law in both their planning and waging of war, as well as for their crimes against humanity in their treatment of populations under their control.[3] The trials at Nuremberg and Tokyo that resulted were important efforts, however flawed from the standpoint of constituting victors' justice. They asserted that standards did exist prohibiting the unlimited and arbitrary use of governmental power against human beings, whatever the orders of state officials. Many of the civilized standards violated by the war criminals simply had been assumed to exist by generations of officials and the public. Therefore, comparatively few of the crimes against humanity had been codified in generally binding treaties. Prosecutors were forced to rely heavily on various national standards protecting human rights, which together, they argued, formed evidence of a customary international standard. But the ambiguity of that assertion for a determinedly legalist opponent caused many to insist that the time had come to develop treaty commitments that would define world community standards for the rights of all humanity.

Within this context, the organizing conference for the United Nations, which met in San Francisco in 1945, considered the creation of an international bill of rights to be incorporated into the UN Charter, even as such a bill had been attached to the U.S. Constitution before its adoption. In the end, the framers of the Charter concluded that such a bill was too complex for quick formulation. But from almost the moment the United Nations came into being, much of its attention was turned to the issue of creating treaty standards for the protection of various human rights.

As expected, that effort has proved to be neither simple nor noncontroversial, most basically for two reasons. First, it is a clear and direct challenge to statist assumptions of sovereignty, for above all it implies the sovereignty of all members of the species above that of individual governments, reminding states that they and not human beings are the abstractions that must be made to advance human welfare. Second, the articulation of universal standards inevitably requires agreement on specific values relevant to the advancement of human well-being. But that agreement is not easily reached in a world where competing ideologies about what is best for humankind reflect different political and social priorities, too often even serving to hide perceptions of our common humanity.

Other complications have followed from these two most basic ones. For example, the temptation is often irresistible for a government to point the finger of blame for human rights violations at its opponent and to overlook injustices to individuals within its own jurisdiction. Even governments with relatively good records in enhancing human rights may, as a result, fear that submitting to international standards will make that record something of a political football to its opponents, thus inducing them to shy away from international obligations.[4] In addition, the process can lead to cynicism when governments with little to applaud in the human rights field submit to international standards in the expectation that they will not really be called to account, except perhaps rhetorically, for their behavior. The Westphalian state remains too hard-shelled for easy penetration from the world community to correct unjust treatment of individuals or groups within. The international system itself invites self-righteousness in the assertion of a government's adherence to human rights, for government leaders know a state is unlikely to be challenged effectively. Conversely, it may withdraw from the fray on grounds that it will be the object of political attacks from without rather than judicious and objective judgments of its real performance.

Despite these difficulties, the creation of international standards that articulate acceptable treatment of individuals and groups has proceeded apace over the past several decades. As a result, a sizable body of treaty law has come into existence, which in toto amounts to a remarkable agreement by the representatives of world society about how human beings ought to be permitted to live their lives.

The first historic step toward consensus was the adoption by the UN General Assembly, on December 10, 1948, of the Universal Declaration of Human Rights. No member state at the time voted against the goals it espoused, and in the years since, the precepts it contains have taken on greater norm-setting importance in two ways. First, at the informal level of value formation, the Universal Declaration has remained an attractive magnet for all groups, by no means limited to governments, interested in asserting their aspirations for the decent treatment of human beings. Constant reiteration of its precepts over time has had a discernible effect, in itself, in adding to their stature, their perceived authority as obligatory standards. Over the years, too, citation of the Universal Declaration has been accompanied by numerous other declarations and resolutions, often in the General Assembly, that proclaim acceptable standards of behavior regarding specific aspects of the treatment of humans.

That informal value formation has been supported by the second kind of evidence of the growing strength of these standards. In the years since 1948, a great many states have accepted legally binding obligations through formal conventions that include the concepts of the Universal Declaration.[5] Out of the UN context have come the International Covenants on Civil and Political Rights, and on Economic and Social Rights, both of which entered into force in 1976. Together they make up the explicit obligatory instruments embodying the standards of the Universal Declaration. By the 1990s, a substantial majority of states had signed or ratified these two covenants. Other treaties containing very broad sets of obligations are applicable to limited groups of states, most notably, the European Convention for the Protection of Human Rights and Fundamental Freedoms (which entered into force in 1953) and the American Convention on Human Rights (which entered into force in 1978). Moreover, a great many limited-purpose conventions are now in effect to afford protection against a considerable variety of human rights issues, such as those prohibiting forced labor and racial discrimination, providing equal rights for women, and the like. Many of these treaties contain supervisory and enforcement provisions that, at a minimum, require signatories to submit annual reports to international bodies on their compliance with the relevant human rights standards. As a result, concrete attention to the ways in which humans are treated across much of the globe have become the routine business of the world community.

In the words of one authority assessing the results of this situation as of 1982,

> no matter what their practices, governments throughout the world have accepted the norms embodied in the many international declarations and conventions that have been adopted by international institutions as a legitimate definition of the conditions of human dignity and justice. About half of the sovereign states that comprise the global system, including within their borders more than half the world's population, have explicitly formally agreed, by signing or ratifying the relevant conventions, to be judged by the standards that have been set forth.[6]

Those facts are impressive in themselves, but the implications are greater even than that: "By according these standards legitimacy in international fora, the remaining states have implicitly accepted them as appropriate criteria for their judgment." That is, a genuine worldwide *consensus* has been emerging in recent decades on explicit and wide-ranging standards for the acceptable treatment of human beings. That consensus does not reflect perfect agreement as to priorities, as charges of cultural biases still abound in some human rights discussions. But neither can states any longer hide behind sovereignty doctrines to ignore the authority of these standards.

What Are Human Rights?

As the representatives of governments have struggled to create the conventions and declarations setting forth these standards, they have been forced to probe deeply into what it means to talk about, let alone protect, such a concept as human rights. People reared in the Anglo-American political culture are probably inclined to suppose that rights are those human demands that no government can take from us, that are "unalienable," in Thomas Jefferson's classic description. Americans are informed by the first ten amendments to their Constitution that they have a right to free speech, to freedom from false arrest, to keep and bear arms—all of which are limitations on the powers of their government over them. So a right is likely to appear to Americans to be some kind of guaranteed freedom *from* governmental interference in their lives.

These examples suggest that when we use the term "right," we are referring to particular human values that we regard as so fundamentally important that they must be upheld if we are to achieve what we regard as our essential aspirations within the social order. Such a conception is useful inasmuch as it need not address arguments as to *where* rights come from, from God or nature, as the natural law tradition supposes, or from their authoritative establishment by states, as strict positivism suggests. These are not trivial differences of viewpoint, as has been made dramatically clear by the horrendous deprivations of human rights in our time by state actors asserting their unaccountability to any authority higher than their own. Rather, a value-based conception of human rights helps us to focus on rights as human aspirations and then explore differing views as to the relative importance of various human goals, wants, and needs.

If rights are defined as those fundamentally important human values that must be secured if others are to be sought, does this mean that rights are restricted to the base values that must be maintained for every human being—the minimal needs of food, shelter, and clothing that are essential to survival? That is obviously not the assumption that underlay the traditional U.S. conception; indeed, the Bill of Rights does not even mention a right to, say, an adequate food supply for every citizen, sufficient clothing, or sound housing. Yet we know that arguing the benefits of freedom of the press is not very satisfying to individuals whose families are starving to death. They will regard the need for food as more important than their ability to read uncensored news. Why then did America's founders fail to address these basic rights—survival values—while granting constitutional protection to what must be considered certain of the higher values?

Several explanations are possible. First, the U.S. republic was not created, metaphorically speaking, out of a state of nature. The level of social and economic development in the United States at the time the Constitution was adopted was such as to make it reasonable to suppose that survival needs already were generally secured or that they could be through the creative initiative of each able-bodied citizen. That latter possibility leads directly to the second explanation, namely, that Lockean and Enlightenment precepts about the creative potential of unrestrained human beings dominated the thinking of the time. It was regarded as more important to get the government out of the way of the people, so that the people could provide for their own material needs, than to commit the government to providing them, no doubt at the expense of greater individual freedom. The third explanation for the limited content of the U.S. Bill of Rights is inherent in the second: The founding fathers were much more preoccupied with how to limit a capricious and authoritarian government from interference with the higher aspirations of its citizens than they were with giving it the kinds of commitments to intervene in the social order that, they feared, would encourage the growth of too much governmental power.

All of these arguments are familiar, but they are repeated here as a reminder of the fairly limited and special conception of human rights in the U.S. context. One additional conclusion can be drawn: The U.S. conception of rights typically sees them as the equivalent of ironclad guarantees. Since they are prohibitions on the government, they can be secured as long as that government is committed to honoring them. Their achievement requires no outlay of governmental funds, no hiring of workers, no governmental action of any kind. Rather, they are secured specifically by nonaction from the government. Although the history of the United States makes clear that constant vigilance by private citizens, courts, and all others sworn to uphold the Constitution is needed to prevent both officials and private citizens from infringing on these rights, the fact remains that it is almost certainly easier to secure and maintain these kinds of rights than to guarantee that no child within a polity shall suffer malnutrition, that every citizen shall be adequately housed, or that all who are capable of work shall have useful and remunerative work to do.

Many societies do not fully share the Western conception of human rights. More precisely, if these rights are regarded as the fundamentally important values in many Western states, deserving of the name "rights," they have not been so regarded by many, even though they may be widely considered as desirable values for a society that has the luxury to promote them. Socialist ideologies have tended to reverse the relative priorities, insisting on the fundamental importance, to the point such matters should be considered as rights, of securing basic needs for all members of the society, even if this required a large measure of governmental intervention to ensure such things as distributive justice. Indeed, all socialist thought arose as a critique of what were perceived to be the injustices and inequalities perpetuated by political liberalism. Socialism's Marxist strain, in particular, has tended to regard Western-style rights as essentially serving the interests of a dominant capitalist class, since that class need not worry much about its survival needs and instead will benefit most from keeping its government from interfering in its entrepreneurial activities.

What is described here is a generational shift from emphasis on individual rights in the revolutions of the late eighteenth century in America and France to social rights in, especially, the Soviet, Mexican, and Chinese revolutions of the early twentieth century.[7] Yet as the political systems resulting from both sets of revolutions have matured, they have tended to extend the kinds of protections to their citizens each had previously been charged with neglecting. That evolution toward a more universally understood experience of human rights has been clouded by the ideological charge and countercharge of the past. Now, although it is far from complete, a wider consensus on standards and protections is at last a real prospect.

For a start, every major Western democracy has moved to implement substantial numbers of welfare values during the twentieth century. They generally have chosen to regard these protections as matters of legislation rather than constitutional guarantees. But no one in the democratic West seriously supposes that such matters as minimum-wage standards, the right to bargain collectively, health and medical provisions, or old-age security are not now fully embedded in the fabric of protections we expect from our governments. Western democracies clearly regard governmental support of these kinds of basic values as fundamentally important, even if they do not always choose to define them as rights.

Conversely, almost everywhere that socialism retains influence today, it has reaffirmed its support for the traditional libertarian rights once associated largely with the West. This has long been true where social democratic parties have governed in the highly developed societies of Europe. With the collapse of the Soviet Union, it is now also the case, if more tentatively, across most of the vast region that made up the Soviet bloc. Indeed, the end of the cold war seemingly produced the triumph of democratic values on a scale never before reached in the world's history; single-party rule—often that of ostensible socialists—also began to crumble in other regions, including much of Africa and Asia. That suggested to some a convergence on civil libertarian principles and values that foreshadowed an end to real conflict over the goals of civilized government.[8]

Yet such a view seemed to flow from a naive assumption that humanity's life on earth was somehow transcending social conflict and, therefore, politics itself. Evidence abounded in the closing years of the century of the continuing abuse of higher human values. The crackdown at Tiananmen Square in the spring of 1989 was one shocking reminder that determined political elites could still repress citizens who had absorbed civil libertarian values. In contrast, a reaction against social democracy in some Western states brought a widening gap between the richest and poorest members of these societies, along with unprecedented numbers of children living in poverty, a rise in homelessness, and the growth of an ever more desperate urban underclass. And where governments themselves were no longer able to provide security because they had tottered or collapsed, the basic right to life itself was too often violated as a consequence of the very competition between rival groups for power.

Considering rights as nothing more or less than fundamentally important human values allows us to see more clearly why the relative priority given them in various societies will very likely reflect the level of a society's economic and social development. The fulfillment of basic needs, no doubt, should constitute a real priority for the governments of impoverished societies. Ideally, we may wish that these values would be advanced without simultaneously denigrating the higher aspirations that allow individuals to realize as much as possible of their human potential free from authoritarian restrictions. But we should at least not be surprised or unduly critical of governments that may inhibit fulfillment of some of the higher values in the interest of securing basic values for all members of their societies.[9] In the imperfect material world in which we live, such judgments must weigh relative costs and benefits to all. The matter of balancing human freedom against governmental protection to support minimal human needs is at the very core of those social problems requiring divergent solutions, solutions that must constantly be reexamined to meet the evolving technological and desired situation.[10]

In spite of current tremors and reversals—the timidity of the West in its effort to halt the atrocities associated with the Bosnian war is a case in point—future generations may nonetheless look back on our era as one in which a seismic shift occurred toward the wider sharing of some fundamentally important human values. If so, it is a shift produced by far greater interaction among the world's peoples than has ever before occurred in human history, resulting in an ever wider sharing of material goals, outlooks, and behaviors. In such an analysis, even the bloody repression at Tiananmen Square may come to be seen as an exception that proves the rule. For China, that event may have been the last, desperate reaction of aged leaders whose authoritarian regime might not long outlive them, thanks to the profound economic and social changes that they themselves unleashed and that continued after 1989. The real lesson may be the one learned by the last generation of Soviet leaders, that neither the Soviet Union nor China could become truly productive in this late-twentieth-century stage of its development without the kind of increase in the dignity and well-being of its citizens that can come only with greater political and civil rights.[11]

Government Violations of Individual and Group Rights

Because tragic setbacks in human rights protections have marred dramatic instances of progress in recent years, we may feel cynical about the real value of international efforts in the human rights field. Great powers whose moral leadership of others is meant to rest mainly on the acceptability of their treatment of those they govern have conducted brutal foreign interventions with methods that too often have produced extreme violations of the human rights of others, conduct that they would not likely try to justify in the treatment of their own citizens. Do such developments suggest that efforts to define acceptable standards of conduct toward individuals throughout this period have been in vain? Before seeking an answer, we need to try to assess the characteristic causes and features of human rights violations by sovereign governments today.

We should remember that *all* government is more or less restrictive of individual freedom, seeking, in the interests of the whole society, to restrain the untrammeled liberty of each one of us to do exactly as we please. In that process, government—*all* governments—necessarily promotes and protects some human values and the values of some people within the society more fully than it does others. Decisions as to the allocations of values are at the very core of the political process. A society in which no arguments remained as to which should be advanced would be, by definition, a utopian society. In the real world of conflicting social interests, no such condition has been attained, except, arguably, for brief periods within very small groups of people who largely cut themselves off from the larger society, maintaining their isolation because of their prior commitment to the same values.

In larger societies, such as nation-states, the justification for a pluralistic democracy is that it permits a great amount of competition for the allocation of values among diverse groups, based as pluralism is on a conviction that no individual or group of individuals can ever be in sole or final possession of the truth about what is good for the society as a whole. The results of such competition can never be wholly satisfactory to all, or even to any, members of the society. But in protecting the right to compete through the political process, democratic societies strive to keep repression of particular groups to a minimum and thereby to open the possibilities for human aspiration and advancement to all. To the extent that democratically governed states achieve the consent of the governed, they presumably do so because of the people's confidence that value competition will be maintained through the political process, which potentially can be made to serve them.

The argument against authoritarian regimes is that they suppress that competition, enshrining some social values at the expense of others, maintaining social order in patterns acceptable to the governing elite at the expense of justice for those within the social system whose lives are degraded as a result. The more authoritarian a regime is, the more it represses the goals of any within the society who are not themselves served by maintenance of the elite in power. Such a government's authority rests not on consent but on its ability to maintain control over potentially disaffected groups.

The ethnic conflicts that emerged with the coming of glasnost in the last years of the Soviet Union were an especially vivid—if, at first glance, apparently paradoxical—lesson about the challenge many states pose to the rights of ethnic and cultural groups combined under their rule. They told us, first, that government does not merely restrict the freedom of individuals in various ways; it restricts the freedom and power of groups within the state unequally. This is a fact that has been masked by Westphalia's often very tenuous linking of sovereign statehood to what is presumably a single nation but is often in reality a congeries of status groups, different in culture, separate in organization, and unequal in resources.[12] As was clearly illustrated with the collapse of the Soviet empire, some of these status groups have been inferior to others. National unity thus may hide "subnational" diversity that when allowed to express itself speaks of injuries to important human values.

The second part of the lesson from the former Soviet world is that the end of the empire produced a centrifugal effect, spinning off repressed demands for ethnic rights that still threaten the integrity of successor states, from Russia through the Caucasus republics and beyond. Human rights in such situations are in double jeopardy: As the minority nationality attempts to assert its right to greater equality with the dominant ethnic group, it may trigger a repressive backlash from a governmental elite unwilling to lose control over a social order that seems to be disintegrating.

The tendency to deal harshly with dissident minority groups is of course greatest in authoritarian societies. Kurdish populations in Iraq and Tibetans under Chinese rule have found their demands for greater freedom ruthlessly suppressed in recent years. But just as troubling is the evidence that the governments of democratic and pluralistic societies also lose their bearings and turn most repressive when they feel compelled to reassert control over dissident minorities. The government of India was not above storming the Golden Temple at Amritsar and killing many Sikhs charged with plotting separatism. And more than once, the British government has had to answer charges that certain of its laws enacted to aid police in the suppression of Irish separatism in Northern Ireland were in violation of the European human rights convention. In classifying states, we have customarily distinguished between the self-governing nation that may happen to contain minority groups and the imperial power that quite clearly has imposed its rule over alien peoples. Now that anti-imperial values are dominant in the late twentieth century, conventional wisdom says that rule by the former is more benign than the latter. Yet when it comes to the impact on the subordinate group of rule by a dominant class or nationality, the distinction may be blurred, as all these examples show.

Recent Trends in State Responsiveness to Human Rights

The only progressive alternative to governmental repression is the encouragement of self-help and self-expression that is tolerant of the rights of others. That explains the importance of restraining governments through an emphasis on the political and civil rights of individuals. But without minimal economic and social well-being throughout a society, such restraints will seem far less meaningful and, where they exist, far more fragile than in a state where greater social justice is the rule. So the sturdy democracy in today's world is a society with safety nets for its most seriously disadvantaged and tangible economic and social opportunities for the members of its underclasses. That is a lesson that, in spite of periodic political reactions that seek to deny it, is no doubt widely understood and deeply embedded in the thinking of political elites in the Western democracies. Now we are learning that the converse may also be true: The postindustrial economy, if it is to become truly sturdy and vigorous, demands more meaningful political participation—and more self-help—than has traditionally been permitted in a centrally planned economic system.

For the most highly developed societies on earth, we can begin to see that a common stage may soon be set for the first time in the modern age, a stage characterized not by a nearly exclusive attention either to political and civil rights or to economic, social, and cultural rights, but to both. That convergence is by no means in place yet. It is still a matter of contest and, perhaps, continuing polar swings in some of the states that were once under Soviet domination. It continues to meet resistance on the part of many in the United States and in parts of Western Europe. There is nothing inevitable about its success. And even if it does proceed among the most advanced postindustrial states, it may do little to touch the problems of grinding poverty and ruthless oppression in other parts of the world. Even though remarkably important democratic reforms have begun to take root in a number of countries in recent years, the world's continuing failure to improve economic well-being in many of the poorest countries makes these developments still tenuous.[13] What follows is a sketch of recent trends in a number of states that appear to affect human rights most directly, starting with the comparatively rich countries of the northern hemisphere.

In *Western Europe*, the fragile democracy established in *Portugal* and *Spain* in the 1970s grew strong and secure by the 1990s. Both nations, along with a redemocratized *Greece*, were members of the European Union. Developments in these countries suggested that the EU itself seemed to have become a major instrumentality of civil and political rights across Europe. Membership in the Union demanded the existence of a pluralistic, libertarian polity as a prerequisite to joining in the EU's generally liberal economic policies. With the collapse of the Soviet empire, the EU was suddenly a beacon to states to its east. If, as expected, a much expanded European Union is the eventual result, it presumably will be built by casting a much wider net to advance and protect the human rights long associated with the West.

The experience of European integration may be instructive in another respect. Fractious conflicts between majority populations and minority ethnic groups seem actually to be diminishing as the integration of the larger whole continues. Perhaps the pluralism of that process is the key. Over the past two decades, a number of minority communities—including the Scots and Welsh in Great Britain, Basques in Spain, the Flemish and Walloons of Belgium—have been given a greater voice in running their own affairs. Through most of that same period, vigorous economic growth has helped "to lift all boats" so that material gains have been felt by minority as well as dominant groups within the EU membership. Even the more complex effort to resolve the "troubles" in Northern Ireland may have been given a push by the rising prosperity of both Protestant and Catholic communities there. This experience suggests that the long-term solution to the ethnic conflicts that have broken out in Eastern Europe and elsewhere may lie only in more pluralistic governance combined with a sustained and widely shared increase in economic well-being.[14]

The experience of the *United States* in the last quarter of the century also showed the social pitfalls on the path to material enrichment. After the "stagflation" of the 1970s, the early 1980s brought strong economic growth overall for the United States. But it was achieved through a marked increase in social and economic disparities. Although incomes for the richest 10 percent of Americans rose steadily, a total of 32.5 million, or some 15 percent of the population, were living below the officially defined poverty line. That group included one-fifth of all the children in the nation and one-third of all African-Americans. A huge increase in school dropouts, teenage pregnancies, homelessness, and rampant drug abuse caused some of the most serious social problems of the period. All were human rights deprivations due to neglect, not the repression of the mailed fist. By the end of the decade, what was to become the most sustained recession since World War II no doubt deepened the misery of those already sunk in poverty, spreading it upward.

All these factors set the stage for the most destructive explosion of urban unrest in the nation's history. The Los Angeles riots of April 1992 erupted after several white police officers were acquitted of charges that they had used excessive force in nearly beating to death a black man while taking him into custody. As economic growth returned to the United States in the 1990s, the social disparities of the country seemed largely untouched. Many corporations downsized drastically while reaping high profits; their executives drew multimillion-dollar salaries while the poor were cut from relief rolls by changes in the welfare system. Laws helping minority groups to find education and employment came under increasing attack. Under such conditions, social solidarity remained fragile, as was tacitly acknowledged by President Clinton when he launched discussions on racial issues during his second term.

Within a year after the death of the *Soviet Union,* which came on December 31, 1991, political and civil liberties had been formally extended across much of the vast region in the collapse of the repressive Soviet system. Struggling at times against difficult odds, they generally were becoming rooted as the decade lengthened. The forms of political democracy were established everywhere, including, most importantly, in *Russia,* where the first popularly elected head of state in that country's long history, President Boris Yeltsin, was the chief hero in rallying opposition to the would-be coup in August 1991 against Mikhail Gorbachev and his policies of *perestroika.*[15]

Yet Russia and, in varying degrees, all the other former Soviet republics were confronted with two massive sets of problems that challenged democratic processes. The first of these included a dizzying array of minorities issues, long buried under the authoritarian hand of Soviet rule, that burst out when that rule was lifted. The second stemmed from the potential social explosions resulting from the effort to liberate the economies of these republics from more than seventy years of centralized control. Either phenomenon alone would have been a serious test of even a well-established democratic system. One set of the difficulties posed for Yeltsin came to a head in October 1993, with supreme irony for the allegedly democratic president, when he ordered a military assault that ended the life of the Soviet-era parliament. Another arrived with the onset of his effort, late in 1994, to thwart Chechnya's independence through the use of force. That led to a bloody conflict in which Russian troops were humiliated, Chechnya's capital was destroyed, and many civilians were driven from their homes before a large measure of independence was conceded to Chechnya.

Outside the former Soviet Union proper, in Eastern Europe the reform and collapse of the Soviet empire typically brought similar problems to the fore. With the exception of *Poland,* no country of that region was without substantial minorities issues, a number of which surfaced with the demise of the Soviet Union. Most grimly destructive of human rights was the disintegration of *Yugoslavia* as one after another of its constituent republics voted for independence in 1991 and 1992, and civil warfare resulted. The outcome was the most tragic experience in our time of whole communities being ruthlessly deprived of their most basic rights as the result of ethnic hatred abetted by governmental forces desperate to keep their states intact and themselves in power. After *Slovenia* and *Croatia* fought their way to independence, multiethnic *Bosnia* was hardest hit by Serbian forces, which bombarded its capital, Sarajevo, for many months in a siege that destroyed much of the city, made refugees of many thousands of its citizens, and threatened the rest with mass starvation. Yet for centuries, Sarajevo had been prized as a cosmopolitan city where different ethnic and religious communities lived side by side as friends. Meanwhile, Serbian irregulars engaged in what they called "ethnic cleansing," the chilling euphemism for murdering or driving from their homes all non-Serbian citizens of Bosnia. Finally came the massacre of many thousands by Serb militias within the UN "safe haven" of Srebrenica, action that chillingly revealed the impotence in the international community's modest effort to protect the victims of the conflict. That unspeakable tragedy was one of several dramatic events in Bosnia in the summer of 1995 that helped propel the belligerents to an uneasy peace by the end of that year. In 1998, the government of Yugoslavia turned to attacking ethnic Albanians in its province of Kosovo, raising new human rights abuses.

Within the former Soviet empire and sphere of influence, the record of political reform was mixed by the late 1990s. The *Czech Republic, Hungary, Poland,* and *Slovakia* took the lead in binding themselves to the political and economic systems of the West (all but Slovakia were invited to join NATO in 1997). The three *Baltic Republics,* along with *Romania* and *Slovenia,* were in the next rank in terms of progress on reforms. But in *Belarus, Kazakhstan,* and *Kyrgyzstan* came a turning back toward authoritarianism after early liberalization, and little democratization in the other central Asian republics of *Tajikstan, Turkmenistan,* and *Uzbekistan.* In *Albania* (not under Soviet influence since the earliest days of the cold war), virtual anarchy broke out in 1997 as the result of public anger over an investment scam for which the government was blamed. By late summer, a new and popularly elected government had come to power. It was faced with trying to restore a country that had nearly been destroyed by economic and political chaos.

Countervailing pressures over civil liberties issues within what had been the Soviet bloc were symbolized in a Russian development in that same summer. President Yeltsin vetoed a bill that would have restricted "nontraditional" religious groups in the country—recently arrived, frequently evangelical sects—by requiring them to register with the government in order to own property or conduct public worship. Many in the West viewed the presidential veto as "a definitive moment for Russia's . . . future as a secular and liberal state."[16] But for many Russian nationalists, Yeltsin had capitulated to Western pressure. Critics of the veto pointed to the U.S. Senate's vote, days before Yeltsin's action, to cut off all aid to Russia if the bill became law. Once the bill was revised to make it slightly less restrictive, Yeltsin signed it into law, to the dismay of many.

The link between economic welfare and civil and political rights had again become ominously apparent in a reunified *Germany* by 1992. Reunification of East and West Germany came in October 1990, as the end result of an election campaign that triumphantly promised that adjusting to the new union would bring little economic pain to the much wealthier citizens of the western two-thirds of the reunited nation. The promise proved overblown, at least for the short run. A general economic downturn had already set in across the North; economic dislocations, including terrible problems of industrial pollution, in eastern Germany were much more severe than had been anticipated; and, most stressful of all, civil unrest in, especially, Yugoslavia brought huge numbers of refugees pouring into Germany in search of often-scarce employment. By autumn 1992, outbursts of violence against foreigners alarmed the world with the prospect of a neo-Nazi resurgence. Even so, after the murder in November of three Turkish nationals by right-wing youths, hundreds of thousands of German citizens came out in demonstrations against the xenophobic extremists in cities across the nation. That seemed a turning point in demonstrating what became clearer in following years, that a democratic culture was well rooted in Germany, even though it came under serious attack as the result of severe social and economic strain.

While liberalization in the Soviet Union had been leading to that nation's eventual disintegration, in *China*, a harsh authoritarianism was reestablished in spring 1989. The bloody crackdown at Tiananmen Square made clear that China's aged rulers were not prepared to allow the seeds of political pluralism and dissent to grow along with the flourishing market system they had encouraged. That situation posed serious questions, not only for human rights in China but also for the even larger matters of the connections between society's economic and civil development. As we have seen, many in the West clearly believe that the very libertarianism of market economics encourages an emphasis on individualism and decisionmaking at the grass roots—certainly where the issues are purely economic. But the Chinese government seemingly remains convinced that it can encourage spectacular economic growth indefinitely without regard for political liberalization.[17]

Whatever the relative merits of these positions, the fact is that China's prodemocracy movement itself would have been unthinkable without the preceding economic liberalization that opened the country to the rest of the world. What students attempted in spring 1989 seemed light-years from the student adulation of Mao Tse-tung that accompanied the Great Proletarian Cultural Revolution only twenty years earlier. The difference may be mainly explained by the fact that the Cultural Revolution came at a time when China was still a thoroughly closed society whose leaders could manipulate the masses for their own ends. China was transformed in the intervening years, and the suppression of the prodemocracy movement seems a tragic example of structural resistance to inevitable change within the Chinese system—inevitable, that is, if a link truly does exist between economic and political development.

Meanwhile, the divergence between China's economic and political development heated the formulation of policies elsewhere. Throughout the 1990s, the Chinese government worked assiduously to avoid being rebuked by the UN Human Rights Commission for its human rights record. Each year, a varying majority of Commission members blocked criticism of China. Some states, particularly Southern ones, shared the Chinese view that economic well-being superseded civil liberties as a social value. Others, including a number of Western countries, voted against a critical report on grounds that trade and dialogue were more likely to persuade China to become more tolerant of pluralism. All in all, China was by far the most important country where different trajectories in the political and economic spheres remained so disparate a decade after the close of the cold war.

It may be that *South Korea's* evolution since the 1950s is instructive for China. What was, at the close of the Korean conflict, a state run as a virtual dictatorship in a poor and underdeveloped society has grown into an economic power that is now among the economic leaders of the world. More than once over the past thirty years, the government silenced and jailed its opponents, sometimes in the face of violent protests. The South Korean political system remained authoritarian by Western standards into the 1980s, although by then it was also slowly becoming more open and competitive. In 1992, a onetime dissident political figure was elected president, strengthening democratic processes immeasurably. With national variations, several other Asian states—*Japan* perhaps was the earliest model—appear to fall into this pattern of economic development directed from the top and followed by the gradual evolution of greater political pluralism.

The slide toward dictatorship and military rule that characterized a number of *less developed* states in the 1960s and 1970s was largely stemmed in the 1980s. The diversity of states involved rules out a simple or single explanation, although the collapse of single-party rule across what had been the Soviet sphere clearly inspired dreams of popular government elsewhere in the world as well. Across much of sub-Saharan Africa, single-party systems that had dominated their nations since independence were challenged in multiparty elections, with independent experts from abroad observing and monitoring the results. Yet there and elsewhere throughout the 1990s, economic life often remained as fragile as political freedom, and in such places as *Burma* and *Nigeria*, military juntas silenced their numerous critics through intimidation and arbitrary arrest. *Somalia*, meanwhile, made little progress in recovering from the civil strife and anarchy that had replaced rule by strongman at the start of the decade, and the people of *North Korea* suffered a catastrophic famine brought on in large part by the isolation and skewed priorities of its single-party dictatorship.

After decades in which *South Africa*'s apartheid system presented a special human rights challenge to the world, momentous changes have been taking place there since 1989. In that year, leaders of the outlawed African National Congress (ANC) were released after decades of imprisonment. Then came negotiations to hammer out a constitution extending equal citizenship to all. The result was a "negotiated revolution." Under universal suffrage for the first time in the nation's history, Nelson Mandela of the ANC was elected president in 1994. Momentous change continued as the new leaders struggled to create a multiethnic participatory democracy against incredible historical odds—three hundred years of racism in which a white minority reaped the rewards of the system by exploiting the people of color who made up the majority. Conflicts within the society during the 1990s, including a very high incidence of violent crime, suggest that it may be many years before widespread material improvement in the lot of many becomes apparent.

But the new South African government began with an unprecedented effort to come to terms with its nation's past with help from its Truth and Reconciliation Commission. This multiracial body began its work at the end of 1995. Its members were appointed by President Mandela, who himself embodied the commission's conciliatory purpose, to hear from both victims and officials of the apartheid era, and to grant amnesty to individuals who, in the commission's view, told the truth in their testimony about their past role in maintaining the apartheid system.[18] Archbishop Desmond Tutu was widely credited with effectiveness as the commission's chair. "Once we have got it right," he said in reference to the whole effort to create a successful, multiethnic state, "South Africa will be the paradigm for the rest of the world."[19]

Starting in the 1970s, some saw evidence of a trend toward more repressive government in some states as a reaction against the spread of Western-style freedoms accompanying Western culture. Still, the prime evidence for this argument, the growth of Islamic fundamentalism, seems less visible today than when the mullahs first came to power in *Iran*. Iran's government itself is somewhat more accommodating in its relations with the West than it was in the 1980s. Nor have similar regimes swept the Islamic world. In those few cases where they have come to power—as in *Pakistan* until 1988 and in *Afghanistan,* with the Taliban victories of the mid-1990s—they have had little anti-Western impact even while constricting the freedoms of those over whom they ruled. In that part of the world embraced by Islam, it is not a government of religious fundamentalists but the secular one of Saddam Hussein in *Iraq* that has been most repressive and most damaging to the rights of minorities and to neighboring populations.

Nonetheless, attacks on human dignity and happiness continue to be justified in the contemporary world in the name of religion. South Africa's racist system of apartheid was rationalized until its end by some within the white population on biblical grounds. In *India*, Hindu extremists destroyed a six-hundred-year-old mosque in 1992, unleashing a chain of events that left more than a thousand dead and a number of Hindu temples destroyed by vengeful Muslims in neighboring Pakistan. In Europe, violent outbursts of anti-Semitism and xenophobic nationalism have been launched by professed Christians who are at the same time admirers of the Nazis. Nor are the xenophobic fires of the immediate post–cold war world entirely extinguished. Xenophobia is itself a kind of religion, for it makes a sacred icon of the nation, fueling intolerance for all who are apart from it.

Intervention in the Name of Human Rights

The realization that power over others cannot be exercised without some measure of oppression has led to humanity's age-old struggle to make government responsive to the desire for freedom by the governed. Yet at the present stage of world development, that struggle has produced far more tangible and beneficent results within certain societies than it has where governments, including those that are comparatively restrained at home, exercise power outside their own territorial scope. We would not suppose it within the realm of possibility that a U.S. president might send several thousand troops into, say, Topeka, Kansas, to topple a mayor whose policies were unacceptable to the administration in Washington. Yet when President Reagan invaded Grenada for a comparable purpose in 1983, the public generally accepted the action as falling within the foreign policy prerogatives of the president.

This case reminds us that great powers have a potential impact on the rest of the world that is not achievable by the governments of small powers, even when the latter may behave abominably toward their own citizens. Great powers can always make their presence felt—for good or for ill—beyond their borders.

Throughout the cold war, this capacity was illustrated by the two superpowers with their global interests, which they often advanced with idealistic-sounding arguments in the name of protecting human dignity. Yet because their interests were typically in direct opposition to each other, those claims could usually be derided by their opponents as far more self-interested than selfless. At times—as in the U.S. intervention in Vietnam and, later, the Soviet engagement in Afghanistan—the depth of the resistance to their claims to be policing law and order made untenable their self-justifications for such coercive actions beyond their borders. Nonetheless, competition between the two superpowers at least produced ordering arrangements within each of their blocs, however inadequate the justice that resulted. And, more often than not, that same competition restrained them from military interventions outside their blocs. Vietnam and Afghanistan were the principal, traumatic exceptions.

With the end of the cold war, these patterns and the expectations that accompanied them all disappeared. The world very quickly became more unruly than it had been during much of the cold war. The divergent human desires for order and freedom tipped rather suddenly to freedom. This was particularly so where the heavy hand of Communist rule was lifted, and the narrow tribalist mentalities that had been suppressed by that rule rose to the surface. In such places as Yugoslavia and the Caucasus, the end of repressive order produced a new freedom to coerce, oppress, and kill. Although a new and more benign police power was needed to replace the one that had died, the first decades of the post–cold war era did not make very significant strides in that regard. Real opportunities for improving global police power remain, nonetheless, and to the extent that they are built on freedom and order, they may enhance rather than destroy human rights in the coming era.

Meanwhile, three interconnected factors now are having the most critical impact on the way in which intervention in the name of human rights unfolds in the years immediately ahead. They are, first, the unprecedented ability of the United States to play a dominant, if still limited, role in these matters today; second, the authorization of multilateral operations to provide humanitarian assistance where innocent life is threatened; and third, the spate of efforts in recent years to make individuals responsible for the atrocities they commit in the name of some cause or other.

Since the end of the cold war, the dominant position of the United States has made it the principal state agent for law and order in the world.[20] The record of that agency to date is mixed. It reveals the difficulty in trying to square a principled role in which universal standards are enforced with a single sovereign's self-interest. By the same token, it shows many of the tensions and ambiguities that still exist when the principled role requires, as it always does, as much multilateral sharing of the terms and purpose of the police action as possible. In other words, the first and second factors listed above are very much in mutual tension even though they are intertwined today. To the extent that the United States acts unilaterally, it retains flexibility, freedom of choice, and a more direct responsiveness to its own citizens. To the extent that it seeks the authority to act from other sovereigns, it submerges those attributes in a larger quest for justice.

Three cases from the cold war's aftermath are illustrative. The first came shortly after the defeat of Saddam Hussein's Iraq in the Gulf War early in 1991. After the Iraqi army withdrew from its occupation of Kuwait, Saddam turned it on a dissident minority, the Kurds, in northern Iraq. President Bush then ordered an American force to intervene to protect the Kurdish population from its own government. The second case, in which the United States asked for UN authorization to lead a multinational force, began at the end of 1992. It was intended to make possible the provision of food to starving Somalis who were being victimized by civil war, anarchy, and the looting of relief supplies by armed gangs of citizens. The third action involved the American airlift of food and medicine to besieged Bosnians in 1993. That was soon overshadowed by the evolving role of a peacekeeping force, the UN Protection Force (UNPROFOR), that had been authorized by the United Nations a year earlier to police a cease-fire in Croatia. There its mandate was extended to provide humanitarian assistance to Bosnia, where it was also expected to police a nonexistent peace.

All of these came about because of initiatives from the United States, but each received the tangible support of many other governments, including official authorization by the Security Council of the United Nations. These operations also revealed the frustrations and the ambiguities of humanitarian interventions to protect a target population from internal lawlessness (including, in the first case, that justified by Saddam's brutal authoritarianism). It may be a paradox of world politics that the moral or ideal force of these interventions seemed inversely proportional to their impact on real political power in the region. That is, they were tolerated, if not enthusiastically supported, by the U.S. public only as long as they did *not* effectively lead to prolonged occupation and political control of the target population—as long, that is, as they ran little risk of altering the fundamental political equation in the area.

The Iraqi intervention evidently accomplished its immediate goal, but certainly it had no impact on the larger political situation in Iraq, that of Saddam's authoritarian control of the state. Moreover, it can be argued that relative security for the Kurds has only been possible since U.S. intervention ended because of the whole context of UN restraints that remained in place on Saddam after the Gulf War. The authority of the United Nations was exercised to keep Saddam within acceptable bounds, not to overturn him. In Somalia, the U.S.-led force soon changed its mission from providing humanitarian aid to bringing greater order to the country by corralling fighting warlords. That proved disastrous. Not only did it fail but it also turned large numbers of Somalis against the Americans. By the time eighteen U.S. soldiers were killed, the body of one being dragged through the streets of Mogadishu, the mission was doomed. The agent of the world community essentially tossed the problem of Somalia

back to the United Nations, which was left without the mandate or the resources to rescue the nation. The Bosnia case (as explained in Chapter 5)
proved an even more dismal reminder than Somalia that it is not enough
to have legitimate authorization for humanitarian intervention, not if
what is commanded fails to address the reality of the situation it is meant
to correct. Here, as UNPROFOR took center stage, the United States refused to participate with peacekeeping troops of its own. Neither did it
consistently push for a police power effective enough to coerce the disputants into ending the fighting. The result was continued suffering as local warriors fought against the UN Force and what it stood for until such
time as shifting military fortunes, along with stepped-up pressure from
the United States, produced a shaky peace.

These cases show plainly that there is probably no such thing as a
"purely" humanitarian intervention, that is, one with no political ramifi-
cations in the target state. But we may describe as relatively humanitarian
those that do not threaten powerful local interests in a way that incites
them to inflict large numbers of casualties on the intervenors' forces. That
is what makes them less controversial as the foreign policy initiatives of
one or several states. As the political stakes and thus the risks grow
higher, we should naturally expect relevant decisionmakers to seek both
the views and the participation of others. While that legitimizes the police
role and shares its burdens, it does not guarantee a justice-producing outcome. At the end of the twentieth century, we are caught, more
poignantly than ever before, between the conflicting imperatives of self-
interestedness on the one hand, with all its incentives for not getting involved in the troubles of others, and wanting to redress the wrongs inflicted on fellow human beings on the other, where a principled resolve
commands us. Our recent history speaks clearly of our shortcomings in
the effort to move toward the second pole. Even so, we are caught because we at last have that pole clearly in sight, not simply as an ideal but
as a viable goal of our politics. With effort, such a goal should no longer
lie beyond our reach.

Governments by their very nature can play constructive roles in advancing human rights internationally only to the extent that they are
prodded by publics that are both informed and committed to the universal imperatives of human rights considerations instead of parochial or
partisan advantages. Governments will always be inclined to reach for
the self-serving outcome. Private groups and individuals whose goal is
the universal enhancement of human dignity need labor under no such
constraint. The recent trend in awarding the Nobel Peace Prize is an interesting indicator of the implications of such a conclusion because the work
of a number of recipients in recent years has been closely tied to human
rights issues, which says volumes about the intimate connection between

the advancement of important human values and the establishment of peaceful societies. But even more significant is the fact that Nobel awards have gone to private individuals or organizations whose efforts often have run directly counter to the practices of governments or important political parties.[21] In a world where such recognition is possible, governments and their spokespersons no longer are without effective gadflies from within their societies to push them toward the fuller enhancement of the rights of human beings.

International Criminal Tribunals

The third factor of the current period that relates to human rights enforcement is the effort to bring to justice individuals charged with crimes that violate universally recognized rights. In the 1990s, this effort has developed along two tracks. One has established war crimes tribunals in two societies where rights abuses have been most egregious and the other has brought progress toward creating a permanent international criminal court.

The two ad hoc tribunals constituted the first such effort in nearly fifty years, since the prosecution of German and Japanese war criminals at Nuremberg and Tokyo after World War II. In 1993, the Security Council created an international tribunal for the former Yugoslavia, giving it jurisdiction over war crimes and crimes against humanity, including genocide, committed after January 1, 1991, when Yugoslavia began to disintegrate.[22] The gravest punishment it may impose is life imprisonment. Some critics of great power leadership were inclined to see this initiative as little more than a symbolic gesture and a cheap alternative to committing troops in sufficient numbers to halt ethnic cleansing and other aggressive behavior in Bosnia. Others wondered how the tribunal would overcome its greatest impediment—not being permitted to conduct trials in absentia—since, while the war raged, the worst offenders remained firmly in power and thus beyond the tribunal's reach.

By the time of the Dayton agreement, in December 1995, the tribunal's prosecutor had prepared indictments against dozens of participants in the conflict (there were 76 indicted suspects by 1997, of whom more than 60 were at large). Among them were the civilian and military leaders of the Serb faction in Bosnia, Radovan Karadzic and Ratko Mladic. Both men were stripped of their political power at Dayton, and all parties to the accord were ordered to cooperate with the tribunal in return for economic assistance. Meanwhile, trials began in the Hague of several individuals of lesser rank who had come into the tribunal's custody. Yet little effort was made in Bosnia, either by local officials or NATO peacekeepers, to arrest the others. Not until some nineteen months after the Dayton agreement came into effect did the NATO Stabilization Force move to make some arrests. That action in July 1997 resulted in the capture of one man. The other was killed in a shoot-out. It was not at all clear, however, that this exercise of police power meant that it would soon be used to capture the most important of those indicted. That, said a senior White House official, would be "a different kettle of fish. Using troops in a hunt-them-down mode is still not our policy."[23] Reports suggested that some within the Clinton administration had pushed strongly for NATO to take such action on the grounds that peace in Bosnia depended on successful prosecution of leading war criminals. Others were leery of making U.S. and other NATO troops the potential targets of revenge. With such conflicting pressures still at work, it would be some time before an appraisal of the effectiveness of the Yugoslav tribunal would be possible.

Toward the end of 1994, the Security Council established a similar tribunal for Rwanda, which had been devastated by a genocidal conflict earlier that year in which 500,000 to 1,000,000 people had been murdered. Most of those massacred were members of the Tutsi minority, killed in vengeance during the anarchic period when the Hutu-dominated government was being overthrown by one whose members came from both these major ethnic groups. Once again it could be argued that leading states created this tribunal to save face when they failed to undertake the harder job of intervening to stop the massacres in the first place. Criminal punishment becomes the goal by default when there is insufficient will to halt criminal action before it has run its course. Here the issue of gaining custody over those indicted was less acute than in Bosnia, although other problems, including charges of incompetence leveled against several administrators of the tribunal's work, slowed its progress. And when the first case opened early in 1997, nearly a hundred Rwandans were soon murdered, evidently to prevent them from testifying. This tribunal's trial chamber is separate from the one for former Yugoslavia, but it shares with it a common appellate chamber. That is designed to encourage development of a single body of law as it relates to such matters as defining genocide and applying the principle of individual responsibility.[24]

The creation of these two tribunals—and the horrifying histories that produced them—have spurred new interest in the 1990s in an idea first considered half a century ago, namely, the creation of a standing international criminal court (ICC). Such a court could serve the human rights agenda in a number of ways. Most important, perhaps, is that it would punish individuals, not the states or other groups for which they purportedly acted, for such criminal actions as war crimes. One of the greatest ethical flaws in the Westphalian conception of order has always been its tendency to hide individual responsibility behind the doctrine of *raison d'état*; its converse is that whole nations are blamed for the sins of their leaders. If destructive and vengeful forms of nationalism are to be tamed and ended, the individuals who commit crimes in their name must know that an impartial justice system, not the threat of victor's justice, awaits them. An ICC would make fully credible the view that some kinds of criminal actions violate universal norms, not simply a particular national law expressing behavioral standards different from others. By providing a standing alternative to national trials, it presumably would undermine the arguments that suspects in highly charged "political" crimes, such as airline hijacking, would not receive fair trials in countries where feelings ran strongly against them.

A treaty to create an ICC may be ready for acceptance before the end of the century. If and when such an institution comes into being, it will mark another innovative and constructive step out of the straitjacket of sovereignty. It should do much to reinforce the principle that the world community has struggled to advance, particularly over the past fifty years, that the rights of human beings are universal, and that every agent of the world community is obligated to defend and help advance them.

Protecting Human Rights
Through International Institutions

The international community has in fact articulated many human rights standards since the end of World War II. The period of standard setting that constituted most of the human rights effort worldwide for the first two and a half decades after the war has given way to an era of more attention to enforcement of those standards, as the previous section suggested. The creation of an international criminal court may mark the culmination of this effort through the 1990s. The world has now produced an impressive array of new machinery for protecting human rights.

The United Nations

The last great standard-setting work of the United Nations came with the completion of the International Covenants on Civil and Political Rights, and on Economic and Social Rights in 1966.[25] Comparatively more attention since has been devoted to investigating alleged human rights violations in particular countries. Given the fact that the United Nations is a highly political body, its treatment of human rights issues often has been highly charged, selective in its targets, and inflammatory in its results. Actually, UN human rights activity has often been highly political because of two inherent features: its constitutional structure, in which only sovereign states are represented, and its nearly universal membership. It was able to create human rights treaties during its norm-setting phase because it spoke for governments *and* most governments of the world were its members.[26]

Throughout the cold war, human rights matters frequently seemed hostage to East-West antagonisms and often were complicated by the politics of North-South divisions. For decades, the intergovernmental nature of the United Nations seemed to frustrate its ability to deal effectively with the policies of racial discrimination practiced by the government of South Africa. Although that government of South Africa was increasingly made a pariah within the community of nations, it yielded almost nothing to the nonwhite majority of its people.

With Israel's occupation of Arab territories following the Six-Day War in 1967, its government frequently became the target of harsh criticism in the UN General Assembly, much of it in terms of human rights violations. In 1975, that criticism burst out in a resolution equating Zionism with racism.[27] For many in the West, this action seemed a hopeless perversion of how the world organization ought to engage in promoting human rights, with dispassion and justice, as the only way to bring them under the protection of governmental norms.

Inherent in everyone's view of the world is the tendency to accept votes that support the policies we espouse as not only good but also just and fair-minded. Votes that are critical of our actions or the actions of our presumed friends we brand as arbitrary and unjust. Nowhere is that tendency thrown into sharper relief than in matters relevant to human rights, which should, because we have defined them as such, be enshrined beyond the reach of politics. Partisan judgments here are likely to arouse us to self-righteous denunciations of the entire effort at evaluation. But even after we have observed that General Assembly resolutions naturally express what is politically acceptable to the majority, we should also note the extent to which they may reflect some legitimate objections to the policies of certain states. For decades, until the sanctions movement finally became irresistible in the mid-1980s, South Africa's racist government was a reliable trading partner of the Western democracies, supplying them with strategic minerals and welcoming their investors. It was not far-fetched to suggest that these economic ties perpetuated the ruling elite and the social system it defended. Israel, in addition to its strong economic and military ties with South Africa, was viewed by the UN majority as in open violation after 1967 of a fundamentally important Westphalian standard—the illegitimacy of occupying by conquest the territory of other states.

The end of the cold war helped to transform both these cases. UN-sponsored trade boycotts of South Africa were followed at the end of the 1980s with the dramatic, largely peaceful fall of the apartheid system and the creation of a pluralistic democracy. At roughly the same time, the seemingly intractable impasse between Israel and the Palestinians developed fissures, which arguably began with an uprising on the West Bank

and Gaza against continued Israeli occupation. Then the Palestine Liberation Organization (PLO) reaffirmed its renunciation of terrorism and recognized Israel's right to exist. Arab-Israeli peace talks began as the Middle East increasingly was disinfected of the East-West rivalries that long
had worked against a negotiated peace. One symbol of the change was
the General Assembly vote late in 1991 to rescind the resolution enacted
sixteen years earlier equating Zionism with racism. A dramatic breakthrough in talks came in September 1993, when an accord was reached to
produce Palestinian autonomy in stages, starting with limited self-rule in
Gaza and Jericho, which many hoped would lead to a general settlement.
Progress in its implementation was delayed following the assassination
of Prime Minister Rabin in 1995, periodic acts of terrorism by extremists
on both sides, and the election of a more resistant government in Israel in
1996. Obstacles such as these sometimes obscured the powerful vision toward which the peace process was directed, that of ending Israel's occupation of the West Bank and Gaza. As the Jewish people themselves had
learned when they were the victims of oppression, to wield power over
another people invites inhumane coercion of the vanquished. Occupation, sooner or later, leads to a corruption of the very moral standards by
which the occupation was rationalized in the first place.

In the years of greatest controversy about the human rights issues
raised in these cases, the UN General Assembly often appeared less than
objective in its treatment of them. The Assembly is, after all, an essentially
political forum.

Because world order will continue to be shaped in such forums, it cannot be assumed that blind justice is the only actor or even the most important one. Thus it is doubly important to keep human rights standards and
concerns high on the international agenda. No political body can be expected to disregard other important political values when it considers human rights, which is to say that the boundaries between those values and
what are distinguished from them as rights tend, in the political arena, to
become more or less indistinguishable. Does this serve to promote universal rights qua rights? Only if men and women of goodwill can detach
themselves sufficiently from their partisan outlooks to seek justice for all,
to recognize the imperfections in their own states' treatment of human
rights issues, and to fight partisanship with a quest for universally applied standards. Given the conflict-inducing imperatives of a Westphalian
structure such as the UN General Assembly, that is a very large *if*.

From the earliest days of the United Nations, its Commission on Human Rights (UNCHR) has been the principal body charged with pursuing human rights issues. The Commission hammered out most of the
standard-setting treaties and can be expected to create additional ones in
the future. In recent years, the UNCHR has taken on an increasingly im-

portant role in investigating and publicizing human rights abuses. It has now developed a variety of subunits—including working groups, independent investigators known as rapporteurs, and supervisory committees—to monitor compliance with human rights treaties. It provides advice on technical matters relevant to human rights issues and expanded information to a worldwide public about available UN machinery—all of which are helping individuals to claim their rights. These developments brought change in the 1990s to what was long an unwritten taboo in the Commission, that is, publicly naming violator states.

This shift has been supported by the greater convergence on values that characterizes the post–cold war period. It has been encouraged by effective exposure to the critical reports and lobbying efforts of such NGOs as Amnesty International and the International Commission of Jurists. One remarkable indication of this more aggressive stance on the part of the UNCHR came in August 1992, when the Commission met in its first special session to consider the human rights situation in the former Yugoslavia. One observer called the resulting resolution "unprecedented in the strength of its language and in its timeliness."[28] After condemning all human rights violations and expressing the Commission's *"particular abhorrence* at the concept and practice of 'ethnic cleansing,'" the resolution established a special rapporteur to visit the territories in question and asked that other standing mechanisms of the UNCHR and all other UN bodies should cooperate fully with this investigation.[29]

Clearly, this resolution did not in itself stop the human rights abuses that accompanied the dismemberment of Yugoslavia. But it marked an important articulation of the standards by which the bloody actions in the Balkans increasingly would be judged. It no doubt helped push the Security Council toward creating the war crimes tribunal for the region in the following year. It thereby committed the world community more fully to a solution on a higher order than that of the survival of the most ruthless.

In 1994, the General Assembly created the post of High Commissioner for Human Rights, which many human rights advocates had long desired. Their hope was that such an official could increase the organization's effectiveness in this area, both by overseeing and coordinating the disparate UN activities, and by providing them with greater visibility and clout as the result of the High Commissioner's stature within the UN bureaucracy. As has become commonplace in the United Nations, the new office was plagued from the start by inadequate resources and what some thought was a less than well-focused mandate. In 1996, the Assembly pleaded with the secretary-general to make available additional financial resources to the work of the High Commissioner.[30] The first High Commissioner, Jose Ayala Lasso, who had been Ecuador's ambassador to the UN, had to cope with massive reorganization efforts in the midst of funding problems. In 1997, he was replaced by Mary Robinson, the popular former president of Ireland, who had resigned that position in order to become High Commissioner. Whether or not this office would eventually fulfill the highest hopes for it, its creation was yet another indication of the growing centrality of human rights issues in world politics.

The United Nations now seems poised to become a far more important instrumentality of human rights protections than it has ever been before. A conjunction of factors—the end of the cold war, the reassertion of human rights in the foreign policy of a number of countries, the creation of tribunals for prosecuting some charged with human rights violations, and the growth in the effectiveness of a number of NGOs working on these matters—have greatly increased this prospect in the last years of the century. Such a takeoff, if it occurs, will be built on what has gone before. The trend for nearly five decades shows a considerable, if often nearly unseen, accretion of advances. In the most general terms, we moved during the period from the almost complete absence of universal standards for human rights conduct to the widespread and commonplace assumption that such standards now clearly exist. Frustration still flows from their inadequate and uneven enforcement, from the self-serving and self-righteous attempts of some to assert that it is only their opponents who fail to live up to the standards. But those are frustrations that the champions of human rights have always known as they battled the oppressions of governments from within. Now that the universality of fundamental human values is so widely recognized, the power of such advocacy can no longer be restricted to what domestic political systems may allow. That is a potentially revolutionary new advance and its power for world order is just beginning to be felt.

Regional Human Rights Law

In recent decades, developing regional systems for the protection of human rights have also promised to move the subject from the realm of political partisanship to that of generally authoritative law. Here the prospect—and in the case of Europe, much of the reality—is the creation of a supranational body of guarantees for individuals that are binding on their own states. As such goals are being realized, the member states are moving out of a purely Westphalian world.

In one sense, the fact that the states of Europe have moved farthest in this direction is ironic, since Europe probably is "the area of the world in least need of international support for human rights."[31] Such a system would be most easily established there, since the governments that created it felt basically unthreatened by it. In addition, those governments consciously chose to build a regional human rights system as yet another path toward the closer integration of their separate polities after World War II. Their widely shared common values, their friendly relations, and their general desire to demonstrate the importance of human rights to the world in the aftermath of Hitler all contributed to the building of an effective system.

Even in this area of the world where expectations for the creation of effective regional human rights law have proved most justified, it is intriguing to note the essential caution in the way the region has moved in this direction. A vast majority of the petitions from individuals that have come before the appropriate European institution have been ruled inadmissible, usually on grounds that national remedies have not yet been exhausted. Of those accepted, most find satisfactory resolution within the European Commission on Human Rights, rather than the European Court, where decisions are likely to be based on mutually acceptable compromise as opposed to the enunciation of binding legal precedent. Thus a large percentage of the cases, real and potential, that enter the system are resolved without contributing notably to the supranational body of relevant law but defer to the more traditional political sensibilities of member states.

This essentially slow-going process has produced notable results. One observer, writing in the 1970s, would have a considerably larger body of case law to appraise today:

> It was not, in fact, idle or merely cosmetic European institutions that stood out against Greek unlawful detentions, torture, and political repression during the rule in the 1970s of "the Colonels." These institutions have called Great Britain to account for tolerating torture and unlawful detention in Northern Ireland. Less dramatic cases have involved challenges to criminal procedures and punishment and to limitations on freedom of expression and publication and on the scope of trade union legislation, and compulsory education laws. . . . A jurisprudence of substantive law and of procedure has been growing for European use and for example to others.[32]

The European Court is an arm of the Council of Europe, which dates from the post–World War II effort to build a normative system to preclude the recurrence of a fascist antihumanism on the continent. Long identified with the states of Western Europe, the Court's jurisdiction in the 1990s was expanded as the Czech Republic, Slovakia, Hungary, and other states of Eastern Europe were added to the Council's membership. Significantly, most of these new members viewed the Council as a waiting room for membership in the European Union. That was a clear indication of how community building was taking on new dimensions across the continent in the aftermath of the cold war. This expansion of uniform protections for individual rights was a principal measure of the phenomenon. Another feature of the trend came with the signing of the Charter of Paris in November 1990 by the members of what is now the Organization of Security and Co-operation in Europe (OSCE).[33] The Charter affirms that protecting human rights is a valid international concern among the members and obligates their governments to respect and protect such rights at home.[34]

The American Convention on Human Rights entered into force in 1978 and by 1996 had been ratified by twenty-five of the thirty-five members of the Organization of American States (OAS). Although the treaty was submitted by President Carter to the U.S. Senate for its advice and consent, the Senate did not act favorably on it at the time. Proponents of an inter-American human rights system, with this treaty at its heart, have long urged that "the international protection of the rights of man should be the principal guide of an evolving American law."[35] They argue that such law needs cultivation in a region with an unfortunate history of human rights violations through frequent coups d'état, rule by military juntas, political imprisonment, and the like. Somewhat like the European system, this Convention provides for both an Inter-American Commission of Human Rights and an Inter-American Court. When the Court began its work in 1978, most OAS members were under authoritarian rule. Today almost none are. The regime established by the American Convention and related documents appears to be growing with some vigor, increasingly articulating the regional consensus regarding evolving standards of decency. Its caseload increased dramatically in the Court's second decade.

A start has also been made at constructing a human rights regime for Africa. In 1981, the Organization of African Unity (OAU) adopted the African Charter on Human and People's Rights, known as the Banjul Charter. Late in 1987, the Commission established in the charter began its work. By the 1990s, all but a handful of OAU members had ratified the charter. Patterned in part after the UNCHR, the work of the Banjul Charter's Commission has been modest to date. In the view of one observer, it has been hampered by the fact that the obligation accepted by member governments, to submit detailed reports on their human rights compliance, has not yet been taken very seriously. Moreover, the Commission has been starved for adequate resources to work effectively.[36] To the extent that competitive political systems develop and spread across Africa, the Banjul Charter's human rights regime, like that of the Americas, should grow more salient.

Toward Greater Human Dignity?

It is easy to be pessimistic about the prospects for enhancing human rights protections worldwide. In recent years, what seemed intractable problems in cracking the power of governments to oppress their people have succeeded only at the cost of new dangers, even calamities, with regard to other human rights. Within the first decades after an international treaty prohibiting genocide entered into force, genocidal acts of governments raged largely unchecked on more than one continent. Still, the most negative observations must be balanced by a sense of what may have been accomplished and, more importantly, may be done in the future to increase the dignity of all members of the species. It is simple realism, first, to note that the protection of human rights is never won in any lasting sense, not even in the societies that are recognized as having the best records of achievement. The struggle is like that of Sisyphus in his eternal effort to heave his burden to the summit.[37] Without the struggle, humanity is lost, although the effort itself is endless and not necessarily obviously progressive to those engaged in it.

Part of the sense of discouragement many people feel no doubt arises from their dismay at the way in which human rights charges and countercharges fly between political opponents, poisoning the prospects for their improved relations and enhancing not one whit their human rights conduct. Sometimes including human rights issues on the global agenda appears merely to have provided states with yet another issue to divide them. But as we have seen in other matters, this politicization of human rights—bringing them into the arena where important values compete for power—appears to be an essential first step toward their advancement, however divisive and even retrogressive that process may first appear. Because we are beginning to sense for the first time in human history that we must develop the capability to correct gross injustice everywhere and not only in our own neighborhoods, the international human rights movement has arisen. That is a potentially revolutionary new perception of our real political obligations to our fellow humans, and it is only beginning to make itself felt. Little wonder that at this stage its results have been erratic and often disappointing. The kinds of concerns embodied in attention to human rights have begun to alter the ways in which both governments and informed individuals think about and evaluate international political behavior.

In considering the importance of the various human rights standards written over the past several decades, it is useful to consider the analogy of Magna Charta.[38] That great constitutional landmark for the Anglo-Saxon world did not have a clear and decisive impact on all British subjects until many years after the barons forced King John to sign it at Runnymede. Its legitimacy gradually emerged as the result of the long-standing determination of the people of England to rein in the arbitrary exercise of power by the sovereign (a determination that is widely shared by human beings in all times and places when confronted with oppression). The document's existence helped clarify the purpose and, over the course of centuries, legitimize it. In much the same way, the Universal Declaration and skein of human rights treaties that followed it have provided a foundation of law for protecting human beings that is clarifying and directing our worldwide task, not just within our lifetimes but conceivably for generations to come. Efforts in just the decade of the 1990s to make individuals accountable under these standards for their treatment of others are building on that foundation.

Other evidence of this process at work is appearing in the international legal order. In general, it is most visible at the nexus between customary and positive international law, between doctrines of consensus versus consent as the basis of international legal obligation. It is a matter of logical consistency that strict legal positivists should look at a purely Westphalian world and conclude that sovereign states may only be bound by laws to which they have specifically consented, which is most clearly done through treaty making. According to such a view, in the absence of that consent, no state can be bound by the will of others, even when an overwhelming number of them are committed to a particular multilateral treaty. Yet when that view is carried to its logical conclusion, it denies the efficacy of custom as a binding source of the law, even though a substantial amount of contemporary international law, including much that is now codified, has grown directly from the customary practices of states. At the very least, the long acceptability of a particular practice to sovereigns has always seemed tantamount to their general consent to it.

In the contemporary world, these considerations have been put into a new light, essentially for two reasons. First, a great many more sovereign actors are present in the world today than in the past, which complicates enormously the problem of securing their consent to every issue for which all of them appropriately should be bound. Second, the growth of international organizations provides ongoing arenas in which governments may express their views officially, although without engaging in treaty making, through roll-call votes. As a result, one can often find the international consensus on an issue whether or not consent has been expressed through ratification of a treaty. In the General Assembly, for example, certain widely adhered-to resolutions (particularly, as in the human rights area, those specifically labeled *declarations*) may serve as the basis for creation of a treaty. Others, such as the numerous condemnations of apartheid from 1950 to 1990, may recur so often that they take on the general character of an international social standard on a particular issue. Because so much of the modern world is influenced by the legitimacy of representative institutions and majority rule, it seems only logical to extend that legitimacy, gradually and organically, to the international life of states. As a result, we may expect world community consensus to matter increasingly in the determination of specieswide standards in the near future.

Perhaps no area of international life is supported by the consensual view of obligation so forcefully as that of human rights. After all, if these rights apply to human beings as humans, then presumably no minority of governments should be permitted to deny their local application. As evidence, the Universal Declaration is now widely regarded as at least a quasi-obligatory set of standards, even though it is not a binding treaty,[39] and authoritative decisionmakers are beginning to assert the existence of relevant new norms as having emerged, at least in part, through international consensus in the human rights field. One of the most dramatic examples of the latter trend came in a 1980 decision within a U.S. Court of Appeals, when the judge held that deliberate torture engaged in by governmental authorities is a violation of the law of nations. For the principal evidence that such a standard now exists, the judge had to look to a wide variety of international statements on the subject. Together these marked a clear international consensus on the unacceptability of torture, although taken singly, none would have seemed to bind relevant government officials—in this case, Paraguay's—on the basis of their overt consent to a treaty standard.[40]

Much of what has been discussed here describes a global socialization process of growing agreement on what is and is not acceptable conduct. In 1985, one student of this subject could say, "It can be persuasively argued that in some cases—for example, Anastasio Somoza's Nicaragua, the Shah's Iran, perhaps Ferdinand Marcos's Philippines—the ruling regime lost its legitimacy in the eyes of important actors because of human rights violations."[41] Within another few years, one could add dramatically to that list. Across the vast lands of the Soviet empire, for example, the transformations that ended Communist rule had been fueled by years of human rights abuses.

In the broadest sense, this discussion of human rights as a world order concern has focused on the way in which a popular-based legal order develops within any society. Relevant values must be formulated before they can be agreed on, and the process of their formation elucidates where agreements lie or may be formed. Value formation is the first step and one that, at the international level, has been entered into with considerable energy and impressive results over the past thirty to forty years. The second part of the process is to work to secure those agreed-on values that, given the political factors inherent in Westphalia that act against such an effort, cannot be expected to be attained quickly. The mountain of injustice on which the human rights movement labors may even grow higher before it is conquered, but every step in the direction of taming it is a victory for each of us, adding hope to our future as a species.

Notes

1. International law also has addressed the problem of what to do in the event of unacceptable deprivations of human rights by governments over individuals

within their jurisdiction. That has mainly taken the form of justifications for humanitarian intervention by other states. But Westphalia's insistence on the hard-shell quality of the state inevitably meant that human rights violations principally had to be addressed from within through domestic law and not through the international legal order.

2. In one of his typical writings on the subject, Mussolini argued, "The keystone of the Fascist doctrine is the conception of the State, of its essence, its purposes, its ends. For Fascism the State is an absolute, before which individuals and groups are relative. . . . The Fascist State organizes the Nation, but then leaves sufficient margins to the individuals; it has limited the useless and noxious liberties and has conserved the essential ones. The judge of such things cannot be the individual but only the State" (*Essay*, pt. 2, quoted in Herman Finer, *Mussolini's Italy* [Hamden, Conn.: Archon Books, 1964], pp. 204–205).

3. Crimes against humanity included murder, extermination, enslavement, deportation, and other inhuman acts committed against any civilian population, before or during the war, or persecutions on political, racial, or religious grounds in execution of or in connection with any crime within the jurisdiction of the Tribunal, whether or not in violation of the domestic law of the country where perpetrated (Article 6 of the Charter of the International Military Tribunal, 1945, reprinted in Jay W. Baird, ed., *From Nuremberg to My Lai* [Lexington, Mass.: D. C. Heath, 1972], pp. 12–13).

4. This has been characteristic of the international role of the United States. Its record of ratification of human rights conventions remains comparatively poor, which is particularly ironic when one considers that the standards to which the United States has been unwilling to submit through treaty obligations are very often those already established and enforced in U.S. domestic law. Those set forth in the UN Convention on the Elimination of All Forms of Racial Discrimination are a case in point. The reasons for the reluctance of the United States to be bound by relevant treaty law are complex, but they no doubt include, in addition to a possible residue of isolationism, constitutional jealousies over the division of legislative and treaty-making powers between Congress and the executive. See, for example, William Korey, "Human Rights Treaties: Why Is the U.S. Stalling?" *Foreign Affairs* 45, 3 (April 1967):414–424, and Vernon Van Dyke, *Human Rights, the United States, and World Community* (New York: Oxford University Press, 1970). It is notable that since the first edition of this book, the United States finally ratified the Genocide Treaty, almost exactly forty years after President Truman had first submitted it to the Senate early in 1949. Its ratification became something of an obsession for Senator William Proxmire, who delivered more than 3,300 speeches in the Senate over the course of nineteen years calling for ratification. In 1992, the United States ratified the UN Covenant on Civil and Political Rights. That action came twenty-six years after that treaty was completed and fifteen years after President Carter asked the Senate to consent to its ratification. Carter submitted the Covenant on Economic and Social Rights to the Senate at the same time, but that remained unratified in 1997. By that date, the United States had adhered to only about one quarter of the twenty to twenty-five most important human rights treaties.

5. For an imaginative early essay on the evolution of human rights law out of the general deference to the Universal Declaration, see Egon Schwelb, *Human Rights and the International Community* (Chicago: Quadrangle, 1964).

6. Harold K. Jacobson, "The Global System and the Realization of Human Dignity and Justice," *International Studies Quarterly* 26, 3 (September 1982):322–323.

7. Stephen P. Marks, "Emerging Human Rights: A New Generation for the 1980s?" *Rutgers Law Review* 33, 2 (Winter 1981):435–452.

8. See, for example, Francis Fukuyama, *The End of History and the Last Man* (New York: Free Press, 1992).

9. At the UN World Conference on Human Rights in Vienna, in June 1993, China and several other Asian nations failed to gain much support for their argument that libertarian democracy was simply a Western cultural preference rather than a matter of human rights. They were more persuasive, however, in insisting that economic development was a more immediate priority than Western-style democracy for many nations. Also at that conference, the United States recognized for the first time a "right" to development.

10. The balancing act reflected in these divergent values is also clear in the separation of the UN covenants into one that treats political and civil rights and another that treats economic, social, and cultural rights. The former covenant contains, in its Part 4, elaborate provisions for enforcing political rights, largely through a system of reporting to an independent international committee of experts. Its optional protocol even permits that committee to receive petitions from individuals who wish to go over their own governments with human rights complaints. In contrast, the second covenant contains no such comparable provisions. State compliance with its standards is addressed only through the annual reports that ratifying states are asked to submit to the UN Economic and Social Council.

11. This has become almost the standard argument of Western liberals since the cold war's end. Chinese leaders have seen the issue otherwise. As China's deputy foreign minister, Liu Huaqiu, put it bluntly at the Vienna Conference, "The argument that human rights is the precondition for development is unfounded" (*Christian Science Monitor*, June 20, 1993, p. 1). The liberal argument is that at some point, successful economic development must induce political liberalization.

12. This paraphrases the words of Professor Lev Gonick to the author in an undated memorandum of 1988.

13. In the first edition of this book, I cited Richard Falk's *Human Rights and State Sovereignty* (New York: Holmes and Meier, 1981), which described nearly a tripling of militarized governments throughout the world between 1960 and 1979, from about sixteen to more than forty, and a significant increase in military influence in many others so that more or less oppressive regimes had grown in that nineteen-year period from between thirty and forty to about ninety. During the 1980s, perhaps a dozen of these regimes either were replaced with more progressive ones—as in Argentina and the Philippines—or were made somewhat more accountable to their own citizens—as in South Korea and Chile. Yet none of these governments had yet made much more than a start toward creating vigorous participatory systems. By the 1990s, the above countries generally saw democratic processes strengthened, even as more pluralistic politics also grew apace across much of sub-Saharan Africa. Freedom House measured a 20 percent increase in the number of democracies from 1985–1986 to 1995–1996, from 41 percent of the world's total in the earlier years to 61 percent in the latter. That meant that a majority of the world's governments were democratic for the first time in history.

"Comparative Survey of Freedom," Freedom House press release, December 19, 1995.

14. Flora Lewis, "The G-7 $\frac{1}{2}$ Directorate," *Foreign Policy* 85 (Winter 1991–1992):37.

15. Gorbachev's reforms had included a decree under which the Soviet Union recognized the binding jurisdiction of the ICJ in respect to the six human rights treaties to which it was a party. See *American Journal of International Law* 83, 2 (April 1989):457.

16. *New York Times*, July 23, 1997, A5.

17. See note 11.

18. The Promotion of National Unity and Reconciliation Act of 1995 gave the Commission six tasks to establish "as complete a picture as possible of the nature, causes, and extent of gross violations of human rights" from the 1960 Sharpeville massacre to the end of 1993; to grant amnesty to "persons who make full disclosure of all the relevant facts relating to acts associated with a political objective" during those years; to give victims "an opportunity to relate the violations they suffered"; to assist in restoring "human and civil dignity" to the victims; to report to the nation on its findings; and to make recommendations aimed at preventing such violations of human rights in the future. Cited in Timothy Garton Ash, "True Confessions," *New York Review of Books*, July 17, 1997, p. 34.

19. Quoted by Timothy Garton Ash, "The Curse and Blessing of South Africa, *New York Review of Books*, August 14, 1997, p. 11.

20. Although the United States is not the only such agent. In 1991 and again in 1997, Italian forces were invited into Albania to provide humanitarian assistance where civil order had largely collapsed. The Russian government has asserted a humanitarian purpose for its interventions in several of the now independent countries (the "near abroad") of the former Soviet Union. And the French government has intervened from time to time in some of the francophone states of Africa to restore the peace.

21. Fourteen of the winners between 1975 and 1997 clearly fall in this category. They include Andrei Sakharov of the Soviet Union (1975); Mairead Corrigan and Betty Williams (Northern Ireland, 1976); Amnesty International (1977); Mother Theresa of Calcutta (India, 1979); Adolfo Perez Esquival (Argentina, 1980); Lech Walesa (Poland, 1983); Bishop Desmond Tutu (South Africa, 1984); Elie Wiesel (United States, 1986); the exiled Dalai Lama of Tibet (1989); Daw Aung San Suu Kyi (Burma, 1991); Rigoberta Menchu (Guatemala, 1992); Joseph Rotblat (United Kingdom, 1995); Bishop Carlos F. Ximenes Belo and Jose Ramos (East Timor, 1996); and Jodie Williams (United States, 1997). It is potentially important too that the number of nongovernmental organizations concerned with promoting and protecting human rights has increased greatly in recent years. Conservatively estimated at several hundred today, most are Western based. However, as two students of this subject noted even before *perestroika*'s advent, "In Eastern Europe, the emergence of private, nongovernmental human rights organizations—a Moscow-based Amnesty International Group, a Moscow Committee for Human Rights, the Charter 77 Movement in Czechoslovakia, the Polish Workers' Defense Committee—is an entirely new phenomenon in the evolution of East European Communist development" (Laurie S. Wiseberg and Harry M. Scoble, "Recent Trends in the Expanding Universe of NGOs

Dedicated to the Protection of Human Rights," in *Global Human Rights: Public Policies, Comparative Measures, and NGO Strategies*, ed. Ved P. Nanda, James R. Scarritt, and George W. Shepherd Jr. [Boulder, Colo.: Westview, 1981], p. 235).

22. For an analysis of the tribunal's history and powers, see James C. O'Brien, "The International Tribunal for Violations of International Humanitarian Law in the Former Yugoslavia," *American Journal of International Law* 87, 4 (October 1993):639–659.

23. *Philadelphia Inquirer*, July 11, 1997, A18.

24. Lori Fisler Damrosch, "The Role of International Courts in the Control of Violence," *Report*, The Joan B. Kroc Institute for International Peace Studies, Spring 1995, pp. 2–3.

25. Those two treaties came into effect among the countries that had ratified them in 1976.

26. The United Nations treats human rights issues principally in two different arenas. The forty-three-member Commission on Human Rights, which includes most of the democratic states of the North, has originated most human rights treaties and in recent years has examined human rights violations in a variety of countries. In contrast, the General Assembly's Third Committee, which includes all 185 members, is dominated by the nonaligned group. The voting power of that coalition, combined with the need to strike bargains in so vast a body, typically ensures that its investigations will be restricted to a few universally acceptable targets.

27. The political trade-off was clear in the Zionist resolution, when reportedly, for example, the Chilean government of the authoritarian General Pinochet agreed to support it in exchange for Arab states' agreement to side with Chile in defending itself against charges of torturing political opponents. See *New York Times*, October 19, 1975, A1.

28. Laurie S. Wiseberg, review of *Behind the Disappearances: Argentina's Dirty War Against Human Rights and the United Nations*, by Iain Guest, *Human Rights Quarterly* 14, 4 (November 1992):585.

29. Resolution of the Commission on Human Rights, First Special Session, Agenda Item 3, UN Doc. E/CN.4/1992/5–1/L.2 (1992) (passed August 14, 1992).

30. For a more detailed account, see Stephen P. Marks, "The Politics and Bureaucracy of Human Rights," in *A Global Agenda: Issues Before the 51st General Assembly of the United Nations*, ed. John Tessitore and Susan Woolfson (Lanham, Md.: Rowman and Littlefield, 1996), pp. 175–177.

31. Louis J. Henkin, *The Rights of Man Today* (Boulder, Colo.: Westview, 1978), p. 104.

32. Ibid. In 1987, the Council of Europe added to this human rights regime for Europe by concluding the European Convention for the Prevention of Torture and Inhuman or Degrading Treatment or Punishment, which creates a standing committee with the right to conduct visits where persons are deprived of their liberty by a public authority in order to assure their protection from torture. See Antonio Cassese, "A New Approach to Human Rights: The European Convention for the Prevention of Torture," *American Journal of International Law* 83, 1 (January 1989):128–153.

33. The OSCE, with more than fifty members, comprises all the states of Europe except for Serb-dominated Yugoslavia, as well as Canada, the United States, and the republics of the former Soviet Union.

34. Lewis, "The G-7 $\frac{1}{2}$ Directorate," pp. 27–28.

35. Res. 30, 6, Ninth International Conference of American States, Actas y Documentos 297 (1953), quoted in Donald T. Fox, "Inter-American Commission on Human Rights Finds United States in Violation," *American Journal of International Law* 82, 3 (July 1988):601–603. See also Lynda E. Frost, "The Evolution of the Inter-American Court of Human Rights," *Human Rights Quarterly* 14, 2 (May 1992): 171–205.

36. Claude E. Welch Jr., "The African Commission on Human and Peoples' Rights: A Five-Year Report and Assessment," *Human Rights Quarterly* 14, 1 (February 1992):43–61.

37. See Jerome J. Shestack, "Sisyphus Endures: The International Human Rights NGO," *New York Law School Law Review* 24 (1978):89.

38. See opening pages of Chapter 3.

39. See Schwelb, Human Rights.

40. *Dolly M. E. Filartiga and Joel Filartiga, Plaintiffs-Appellants, versus Americo Norberto Peña-Irala, Defendant Appellee,* No. 191, Docket 79-6090, U.S. Court of Appeals, Second Circuit, June 30, 1980 (630 F. 2d 876). See also Matthew Lippman, "The Protection of Universal Human Rights: The Problem of Torture," *Universal Human Rights* 1, 4 (October–December 1979):25–55.

41. David P. Forsythe, "The United Nations and Human Rights, 1945–1982," in *The Politics of International Organizations,* ed. Paul F. Diehl (Chicago: Dorsey, 1989), pp. 340–341.

Suggested Readings

Alston, Philip, ed., *The United Nations and Human Rights*, Oxford: Oxford University Press, 1992.

Baird, Jay W., ed., *From Nuremberg to My Lai,* Lexington, Mass.: D. C. Heath, 1972.

Bassiouni, M. Cherif, *The Protection of Human Rights in the Administration of Criminal Justice,* Irvington, N.Y.: Transnational, 1994.

Dahl, Robert A., and Edward R. Tufte, *Size and Democracy,* Stanford, Calif.: Stanford University Press, 1973.

Donnelly, Jack, *Human Rights and World Politics,* Boulder, Colo.: Westview, 1993.

Gurr, Ted Robert, *Minorities at Risk,* Washington, D.C.: U.S. Institute of Peace Press, 1993.

Hannum, Hurst, ed., *Guide to International Human Rights Practice,* Philadelphia: University of Pennsylvania Press, 1992.

Jacobs, Francis G., and Robin C.A. White, *The European Convention on Human Rights,* 2d ed., Oxford: Oxford University Press, 1996.

Juviler, Peter, Bertram Gross, et al., *Human Rights for the 21st Century,* Armonk, N.Y.: M. E. Sharpe, 1992.

Lawson, Edward H., ed., *Encyclopedia of Human Rights,* London: Taylor and Francis, 1989.

Luper-Foy, Steven, ed., *Problems of International Justice,* Boulder, Colo.: Westview, 1988.

Morris, Virginia, and Michael Scharf, *An Insider's Guide to the International Criminal Tribunal for the Former Yugoslavia,* Irvington, N.Y.: Transnational, 1995.

Robertson, A. H., and J. G. Merrills, *Human Rights in the World*, New York: St. Martin's Press, 1996.

Rubenstein, Richard L., *The Age of Triage: Fear and Hope in an Overcrowded World*, New York: Beacon, 1982.

Schwelb, Egon, *Human Rights and the International Community*, Chicago: Quadrangle, 1964.

Snyder, Louis L., *Global Mini-Nationalisms: Autonomy or Independence*, Westport, Conn.: Greenwood, 1982.

Taylor, Telford, *Nuremberg and Vietnam: An American Tragedy*, Chicago: Quadrangle, 1970.

Van Dyke, Vernon, *Human Rights, the United States, and World Community*, New York: Oxford University Press, 1970.

Vincent, R. J., *Human Rights and International Relations*, Cambridge: Cambridge University Press, 1986.

Winston, Morton, *The Philosophy of Human Rights*, Belmont, Calif.: Wadsworth, 1989.

CHAPTER 8

The Closing of the World Frontier

It is (the) ratio of population to land which determines what are the possibilities of human development or the limits of what men can attain in civilization and comfort.

—**William Graham Sumner,**
"Earth-Hunger or the Philosophy of Land-Grabbing"

In 1952, U.S. historian Walter Prescott Webb published an important book exploring the political and social consequences of the fact that the four-hundred-year period of European discovery and exploration at what he called the world's frontier had very recently come to a close.[1] From the time of Columbus's discovery of the New World until about the beginning of the twentieth century, Europe had succeeded in dominating the globe once it entered the planet's great frontier of the Americas, the South Pacific, and southern Africa. Together, these lands had an area five or six times the size of Europe, they were comparatively thinly populated, and they were filled with the abundant material resources that would make the European peoples increasingly rich and powerful in the modern age. Webb's thesis was that this period had produced "a business boom such as the world had never known before and probably never can know again," for he concluded that the period of expansion then ending was an unusual and perhaps unique phenomenon in human history.[2]

Webb did not seem to question the legitimacy of the fact that the "business boom" to which he referred had primarily enriched the Europeans or that the enrichment had been made possible by treating much of the rest of the world—including its other peoples—as an abundant and potentially productive gift from nature to the Western world for its exploitation. However Eurocentric his analysis, Webb nonetheless described how a social system that had been open and expanding for four hundred years had become a closed one, with consequences that in his day were only beginning to be dimly perceived.

Several decades later, we may ask how much better we are at perceiving them, for many of our behavioral patterns and values still seem to reflect the mindless habits of creatures living in an expanding, largely boundless system—habits dangerously learned from that long era of Western domination of the planet. Reason tells us that when something is closed that has always seemed open, the resulting difference could not be greater. Yet even when we understand the facts regarding the planetary limits we have reached today, we seem to have difficulty in adjusting to them. Because we cannot yet, for the most part, sense the closing in a way that tangibly touches our lives, we tend still to live as if we were more or less free agents in an ever expandable world.

Humanity's Impact on a Shrinking Planet

The facts dramatically prove the speed at which our planet is shrinking, which is simply the metaphorical way of saying that population growth and the demands being placed on the earth and its resources are clearly outstripping the planet's ability to sustain many people, particularly in the richest societies, in the way to which they have become accustomed.

When Rome fell, some 1,500 years ago, the total human population of the world may have been about 400 million. It doubled in about another 1,000 years, and by the dawn of the industrial revolution in Europe may have reached 1 billion. Then population growth began to take off, first in Europe and more recently worldwide. The globe's population reached 2 billion, not in a thousand, but in a scant hundred years, by about 1900. The world's population doubled again in a little more than three-quarters of a century, with more than 4 billion humans on the earth by 1980. The number will surpass 6 billion by the end of the century. This vast acceleration in population growth began to show the slightest signs of slowing down by the late 1980s, although the world's population almost certainly will reach about 8 billion (double the 1980 figure) before the time, midway through the twenty-first century, when achieving zero population growth throughout the world may first be possible. Projections that do not anticipate that leveling-off foresee populations of almost 20 billion by the end of the twenty-first century.

Although these facts are startling enough, they are only the beginning of the story of humankind's impact on the planet. That great frontier of which Webb wrote has been filled up and closed off with the booming growth in population. The nearly limitless potential abundance it once held is drying up as mineral resources are mined and otherwise exploited at a rate that surpasses even the increase in population. Each of the 2 billion people alive in 1900 on average consumed less than one-sixth the amount of energy a person used in 1995—and there were some three times as many people on the planet in the latter year!

This enormous increase in the consumption of nonrenewable resources raises questions about our place in nature's scheme of things that go beyond our sheer numbers—which we conceivably can learn to limit—to ask about our social and material values. The population and energy consumption trends together suggest that some of our favorite human desires, for wealth and for power over the physical universe, may yet prove suicidal for our species. We must make no mistake; these "natural" desires for wealth and mastery demand insatiable amounts of energy, which in turn generate the technology and the productivity that have so greatly enlarged our range of material goods and comforts. To have these things in the greatest possible abundance has seemed natural to us, never mind that the overwhelming number of our ancestors would have regarded acquiring them an impossible dream. Our generation, for the first time in human history, is being forced to understand the dangers now inherent in the materialism most of us have taken as a good, especially since more of it became possible at the dawn of the industrial revolution.

The industrial revolution was built from the beginning on the exploitation of nonrenewable resources, specifically the fossil fuels created in the earth's surface over the course of billions of years. That they are finite is unarguable, even though some of them, notably coal, clearly exist in much greater abundance than do others, such as oil. The other chief characteristic of the fossil fuels on which we rely so heavily is that they are never literally consumed but are used and then passed back into the natural world in other forms, mostly as pollution.

Resource scarcity and environmental degradation—these twin dangers of our lust for power over the material world—have put us on a collision course with nature itself. How well do we yet understand that our way of life, not nature, must ultimately give way? That is the only reasonable conclusion we can reach when we reflect that we are helpless apart from the natural world. Learning to live in greater harmony with nature is a matter of our life and death, if it is not already too late. Modern technology is proceeding in a way that is altering, perhaps irreversibly, the natural systems of the planet on which humankind's biological survival depends. As Ward and Dubos noted in the early 1970s, such dangers were already apparent "when only a third of humanity has entered the technological age."[3] Yet we have scarcely begun to shift our development strategies away from the assumption that the aspirations of the rest of our species for technological progress are as meritorious as our own and should be met. Now it seems that we may have understood it backward. What we have regarded for centuries as our road to progress is in fact the road to ruin.[4]

The reasons for this colossal misconception seem to lie deep within our very humanity. As Ward and Dubos pointed out, "Man inhabits two worlds. One is the natural world of plants and animals, of soils and airs and waters which preceded him by billions of years and of which he is a part. The other is the world of social institutions and artifacts he builds for himself, using his tools and engines, his science and his dreams to fashion an environment obedient to human purpose and direction."[5] That first world of nature is appropriately named the *biosphere,* since that term reminds us that the life-sustaining component of the planet is indeed a sphere, closed and finite. The second world, made by humans, is therefore the *technosphere,* although the more general term often associated with it is *civilization.*

Traditionally, we have tended to see nature as a force to be tamed, used, and exploited for our needs. We have seen our achievements in the technosphere as a means of conquering the biosphere and bending it to our purpose. We have counted ourselves civilized to the extent that we have mastered and escaped from raw nature. Such a tendency in our thinking over the course of many millenniums has given rise to our attitude that we are somehow apart from or even superior to nature (an attitude that may constitute our ultimate hubris). To the extent that we have succeeded in subduing nature, it has seemed to us a positive good. The march of human civilization has been marked by the ever greater supremacy of the technosphere over the biosphere. Not until very recently have many of us begun to worry about the consequences of that drive to conquer nature.

The essential lesson of the biosphere is that it is neither indestructible in the face of human intervention nor replaceable by human effort. Indeed a delicate balance of nature throughout the ecology of the planet forms a life-sustaining system through an infinitely complex web of connections among the biosphere's components. Strands in the web may appear to be inconvenient (if not clearly hostile) to human purpose, as seems obvious in the case of insect pests that traditionally have devoured half or more of the food crops humans have labored to produce to keep themselves alive. We have used our godlike technological power to create pesticides that work remarkably well at wiping out many of those pests. Then belatedly we have been forced to see that unintended results have been less beneficent. Our pesticides may also have eliminated the insect's natural predators, which played an essential role elsewhere in the food chain. Hardy specimens that survived poisoning may give rise to future generations that are impervious to the same chemical. Meanwhile, the insecticide may have run off into nearby rivers and streams with potentially disastrous results for still other plant and animal species.

It is even more disturbing to be reminded that the thin layer of atmosphere around the earth, which is the product of eons of development, is all that protects us from the lethal radiation of the sun. We now know that our activity in the technosphere in the industrial age, principally the burning of fossil fuels, has tampered with the atmospheric layer, releasing huge amounts of carbon dioxide that may be altering climates around the globe. If that were not enough, the production of chlorofluorocarbons (CFCs) is destroying the earth's ozone layer. By the last decade of the century, the alarm bells were sounding so that all could hear. It was argued that the greenhouse effect resulting from the release of carbon dioxide was causing a catastrophic warming of the earth,[6] and the rapidly growing holes in the ozone layer over the polar regions were allowing increased penetration of the sun's ultraviolet rays to occur. In the words of Lester R. Brown, the president of Worldwatch Institute, a nongovernmental organization concerned with environmental protection, "Time is not on our side. We have years, not decades, to turn the situation around."[7]

It is clear that the highly developed societies of the North must take the lead today, if the situation is to be turned around. Those who are comparatively rich are a much greater burden for Mother Nature than are their poor brethren. The rich remain seemingly insatiable in their demands for nature's resources and in using them have most seriously affected the biosphere's ecology, with disastrous results. The citizen of the United States, by most measures the richest society in the world, carries around the equivalent of eleven tons of steel in cars, household appliances, and other machines, which give power over the physical universe.[8] A dozen of the world's poor demand less in the way of nonrenewable resources than does a single North American, however unpleasant the implications of that fact for Northern modes and styles of life.

Because the implications *are* so unpleasant, it is not enough to insist that the way of life rich societies have created is quite literally unnatural. Equating that way of life with progress is too deeply ingrained in people for them to forego voluntarily the power over the material world that gives them pleasure. "It is a fairly general characteristic of human nature that [people] seek to avoid back-breaking and monotonous work, that they like comfort, are fascinated by personal possessions, and enjoy having a good time."[9] Even more fundamentally, Homo sapiens' creation of a technosphere more than anything else defines us as human beings. The alternative to the highly exploitative system of production that the industrialized world has produced is not a plunge into a state of nature but rather a conscious modification of our technosphere to bring it into greater harmony with nature's laws. If we can do that, we shall truly progress. If we resist doing that, change will uncomfortably, probably even tragically, be forced on us by nature itself.

The End of Limitless Abundance

If we are to understand the magnitude of the change required in many of
our long-standing values, we need to see how and why such a polar opposition has grown between our way of life in the technosphere and the demands made by our rootedness in the biosphere. Essentially, the answer
lies in the fact that not until our time, to paraphrase a prominent environ-
mentalist, has the closed circle of nature begun to redirect fundamentally
the way we must live.[10] More precisely, the *planet* has become closed for all
human beings today, whereas in the past it has been treated as open for
some *societies* during long historical periods, whereas it seemed much more
nearly closed to others. The fact that the world was open to Europeans
from the time of the Renaissance until this century has been critical in the
formation of values and behavior based on unnatural assumptions of an infinitely abundant planet earth. That period of expansion and growth produced the Westphalian international order along with its counterparts of
Lockean liberalism and laissez-faire capitalism in domestic political and
economic theory. For many centuries before about 1500, Europe had been a
closed and crowded place. As W. P. Webb noted, "There was not much
food, and practically no means of escape for those people living in a closed
world. The idea of progress had not been born. Heaven alone, which could
be reached only through the portals of death, offered hope to the masses of
the European Metropolis."[11] Then came the discovery of the nearly empty
New World, with its unimaginable resources there for the taking of any European actor with the will to exploit them.

The change in the European environment from scarcity to great abundance is what essentially defines the shift from the medieval to the modern
age. Scarcity (as explained in Chapter 2) demands more authoritarian decisionmaking to allocate resources fairly than does enormous abundance,
where a "come one, come all" spirit can be encouraged without inducing
chaos. And so came the gradual shift from the hierarchical political order of
the Middle Ages to the horizontal system of sovereign equals called Westphalia. Within the context of potential abundance, every diligent sovereign
society could enrich itself without undermining the ability of others to do
likewise, as long as each left the others largely alone and focused on their
own internal advancement. It was also critically important that the sovereigns maintained the mutual fiction that the new, non-European territories
were literally no one's lands, subject to appropriation by whichever "civilized" sovereign undertook to make them productive.

The world's frontier began to close to continued European exploitation
at about the beginning of the present century. Meanwhile, however, the
laissez-faire ordering principles of Westphalia had been exported to the
entire world. European modes of economic and political organization be-

came those of the entire planet, a phenomenon that finally became clearest in the aftermath of the colonial period, when the Westphalian system covered the globe.[12] Yet another irony of our time, and a further example of the structural lethargy that inhibits complex social change, is that an international normative order based on assumptions of limitless abundance should have become the universal order at precisely the moment when it was beginning to be ill suited to global conditions of scarcity.

As a general principle, when the limits on abundance become evident to the members of a society, the rational political response is greater central planning for the careful and socially acceptable allocation of scarce resources to its individual subjects. That applies for the fulfillment of economic or political values, whether the social system involved is local or global. Within the Western world, moves away from complete laissez-faire came first within the economic realm of advanced industrial states, where the "dismal science" has, from the time of Malthus, understood the underlying reality of scarcity beneath the surface of potential abundance. The socialist critique of pure laissez-faire capitalism assumes at a minimum that distributive justice requires some measure of centralized intervention in the marketplace. At the regional international level, moves toward economic integration, as in Europe, have been induced partly by the lure of economies of scale and have required centralized guidance at new supranational levels. At the global level, sovereigns have been disinclined to move away from Westphalia's laissez-faire system in any formal way. And yet in limited but important areas, they have begun to plan for the allocation of resources along lines that reveal the newfound limits to nature's abundance. Perhaps the most revealing of these is in the emerging law of the sea, which departs considerably from the Grotian laissez-faire approach.

The Changing Law of the Sea

When he wrote at the dawn of the modern age, at a time when Europeans were just beginning to move about the world's frontier in great numbers and to enrich themselves from its treasures, Grotius took as his basic premise that the oceans of the world were limitless in their bounty, incapable of being exhausted or destroyed by any human activity then imaginable. He noted further that the oceans formed the essential highway out of Europe to the world's frontier. Therefore, he built his law of the sea on a classic laissez-faire principle: The oceans should be open to all who were capable of access to them on a mutually reciprocal basis. Sovereigns could claim as their own territory no more than a narrow band of the waters immediately off their coasts, in keeping with the premise that they had a primary duty to provide security to their societies.[13] No security argument for wider claims could outweigh the obvious mutual benefits to be derived by all sovereigns if given easy access to the world's great highway.

The resulting system of laws governing the seas was simplicity itself. All the waters beyond territorial boundaries were to be regarded as *res communis*, or community property, much like the common grazing lands established by many European towns and villages for their residents' domestic animals. Any sovereign actor might travel on those waters, fish them, and take whatever resources were available there, which were what later generations would call free goods, supplied in apparently endless abundance by nature itself. About all that was required of those exploiting these resources was that their oceangoing vessels be properly licensed and regulated by appropriate sovereign authorities, since they were in effect bits of sovereign territory afloat on the high seas.

It is instructive to consider why the Grotian doctrine of an open sea came to be accepted within the Westphalian legal order. If we consider claims to sovereign and exclusive jurisdiction the chief characteristic of Westphalia, it may seem surprising that states did not extend those claims to huge chunks of the sea, effectively closing them off to rival actors. Such claims underlay the argument of one of Grotius's contemporaries, John Selden. But an effective claim to exclusive sovereignty over any piece of territory, including an expanse of water, demands an ability to control it and to keep rival claimants out, with force if necessary. Europe's greatest naval powers possessed that ability by Grotius's day. Yet some thirty years before he wrote, Queen Elizabeth I had proclaimed Britain's determination to enforce freedom of the high seas and then had made good on that claim after defeating the Spanish Armada. Why had Elizabeth moved in anticipation of Grotius's argument instead of attempting to claim vast stretches of the sea for her realm, as she no doubt now could?

The reason was that the British were beginning to see the possibilities for their own considerable enrichment through trade abroad and exploitation of the world's frontier. They above all would benefit from easy access to all the world's oceans because of their island position and lack of resources at home. They above all could be assured of winning the competition with fellow traders and explorers from other European states in the larger world. Thus British entrepreneurs would gain less from the expensive effort by their government to maintain a credible claim to exclusive jurisdiction over a piece of the ocean than by the much cheaper policing of the oceans to ensure British access to its resources and its ports throughout the globe. What made that policing very much cheaper was that it was built on the laissez-faire principle that requires the very *least* governance, the notion of reciprocity or equal rights for all subjects of the law. As a result, the doctrine of freedom of the seas became enshrined in the international legal order thanks to the wedding of laissez-faire economics to British gunboats.

Not until the mid-twentieth century was the Grotian system seriously challenged. That it has been both challenged and radically altered in recent times is a reflection of the closing of the circle on the ocean's free goods. The first clear signs of change came at the close of World War II, when President Truman issued a set of proclamations asserting exclusive U.S. jurisdiction over the living and nonliving resources of its continental shelf, while maintaining that the traditional freedom of the seas above the shelf was not to be affected.[14] Truman's action was principally a response to pressures from U.S. oil companies, which were acquiring the technology to drill for oil under the comparatively shallow offshore waters where rich oil deposits existed.

By 1945, the United States had inherited Britain's role as the world's greatest naval and commercial power and so had no interest in claiming actual sovereignty over the continental shelf and superjacent waters, since that would have invited reciprocal claims by nonmaritime states mainly bent on restricting the access of greater sea powers to waters close to their shores. Nonetheless, the Truman Proclamation soon had exactly that effect, most notably in 1952 when Chile, Ecuador, and Peru asserted their right to claim as exclusive "conservation zones" the waters off their coasts to a distance of two hundred nautical miles.[15] Significantly, these Pacific coast states had virtually no continental shelf (which, in the Americas, lies mainly on the Atlantic side of the continents) and so could not copy what must have seemed to their governments the sophistry of the Truman declarations. In fact, in the eyes of most other governments, the Latin American countries' treatment of these two-hundred-mile zones made them virtually indistinguishable from territorial seas. In practice, therefore, a doctrine of *mare clausam* was implemented for the first time in several centuries. In spite of frequent clashes with, especially, North American fishing boats and protests by the United States, the Latin American states showed their determination to police their claims, arguing that increasing pressures on the resources of these waters from abroad demanded their conservation.[16]

Meanwhile, other states were beginning to experience similar conflicts and to recognize the need for new multilateral agreement as the result of ever growing demand for the resources of the sea and its subsoil. In 1958, an eighty-six-nation conference was convened in Geneva to further codify the law of the sea. It succeeded in producing four conventions that clarified much of what previously had been customary international law, largely endorsing the traditional practices of states. Yet its Convention on the Continental Shelf, unable to define the absolute limit of the shelf area, specified that it might extend beyond two hundred meters "to where the depth of the superjacent waters admit of exploitation of the natural resources of the said areas."[17] Such an expandable definition ensured that as technology capable of exploiting underseas resources increased, so would the legal limit of the continental shelf, and with increased exploitation much of the sea's subsoil would gradually be eliminated from the global commons. Sure enough, undersea technology continued to develop so rapidly that by the mid-1960s it was apparent that a more radical rethinking of the law of the sea was needed.

The UN Conference on the Law of the Sea

That rethinking began in earnest when Dr. Arvid Pardo, Malta's ambassador to the United Nations, proposed in 1967 that the governments of the world create a new seabed treaty based on the premise that the seabed and its resources constituted the "common heritage" of humankind. That new phrase came to be the subject of much discussion in the prolonged negotiations that followed in the Third UN Conference on the Law of the Sea.[18] The common heritage concept is in large part symbolic of the world's perceived need in the late twentieth century to move beyond the Grotian conception of a laissez-faire order for the seas and to create a real governing authority where none has existed before. Yet countries with the technologies and capital currently available for investment in deep-sea exploitation are also those most enamored with continuing laissez-faire and those most reluctant to acknowledge that if the sea's resources are our common heritage, they should no longer be appropriated by the most powerful.

At the conference a basic division quickly developed between highly advanced industrial states on one hand and most third world countries on the other. Among the former group the most extreme view held that the seabed was effectively *terra nullius*—much like the New World in 1492—and was available on a first-come, first-served basis to any who could claim it. The entire Group of 77 opposed that assumption, arguing that if the common heritage principle meant anything, it should justify the greater equalization of wealth as the world's new frontier came to be exploited rather than a furtherance of inequality. To advance the development of the world's poor societies, they argued, an international authority must be created with the power both to license (or in effect tax) state enterprises exploiting the seabed's resources and to engage in deep-sea mining on its own, with both kinds of revenue to be distributed equitably on the basis of need.

In the effort to secure the North's agreement to that position, the G-77 gave away much of the substance to the unilateral jurisdiction of states. The final treaty provided for the creation of two-hundred-mile exclusive economic zones (EEZ) for every coastal state on earth. These are not quite territorial seas in the traditional sense, since only economic rights, not all other marks of sovereignty, are granted to coastal states. This provision nonetheless legitimizes national economic expansion for most nations in a way unmatched at any previous time. The creation of EEZs excludes one-third of what traditionally have been high seas from the logic of *res communis* and, of course, from the common heritage as well. Although the two-thirds that remain do fall under the regime of the treaty's new International Seabed Authority (ISA), the overwhelming percentage of the sea's exploitable resources fall within exclusive zones. Ninety percent of the world's fisheries and at least that amount of the seabed's extremely valuable oil and gas deposits are removed from direct global competition. Moreover, most of the territory enclosed by the EEZs is gained by the world's biggest or richest countries; of the eight states with the largest EEZs, only two are not already highly industrialized.[19]

Even with this enormous underwater land grab, the Law of the Sea Treaty looked for a dozen years as if it might be stillborn, thanks largely to the refusal of the United States to accept the considerable autonomy of the ISA. When the treaty was signed in 1982 (signing signifies a state's intent rather than its formal commitment), the United States was one of only four states to vote against it, although a number of important industrialized states abstained.[20] That amounted to a reversal by the Reagan administration of the policy of the three previous U.S. presidents, whose representatives had all participated in drafting the treaty. Nonetheless, the American objections remained in place over the next decade and exerted an increasingly chilling effect on the ratification process generally. While many developing states slowly ratified it, those that had abstained in the vote typically did not. It became increasingly apparent that the refusal of the world's leading economic powers to enter the treaty's regime would cripple it from the start. Specifically, without their technology and capital, it would not be possible to create the ISA's mining authority—the Enterprise—or regulate the mining activities of states on the deep seabed.

In 1990, the UN secretary-general initiated informal discussions to try to meet the objections of the industrialized states. These gained urgency by 1993, when it became apparent that the minimum number of required ratifications (60) would allow the treaty to enter into force by the following year, but without the states that could make the ISA effective. In June 1994, the secretary-general informed the UN General Assembly that an agreement had been reached that should permit general adherence to the treaty. It effectively amended the treaty's provisions for deep seabed mining.[21] The Assembly was asked to adopt a resolution urging states to adhere both to it and to the treaty. That done, overwhelmingly, the United States and virtually all other industrialized states then signed the agreement, along with the 1982 treaty, and began their various ratification processes.

This outcome was a clear victory for the major industrialized states, which is to say that its main thrust was to rein in drastically the considerable autonomy that the ISA would have had under the treaty's original terms. More specifically, the agreement assures the Northern states of greater control over the ISA's policymaking; it provides for a more market-oriented regime, eliminating the prospect some saw that the Enterprise could establish a monopoly over mining on the deep seabed; it eliminates mandatory financing and technology transfers from rich states to the ISA as a way of assisting the development of the great majority of treaty members. In short, it reveals that the original terms for the International Seabed Authority, which looked like the most ambitious example of functional government at the global level to date, were too ambitious in terms of creating supranational authority to find acceptance by the world's most powerful economic actors.

For the foreseeable future, economic exploitation of the sea and its resources will be largely confined to the EEZs—those huge offshore areas that the treaty excluded from the area defined as high seas. Pardo, among others, was quick to understand the significance of this fact during the UNCLOS negotiations. In his view, if exclusive coastal jurisdiction had been limited to twelve miles, as he originally proposed, rather than two hundred miles, developing countries eventually could have expected some $20 billion annually from the ISA's proceeds.[22] That expectation was radically reduced by the encroachment on what had been high seas by the original terms of the treaty. The 1994 agreement will cut that already diminished allocation of profits still further. Nor will there be proceeds to distribute until some distant date when the Enterprise is up and running.

This lengthy conflict holds lessons about politics as the art of the possible. The success of new regimes is measured in terms of their ability to transform what have been the diverse or conflicting interests of those they govern into more cooperative ones. But before they can be established, there must be deference to those actors that alone can give them life. In this still largely Westphalian world, that means that the powerful few command far more influence than the semipowerless majority. In the post–cold war world, the proponents of laissez-faire have an even stronger voice and, hence, greater influence than they had when the treaty was completed. One consequence may be that, in spite of rhetoric to the contrary, the revised treaty will largely repudiate common heritage as a legal doctrine meant to provide some distributive justice in the exploitation of the sea's resources.

It will no doubt be many years before we are able to assess the full impact of the Law of the Sea treaty on the mix of power and values in world politics. But we can soon begin to see if the novel behavior allowed by the unprecedented extension of state controls offshore serves to reinforce values of exclusive sovereign jurisdiction, or whether the treaty's combination of some sovereign jurisdiction with *res communis* principles will produce novel conceptions and novel doctrines for governing many of our shared planetary resources. It seems clear at century's end that this will become a regime that is unlike any the world has seen before and that it will form the foundation for governing the exploitation, management, and conservation of the sea's resources well into the future.

Antarctica as a Global Commons

Developments in the law of the sea exhibit some interesting parallels with and some remarkable differences from those that have occurred in recent years in the shaping of a regime for Antarctica. In this case too the most provocative action was fired by the twin prospects of a new capability to extract minerals where that had never before been possible and the economic feasibility of such mining in a world of ever shrinking mineral resources. In 1988, some two dozen states produced a draft Convention for the Regulation of Antarctic Mineral Resource Activities (CRAMRA) that would have permitted mining on this last pristine frontier on earth.

Although CRAMRA also contained strong provisions for protecting Antarctica's environment, the agreement met with so much opposition that even many of those who had helped create it almost immediately had second thoughts. What happened next seemed to reflect a seismic shift in world opinion, as environmental concerns grew at the end of the 1980s. By 1991, the very states responsible for CRAMRA rejected it, meeting in Madrid to conclude instead a Protocol on Environmental Protection (the Madrid Protocol), which bans mining in Antarctica.

All of these developments had their roots in the Antarctic Treaty that went into force in 1961. That agreement had been an important world order advance at the time, for it effectively froze the conflicting territorial claims of various European and South American nations over pieces of the continent, and it established a mining moratorium and a framework for international scientific cooperation on the part of the signatories. In short, the treaty went some distance to create an alternative to the traditional territorial rivalries of states, with the land grabbing and resultant warfare that have been so integral a part of that history.

During the energy crisis of the 1970s, the search for oil led major petroleum companies to lobby the treaty states for a lifting of the moratorium on exploration and mining in Antarctica. In 1979, the U.S. Geological Survey estimated that 45 billion barrels of oil could exist off the Antarctic peninsula. Huge oil reserves were said to lie in the sedimentary basins of the western Antarctic continental shelf. Geological studies also proved the existence of strategic mineral deposits. For these reasons, a number of countries—including Brazil, China, Ecuador, Finland, India, and South Korea—rushed to establish scientific research stations on the continent so that they might become full treaty members themselves, in keeping with the treaty's provisions. Those requirements for establishing permanent research bases on the continent explain why membership in the Antarctic club has been limited to states with the capability to explore and exploit the continent's resources.[23] As of 1996, only twenty-six states had achieved such status, constituting the "consultative parties" to the Antarctic regime.

Throughout the 1980s, this exclusivity with regard to decisionmaking for Antarctica brought growing criticism and pressure from the Group of 77. For some years that conflict was manifested in UN General Assembly debate, where Antarctic Treaty members generally refused to agree that they should be swayed by the votes and opinions of this much larger group of "nonconsultative" states. The latter repeatedly pushed for application of the common heritage principle to Antarctica. Many of them viewed the International Seabed Authority as the obvious precedent, asking that the Antarctic Treaty regime be widened to give all states a voice in the management and protection of the continent's resources. When the treaty states nonetheless asserted their right to create CRAMRA without opening it up for much wider ratification (thus tacitly refusing to apply the common heritage principle to Antarctica), many supposed that the exploitation of the continent's mineral resources was all but certain.[24]

Then, remarkably, the members of the treaty regime backed away from the prospect they had just created. In May 1989, the government of Australia, which had played a key role in negotiating CRAMRA, announced its opposition, stating a preference for making Antarctica a world park or wilderness reserve. France, India, and Belgium associated themselves with that change of heart, Belgium even describing CRAMRA as "dangerous and inappropriate."[25] Soon France joined Australia in drafting a new treaty to replace CRAMRA, which was accomplished with the adoption of the Madrid Protocol on Environmental Protection in 1991.

The unanimous consent of all the consultative states is necessary to bring it into force, and as of mid-1998 several of the twenty-six necessary ratifications were still pending. The major shift that occurred with the abandonment of a treaty that would have permitted mining near the South Pole no doubt had been encouraged by the oil glut of the late 1980s. Even so, it probably would not have been feasible were it not for the habit of cooperation that had developed over the lifetime—soon approaching forty years—of the regime for Antarctica.

Pollution and World Politics

From the time of Grotius to the twentieth century, the doctrine of *res communis* for the high seas carried with it the assumption that individual actors had an obligation not to use that resource in ways injurious to the common interests of others. Until very recently, that meant little more than a ban against piracy—which is simply conduct unregulated by states on the high seas—and a commitment to honor the "peace of the port," and so on. The rules were few because the seas were so vast and abundant that it was nearly impossible to jeopardize them as a commons by mistakes or lack of deference to community rules by one or a few actors. At a time when human industrial wastes and use of chemicals scarcely existed, the high seas were nearly impervious to pollution on an extent that could cause obvious injury to others. Until well into this century, the oceans continued to be viewed by most as a vast, self-cleansing sewer with a limitless capacity to absorb the effluents of affluence.[26]

This attitude toward the oceans is one indication of our long-standing tendency to regard the biosphere as a bottomless storehouse of resources free to the taker who is willing to use and develop them. The land and the resources it holds are particularly susceptible to exclusive appropriation and private ownership, which have been the hallmark of the Western approach to land as territory. In contrast, the air and to a lesser extent the water cannot be demarcated and fenced off as neatly as the land. Both therefore have tended to be regarded as free goods, available for anyone's use. Of course, they have always been common goods, since both air and water are essential not only to our lives but to all life on the planet. But our long-held assumption that they were free reflected the apparent facts that more than enough of both resources were available for everyone and that their use by some could not jeopardize the others' interests in enjoying them in unspoiled abundance. Little attention had to be paid to the allocation of these resources, since there were more than enough to go around.

Just as industrialization began the process that led to a population explosion in recent centuries, it also began the process of exploiting the planet's free goods of air and water in ways that at last raised questions about our long-held assumptions. We began to notice belatedly that they were not free, for social costs had to be paid for their expropriation by the industrial entrepreneur. Until quite recently we have tended to view those costs, often in the form of polluted air or water, merely as nuisances that we could live with or as the necessary price of progress, even when we could no longer fish in our favorite stream or venture into the streets of many of our cities without experiencing stinging eyes and raspy throats. Today, however, we realize that the costs are serious. They may lead directly to death, as when a giant oil spill occurs in a shallow sea teeming with marine life. They may result in long delayed death, as when a century-old slag heap from a coal mine collapsed in Wales in the 1960s, literally burying in a little schoolhouse the descendants of those who had dug the coal. They may accumulate so slowly that their impact will not be apparent for many years, as when rampant deforestation so depletes the planet's oxygen supply that it threatens not only an isolated species but all oxygen-breathing animals, including humans.

Governmental authorities at various levels have begun to respond to some of the most egregious assaults on the biosphere through environmental regulations. Yet the very nature of nature itself has tended to make those responses somewhat timid, scattered, and less than fully satisfactory cures for the disease. In environmental connections a complex distance may exist between cause and effect. If a terrorist enters a public place and begins killing innocent people at random, the cause of their deaths is immediately and dramatically apparent, and something will surely be done to try to prevent the killer from wreaking such mayhem again. But if the same number of deaths occurs from cancer over a period of many years among the same size population of workers in a large industrial plant, not only is the effect less dramatic but it is far more difficult to prove that the deaths resulted from a particular cause in the plant's working environment. In general, the public must see a clear and overwhelming threat to the quality of people's lives from environmental degradation before they are likely to urge action to stop it. Until the threat is dramatic, no effective constituency in favor of a clean environment is present. Meanwhile, a powerful and vocal constituency does exist among the exploiters of nature's "free" goods, insisting on a continued right to use them without paying for the resulting social costs.

The biosphere, many of us may still suppose, is there to be exploited as we create still more human products in the technosphere. In spite of our increased environmental awareness, that still remains the unexamined premise of most economic development activity. In the late 1960s, the United Nations began to talk seriously about international action to support the environment. Many third world governments reacted with suspicion. For them, the rich states' sudden concern with the added costs of environmentally sound industrial practice seemed to be just another excuse for nonsupport of economic development programs on their behalf. Some Northern spokespersons may have been secretly pleased to have another argument to use against pleas for their greater largess. But the interesting point here is that this conflict demonstrates how completely third world actors had embraced the classic Western attitude that humankind's material goals are in opposition to nature's own demands—demands that humankind has thought it could ignore.

Discussions continued at the United Nations, and in 1972, the Stockholm Conference on the Human Environment brought together nearly all the world's states to determine, for the first time in history, what cooperative efforts they might make on behalf of their mutual life in the biosphere. The tangible accomplishments of the Stockholm meeting were modest, although with hindsight the conference may be seen as a small landmark in a shifting of dominant values toward greater ecological sensitivity. The representatives at Stockholm agreed to create a permanent United Nations Environmental Programme (UNEP) with its own executive director, staff, governing council, and modest budget. By 1972, a number of UN agencies had undertaken environmental programs relevant to particular issues, as had several regional authorities, such as the Rhine and Danube River commissions in Europe and a great many governments in advanced industrial nations. A kind of umbrella authority therefore was needed to coordinate much of what had begun piecemeal. UNEP was created as a tiny step in that direction, although (as is typical of our Westphalian world) state governments gave it no real power to override their own policies. Since the relationships of nations obviously interlock on environmental problems, states began to recognize their common interest in a global perspective here more readily than they yet had done in, say, matters of their military policies.[27]

Drawing serious international attention to environmental issues required making them politically salient in much the same way that human rights began to be advanced throughout the world. Such issues are no more politically controversial than motherhood until the prospect grows that they be acted on and their relevant values protected in the political system in ways that have not been thought necessary or possible before. When a worldwide effort was launched for a cleaner environment, the issue quickly became a matter of high politics for the international community. In the course of preparing for Stockholm, governments were forced to develop policies in a new area to counter—in the case of Northern governments—arguments advanced by many of the poor, who viewed these concerns as a subterfuge for continued social stratification. Many Southern governments had to try to come to grips with the implications of their own goals for the biosphere.

The Destruction of the Ozone Layer and the Greenhouse Effect

Late in the 1980s, humanity's rapid destruction of the ozone layer suddenly became a matter of high politics. The production of CFCs—used in aerosol sprays, as coolants in refrigerators and air conditioners, in foam insulation, and as solvents in the electronics and computer industries—had long been identified as a major contributor to the destruction of the earth's ozone layer. In 1987, in an effort to cut production of CFCs in half by 1998, the Montreal Protocol on Substances That Deplete the Ozone Layer was negotiated. Then came the widely publicized findings of an international team of scientists: Half the ozone over Antarctica was disappearing each spring. They pointed to CFCs escaping into the atmosphere as the principal cause. A year later, another scientific team reported severe disturbances in the ozone above the Arctic as well.

Those findings seemingly shocked governments into ratifying and even expanding on the Montreal Protocol early in 1989. First, the treaty itself came into force on January 1 of that year with the ratification of the then twelve-member European Community (today's European Union). That made the world's major CFC producers signatories and started a bandwagon effect that quickly brought commitments from dozens of additional governments to give serious thought to ratification (forty had ratified by March 1989). Second, some of the signatories pledged themselves to try to surpass their obligations under the treaty. The European Community, responsible for the production of 768,400 tons of CFCs at the time the treaty entered into force, first agreed to end all CFC production by the year 2000. A week later the goal was moved up to 1997. The United States, the producer of 694,600 tons of CFCs, meanwhile pledged to phase out all production by 2000 if adequate substitutes could be found. Third, discussions with a view to enlarging the terms of the Montreal Protocol began in Helsinki later in the spring of 1989. Under consideration were restrictions on the production of methyl chloroform and carbon tetrachloride, two common chemicals not covered under the Protocol. Recent evidence suggested that they were responsible for some 13 percent of the emissions that were damaging the ozone blanket.

In spite of this increased concern and action, the alarm bells grew louder. Early in 1992, a study by an agency of the U.S. government measured ozone-harming chemicals above northern New England and eastern Canada at the highest levels ever recorded there. High-altitude layers of one of the most harmful CFCs, chlorine monoxide, had never before been recorded at such levels in either hemisphere. The report prompted new proposals for faster phasing-out of CFC production from the Bush administration and Congress. On February 11, 1992, President Bush issued an executive order directing that the deadline for ending all CFC production in the United States be moved up another two years, to 1995. Soon other CFC producers began to follow suit.

As a result of these more stringent commitments and agreements, CFC production plunged dramatically. From a peak in 1988, when an estimated 1,260,000 tons of CFCs were produced worldwide, a 77 percent drop occurred over the next six years.[28] Industrialized countries eliminated their production entirely by the end of 1995, although developing countries were allowed an additional ten years to do likewise. Given their historically much lower levels of CFC production and use, that did not seem a particularly serious concession in 1992. Industrial countries created a fund to help the countries of the South develop alternatives to CFCs. Their payments to this fund, however, have consistently fallen short of their commitments. Meanwhile, consumption of CFCs in parts of the South began to increase.[29] Even with these problems, however, the effort to protect the ozone layer has begun to pay off. We may have passed the peak year in the late 1990s for concentrations in the lower atmosphere of chlorine and bromine—the agents responsible for destroying ozone. In the words of one analyst, "Through international cooperation, therefore, millions of skin cancer cases will be averted, and untold damage to agricultural productivity and ecosystems prevented."[30]

The greenhouse effect also became an issue of high politics late in the century, promising to become the overriding environmental issue of our time. That is partly because its causes seem to be more complex and wide-ranging than those responsible for damaging the ozone layer, and partly because it is a phenomenon so bound up in much of what characterizes the place of humanity in the modern world. These complexities have produced a situation that, in contrast to the ozone issue, allows for more skepticism, more resistance, and more foot-dragging on the part of those who must make painful choices. Global warming is caused by the release of carbon dioxide into the atmosphere, trapping heat in the lower atmosphere and causing temperatures to rise. The burning of fossil fuels in ever greater amounts is one cause. Another is the large-scale clearing of tropical forests, which has other disastrous effects as well: increased rainfall runoff, flooding, erosion, desertification, and the probable extinction of many plant and animal species by eliminating their natural habitats. More generally, global warming is linked, at least indirectly, to the rapid growth in human population. Growing more food, using more water, applying more chemicals to the soil all are activities likely to contribute to the greenhouse gases in the atmosphere.

Debate continues over whether the activities of humankind within the technosphere have actually produced a greenhouse effect in the biosphere, since it is difficult to measure a clear trend in global warming. It is significant that skeptics now appear to be in the minority.[31] Evidence of a coming ecological disaster continues to mount. It is ominous that the ten warmest years on record all fell after 1982, that the twentieth century is the warmest in six hundred years, that in the past hundred years sea level may have risen as much as ten inches and is projected to rise an additional nineteen inches over the coming century. Since, in general, a one-centimeter rise in the ocean's level produces a one-meter extension of the sea onto the land, it is evident that we may face widespread coastal flooding in coming decades, perhaps leading even to the obliteration of such low-lying island nations as the Maldives.

A disaster of that magnitude may have to occur before we act to safeguard the life of the planet. The most meaningful action many Northern societies could take would be to drastically reduce carbon dioxide emissions by eliminating their energy gluttony and moving toward strategies of sustainable growth.[32] The United States, easily the most gluttonous member of the world community, presents the issues most sharply. With less than 5 percent of the world's population, the United States nonetheless emits nearly 24 percent of its greenhouse gases. Automobiles account for much of these emissions—there is one car for every 1.8 Americans. Controls on these emissions relaxed throughout the 1980s as the federal government put less emphasis on fuel efficiency standards and gasoline prices declined. Thanks to low gasoline taxes, Americans paid less for gasoline than did drivers in any other developed nation of the world. Meanwhile, investments in mass transportation systems and cleaner fuel technologies were cut back radically, thereby ensuring that cars would remain the dominant form of transportation in the United States at a time when their damage to the global environment was becoming better and more widely understood. And of course, before gasoline can reach the filling station, oil must first be drilled for, increasingly in such once undisturbed sites as Alaska's Prudhoe Bay, and transported at great risk through fragile and pristine ecosystems. The Shetland Islands, one such ecosystem, were devastated by the largest oil spill in history in January 1993. The nation's energy gluttony is a threat to the biosphere even while it contributes to the greenhouse effect.

During his first year in office, President Clinton proposed an energy tax that would have reduced greenhouse emissions by driving up the cost of fossil fuels for Americans. The proposal went nowhere in Congress. As a result of economic recovery and growth spurred in part by the continued availability of cheap fuels, it seemed probable by Clinton's second term that the decade of the 1990s would see a 13 percent *increase* in carbon dioxide emissions in the United States.[33] This would reverse its government's commitment at Rio de Janeiro in 1992, which was to reduce the output of greenhouses gases to 1990 levels by 2000. The problem was exacerbated when it was learned late in 1997 that carbon emissions in the United States had risen by more than 3.5 percent in 1996 alone. That seriously complicated Clinton administration efforts to craft a proposal for the Kyoto conference on global warming that would reverse the buildup of greenhouse gases and still find acceptance by American business interests.

The Environment and Global Order

Starting with the 1972 Stockholm Conference, we have been building a rather impressive array of authoritative standards and mechanisms reflecting our growing awareness that we constitute a planetary society with shared responsibility to manage global resources, clean up our polluted environment, and protect the biosphere.[34] Yet strong currents of re-

sistance powerfully convey a sense that the costs of environmental protection can continue to be deferred as they have been in the past and that
paying them requires an unacceptable sacrifice of self-interest. From the
perspective of the late 1990s, it is apparent that the environmental
pledges we have been making on paper are not yet fully honored in our
practices.[35] Much as in the human rights field, the coming test of our environmental commitment will be in how it is implemented. To the extent
that we can close the existing gap between rhetoric and real behavior, we
shall also have taken important steps toward greater social justice.

We can get a greater sense of what has and has not counted as environmental progress by considering the commitments made, as well as the
follow-up to, the so-called Earth Summit (the UN Conference on the Environment and Development, or UNCED) held in Rio de Janeiro in 1992.
The summit attracted unprecedented attention throughout the world.
High political controversy abounded in a conference attended by 178
governments and some 15,000 individuals representing NGOs. The environmental action attempted at Rio was notable for its scale and diversity.

The commitments made at Rio were impressive and included the signing of two major treaties. The biodiversity treaty committed signatories to
protection of endangered species and to cooperation on genetic and biological technology. States situated in the tropics are particularly crucial to
the protection of diverse species, thousands of which may be essential for
future food supplies, medicines, and scientific research generally. To induce such states to participate in the treaty regime, the convention provides for a trade-off of aid. The convention on global warming was intended to reduce greenhouse gases by returning signatories to their 1990
levels of emissions.

Other important measures taken at Rio included Agenda 21, which outlined global environmental cleanup strategies and measures to foster environmentally sound development; a statement on forest principles,
which recommended preservation of the world's forests and the monitoring of development's impact on them; a declaration on the environment
and development, which is a statement of principles emphasizing how
economic and environmental concerns can be coordinated; the establishment of a new UN agency—the Sustainable Development Commission—
to monitor international compliance with environmental treaties; and a
commitment from the North of about $60 billion per year in new aid to-
ward so-called green projects in the developing world. (Connected to the
last commitment was that made by most developed countries, although
the United States was not among them, to try to increase development assistance to the South by about 55 percent—to 0.7 percent of their GNPs.
That 0.7 percent target had been advocated by the United Nations for
more than two decades, although in 1992, only a handful of countries had

met it.) The aid commitment made at Rio soon proved to be particularly hollow. Not only was the target not reached, but development assistance actually fell over the next several years, from the 1992 average of 0.33 percent of GNP for all donor states to 0.27 percent in 1995. The United States provided the lowest percentage among developed nations, just 0.1 percent of its GNP.

At Rio, President Bush drew much criticism for opposing a number of the measures that had been hammered out in advance of the summit. He refused to sign the biodiversity treaty or to commit the United States to specific emission controls in the effort to curb global warming. Soon after President Clinton came to office in 1993, those policies were reversed by the new president. He signed the biodiversity treaty and agreed to try to meet the greenhouse gas cutbacks set at Rio. Yet neither of those pledges had come to fruition by Clinton's second term.

As we have seen, the United States actually increased its greenhouse gas emissions during the 1990s, given its failure either to raise energy taxes or to enforce greater fuel-efficiency standards on automakers. By the time of the UN five-year review of Rio's progress, in June 1997, a number of other industrialized countries—Germany, Russia, and the United Kingdom among them—had met their Rio targets. The European Union proposed a new, binding treaty that would cut greenhouse gases an additional 15 percent from 1990 levels by the year 2010. But President Clinton deferred any further American commitment until the treaty conference on the subject at the end of that year. At that conference in Kyoto, the divisions seemed for a time too deep to permit agreement on a treaty. But at the eleventh hour, the delegates were able to conclude the Kyoto Protocol, which then faced ratification by some 150 countries. The Protocol provided for differentiated targets in controlling greenhouse emissions. The most highly industrialized countries would cut back those emissions, on average, by 5.2 percent below 1990 levels. Incentives were to be developed that would encourage TNCs from the North to invest in emissions-reduction projects in the South. Delegates left until late 1998 a determination of how reduction targets might be traded between countries that more than met their targets with those that otherwise would not do so. Given the fairly drastic reversal in carbon dioxide emissions to which the United States was committed—requiring an average annual reduction of 7 percent from 2008 through 2012—it was clear that the Protocol faced an uphill fight for ratification in the U.S. Senate. Yet without some such commitment to controlling greenhouse gases globally, it was estimated that these emissions would increase about 30 percent over 1990 levels by 2010.[36]

As for the biodiversity treaty, although President Clinton asked the Senate for its advice and consent to the treaty, hostile opponents in the Senate's Foreign Relations Committee kept it bottled up there. That inaction prompted India's environment minister to announce in 1995 that his country would work to prevent U.S. pharmaceutical and cosmetic companies from gaining access to medicinal plants and other resources throughout countries in the South if the United States did not endorse the treaty—which had gone into effect among those who had ratified it at the end of 1993.

Thus the record to date is decidedly mixed. Where substitutes for harmful practices do not cause dramatic shifts in lifestyles for millions— as in curtailing CFC production—we can measure positive results. Where those factors are missing—as is the case where greenhouse gases are concerned—our environmental practices are often abysmal. We have not even begun to ensure the sustainable development—the environmentally sound development—of all human societies. To do so will require real departures from the global laissez-faire principles from the past that still dominate much of our thinking.

Two contrasting images of the future may help illustrate the possibilities that still confront us. The first assumes unprecedented forms of competition among the decentralized sovereignties of states. In such a world, rich states grouped into trading blocs possibly may maintain traditional policies of growth and development for quite some time. Yet even for them, such policies will only be sustained with ever greater difficulty and ever more paltry results as the costs of resource exploitation continue to rise along with pressures for more and more material goods. Increasingly powerful economic actors may keep the local engine of production humming for a time, although with ever greater stratification of wealth and abandonment of the public goods required for harmonious social relations. We should probably expect matters of environmental quality to be the first victims. For instance, as oil became unavailable, countries like the United States with huge coal reserves almost certainly would be tempted to exploit them as cheaply as possible, regardless of the resulting scarification of the earth produced by strip or open-pit mining. Meanwhile, embargoes and perhaps even shooting conflicts could be expected to occur with some frequency in the contest for ever more tempting resources in Antarctica, on the ocean's floor, beneath the surface of the moon, or, more immediately, within the territory of weak and vulnerable third world countries, whose own economic status would become ever more precarious.

The second image assumes a world in which effective resource management and antipollution structures are evolving rationally. These structures almost surely would include some arrangements already in place, such as international river commissions, an effectively functioning International Seabed Authority, and regimes to protect the ozone layer, reverse global warming, and ensure biodiversity. They might include a UNEP with the power to force polluting countries to pay to clean up the environment and to regulate the burning of fossil fuels, national EEZs so carefully managed that they create models for marine resource and pollution management, and economic activities under way in space whose benefits were widely shared on earth, particularly with those without the means of venturing onto this new frontier themselves. As such authoritative structures evolved for effective environmental management, they could no doubt be expected to breed still others as the need arose. Somewhere in the process, a global network of precedent, law, and effective management would have been produced that transcended without displacing the separate sovereign arenas for relevant decisionmaking. New loyalties would have begun to emerge wherever new authority was effectively protecting important human values. Nor would they be identical with the acquisitive values of the industrial age, even though the quest for material wealth would scarcely have disappeared. Most important among them would be those supporting renewed understanding of our inextricable dependence on nature, those favoring a style of human life "which accords to material things their proper, legitimate place, which is secondary and not primary."[37]

Whether one image more nearly fits the reality of the future than the other depends on how we all behave in the effort to reconcile our technosphere more fully with the biosphere. Note that neither image assumes much chance that the laissez-faire approach to allocation of goods can continue unabated, even though the first seems to defer to it. That conflict-ridden scenario suggests more authoritarian control at various sovereign centers in opposition to each other, whereas the second image tends to diffuse that possibility by support for a more pluralistic system of authority. As a result, even though the second image assumes more effective global centers of control than the first, it paradoxically may allow for greater choice and variation in the pursuit of localized goals.

The environmental degradation we are experiencing today is largely a disease of the rich in the sense that the material demands of rich societies have produced some of the most obvious damage. Yet poor or traditional societies are capable of assaulting the biosphere too. Such an assault is evident to any visitor to Calcutta or Cairo who has witnessed how much of the pollution of those cities comes from the open cooking stoves of millions of households rather than from modern industry. In Nepal the mountains have been nearly denuded by people who need fuel and building materials for a booming population. The disease is now global, the victims ourselves. The reasons for its onset, growth, and development are the strongest imaginable argument against our tendency to divide ourselves off from nature as we divide nature up among ourselves. In both respects, we must learn to replace that division with the search for greater unity.

Notes

1. Walter Prescott Webb, *The Great Frontier* (Austin: University of Texas Press, 1964).

2. Ibid., p. 13. Webb acknowledged his intellectual debt for this thesis to that of Frederick Jackson Turner some sixty years before. Turner had addressed the impact on the United States of the closing of its own western frontier. (See Chapter 3, note 29.) Webb applied that thesis to the global level.

3. Barbara Ward and René Dubos, *Only One Earth* (New York: W. W. Norton, 1972), p. 11. This study was an unofficial report commissioned by the secretary-general of the United Nations Conference on the Human Environment, which met in Stockholm in 1972.

4. For wide-ranging and sometimes startling analysis of humanity's impact on the earth's ecosystems, see five articles in *Science*, July 25, 1997, pp. 494–525.

5. Ward and Dubos, *Only One Earth*, p. 1.

6. By the late 1990s, evidence had mounted that global warming was being proved. In 1997, President Clinton was persuaded to say that "the overwhelming balance of evidence and scientific opinion is that it is no longer a theory but now a fact that global warming is real." Sandra Sobieraj, *Philadelphia Inquirer*, July 25, 1997, A14.

7. *New York Times*, February 12, 1989, A4.

8. Ward and Dubos, *Only One Earth*, p. 7.

9. Ibid., p. 9.

10. Barry Commoner, *The Closing Circle* (New York: Alfred A. Knopf, 1971).

11. Webb, *Great Frontier*, p. 9.

12. Arnold Toynbee pointed to the irony of that in an introduction he wrote to Webb's *The Great Frontier*: "The Western orientation of the leaders of the non-Western liberation movements is remarkable. Their objective in struggling so persistently to throw off the domination of the Western peoples turns out to have been to go Western, themselves, in a radical way" (p. ix).

13. Grotius's book, *Mare Liberum* [Freedom of the Sea] dates from 1609. The three-mile limit to the territorial sea is attributed to Dutch jurist Cornelius van Bynkershoek (1673–1743), who held that control of the sea off a nation's coast could extend only to the range of a shot from a cannon fixed on the shore. "This principle, almost universally accepted shortly after its formulation, became the basis of the three-mile limit of territorial waters when the range of coastal artillery remained fixed, for an appreciable period of time during the late eighteenth century, at about one marine league [about three miles]" (Gerhard von Glahn, *Law Among Nations* [New York: Macmillan, 1965], pp. 46–47).

14. Truman Proclamation, September 28, 1945, 59 Stat. 884.

15. Joint Declaration on Maritime Zones (Declaration of Santiago, August 18, 1952). Costa Rica later adhered to the declaration as well.

16. The United States of course had the military capability to overpower the merchant militias of these Latin states and thereby enforce its insistence on non-recognition of their claims. But that option seems never to have been considered by any U.S. president, for the simple reason that the states in question were potentially important allies of the United States, and that fact was always more impor-

tant for U.S. policy than the annoyance of these conflicts over fishing rights. The example is a good one of the frequent lack of any simple correlation between a state's potential power and its will or ability to apply it in a world where orderly relationships are also important to each actor.

17. Geneva, Convention on the Continental Shelf, 1958. Text in *American Journal of International Law* 58, Supplement (1958):858–862.

18. The Third UN Conference (UNCLOS) convened its first substantive session, after several years of preparation, on June 20, 1974. Ten additional sessions followed over a period of more than eight years.

19. The only less developed countries in this group are Indonesia and the Philippines. The United States gains the most and largely in a temperate zone—unlike the EEZs of much of Canada, Russia, and Denmark (Greenland): some 3 million square miles of ocean and continental shelf area.

20. Those voting no in addition to the United States at the signing on April 30, 1982, were Israel, Turkey, and Venezuela. Abstaining were Belgium, Bulgaria, Czechoslovakia, German Democratic Republic, Federal Republic of Germany, Hungary, Italy, Luxembourg, Mongolia, Netherlands, Poland, Spain, Thailand, Soviet Union, and United Kingdom.

21. For a full account of the terms of the 1994 agreement, see three articles by Bernard H. Oxman, Louis B. Sohn, and Jonathan I. Charney, "Law of the Sea Forum: The 1994 Agreement on Implementation of the Seabed Provisions of the Convention on the Law of the Sea," *American Journal of International Law* 88, 4 (October 1994):687–714.

22. This conclusion is attributed to Pardo by John Logue, "Law of the Sea Will Enrich the Rich," *Philadelphia Inquirer,* December 8, 1982, 25A.

23. Although the treaty is theoretically open to any state, signatories are unwilling, in the words of an official from one member state (Chile), to "accept countries claiming the right to participate without assuming any duties in research and the sharing of scientific information and communication systems and logistics such as roads and airports." *Philadelphia Inquirer,* May 1, 1988, 18A.

24. Including this author, as indicated in this book's second edition (1990), pp. 222–223.

25. As reported in S. K. N. Blay, "New Trends in the Protection of the Antarctic Environment: The 1991 Madrid Protocol," *American Journal of International Law* 86, 2 (April 1992):378.

26. The pun is suggested by Paul R. Ehrlich's reference to the United States as "the effluent society." *The Population Bomb* (New York: Ballantine Books, 1969), p. 140.

27. UNEP consists of (1) a small secretariat headed by an executive director, (2) a fifty-four-nation Governing Council for Environmental Programmes to provide policy guidance (which reports to the UN General Assembly through the UN Economic and Social Council), and (3) an Environmental Fund of several hundred million dollars to pay for UNEP's programs.

28. Megan Ryan, "CFC Production Plummeting," in *Vital Signs,* ed. Lester R. Brown, Nicholas Lenssen, and Hal Kane (New York: W. W. Norton, 1995), p. 62.

29. Ibid.

30. Hilary F. French, "Environmental Treaties Grow in Number," ibid., p. 90.

31. A good discussion of the history of this debate is Bill McKibben, "Is the World Getting Hotter?" *New York Review of Books,* December 8, 1988, pp. 7–11. But by 1997, the president of the United States had joined those who now viewed global warming as a fact. See note 6.

32. The term and the strategy form the basis for a report, "Our Common Future," published in April 1987 by the World Commission on Environment and Development, an independently funded body of the United Nations. For a thorough exploration of the earth's carrying capacity, see Joel E. Cohen, *How Many People Can the Earth Support?* (New York: W. W. Norton, 1995).

33. John H. Cushman Jr., "Pollution Politics: Clinton's Choice," *New York Times,* June 27, 1997, A11.

34. The number of generally binding environmental treaties grew from 64 in 1972 to 173 by 1994. See Hilary F. French, "Environmental Treaties Grow in Number," p. 91.

35. This is also Hilary French's assessment. Ibid.

36. *New York Times,* December 11, 1997, A1, A10.

37. E. F. Schumacher, *Small Is Beautiful* (New York: Harper and Row, 1973), p. 294.

Suggested Readings

Benedick, Richard Elliot, *Ozone Diplomacy: New Directions in Safeguarding the Planet,* Cambridge, Mass.: Harvard University Press, 1991.

Carson, Rachel, *Silent Spring,* Boston: Houghton Mifflin, 1962.

Commoner, Barry, *The Closing Circle,* New York: Alfred A. Knopf, 1971.

Fischer, Frank, and Michael Black, eds., *Greening Environmental Policy,* New York: St. Martin's Press, 1995.

Johnson, Lawrence E., *A Morally Deep World: An Essay on Moral Significance and Environmental Ethics,* Cambridge: Cambridge University Press, 1991.

Lipschutz, Ronnie D., with Judith Mayer, *Global Civil Society and Global Environmental Governance,* Albany: The State University of New York Press, 1997.

Mathews, Jessica Tuchman, ed., *Preserving the Global Environment: The Challenge of Shared Leadership,* New York: W. W. Norton, 1991.

Mintzer, Irving M., *A Matter of Degrees: The Potential for Controlling the Greenhouse Effect,* Washington, D.C.: World Resources Institute, 1988.

Pirages, Dennis, *Global Technopolitics: The International Politics of Technology and Resources,* Pacific Grove, Calif.: Brooks/Cole, 1989.

Porter, Gareth, and Janet Welsh Brown, *Global Environmental Politics,* Boulder, Colo.: Westview, 1991.

Sands, Philippe, Richard Tarasofsky, and Mary Weiss, eds., *Principles of International Environmental Law,* 4 vols., Manchester: Manchester University Press, 1995.

Simpson, John A., *Preservation of Near-Earth Space for Future Generations*, Cambridge: Cambridge University Press, 1994.

Stokke, Olav Schram, and Devor Vidas, *Governing the Antarctic,* Cambridge: Cambridge University Press, 1997.

Ward, Barbara, and René Dubos, *Only One Earth,* New York: W. W. Norton, 1972.

Webb, Walter Prescott, *The Great Frontier,* Austin: University of Texas Press, 1964.

Weiss, Edith Brown, *In Fairness to Future Generations,* Irvington, N.Y.: Transnational, 1989.

Westra, Laura, and Peter S. Wenz, eds., *Faces of Environmental Racism,* Lanham, Md.: Rowman and Littlefield, 1995.

World Resources Institute, *Greenhouse Warming: Negotiating a Global Regime,* Washington, D.C.: World Resources Institute, 1991.

Young, Oran R., *International Cooperation: Building Regimes for National Resources and the Environment,* Ithaca, N.Y.: Cornell University Press, 1989.

CHAPTER 9

Toward Better Times

The first requisite of civilization . . . is that of justice. . . . The final outcome should be a rule of law to which all . . . have contributed by a sacrifice of their instincts, and which leaves no one . . . at the mercy of brute force.
—Sigmund Freud, *Civilization and Its Discontents*

For the first time in human history, the possibilities for creating a globally integrated civilization seem to be within the grasp of those of us living on the earth today. In fragmented aspects of our lives, the age-old dream of human unity has become a reality through instantaneous communications and growing interdependence on the products of the ongoing life of our biosphere—and through the common threat of extinction that we and other species face, thanks to our behavior. Therein lie both our best and worst of times. That which is so clearly within our grasp can easily elude us if we allow our traditional modes of thought and behavior to command us. Should we fail to change those habits, the result almost certainly will be unprecedented disaster.

It is easy to see the apocalyptic implications of our current condition, but often much more difficult not to allow them to overwhelm us with a sense of impotence to effect the kind of radical alterations that rational analysis demands. In spite of headlong political change on our planet in recent years, we may feel powerless in the face of the most incredible power our technology has created, helpless to improve the human condition when so much in our era seems to conspire to degrade it. The "little matter" of how we get to where we would prefer to be from our present situation, which defines the sense of purpose that gives life meaning, may seem a cosmic problem when our goals encompass the globe. Few of us individually possess the kind of power that determines real social change. What is worse, we must conclude that most of the politically powerful individuals in the world, precisely because they hold power, have the greatest stake in the established order and therefore the greatest resistance to change.

But each of us can try to act in accordance with Kant's categorical imperative, namely, as if we wished and expected our individual actions to become universal laws. That command remains as powerful for the ethical behavior of individuals today as in the past because it expresses the universal sense of the ends of equal justice for all members of the human family. It has political application as well, for we measure the justness of societies by the extent to which their laws bind individuals equally, permitting and even encouraging them all to achieve the full measure of their human potential. The comparatively just society is one that has been able to make universal laws govern the behavior of those within it.

Under the name of reciprocity, this principle has formed the basis for all our efforts to advance the quality of order and justice beyond the nation-state in modern times. Reciprocity encouraged by a vision of universal justice is the expression of the Kantian categorical imperative as applied to international life. In a world with so little hierarchical allocation of socially acceptable values, the reciprocal implications of the behavior of each (especially each state) actor are especially important. To the extent that each behaves in ways acceptable to other actors, their actions are likely to be emulated, to persist, and to become predictable, that is, to be mutually recognized as lawful. In Kantian terms, although no single actor can control the behavior of others, each can behave as it wills others to behave and thereby lead the way to a more just world order through the force of its example.[1]

Much of what follows may suggest to the reader who would try to live by the categorical imperative how that same precept might become an example to international actors for behavior that can advance justice in world order. Although most of us do not have the power to command international actors to do our bidding directly, we too can show the way by our own action, for it is men and women motivated by a vision of greater justice who have the power to improve the world. That action must no doubt take a multiplicity of forms, depending on the particular situations of each of us. The following thoughts about our priorities and sketches for policies are meant to stimulate the reader to think and act on the innumerable possibilities for improving global order.

Our basic priorities should be clear, for our worst-of-times scenario indicates that we are threatened with the actual possibility of severe retrogression and conceivably even extinction, not from one, but two, quarters. The first peril, though pushed from the center toward the periphery of our vision in recent years, has by no means been eliminated. It comes from the continued possession of nuclear explosives by those who delude themselves into supposing that their security is enhanced as a result. The second and now potentially greater threat is from the myriad ways in which we continue to assault our biosphere and thus endanger its capacity to sustain us. Both threats to our existence *can* be addressed and eliminated, and because the maintenance of life is our most basic value, these are the issues that demand the fullest attention of the current generation.

Fortunately, because of the complex interconnectedness of our values and our actions, attention to improving our chances for survival need not mean ignoring issues that may not be so immediately life threatening, such as extending economic justice and protecting other fundamental human rights that allow people to live in greater happiness and dignity. In fact, our best-of-times vision of the near future holds real possibilities for self-fulfillment on the part of more human beings than has perhaps ever before been possible in the history of the world. Political freedoms are putting down roots in places where they never existed before; material comforts are increasingly available to people traditionally trapped in backbreaking toil and abject poverty. Yet these and other civilizing advances remain precarious today, shadowed by the prospects of scarcity, social ruin, disease, and violence propelled by the rage of those who have nothing more to lose. Newfound freedom for millions has threatened its opposing value, order, in the century's last decade. Even as we strengthen the prospects for our survival, we must act to improve the quality of everyone's life globally. To enhance human dignity means to advance world order values on every front.

The Quest for True Security

Our quest for true security through the use of military force brought us finally, in the last years of the cold war, to security's negation: a blueprint for death and destruction out of all proportion to any conceivable human value risked in the process. However great the risks in the prenuclear age of trying to win security for oneself by force of arms, there was at least some calculable chance of success. But the nuclear superpowers of the cold war era built their security strategies on the threat of mutual suicide. Paradoxically, the most powerful nuclear actors became the most impotent, at least in their relations with each other, because they had made themselves and their societies hostages to their own weapons.

That counterpolitical condition at last is being addressed. Cutting back on nuclear arms became, first, a tangible impetus to ending the cold war, then a post–cold war imperative of the new relationship. START II, signed by Presidents Bush and Yeltsin at the beginning of 1993, called for slashing their countries' nuclear arsenals at a magnitude that would have seemed impossibly utopian only a few years earlier. Yet it was not so much the amount of nuclear firepower that would be reduced that brought the cold war's nuclear nightmare to an end. After all, the several thousand weapons that will remain on the assumption that START II will be fully implemented early in the twenty-first century still could turn the planet into a lifeless wasteland. Rather, the nightmare dissipated in the sea change in politics that occurred during the preceding half-dozen years. Almost overnight, the shift in attitudes and intentions on the part of those who commanded these arsenals made their all-out use unthinkable as a design of policy. That was as dramatic an indication as we are likely to see of the fact that human perceptions, values, and goals are ultimately what drive our technology, not the other way around.

Nonetheless, if the nightmare has lifted, we are left with a bad dream in a world where nuclear weapons continue to threaten our future. As Robert McNamara observed, "The indefinite combination of human fallibility and nuclear weapons carries a high risk of destruction of societies."[2] McNamara is only one of an increasing number of opinion makers who now argue for the need to work toward the goal of a world completely free of nuclear weapons.[3] Such a goal has always been in keeping with the normative ideal. Now it has become politically feasible as well.

This goal of a zero nuclear option is strengthened by an advisory opinion handed down by the World Court (ICJ) in 1996 that views the threat or use of nuclear weapons as of dubious legality. Although the decision was somewhat hedged by suggesting the possible lawfulness of their use in self-defense where the survival of a state is at issue, three justices dissented because of that qualification. They argued that the majority did not go far enough in declaring categorically that every threat or use of nuclear weapons is illegal.[4] What is also interesting about this case is that it arose as a grassroots movement of antinuclear activists who lobbied until some forty-five governments were willing to act through the UN General Assembly (which is empowered to ask the Court for advisory opinions on any legal question) to turn to the ICJ. The whole process, in other words, revealed a novel power in international civil society to help shape international law. Once the opinion was handed down, the General Assembly welcomed it and called for negotiations to begin on a treaty to eliminate nuclear weapons.

All of these developments are beginning to energize the effort to control the spread of nuclear weapons technology to those who evidently still must learn that it runs counter to their real security interests. Now that the principal nuclear states are finally cutting back on their arsenals, they stand for the first time in a position of moral authority from which they can persuade others to do as they are doing. Even though we may no longer risk Armageddon, current instabilities probably have increased the risks of nuclear blackmail, or worse, from threatened tyrants clinging desperately to their command of states. Moreover, now that we are faced with the possibility that nuclear materials could fall into the hands of terrorist groups, the folly of nuclearism is becoming plainer even to governments who relied on it in the past.

These dangers alone demand an unprecedented effort in the years immediately ahead to build an effective global structure for security. But even without new specters of nuclearism, the political upheavals that have rocked much of the world once the structure of bipolarity crumbled require new thought and action if we are to secure a more orderly planetary society. If the dangers are unprecedented, so are the opportunities. If we fail to seize them, we are sure to see increased disruption, violence, and disorder in the years ahead.

By way of considering those opportunities, we need to start with a depiction of a security goal or ideal for the people of the earth. That goal should be in harmony with certain universally valid normative generalizations of the sort generally understood to be what justifies and restrains the use of force in civilized societies. The goal posited here is the eventual creation of an integrated security-community encompassing the planet, within which expectations of peaceful change are dependably in place.[5] That in turn presupposes the increasing convergence of core values across societies that historically have viewed each other as being far more unlike than like. To say that such a process appears to be occurring today is another way of describing how the cold war ended.

The first normative generalization relevant to strengthening global security in our time is that *only community authorization should justify the threat or use of force,* which means that force ideally should be wielded in the interests of the whole community. In any humane political system, police power is justified on the assumption that consent on the part of the members of the society supports how and for what purposes it is used. Translated to the world political system, this precept explains the effort to create some measure of community authorization, most importantly through the United Nations, for police action meant to coerce compliance with accepted standards of international behavior.

Throughout the cold war years, the development of a police power for the world community was severely inhibited by the bipolar system itself, which effectively produced two putative world order systems, each with a primitive police power lodged mainly with the bloc leader. That left the global actor, the United Nations, with the secondary role of assisting each of the hegemons to avoid being drawn into the other's sphere in a way that would threaten far greater levels of violence.

The end of the cold war brought far more harmony to the Security Council's great power directorate, and so potentially more agreement as to what kinds of security threats required united action. That has always been the essential precondition to making the United Nations the kind of world police force that its Charter prescribed. Immediately, the Security Council became the locus of authority for an unprecedented police action in the Persian Gulf, an action that was justified, however crudely, in terms of the collective security purposes of the Charter. The crudeness reflected the fact that the coalition effort had to be invented after the fact of Saddam Hussein's occupation of Kuwait, since the collective security structure set forth in the Charter had been an early victim of the cold war, and was not in place. That in turn made the Gulf operation overwhelmingly the undertaking of one member, the United States, and so subject to criticism as serving only the selfish interests of the dominant sovereign of the period. It was an experience that revealed the huge gap still to be closed before the authoritative structure of a global police power could be fully joined to agencies providing it with a genuine capability to police.

The great world order challenge now is to work to close that gap. That task is one that will take generations to complete, for it is multifaceted and complex. And it is confronted at every turn with the structural legacy of our Westphalian inheritance. One piece of it involves the effort to implement the collective security provisions of the Charter's Chapter VII to provide the Security Council with an effective standing military capability (or range of capabilities) to call on when the Council determines that disruptions of the peace require it. This effort is complicated by a number of factors. Among them is the reluctance of the world's greatest military power, the United States, to forego its own freedom to move some of its coercive capability from the realm of foreign policy options to that of a community-based authority, where policing decisions are more constrained by principles agreed to in advance. Another complication is the simultaneous need to make the Security Council a less elitist institution by expanding its membership while greatly improving its effectiveness (not simply its capability) as a policing authority. These two requirements seem to work at cross-purposes with each other, helping also to explain the lack of enthusiasm by current veto holders for a major structural reform of the UN's policing capability.

In the first years after the cold war ended, proposals addressing these and related issues abounded, yet very little progress was made in implementing any of them. Sooner or later, it seems clear, appropriate additional governments will need to be drawn into the work of the Council so that the improvement of the UN police power is a widely shared undertaking.[6] What also is needed is an increased understanding on the part of an informed public of the reasons why a more fully developed police power at the world level will serve the security of human beings everywhere, not simply the interests of the governments that must be the instruments of its creation, as it develops the capacity to enforce universal standards of conduct.

A second normative generalization about security also should inform the effort to improve the world's police authority. It is that *just punishment requires proportionality in the use of force,* fitting the punishment to the crime, not permitting the unrestrained destruction of the wrongdoer. This precept is central to our judgment about what is an appropriate exercise of police power in domestic society. It has been so much more difficult to achieve proportionality in the war system that has been the traditional, crude alternative to a police force internationally, it is little wonder that most of us typically do not imagine that "war" and "police power" share anything at all. But the comparison makes clear that to build ever more reliable structures and processes for collective police action is also to refine and differentiate that capability so that it can be used with proportionality.

In terms of the current challenges, this means in part that the United Nations and other organizations such as NATO and the OSCE now are recognizing the need for a host of techniques and approaches to security that are largely unrelated to the enforcement of a community norm against an outlaw government. These include traditional peacekeeping, that is, the separation of warring antagonists so that the groundwork may be set for the peaceful resolution of their conflict. But they also entail attention to the conditions that reduce the risks that intergroup violence will break out or recur, efforts to focus sanctions as narrowly as possible on offending elites and not their publics, and a determination to make individuals accountable for their coercive behavior under international law.[7]

It is also important to assess the world's security problems by looking through the other end of the telescope, that is, by considering what rightful uses of force states may have that are not directed by a global police authority. Seen from this perspective, the most fundamental normative precept is that *the best security for human societies is defensive.* This rule is fundamental inasmuch as it provides the moral rationale for an individual's right of self-defense as well as that of the state in a Westphalian order. In either case, it means that when force is necessary, it should be used only to defend oneself or one's own community, not to impose one's values on others who resist them.

If such a precept were universally adhered to, a global collective security authority would be left with almost nothing to do. As it is, the primitive ways in which we typically think about the military capability of states have not led most societies to square their military doctrines with a strictly defensive and therefore legitimate purpose. Where uneasy tyrants are in charge of states, military establishments typically are maintained to keep the leaders in power in the face of internal opposition, not to align themselves with the governed in defense against an external foe. And many more popularly based governments maintain military arms capable of defending the society from an external attack, but which they can also turn against another sovereign. Although the governments of the first type will only improve their security postures once they are willing and able to enhance the quality of the lives of their people, those of the second can increasingly be educated to direct their military capabilities in ways that threaten no one.

Although the ability to deter an enemy and defend oneself can take many humane forms, that of civilian-based defense (CBD) is perhaps the clearest and most acceptable normatively. CBD does not threaten the survival of a would-be aggressor but promises an unacceptably high cost for aggression against it. It asserts that the target population of the CBD state will not submit docilely to its own subjugation. Rather, it refuses to be subjugated at all. Since the only point of conquest is control—over population, resources, and therefore capabilities—it loses all meaning when it cannot succeed. The effort simply becomes an unimaginable liability to the would-be conqueror. Civilian-based defense endeavors to make sure that aggression will not succeed, not, that is, without an unacceptable cost to the attacker. Its strength lies in its ability to demonstrate actively the strength of the sense of community on the part of the defending population, which is always and everywhere the most potent justification for taking up arms.

A substantially denuclearized world is difficult to imagine without a simultaneous increase in civilian-based defense, particularly in stable, strong, and democratic countries, where it initially should become one of the guiding doctrines of the next stage of security policy. As such strategies are seriously explored and adopted, the cutting back of more and more of the traditional offensive military components of states, even conventional components, should become an increasingly realistic strategy. The creation of a world in which military force plays no role at all is an impossibility for human society. But it has been the ideal normative vision throughout our history, and we should seek always to approach it as closely as humanly possible. At a minimum, we must be guided by the standard that all humane use of force must be intended to advance important social values, starting most fundamentally with that of the survival of our species and moving, as we advance, up the scale of human needs to protection of the loftiest of our aspirations.

Rewarding Work and Economic Justice

For some two centuries, the Western world has taken pride in knowing that the rapid takeoff in its economic development that began with the industrial revolution has produced ever greater material comfort to larger and larger segments of society. The promise of escape from backbreaking labor for millions undoubtedly has fired development strategies in our time, making economic advancement a first-order issue on the world's agenda. Yet, however commendable the goal, we now see that in pursuing enrichment we have frequently been blind to its consequences for other, divergent values that are also critical to what it should mean to be human. Among the results today in various societies are (1) an obsessive materialism that in its worst effects is decadent, dehumanizing, and antisocial; (2) alienation from the personal rewards of labor through the size and complexity of the economic machine as well as from rigidity in decisionmaking; and (3) increased social stratification that so ignores the disadvantaged members of wealthy societies as to cast them in growing numbers into a netherworld where a desperate turn to parasitic and criminal lives is frequently their only hope for survival.

There may be no such thing as cures in any final sense for these evils, since the forces that give rise to them apparently are grounded in the very material reality of the human condition. But they can and must be fought against if we are to move toward better times as a human society. The normative precept to guide us is that *adult human beings evidently take the greatest sustained pleasure of their lives from a sense of productive and rewarding labor.* That is what apparently is missing from the lives of the bored and idle rich (not to mention the less rich who emulate them) as they seek chiefly to amuse or lose themselves in drink or drugs, at increasing psychic and social costs. It is the loss of a sense of connection between how effectively one works and what one is rewarded for that leads to unhappiness in many sectors of industrial society and that finally brought ruin to the centrally directed economies of the former Soviet world. It is the difficulty in finding or sustaining productive work that turns the underclass of rich societies into discarded refuse whose presence threatens the enhancement of everyone's more civilized values.

We may be able to improve these matters if we start by noting that we generally find labor rewarding when we see it produce a direct, creative impact on our material environment, whether in the form of the raw nature of an unplowed field or the raw canvas on which we have splashed paint. Clearly, as modes of production have changed with our technologies, so has our assignment of social worth to varying kinds of labor. But ever since the industrial age began, a persistent thread of criticism and concern has argued that the mechanization of labor—the interposition of powerful machines between the individual worker and the raw materials—has served to dehumanize the productive process, robbing work of much of its gratification. The man who tends a steel mill's blast furnace by day may enjoy the weekend by cultivating a vegetable patch in the backyard. The woman who earns a wage on an assembly line may knit in the evening. Their hobbies are also productive work, but psychically rewarding in ways their "real" work may not be, for we do not expect to see a craftsman by trade tend a blast furnace as a hobby. It is notable that our typical hobbies resemble much of the kind of "real" work done in premodern societies.

This is not to romanticize the backbreaking toil of much of life in preindustrial societies. It is meant only to acknowledge that our huge-scale and complex technologies have sometimes served to enslave our spirits even while they were liberating our bodies. Such acknowledgment can lead us to a greater respect for, and perhaps a borrowing from, modes of economic organization that do not fit the Northern industrial model. It can suggest the value in efforts to humanize our workplaces, and it can guide those of us moving into postindustrial societies to strive constantly to return to the human scale in our productive lives. It should be heartening, in this regard, that much of what is characteristic about the postindustrial society—with its emphasis on expanding communications technologies and a growing service sector—is more "user friendly" toward its workforce than is true of the characteristic large-scale and impersonal enterprises of the industrial age.

Transnational corporations under private ownership are likely to continue as a vital force in international economic integration. Yet their very vitality increases the gravity of the costs they too pose to world order values. First, many of their activities carry "governmental" weight at least as great as that of the policies of governments. The difference is that profit maximization, not community well-being, is the chief engine of their action. That means that Exxon, for example, decides not to spend the additional money needed to equip its supertankers with double hulls for greater protection. Thus Exxon's profits are maximized, but with wave after wave of costs that radiate outward to engulf others in the event of a disaster like that resulting from the *Exxon Valdez* oil spill. It brought ruin to many economic actors in the vicinity, raised oil prices for millions of consumers, and upset or destroyed the very chain of life over a hitherto unspoiled region. Second, corporate enterprises of this size are no more clearly beholden to the social values of their stockholders than are undemocratic governments to the aspirations of their citizens. Neither provides a setting for the effective participation of ordinary people—stockholders or citizens—in decisions affecting them. Whether a company manufactures napalm or increases its operations in a country ruled by a military dictatorship is strictly a profit-based decision, and one highly impervious to the opposition of its investors or the public at large.

These considerations are a central part of the explanation for the widening of the gulf between rich and poor members of society throughout the world. More and more of the "governing" economic decisions are made to satisfy profit hunger rather than social needs—and the crucial point is that only those with capital to invest are allowed to try to satisfy that hunger. The economically empowered tend to reinforce their position as the politically empowered. They press for policies that sustain their lifestyles (that is, their selfish interests): lower taxes, budgets that slash welfare roles and social services, deregulation of the private sector, and so on. In this post–cold war world, we are perhaps more aware than ever before that wealth equals real political power, and poverty, impotence.

But when the private pursuit of greed becomes the dominant public ideology, the results are bound eventually to transform the misery of those left out of the chase into unavoidable social problems. The current drug crisis in a number of the most fully developed states on the planet is one devastating example. Drugs are, for most users today, a psychic escape from hopeless poverty and despair about ever finding a way into a satisfying life within society. For their suppliers, drugs promise quick enrichment—no matter the illegality or the risk—beyond anything available through socially accepted channels. Similarly, the huge debt of many states in the South in recent years—made possible, let us not forget, by pursuit of the profit motive by rich investors and lenders in the North—is producing an austerity for whole nations for which the price is yet to be paid. Although we cannot see the full dimensions of that price at present, we know that when people see material hopes that have seemed within their grasp elude them, the results can be immensely degrading to the human spirit, producing, in the worst of times, social violence, repression, war, and upheaval.

Whatever the shape of the coming economic age on earth, the economic upturn near the end of the twentieth century still has not eliminated all prospect of what is sketched above. The closing years of the century are marked by a general turning away from the once significant effort to achieve economic fulfillment and justice. That makes it all the more difficult to assess our condition in keeping with what should be the relevant normative concern, which is *how to make the historically inevitable growth in transnational economic life support rather than degrade human well-being and dignity.*

With the dissolution of the Soviet Union, material well-being suddenly and dramatically was threatened in the region it once commanded. The dislocations caused by the shift from central planning to free market economics brought exploding inflation and sudden impoverishment, particularly for the elderly; an often venal entrepreneurship producing sudden wealth, especially for the unscrupulous; and, as a result, a political backlash in parts of the region that threatens the chances for humane social values to put down roots and grow. The resurgent nationalism that accompanied the breakup of the Soviet bloc was a politically salutary response to the economic imperialism of the old Soviet system. Nonetheless, it produced less viable economic units—as in the creation of separate

Czech and Slovak republics and the disintegration of Yugoslavia—that in many cases are still light-years behind the European Union's logic of a borderless marketplace.

Meanwhile, the far wealthier, far more stable states to the west failed to offer very significant help at a moment of unprecedented need and opportunity. They at first were plagued by distracting economic problems of their own, which included a prolonged recession accompanied by rising unemployment for nearly all of them, a huge and mounting debt for the United States, serious social and economic dislocations for a reunited Germany, and a sharp drop in available capital for investment in the case of Japan. Although the economic record of G-7 countries improved in the mid-1990s, that still did not bring a very significant increase in their assistance to Russia. It appeared for a time that a serious political reaction was in the making when extreme nationalists received a sizable vote in Russia's legislative elections in 1993. In the summer of 1996, President Yeltsin had to beat back a challenge from a resurgent Communist party candidate to regain the presidency. By that date, faint signs of economic progress—in privatization, reducing inflation, the slight rebounding of production—all may have helped the incumbent. Even so, it remained the case that, in the words of one observer, "The big unknown is whether there will be enough that is positive to convince the Russian public to remain patient and continue its tolerance of what appears to many as anarchy."[8]

Across the South, meanwhile, the economic record produced more extremes than ever. Some economies in East Asia, including China, Korea, Taiwan, and Thailand, led the world in their rates of growth, which, for some, were in double digits annually. Then, in 1997, Thailand and Korea, as well as Indonesia, suffered sudden reversals that threatened to infect many other economies. But while the boom for these states had lasted, the economic life of others had steadily deteriorated during the last two decades of the twentieth century, typically as their political systems failed. Some of these, such as Cambodia and Burma, were the neighbors of the economic successes. Others—Rwanda, Somalia, Zaire—were among the worst cases on a continent whose recent economic history generally has been the most dismal in the world. For most of Latin America, the 1980s constituted a "lost decade," economically speaking. All but a handful ended that period with per capita gross domestic products (GDP) that were actually lower than they had been ten or even twenty years earlier.[9]

By the mid-1990s, a number of economies in the South had improved, although growth remained uneven. In general, two factors accounted for the increasing variation in the records of these economies. Some that did not fare well nevertheless engaged in essentially nationalistic developmental policies. Instead of targeting foreign markets and encouraging the growth of exports to stimulate their economies, they had tried import substitution, creating their own basic industries and protecting them with subsidies, tax breaks, and tariffs. In contrast, the success stories generally came from those whose strategies were to increase exports, whether of primary products, manufactured goods, or—as in the case of the East Asian "tigers"—high technology.[10]

The second factor inhibiting growth for some countries was their huge debt burden. At the start of the 1990s, debt restructuring had eased the debt crisis of the previous decade—which helped, in particular, several of the larger economies of Latin America. But it provided little immediate relief for many of the poorest countries of the South. It was still the case in 1994 that the debt of sub-Saharan Africa, excluding South Africa, was some 10 percent *higher* than its total annual output of goods and services. The region was required to spend $10 billion that year in debt-service payments, which amounted to some four times what those nations were spending on health and education combined.[11] Even with better economic news from parts of that region in succeeding years, it is still true that the debts the poor continue to pay to the rich make it far more burdensome for them to work their way out of their poverty than hard work alone would require.

The explosive growth in population that continues in a number of societies in the South is both a cause and an effect of their continued poverty. It is a cause in the obvious sense that a growing population offsets by whatever amount it increases annually the same annual increase in its wealth. But it is also an effect of poverty, in the sense that high birthrates typically end once a society has moved through the industrial revolution. That process is revolutionary, in other words, not simply for recasting the dominant modes of production but also for the radical changes it brings in the way people live. The rapid decline in the death rate that is a part of this revolution is eventually matched by a substantial decline in the birth rate. High rates of fertility have been a mark of preindustrial economic life throughout human history. This "demographic transition" from high birth and death rates to far lower ones has accompanied economic development wherever it has occurred.[12] In our day that transition has been completed by the richest countries on earth, including a number of countries in East Asia whose population soared while that transition was under way. But it has scarcely begun in much of the rest of the world.

Those who are privileged seldom look past their conclusion that poor societies are having too many children for their own good. If that is true, the cure is to help those societies through their own demographic transitions toward participation in the material enrichment that the privileged now enjoy. We have found no substitute for the complex social changes that accompany the industrial revolution to give us both greater material well-being and the prospect of zero population growth. Until that process is completed in Africa and Latin America, as one critic has noted, "the resources of these continents continue to fuel the economies of the industrial world. The underdeveloped countries await delivery of the less portable technologies of industrial revolution. Some day, these will permit them to develop the value of their resources for their own uses."[13]

Meanwhile, throughout this uneven record of the state of humanity's well-being runs both the thread of our ever increasing social interdependence and the counterthread of efforts to stop, slow down, or avoid that expanding network of economic relationships. For example, some of Africa's current economic difficulties are attributable to its increased incorporation into the world economy. Giving up their former self-sufficiency in food in favor of such export crops as coffee, tea, cocoa, and rubber has both robbed the economies of many African countries of the greater autonomy they once possessed and made them subject to competition from abroad. In these and other respects, they have been victimized by the growth of the economic marketplace. It is little wonder that advocates for economic nationalism still receive sympathetic hearings in many quarters—especially in times when a focus on scarcity crowds out hopes for growth. But the countervailing effort to stop or correct the injuries done by interdependence brings with it other kinds of economic loss, as was true for much of Latin America in recent years.

Until fairly recently, we have tended to view the growth in transnational interdependence still as largely limited to the most economically advanced societies of the world that espoused liberal economic doctrines. But today, the numbers of sealed-off economies driven by national command are much diminished. Technological change continues to drive economies across the planet, regardless of their level of development, into ever more transnational relationships:

> New technologies are challenging traditional assumptions about the way we make, trade, and even grow things. Automated workplaces in Japan intimate the end of the "factory system" that first arose in Britain's Industrial Revolution and spread around the world. Genetically engineered crops, cultivated in biotech laboratories, threaten to replace naturally grown sugar, vanilla, coconut oil, and other staple farm produce, and perhaps undermine field agriculture as we know it. An electronically driven, twenty-four-hour-a-day financial trading system has created a global market in, say, yen futures over which nobody really has control. The globalization of industry and services permits multinationals to switch production from one country to another (where it is usually cheaper), benefitting the latter and hurting the former.[14]

We have scarcely begun to treat in any adequate way these and other challenges arising from the fact that the material relations of the peoples of the earth make us increasingly a single people. The overriding task for the next stage of history is to attend far more seriously than we have before to issues of equity in those interrelationships.

The Demand for Human Dignity and Justice

At the current stage of world historical development, *advances in human rights, dignity, and justice require participation in the political and social process*.[15] For many decades, democracy, however defined, has received recognition as the ideal that virtually all the world's political elites claimed to espouse. But we have always heard this cynically, since it typically has meant that dictatorships, while paying lip service to the principle, could thrive. Mussolini and Hitler, among many others in this century, proved that dictators could rise to power through the popular institutions of democracy.

Now, however, as we survey the events of the recent past, we see that participatory politics has a strength and an appeal we had not imagined. At one level, the reason for that has been evident throughout human history: Participation is what empowers us, infusing our lives with dignity, a sense of worth, and the possibility of reaching our full potential. But today we have glimmers of something even more powerful. We begin to see that some greater measure of participation has the appeal of realism for many people throughout the world at present, thanks to a complex set of factors that describe the condition of much of human life on earth today. In the Soviet Union under Stalin, forced labor and coercion could produce road building and factory construction. In the Soviet society that induced its last leader, Mikhail Gorbachev, to embrace political liberalization, the requirements of postindustrial growth could no longer be commanded from a population that was disaffected or cowed into obedience.[16] Development itself, then, supports and may eventually require participation:

> Modernization accelerates the circulation of people and information and the evolution of political consciousness. This confronts authoritarian regimes with . . . a "legitimacy contradiction, a kind of Catch-22." If such regimes do not produce socioeconomic dynamism, they lose legitimacy because such progress is their justification for monopolizing power. If they do produce dynamism, it has political repercussions in intensified demands for participation which the regimes cannot satisfy without liquidating themselves.[17]

The world witnessed the dark side of this generalization in the crushing of the prodemocracy movement in China in 1989. As the quotation above suggests, ending the prodemocracy movement was the desperate act of a divided regime determined not to let itself be liquidated. Its success in clamping the lid of repression tightly into place was another stark reminder of the ruthless power that remains available to those who control the reins of the state. During the 1990s, the Chinese government continued to insist that it could maintain freewheeling, vigorous economic growth without granting like freedoms in the political sphere. But the experience of both South Korea and Taiwan suggested otherwise. Once their economies grew dramatically, starting in the 1960s, challenges to authoritarian political control eventually became irresistible. Given the time needed for political liberalization to catch up with modern economic expansion in those societies—some thirty years—the verdict is still out on the Chinese case.

Nor is this to say that there is something inevitable about the liberalization of societies under authoritarian rule. Rather, what looks inevitable today is that if societies living under such rule are not to be left in some backwater of civilization, then liberalization must occur. Modernization evidently cannot be carried past a certain stage under the conditions of advanced economic and social organization without awakening a demand for participation in the political process. The evidence suggests that such a demand must be met, sooner or later, if modernization is to proceed.

We must look at the characteristic features of development for a fuller explanation of this connection between its evolution and the cry for greater individual autonomy. One such feature is ever more rapid and widespread *communication*. In the age of television, it is seldom possible for governments to hide any longer behind bastions of the public's ignorance as to how the rest of the world is doing. In the 1960s, nightly broadcasts from the battlefield no doubt heightened the revulsion of the American public toward the war in Vietnam. In the 1980s, the reach of radio and television encouraged voters across the Soviet Union to elect reform candidates to the Congress of People's Deputies, generally by throwing out longtime Communist party officials. In the 1990s, the spectacle of helpless Rwandans being clubbed to death on the nightly television news summoned outrage that helped push the Security Council to create a tribunal for that country to prosecute those accused of genocide.

Such developments suggest that even though the process is tortuous and sometimes painful, we are witnessing *the creation of a global political and normative culture* as the ideational expression of the emerging global village. Western visitors to China at the close of the Cultural Revolution in the late 1970s were often struck by how little in the way of Western influence seemed left there and by the ignorance of the Chinese people of much that was taken for granted in the outside world. By 1989, it was striking that demonstrators in Tiananmen Square often wrote their slogans in Russian and in English. Even more striking were the signs of a cosmopolitan convergence that was occurring in the world of political ideas (a convergence soon to be denied and opposed by those in command of the tanks and guns). Nowhere was this more dramatically symbolized than in the painted banners held aloft by students that read, "We Shall Overcome!" Thus the Chinese quest for lives of greater dignity had borrowed from the rallying cry of the U.S. civil rights movement, which itself had borrowed proudly from the satyagraha of an earlier day's Mahatma Gandhi.

Significant, too, is communication's solemn other face, *education*, in the urge for participation. The illiterate may be intimidated by magic and brutal displays of force; they are easily led, coerced, and manipulated. But those with a greater awareness of life's possibilities—both material and intellectual—are empowered by their learning. The educated develop confidence in their capabilities and a willingness to question the rule of privilege. Through the power of their ideas and their ideal, they may organize the multitudes, bravely endure hunger campaigns, and speak to the world. Meanwhile, they disrupt the routine life of the society in ways that those who presumably wield power—state officials—are powerless to stop, short of acting with the kind of brutality that renders their rule illegitimate.

The spread of education has the power to put an end to the murderous repressions that we have seen desperate regimes resort to as the century nears its end. Only enlightened individuals are able to assess the extent to which their governments assist them in advancing important values; only such individuals, therefore, have the power to judge the legitimacy or illegitimacy of the actions of those who rule. The spread of education is now extending shared social and political values ever more widely. What education produces most powerfully of all is the quest for the fullest possible realization of one's human potential. In political terms, that requires above all the ability to participate in decisions that affect one's life and aspirations.[18]

These considerations demonstrate that the quest for human rights has progressed to the point that it cannot be trivialized as a pious or romantic venture—a nice ideal with no real hope of cracking the omnipotence of sovereigns. Concern with human rights as a world order value was born out of our horrified awareness of the new cruelties governments were capable of inflicting on their citizens in the modern age. It seemed imperative, in creating what was to be the new international order after World War II, to try to restrain sovereigns by framing universal standards of human rights.[19] Now we see that the norm-setting process that followed has interacted symbiotically with a complex range of developments in the world's social and economic system to further our general integration, that is, our broadly shared agreement on certain core values. Specifically, at this stage in history, the value of participation has become the focus of what the enhancement of human dignity seems all about. It is there, as seen in the increase in democratic governance from the 1980s into the 1990s, that the contemporary human rights struggle is converging in a unified way.

In the upheaval initially accompanying the end of the cold war, these developments have been overshadowed by violent human rights abuses perpetrated by those attempting to assert autocratic control. Ethnic conflicts in the former Yugoslavia in the early 1990s suggested that the region was returning to the murderous conditions that had existed at the beginning of the twentieth century instead of its populations' coming to a wider sharing of compatible values at the century's end. But those conflicts probably reflected a wider truth, which is that for three-quarters of the century—from the outbreak of World War I in 1914 to the end of the cold war in 1989—two world wars and the imposition of imperial control effectively froze real social integration across Central and Eastern Europe, preventing what tended to occur where more pluralistic freedoms prevailed. As frozen positions thawed, change often unleashed violent clashes.

In the 1970s, Greece, Spain, and Portugal effectively made the transition from dictatorship to democracy, although that outcome looked anything but foreordained as their authoritarian governments were toppled. None of the three countries had any more substantial history of democracy than most of the states of Eastern Europe when they cast off single-party rule at the start of the 1990s. But they did have one distinct advantage—they did not have to try to liberalize their polities at a time when their economic well-being was in jeopardy, as was the case for much of the former Soviet bloc in the 1990s. If it is true, as much evidence suggests, that democratic politics flourish best in a context of growing material abundance, then it is surely much harder to maintain the conditions of tolerance democracy demands in societies experiencing serious economic distress. If the current problems in some states of the former Soviet sphere are to be ameliorated, then improved economic life and strengthened democratic polities will march forward hand in hand. Should one front continue to deteriorate, however, it almost certainly will lead to the collapse of the other.

The resurgent ethnic hatreds that are the foe of human rights produced new barbarities after the end of the cold war. The attitudes that gave rise to them stand in a poisonous contrast to a vision of national affiliation that comports much more fully with a civilized humanity at the end of the twentieth century. Vaclav Havel, the last president of a federal Czechoslovakia and first president of the Czech Republic, articulated one of the most eloquent visions of what national citizenship should mean in today's world:

> I am in favor of a political system based on the citizen, and recognizing all his fundamental civil and human rights in their universal validity, and equally applied: that is, no member of a single race, a single nation, a single sex, or a single religion may be endowed with basic rights that are any different from any else's. . . . Today this civil principle is sometimes presented as if it stood in op-

position to the principle of national affiliation, creating the impression that it ignores or suppresses the aspect of our home represented by our nationality. This is a crude misunderstanding of that principle that represents the best way for individuals to realize themselves, to fulfill their identity in all the circles of their home, to enjoy everything that belongs to their natural world, not just some aspects of it. To establish a state on any other principle than the civic principle—on the principle of ideology, of nationality or religion for instance—means making one aspect of our home superior to all the others, and thus reduces us as people, reduces our natural world. And that hardly ever leads to anything good. Most wars and revolutions, for example, came about precisely because of this one-dimensional conception of the state.[20]

Havel's view of what nationality means should stand as the only meaningful definition for increasing numbers of us as our destinies become ever more intertwined on this small and fragile voyager through space that is our common home.

Protection of the Global Habitat

If our values are to continue to converge in greater world order, attention to a host of issues on the "new agenda" of environmental threats almost certainly must act as an important catalyst. Ronald Reagan is reported to have said to Mikhail Gorbachev the first time they met that perhaps their two nation-states would learn to cooperate if ever they were jointly threatened by alien invaders from outer space. The fact was that those "alien invaders" were already making their presence felt in the form of the depredations that all members of the human species were inflicting on their common home. The resulting normative precept is obvious: *Humanity shares environmental responsibilities that require global cooperation if the biosphere is to survive.* That generalization has numerous implications for changes in our behavior.

At the level of formal governmental activity, first, we should expect real compliance on the part of governments with the mounting body of legislation that increasingly has set standards and has created necessary regulatory and enforcement capabilities. But people everywhere must be made to feel the force of serious environmental dangers before they are likely to shake governments from their unwillingness to take what may sometimes seem like costly medicine. Governments have been slow to address what traditionally were matters of the lowest politics precisely because no powerful political interests have supported environmental protections, while many—especially in the most highly industrialized states—have opposed them.

That leads us to the second implication, which is that we who are non-governmental participants need to work within the political process in support of environmentally sound policy. The political process is, by definition, one where conflicting values are advanced and addressed. Only recently have threats to the environment begun to achieve a political saliency that allows them to compete for policy outcomes along with military, industrial, or other more traditional interests. Habitual assumptions about what is or is not politically feasible with regard to the environmental impact of human behavior are beginning to change.[21] Such changes must be encouraged in accordance with ethically reasoned policies. The analogy to guide us lies in the ending of the cold war: What looked romantic and unrealistic in one era became the foundation of revolutionary policies in the next, to the amazement of those who had unthinkingly supposed that such change could "never" come about. Although it is not possible to foresee the exact shape of what that will mean in the world of the future, a number of actions in recent years suggest ways in which human development may be brought more closely into line with nature's imperatives.

First is the growing effort to counter global warming. The Global Warming Convention completed at the 1992 Earth Summit set guidelines for regulating the emissions of "greenhouse" gases that are building up in the atmosphere with potentially disastrous long-term results. Control of this problem requires cutting back on the burning of the fossil fuels that are the primary culprits, which in turn requires tax policies to discourage the burning of coal, oil, and gasoline. Within five years after the Earth Summit, some industrial countries had met their targets for cutting back on carbon dioxide emissions. Others, including the United States, had not. Developing countries were emitting about one-sixth the amount of carbon per person that the industrialized states were emitting in this period. Nonetheless, they accounted for a third of the global total and their emissions were rising fast enough to double every fourteen years.[22] The dangerous, if ironic, reality remains in place: "One group of countries emits most of the carbon; the other has most of the people, and appears bent on matching the first's profligacy as quickly as it can."[23]

A two-front shift in policy is required, especially in the United States, to encourage ever greater energy efficiency and the increasing use of renewable energy resources. New technologies are beginning to assist on both fronts, making it feasible to project a possible 70 percent reduction in carbon dioxide emissions over the next forty years in spite of little progress in the years after Rio.[24] This will require a change in U.S. patterns of automobile use, as well as the increased efficiency of automobiles and the availability of alternative fuels to run them. It will also require the increased use of such nonpolluting energy sources as solar and wind power, which are beginning to have wider, cost-effective applications than in the past. Together, these changes could correct much of America's unhealthy appetite for carbon-emitting fuels and greatly assist the whole world in providing new and far more benign energy technologies.

Second is increased awareness of the need to maintain and protect biodiversity. We are just beginning to grasp the potential benefits to human health to be found in many largely unknown and untapped plant and animal species. This fact puts the protection of species diversity in self-interested terms for Homo sapiens. Yet that interest is threatened, especially in the rapid destruction of tropical rain forests (which also contributes to global warming), since these are the richest habitats for a myriad of species on earth. At the moment, concern over tropical deforestation has been framed largely as another North-South division, since the developing states of the tropics have tended to argue that their rain forests are a renewable part of the national patrimony, the management of which is their responsibility alone.

The debate to date over saving the world's forests has tended to be framed in zero-sum terms, that is, if governments continue to destroy their rain forests, they may "win" economic development for their countries even as all of us "lose" irreplaceable resources. Conversely, if biodiversity is "won" through such measures as forest conservation, then economic development is "lost" in such regions, which are prevented from pulling themselves into the modern world in the way Northern societies did, which has entailed the wholesale destruction of their forests as a by-product. But to maintain biodiversity by protecting its chief storehouses can have non-zero-sum outcomes for all. We must attempt to increase human well-being hereafter in ways that secure the diversity of life instead of threatening it with the kinds of large-scale interventions that traditionally have tended to put the human species in an adversarial relationship with nature.

A recent movement works to mend this conflict. Debt-for-nature swaps have begun to attract attention as a way to bridge North-South differences and to advance common interests over matters of economics and the environment. They loose a financial millstone from around the neck of the poor country by either paying or arranging to forgive some of its debt to Northern banks. In exchange, the debtor typically pledges to conserve forests that are invaluable as a species storehouse and supplier of oxygen to the planet. In this way we are crossing the threshold to solutions for the protection of life's diversity in ways that are both effective and equitable.

Third, new development concepts and strategies must be put in place that foster ecologically sustainable development instead of replicating the environmentally destructive strategies of the industrial age. The Earth Summit's Agenda 21 outlined a number of such measures. Northern governments pledged new economic assistance in line with these guidelines, and a UN Commission on Sustainable Development (CSD) was created to monitor international compliance with environmental treaties. These developments did not immediately produce a dramatic, visible shift in the development priorities of most governments or, seemingly, the general public. The danger, as always, was that new agencies such as the CSD would be so starved for resources as to be powerless to shift global strategies very meaningfully. Yet within just a few years after Agenda 21 was adopted, numerous incremental shifts could be counted.[25] Together, these may someday be seen as the start of specieswide reeducation, teaching us that the human effort to prosper must be made in harmony with, not at the expense of, our planetary home.

Increasingly, conflicting claims and counterclaims to ownership over the earth's resources must be resolved on the basis of the principle that *all the products of the biosphere are humankind's common heritage.* Beginning in the 1960s, many less developed countries asserted their permanent sovereignty over valuable natural resources within their territories in a move that some have viewed as virulently nationalistic and defiantly opposed to the larger view of the biosphere as a single natural system. Yet this assertion was a typically Westphalian reaction to the practice of distant entrepreneurs who exploited nonrenewable resources more for their private gain than for the material profit of the local society, encouraging greater social stratification.

The permanent sovereignty claim is the first defensive step in world order policy toward recognizing the nonrenewability and therefore the preciousness of the earth's resources to all of us, not just the economic elites. That principle was embodied in the provisions of the 1982 Law of the Sea Treaty. To the extent that sound and mutually reinforcing environmental policies are applied to the exclusive economic zones of coastal states, this principle will become public policy for the world. A common heritage awareness also underlies the Madrid Protocol of the Antarctica Treaty as well as the global warming and biodiversity treaties of 1992. As the world's free goods inevitably become more scarce and more susceptible to destruction through misuse, public policies at every level of society must be formulated to provide greater and greater protection over this common heritage.

Nor is policy based on recognition of our common heritage restricted to the activities of transnational corporate actors or others engaged in use of high technology. The rapid desertification of the Sahel region of Africa is principally the result of overgrazing on marginal lands, which came about in turn because of rapidly growing populations and the ever expanding need for food resources. Today 90 percent of the world's rangelands are threatened by overgrazing. But evidence is mounting that the threat can be reversed once we understand nature's own lessons about what particular environments can support and sustain. In the 1980s, a longtime cattle rancher in Kenya turned to the "natural ranching" of native wild animals and found that his rangelands prospered considerably as a result. "Wild animals eat grasses and shrubs evenly, while cattle devastate preferred grasses. Cows suck rangeland dry by drinking 10 to 15 gallons of water a day. African game animals need little or no water. Cows damage the land through heavy tracking, while wild game produces no serious tracking."[26] Not only did this experimental rancher earn far more, he supplied the local market with game meat that has only 1 percent fat (versus 20 percent for cattle) and contains none of the harmful saturated fats, antibiotics, and hormones of the commercially produced beef of many countries.

Natural ranching, like natural farming, is scarcely known beyond experiments like that described above. But as we grow to understand that all our material development must be bound by nature's limits, we must expect and encourage all such ecologically sound practices—in the production of food, material goods, or energy supplies. With his usual breathtaking sense of the time frame of human development, Arnold Toynbee noted in his last major work that "the two million years that have passed since the first stone was chipped into a more useful shape by *australopithecus* is the twinkling of an eye compared with the 2,000 million years more for which, it has been estimated, the biosphere will continue to be habitable if Man permits."[27] Apparently we, the members of a single species, will decide whether life will continue on the planet. Only in this century have we begun to perceive that we hold such satanic power. As we struggle to avoid the kind of apocalyptic catastrophe that could decimate advanced life-forms, we also must reorder our priorities to ensure that our material development proceeds in accordance with nature's law.

Integration, Peaceful Change, and Local Action

As we approach the twenty-first century, the tantalizing possibilities for the advance of global civilization beckon more clearly than they have for many years, although reminders of how we might regress also lie all about us. In the century's last decade, we have seen the end of a global conflict that long consumed too many of our material resources while dehumanizing our politics. A contest of thought-deadening ideology has been replaced with what can be a common search for pragmatic solutions to common problems. We have abandoned the myth that our security can somehow be maintained through the threat of genocidal destruction. But we have watched as ancient hatreds and intolerance have broken out in terrible reminders of events that plunged the world into one, then another, of the global wars that marked the first half of this century.

The world may again be drawn into the kind of vortex that led to so much bloodshed and destruction early in the century. But that would be an unimaginable tragedy at the century's close, when so many social and political developments across the globe have opened the door to what could be humanity's best of times. We have the opportunity today to transform the erstwhile antagonists of the era just passed into members of a security-community whose own conflicts are dependably resolved in peace. We are challenged to do what we can to assure the beneficent orientation of that group toward the larger world. That means, in the current context, that its governments must develop the dependable ability to cooperate as a force for law and order in the world, developing a real authority for peacekeeping and peacemaking. Notwithstanding the disorders that resulted from the end of the cold war, we are now confronted with a realistic possibility for ending, for the first time in human history, large-scale warfare among advanced states.

That is a cause that, until the 1980s, few would have regarded as plausible. Now, however, we have come to a point in world development at which we begin to see that true greatness for societies will increasingly be measured in terms not of the empires or military resources they command, but in the extent and quality of their socioeconomic relationships with others and the mutual enhancement of civilized values that results for all involved. Something like that is the thesis of a number of important recent studies.[28] It is implicit in the connections that currently exist among world order issues today, wherein non-zero-sum strategies are emerging to link world order values that thrive on that linkage. It is more than hinted at in the process by which the European Community has led its members away from their past military and imperial orientations, and has defined well-being for its citizens in terms of economic and social advances. It is strongly suggested in Japan's spectacular rise to prominence in global society. Although Japan was devastatingly thwarted in its effort to achieve geopolitical power through military conquest, it found greatness after World War II through economic prowess and trade. Japan's rich trade demands peaceful and interdependent relationships with many other societies. The results are beneficent for Japan, as they should be for any other states that model themselves on Japan in the future. More broadly, our prospects today should remind us of certain value linkages. Our security is enhanced as material welfare advances and human rights are protected, and living in harmony with nature strengthens aspects of our material well-being that provide us with more secure futures and make us more respectful of life generally.

These conclusions suggest that the nature of *economic organization* for the most advanced states in the world today is the product of one historical trend that makes abandonment of the war system a sensible prospect.

Economic units have grown in scale and complexity throughout the modern age, expanding (with the help of Westphalian ordering arrangements) from village and provincial levels to that of the nation-state and then bursting through many of the constraints imposed by Westphalia in our time. Now that ever more powerful economic actors possess global reach, nation-states are economically permeable in ways they never were before. The resulting development of intricate strands of economic interdependence could be badly damaged or destroyed by war, which means that growing numbers of powerful economic actors today have a positive incentive not to let organized violence disrupt the web of their relationships. Increasing numbers of us rely on and profit from this burgeoning web of economic activities.

A second historical trend, the development of modern *military technology*, has produced a crisis in the timeless connection between politics and the uses of force. As our military technology grew ever more destructive, it made less plausible the view that our most destructive weapons could be used to continue politics by other means. The control of violence by the authorities that unleash it is essential to any political purpose that can be claimed for the use of force. But control is problematic today in two respects. First, our twentieth-century experience makes clear that we frequently can no longer discriminate between military (legitimate) and nonmilitary (illegitimate) targets in time of war and, second, our territorial units, nation-states, can be penetrated militarily and thus are no longer satisfactory places of refuge and security from the very violence whose only legitimacy is to protect the values of social groups. These contradictions were among those that made immediately untenable the nuclear deterrence doctrines of the cold war from the moment the cold war ended. They continue to work against the revival of any notion that a general, if "conventional," war between highly developed states could produce other than a disastrous loss for both societies.

A third historical trend is the rise in *political participation* throughout much of the world. The demand for more participation is dramatically expressed in a number of societies today. Both the demand and the reality are the product, as we have seen, of the imperatives of instant communication, mass education, and of the very nature of advanced economic organization. Those same citizens whose willing participation in economic life is essential to the success of their leaders are increasingly unwilling to become the victims of the organized violence those same elites may lead them into; nor are restive populations, when given the slightest opportunity to express themselves, likely to see such ventures as being worth the sacrifice of their sons and daughters.

Each of these phenomena reflects today's permeability of what once were separate economic units, military actors, and the distinct social and ideological systems of no longer distant peoples. They are the result of converging trends that point us toward a more interdependent world in which many of the thorniest of our traditional security problems should begin to solve themselves. Richard Rosecrance has concluded that an economically interdependent world "is easier to govern than one of military-political sovereign states." With more of the kind of interdependence projected here, "world government—an international Leviathan—is not necessary."[29] As the planet continues to shrink, and as more and more groups derive benefits from mutually peaceful relationships, the incentives for peaceful conflict resolution are bound to grow.[30]

This shrinking of the planet demands that we develop unprecedented understanding of how to advance our values and act on our true interests. UN Secretary-General Boutros Boutros-Ghali, in his keynote address to the UNCED Conference in Rio de Janeiro, suggested how our thinking has to change:

> Mankind has always had to face threats to its security, but security evolves. . . . It is becoming less and less a military matter—since in a world in the process of unification any war becomes a kind of civil war—and rather requires an economic-ecological dimension. . . . A portion of so-called security expenditures, in the old sense of the word—that is, military expenditures—must necessarily be reallocated for planetary development projects.[31]

Achieving security through ecologically sound economic policies, the reorientation of much military expenditure toward planetary development—such goals are the stuff of realistic global politics today.

It is nonetheless a further challenge to move in these directions without leaving the desperately impoverished—whether poor societies generally or the underclasses of otherwise rich societies—farther and farther behind in the dust. Only by acting on our respect for the idea of enhancing human dignity and autonomy can that dreadful prospect of a newly and even more deeply divided world be avoided. There is, as is so often the case, more than a pinch of self-interest in such socially conscious behavior as well. If the rich continue to ignore the needs of the poor and the politically dispossessed, the rich will ultimately fail to achieve the promised advances in world order values for themselves just discussed and eventually will fall back into too familiar patterns of repression, violence, and viciousness. Only such behavior may permit them to maintain their own privileged positions for a time in the face of growing unrest on the part of those who, it must be remembered, will have enough access to the communications media to be made very much aware of the injustice of their own lives. Given the terrifying capabilities modern technology presents for pathological dissent by the disaffected, the result could be a retreat to barbarism on a scale frightening to imagine.

A final generalization to guide us toward a better world reminds us that social unity must not be obtained at the expense of the autonomy and complex diversity that are also essential to what makes our lives good. Our agenda cannot be advanced either through monolithic centralization or by leaving action entirely in the hands of "official" groups. Not only are local action and autonomy possible, they are absolutely essential to the shape of our political and social future. *The best social order would permit very great local control and autonomy in policymaking but link us in a global network of social solidarity.* As Toynbee said, "What has been needed for the last 5,000 years, and has been feasible technologically, though not yet politically, for the last hundred years, is a global body politic composed of cells on the scale of the Neolithic-Age village community—a scale on which the participants would be personally acquainted with each other, while each of them would also be a citizen of the world-state."[32] No doubt we would have to reach the height of idealism to suppose that such a vision could be reliably achieved within our lifetimes, yet we have noted the realistic conditions present today that can take us a number of steps in that direction. We also have seen that the conditions for the opposite of this arrangement, the worst social order we can imagine, are lurking all about us. Those conditions would create repression and political domination at local levels without a corresponding network of authority that would bridge the globe. We may not achieve the best, but we can act every day to ensure that we avoid the worst.

The ideal of achieving human dignity through a recognition of human equality is what underlies much of the quest for an improved reality for humankind. If we, like Hobbes, imagine a state of nature without protection for equal rights, we find ourselves in a situation where might makes right, where only the strongest are afforded what all of us claim in a just social order. In asserting equal rights within civil society, whether local or global, we learn to interact on the basis of that legal fiction, our equality. Even while we develop a respect for our equal rights, we learn to develop simultaneously a toleration for our differences, which can largely be expressed within our various private spheres. The growth of our sense of communal solidarity is the other side of our respect for our separate autonomies, our sovereign capabilities as distinct creatures.

Just as that truth underlies what we regard as acceptable social order among individual human beings, so can it form the basis for acceptable global order among individual states (which, in some cases, might reasonably devolve into smaller units than they are at present). The Westphalian system has always been based theoretically on that insight, but for most of its history, global sociopolitical development had not yet advanced to the point to make it drive international behavior effectively. International social and political intercourse tended to be so limited, so unconstrained by the environment of international politics, that the mutual social obligation of sovereigns could largely be ignored. Most could grow and flourish without paying heed to each other.

The danger in that state of affairs always has been that it hides the social obligation of each sovereign and each sovereign society from view. Each nation-state traditionally has been so isolated from others that its members have been tempted to forget that others are composed of the same species as themselves, motivated by the same biological and spiritual needs. Given the instantaneous communications possible throughout the world today, including the ability we have to wreak unspeakable damage on fellow humans across the globe in a matter of minutes, we find it increasingly impossible to forget our species sameness. A thousand traditional habits and modes of organizing our political lives conspire to try to make us forget. The challenge that we all face is to overcome them.

Notes

1. This adaptation of the Kantian categorical imperative paraphrases Earl C. Ravenal, "The Case for Disengagement," *Foreign Affairs* 51, 3 (April 1973):521, who added, "Admittedly, this is not a self-executing policy but, at least in moral theory, it could be a self-fulfilling prophecy."

2. Robert S. McNamara, "The Nuclear Emperor Has No Clothes," *New Perspectives Quarterly*, Summer 1995, p. 33.

3. McNamara cites a number of these.

4. For analyses of this opinion, see Michael J. Matheson, "The Opinions of the International Court of Justice on the Threat or Use of Nuclear Weapons," *American Journal of International Law* 91, 3 (July 1997):417–435, and Richard A. Falk, "Nuclear Weapons, International Law and the World Court," *American Journal of International Law* 91, 1 (January 1997):64–75.

5. Karl W. Deutsch et al., *Political Community and the North Atlantic Area* (Princeton, N.J.: Princeton University Press, 1957).

6. The Charter provides in Article 47(2) for the Military Staff Committee to invite governments other than of the Permanent Members "to be associated with it when the efficient discharge of the Committee's responsibilities" requires it. That is an obvious way for participation in the collective security functions of the Council to be opened up to appropriate additional members without formally enlarging its membership through Charter amendment.

7. A few of the numerous recent analyses in these areas include David Cortright and George A. Lopez, "The Sanctions Era: An Alternative to Military Intervention," *Fletcher Forum of World Affairs* 19, 2 (May 1995):65–85; Robert C. Johansen, "The Future of United Nations Peacekeeping and Enforcement," *Global Governance* 2, 3 (September/December 1996):299–333; F. T. Liu, "United Nations Peacekeeping and the Non-Use of Force," International Peace Academy Occasional Paper, 1992; and Samuel S. Makinda, "Sovereignty and International Security: Challenges for the United Nations," *Global Governance* 2, 2 (May/August 1996):149–168.

8. Marshall I. Goldman, "Is This Any Way to Create a Market Economy?" *Current History,* October 1995, p. 310.

9. *Economic and Social Progress in Latin America:* 1989 Report (Washington, D.C.: Inter-American Development Bank, 1989), Table B1, p. 463.

10. Paul Kennedy, "Preparing for the 21st Century: Winners and Losers," *New York Review of Books,* February 11, 1992, p. 36.

11. John Darnton, "In Poor, Decolonized Africa Bankers Are Overlords," *New York Times,* June 20, 1994, A1.

12. See Gerard Piel, "Worldwide Development or Population Explosion: Our Choice," *Challenge,* July/August 1995, pp. 13–22.

13. Ibid., p. 18.

14. Kennedy, "Preparing for the 21st Century," p. 32.

15. Western commentators have frequently supposed that calls for democratization are a sham if they do not include demands for multiparty elections, a constitutional system of checks and balances, and the like. These institutional indicators of democratic systems are certainly important but should be expected to follow rather than precede larger amounts of political participation, for in politics as in architecture, form follows function. But because democracy in the West is generally defined in terms of political institutions, I shall speak instead of participation to describe the social and political process that may be an essential prior development.

16. See "Toward Greater Global Welfare" in Chapter 6.

17. Larry Diamond, as quoted by George Will, *Philadelphia Inquirer,* December 19, 1988, 16A.

18. A few comparative figures reinforce much of the story of these links connecting education to a society's economic well-being and level of political participation. Japan, a very rich and politically stable society, has the highest number of scientists and engineers—3,548 per million of its population (the figure for the United States is 2,685); Africa as a whole has the fewest, only 53 per million. In the early 1980s, Angola reportedly had 2.4 million pupils in its primary schools, only 153,000 in secondary schools, and 4,700 in higher education. In contrast, Sweden, whose population is slightly smaller than Angola's, had nearly four times as many students in secondary education—570,000—and 179,000, or some 38 times as many students as Angola did in higher education. Kennedy, "Preparing for the Twenty-First Century," pp. 40–41.

19. So, for example, the comment of a UN civil servant in 1948: "What the United Nations is trying to do is revolutionary. . . . Human rights are largely a matter of relationships between the state and individuals, and therefore a matter which has been traditionally regarded as within the domestic jurisdiction of states. What is now proposed is . . . some kind of supranational supervision of this relationship between the state and its citizens." John P. Humphrey, "International Protection of Human Rights," *Annals of the American Academy of Political and Social Science* 155 (January 1948):21.

20. Vaclav Havel, speech given at Lehigh University, Bethlehem, Pa., October 26, 1991, as published in *New York Review of Books,* December 5, 1991, p. 49.

21. In this respect, it is probably hopeful that in spite of the antienvironmental lobbying of special interest groups in industrialized states, their governments are now more likely to press for environmental protections in international agree-

ments than are the representatives of less developed countries. For one example, see debates over the powers of the new World Trade Organization, as outlined by John Zaracostas, "Environment's Link to Trade Pits Us Against Poorer Nations," *Journal of Commerce*, October 28, 1994, 1A.

22. David Malin Roodman, "Carbon Emissions Resume Rise," in *Vital Signs 1995*, ed. Lester R. Brown, Nicholas Lenssen, and Hal Kane (New York: W. W. Norton, 1995), p. 66.

23. Ibid.

24. Union of Concerned Scientists, *Cool Energy* (Cambridge, Mass.: MIT Press, 1992).

25. See, for example, Gail V. Karlsson, "Environment and Sustainable Development," *A Global Agenda: Issues Before the 51st General Assembly of the United Nations*, UNA-USA (Lanham, Md.: Rowman and Littlefield, 1996), pp. 135–148.

26. David Zucchino, "Kenyan Saves Ranch Raising Game," *Philadelphia Inquirer*, March 28, 1988, 7A.

27. Arnold Toynbee, *Mankind and Mother Earth* (New York: Oxford University Press, 1976), p. 26.

28. Among them are Werner Levi, *The Coming End of War* (Beverly Hills, Calif.: Sage, 1981); John Mueller, *Retreat from Doomsday: The Obsolescence of Major War* (New York: Basic Books, 1989); J. M. Owen, "How Liberalism Produces Democratic Peace," *International Security* 19 (1994):87–182; Richard Rosecrance, *The Rise of the Trading State* (New York: Basic Books, 1986); and Bruce Russett, *Grasping the Democratic Peace* (Princeton, N.J.: Princeton University Press, 1993).

29. Rosecrance, *Rise of the Trading State*, p. 92.

30. Many of the revolutionary possibilities for world political change are implicit in the shrinking planet metaphor. In 1648, the year of the Peace of Westphalia, the speed of travel and communication were identical, and neither had changed appreciably in two thousand years. In A.D. 50 a rider could carry a message from an outpost in Germania to the imperial capital of Rome in about the same time that 1,600 years later, a letter could have gone to the Papal States from Prussian Berlin. In terms of the speed of travel, the airplane today has made the globe perhaps the equivalent in size of medieval Portugal. Nearly instantaneous communications today have placed most of the world's population on the equivalent of a single city block.

31. *New York Times*, June 4, 1992, A10.

32. Toynbee, *Mankind and Mother Earth*, p. 593. Chadwick Alger has frequently urged students of international order today to "think globally and act locally." See his "The Role of People in the Future Global Order," *Alternatives* 4, 2 (October 1978):232–262; "Bridging the Micro and Macro in International Relations Research," *Alternatives* 10, 3 (Winter 1984–85):319–344; and "Local, National and Global Politics in the World: A Challenge to International Studies," *International Studies Notes* 5, 1 (Spring 1978).

Suggested Readings

Arendt, Hannah, *Between Past and Future*, New York: Viking, 1968.

Armstrong, David, Lorna Lloyd, and John Redmond, *From Versailles to Maastricht*, New York: St Martin's Press, 1996.

Beer, Francis A., and Robert Hariman, *Post-Realism*, East Lansing: Michigan State University Press, 1997.

Biersteker, Thomas J., and Cynthia Weber, *State Sovereignty as Social Construct*, Cambridge: Cambridge University Press, 1996.

Ferenz, Benjamin B., *World Security for the 21st Century: Challenges and Solutions*, Dobbs Ferry, N.Y.: Oceana, 1991.

Hollins, Harry B., Averill L. Powers, and Mark Sommer, *The Conquest of War: Alternative Strategies for Global Security*, Boulder, Colo.: Westview, 1989.

Kant, Immanuel, *Eternal Peace*, Indianapolis: Liberal Arts Press, 1957.

King, Alexander, and Bertrand Schneider, *The First Global Revolution*, A Report by the Council of the Club of Rome, New York: Pantheon Books, 1991.

Kotkin, Joel, *Tribes*, New York: Random House, 1993.

Levi, Werner, *The Coming End of War*, Beverly Hills, Calif.: Sage, 1981.

Mittelman, James H., ed., *Globalization: Critical Reflections*, Boulder, Colo.: Lynne Rienner, 1996.

Mueller, John, *Retreat from Doomsday: The Obsolescence of Major War*, New York: Basic Books, 1989.

North, Robert C., *The World That Could Be*, New York: W. W. Norton, 1976.

Our Global Neighborhood, Report of the Commission on Global Governance, Oxford: Oxford University Press, 1995.

Rotberg, Robert I., and Theodore K. Rabb, eds., *The Origins and Prevention of Major Wars*, Cambridge, Mass.: Cambridge University Press, 1989.

Slater, Robert O., Barry M. Schutz, and Steven R. Dorr, eds., *Global Transformation and the Third World*, Boulder, Colo.: Lynne Rienner, 1993.

Strange, Susan, *The Retreat of the State*, Cambridge: Cambridge University Press, 1996.

Tinbergen, Jan, and Dietrich Fischer, *Warfare and Welfare: Integrating Security Policy into Socio-Economic Policy*, New York: St. Martin's Press, 1987.

Wagar, Warren, *Building the City of Man: Outlines of a World Civilization*, San Francisco: W. H. Freeman, 1971.

World Development Report 1997: The State in a Changing World, Washington, D.C.: The World Bank, 1997.

Index